T

GEORGE
HARRISON

ENCYCLOPEDIA

BILL HARRY

To Olivia and Dhani

First published in 2003 by
Virgin Books Ltd
Thames Wharf Studios
Rainville Road
London
W6 9HA

A catalogue record for this book is available from the British Library.

ISBN 0 7535 0822 2

Typeset by Phoenix Photosetting, Chatham, Kent
Printed and bound in Great Britain by Clays Ltd, St Ives plc

INTRODUCTION

In 1964, when I was preparing a series of colour covers on each individual Beatle for *Mersey Beat*, I had to come up with a punchy tag for each of them.

For the cover of George I described him simply as 'The Quiet Beatle'. I don't remember if that was the first time he was referred to in that way but, on reflection, this might not have been the most appropriate tag after all.

George did have that dry sense of humour – John Lennon's was acerbic, George's was definitely dry. He also had that touch of surrealism that young British people developed through listening to *The Goon Show*.

This became evident fairly early on and, later, as George became 'stretched' through his contact with the mystic qualities of Eastern philosophy, his comments acquired a maturity and insight.

At one time George dated Iris Caldwell, sister of popular Liverpool singer Rory Storm. When he was in Hamburg in 1962, he sent Iris's mother Vi a postcard that read:

Darling Vi, We are all missing you very much. To caress your teeth once more would be just heaven. Also to hold your lungs in mine and drink T.B. John sends you his lunch, also Paul and Ringworm greet you too. It's not too much fun here but only one week to go now, so it's not so bad now. Have tea ready on Sunday 18th.

Cheerio, love from George and friends.

George's deadpan humour was obvious right from the beginning. When Paul was late for the first official meeting between Brian Epstein and the Beatles at the NEMS office, Epstein was annoyed at what he considered Paul's tardiness.

'Sorry, Mr Epstein,' said George. 'He's just been having a bath.'

Brian was still angry and said, 'This is disgraceful. He is going to be very late.'

'Late,' said George, 'but very clean.'

It was George's wit that helped them to secure their record contract with George Martin. After their recording audition, Martin called them into the control room to listen to the playback, saying, 'You must listen to it, and if there's anything you don't like, tell me, and we'll try and do something about it.'

George said, 'Well, for a start, I don't like your tie.'

Martin was amused by the comment; it endeared him to the Beatles and their sense of humour.

When the Beatles were in Washington in February 1964, local disc jockey Carroll James was interviewing them when George said to him, 'I wanna be a baggy sweeger.'

'A baggy sweeger?' asked James, wondering what George was talking about.

'Oh, yeah,' said the Beatle. 'You know, in every town there's twenty-five baggy sweegers and every morning they get up and go out to the airport and baggy sweeger all around.'

In 1965, during the Beatles' tour of America, a chartered aircraft developed engine trouble and was replaced by an old plane that was to fly them to the West Coast. Noting the worn fittings in the interior, a worried George began to examine them. He noted a dusty coil of rope on a rack and asked the stewardess what it was.

'It's an escape ladder,' she said.

'How long is it?' asked George.

'About twelve feet, I guess,' she replied.

'I take it we shall fly to California at a steady thirteen feet all the way then,' said George.

Some examples of the Beatles sense of humour were taken seriously. The famous hairstyle was developed while they were in Hamburg, before they became well known. They had been asked about their hair so many times that when an American journalist in Paris in January 1964 asked George how they came up with their distinctive hairstyle, he said, 'We were coming out of a swimming baths in Liverpool and we liked the way it looked.' As a result, the story continued to surface for many years that they discovered the hairstyle after they'd been swimming.

When another American journalist asked George what they called their hairstyle, he said, 'Arthur.' As a result, someone opened a night-club in New York called Arthur's!

When discussing their appearance in Holland, George asked Paul if he remembered the house they stayed in at Harlech. Paul couldn't. George told him, 'Yes you do! There was a woman who had a dog with no legs. She used to take it out in the morning for a slide.'

George also had a serious side. During 1966 he was absorbing the culture and philosophy of India and made a trip to Bombay to study the sitar under Ravi Shankar.

On his arrival in India he gave a press conference, announcing, 'The urge to be something more than a mere Beatle provoked me to come to India. By learning to play the sitar, I can give Beatles fans a little more.'

George had also begun yoga lessons and was to comment, 'I find the philosophy and culture of the East natural and real, unlike Western philosophy, which at a certain stage reached a dead end. I think the Westerners who say the East is a mystery are a narrow-minded lot, not ready to accept its greatness.'

When asked what his own philosophy was, he said, 'Life is a game which one should play the best he can.'

Another reporter asked him whether he would be a Beatle forever and he answered, 'I do not even think about next week.'

In September 1967, on *The David Frost Programme*, George said, 'If everybody took up meditation it would help them to sort out their own problems, put their houses in order, if you like. People cause all the world's problems. So if people fix up their personal problems, that's it, we're well on the way aren't we? It's up to each individual, every person, to make his own move.'

On the death of Brian Epstein, George said, 'There is no such thing as death, only in the physical sense. Life goes on. The important thing is that he is OK now.'

George once said, 'There's high, and there's high, and to get really high – I mean so high that you can walk on water, that high – that's where I'm going.'

Another comment from George was, 'I believe in reincarnation. You keep coming back until you get it straight. The ultimate thing is to manifest divinity and become one with the Creator.'

He was to comment sagely, 'Many people think that life is predestined. I think it is, vaguely, but it's still up to you, which way your life is going to go. All I've ever done is to keep being me and it's all just worked out.'

During an interview for the television show *Good Morning Australia* in March 1982, George discussed the effect Eastern religions and the laws of karma and Krishna had on him, commenting that the soul is in the body for a period of time, but that the body is 'like a suit that you put on'.

When asked whether he knew where the soul went, he laughed and replied, 'Well, the soul – Christ said in the Bible about the three cages of the birds of Paradise, the three bodies that house the soul. And there's the causal body and then around that is the astral body and then there's the gross physical body. So death is really when the physical body falls off, but the soul's still in two of the bodies, so it's then on the astral level.'

In 1987, George told the *Sun* newspaper, 'I'm still very religious. I believe in an afterlife and reincarnation. I believe you keep coming back to this world until you lead such a good and holy life that you escape the mortal world.'

I was conscious when researching this book that, due to its length, I would have to make certain restrictions and a number of songs, most of them unrecorded or existing only as demo discs, have been left out, as have a number of musicians and friends who were associated with George, such as Dave Edmunds. The omissions were purely due to limitations of space.

The entries of Olivia and Dhani are extremely brief, due to George's wish to keep their privacy intact. He was a very private man who hated fame and loved God, who was frustrated at having the shadow of the Beatles fall over the rest of his life from 1970 onwards when he had moved on.

I would like to thank Carolyn Thorne and Barbara Phelan for their editorial support and everyone at Virgin Books for making my book a reality.

Bill Harry.
London. August 2003.

Abandoned Love
A studio demo of a Bob Dylan song that George recorded in 1983 but never released.

Abram, Michael
The man who tried to kill George in his home on 30 December 1999.

Abram was the eldest of three children born to labourer Ray Abram and his wife Lynda. They lived in a council house in Boode Croft, near Stockbridge Village, Liverpool.

At the age of sixteen he found his girlfriend Jeanette had become pregnant with their daughter Vikki, although the couple chose not to live together.

He began work as a telesales executive selling advertising space and began taking LSD and smoking cannabis before graduating to ecstasy, crack cocaine and heroin.

At 21 he set up home with his girlfriend and daughter and they had a son Michael. He then began to display signs of mental illness and in March 1990 was admitted to Whiston Hospital in Liverpool. He was released after two days and treated as an outpatient. The hospital's consultant psychiatrist said Abram was 'psychotic with paranoid delusions about his girlfriend, leading to pathological jealousy'.

The following year he overdosed on prescription tablets and was detained for a short while under the Mental Health Act, but was still treated as an outpatient.

He became a heroin addict, deserting his girlfriend and children and in 1996 moved into a squalid flat in a fourteen-storey tower block in Huyton.

Abram began sleeping on the landing of the building, frightened to enter his flat because he said a fat woman and a man in black were haunting him.

He was readmitted to hospital at his own request in September 1997, but was discharged after eleven days.

In 1999 he took to standing outside a Liverpool record store for hours listening to music on a personal stereo. Then he listened to one of his mother's Beatles albums.

From that time on the Beatles obsessed him. He told his mother that George was 'the phantom menace – the alien from Hell' and began finding 'messages' in the Beatles' lyrics. For instance, he believed that 'Let It Be' stood for: Hell (L) Extra-terrestrial (ET) I've given you tuberculosis (ITB).

His mother, Lynda Abram, said, 'He takes all music literally. It is the Beatles at the moment, but a few weeks ago it was Oasis. He has been running in pubs shouting about the Beatles. He hates them and even believes they are witches and takes their lyrics seriously. He started to wear a Walkman to play music to stop the voices in his head. I could not believe what he had done because he has never been violent. The neighbourhood's children called him "sheephead" because of his distinctive white hair.'

After spraying a shop window with graffiti Abram was arrested and placed in a cell overnight where he began to argue with God and declared that he was the archangel St Michael.

After being discharged he made several trips down to Friar Park.

His mother was to comment, 'Michael told us he believed George Harrison was a witch, a sorcerer, and that he was possessing him.'

On 29 December 1999 Abram borrowed £50 from an uncle and took the train to London.

Although Friar Park was guarded by a wall and razor wire around its thirty acres of grounds, with electronic gates and video surveillance which could be instantly floodlit to deter intruders, Abram still gained entry and broke a statue of St George and the dragon, which he used to smash a window.

That evening George had visited his brother, then watched a film and retired to bed at 2.10 a.m. Olivia woke him at 3.20 a.m. saying that she'd heard glass smashing. She had initially believed a chandelier had fallen down, then realised that an intruder was in the house.

She phoned the police while George put a jacket over his pyjamas, put on a pair of boots and went downstairs. He discovered that two windows had been smashed.

He recalled, 'I retreated hurriedly to the bedroom, shouting at my wife someone was in the house.

'My wife was saying, "Stay in the room," but I decided to look again. As I looked down to the room below me, I saw a person run from the kitchen. He stopped in the centre of the room and looked towards me. He started shouting and screaming. He was hysterical and frightening in his manner. He said words to the effect of "You get down here. You know what it is." I could see he held a knife in his hand and a stick. I recognised it as the spear from part of the statue.

'I made the decision to shout back at him, to confuse and distract him. I shouted, "Hare Krishna, Hare Krishna."

'He rushed towards the bottom of the stairs and looked up towards me. I attempted to go into another room but I couldn't turn the key.

'I took the split-second decision to tackle the man because once he passed me, both my wife and my mother-in-law would be vulnerable. Armed only with the element of surprise, I ran at him. My first thought was to grab the knife and I kicked him slightly off balance, but he thrust the knife towards my body and I was pushed off balance. We tumbled to the floor, I was fending off the blows with my hands and arms. He was stabbing down towards my upper body. He lost grip of his stick. He was on top of me, stabbing towards my upper body.

'I was aware of my wife approaching and striking him about the head with a brass poker. It appeared to have little effect. He stood up and chased my wife. I feared greatly for her safety and hauled myself up to tackle him. I placed my hands around the blade. He struck out blindly.

'He again got the better of me and got on top of me. At that point, I felt exhausted and could feel the strength draining from me. My arms dropped to my sides and I vividly remember a deliberate thrust of a knife and I could feel the blood entering my mouth and hear my breath exhaling from the wound. I believed I had been fatally stabbed.

'My wife struck this man about the head with a lamp. He stumbled over. I took hold of the knife and wrenched it from his grasp.

'He got up in a quite surprising surge of energy and went towards my wife. I watched as he lashed out with part of the lamp that was left at her head. Then he turned towards me as I was still lying on my back and rained down blows on my head as my wife ran from the room.

'Then he stopped and chased after her. I was still lying on my back and I turned to my right and as I did so I saw him struggle and partly collapse. Then I heard other voices and people coming up the stairs and I was aware of a uniformed policeman who handcuffed him and arrested him.

'I have no doubt this person had the intention of killing me and my wife Olivia. There was a time during this violent struggle that I truly believed I was dying.'

In fact, George had been stabbed five times and suffered a punctured lung.

Olivia was to say, 'I saw my husband looking very pale. He was staring at me in a really bizarre manner. I have never seen my husband look like that before.

'I was knocked backwards and the man was up against the wall and I was on my hands and knees by his feet. I reached up and tried to grab his testicles but just got a lot of trouser fabric.'

Olivia described how she felt the attackers hands on the back of her neck and how he then fell when George jumped on the attacker's back.

'There was blood on the walls, blood on the carpet. I realised we were going to be murdered. The man was very determined, very angry, aggressive. He had blood all over his face and had very wild, staring eyes. He appeared crazed and frenzied.

'I turned around and grabbed a lamp. I brought it down on the man's head as hard as I could as many times as I could. He seemed to slump and I said to him, "Stop, stop," because I didn't want to hit him any more – it was not a pleasant experience. My husband said, "Don't stop, hit him even harder," so I hit him again. After I hit him over the head, the man jumped up and faced me. I had the lamp in my hand and was swinging it at him. The cord was too long and he ripped it over my head and gashed my head.

'He began wrapping the cord around his hands and I thought he was going to strangle me. I threw the lamp at him and ran out of the room.

'My husband was fading away. I had to leave my husband there because I couldn't do any more. As I reached the last section of the stairs I realised he wasn't following me any more. I thought he'd gone back to inflict more harm on my husband. At that point the police came in.'

The two unarmed policemen arrested Abram and took him to Henley Police Station. As he had a head wound he was then taken to John Radcliffe Hospital for treatment and then taken to St Aldridge Police Station.

In the meantime, George and Olivia had been taken to the Royal Berkshire Hospital in Reading. A statement was given to the press saying that 'George was stable and there wasn't a life-threatening situation,' although he had a drain in his lung to remove blood, as his lung was partially collapsed.

George was later transferred to Harefield Hospital, Uxbridge, for observation.

A spokesman at Harefield commented that, 'Harrison had remained in good spirits, although he was probably making an effort to conceal his shock in front of his wife and son, who were still believed to be at his bedside last night. He is probably in quite a lot of discomfort. He is on serious painkillers because he has a serious painful injury. He is breathing unaided and did not suffer a large loss of blood as far as I am aware. He has had antitetanus injections and antibiotics, normal in these circumstances, as there is always a fear of infection. I am reasonably confident the treatment he has had is all he will need. Nature will do the rest.'

Abram was put on trial at Oxford Crown Court on 15 November 2000, charged with two counts of attempted murder. On the second day of the trial, Judge Michael Astill instructed the jurors to find the defendant not guilty by reason of insanity. This was due to the Lunatics

Act, which stated that a jury had to return a verdict of not guilty if the offender is declared criminally insane at the time of the offence. Abram had said that he had tried to kill George 'on the orders of God'. He was ordered to be held in a psychiatric institution.

Dhani Harrison was to comment, 'It is tragic that anyone should suffer such a mental breakdown to commit such a brutal act.' He also said, 'The prospect of him being released back into society is abhorrent to us. We hope that the authorities will act with the utmost responsibility in avoiding it in the future and allow us to be consulted before reaching any conclusion. We will ask the Home Secretary to notify us of any attempt to release him.

'We shall never forget that he was full of hatred and violence when he came into our house. We understand that the jury was given no real choice in this matter and that the ancient law of the Lunatics Act provides a loophole. We will now continue rebuilding our lives and hope violence in our society is contained and ultimately overcome by the goodness of most people in the world.'

George provided a written statement and Olivia was in court to testify about the attack.

The court was told that 34-year-old Abram was convinced that the Beatles practiced witchcraft and were flying around on broomsticks. He also believed he was the fifth Beatle and spent days studying their lyrics, believing they contained private messages to him.

Abram had told the psychiatrists that when he broke into George's mansion he had originally intended to kill George and then decided he wouldn't go through with it. But then George began chanting 'Hare Krishna'.

Giving evidence, Dr Philip Joseph said, 'Abram said that George Harrison spoke backwards to him and cursed him in the devil's tongue, which to him proved that Harrison was a witch.

'He said that if Harrison had talked normally to him he would not have gone through with it. But he realised that Harrison was a witch who had possessed him and he believed he was on a mission from God to do this.

'He said that it was all contained in the Book of Exodus. He thought he was doing the right thing by God, that he was St Michael and was justified in killing Harrison because he had possessed him, was making him do things he didn't want to do and he had to stop him.'

After being cleared of attempted murder at Oxford Crown Court on the grounds of temporary insanity, Abram was sent to the Scott Clinic in St Helens. He was released less than two years later.

Olivia was angry to hear of his release and Dhani was to comment, 'We certainly wish Mr Abram no ill, but to be presented with this as a fact after the event is deeply upsetting and insulting, and we feel completely let down by the system.

'It remains the case in this country that the victim simply has no voice. The law must be changed. This was promised by Jack Straw at the last election, and we wonder if it will ever happen.'

In July 2002, Abram said, 'I would give anything not to have done what I did in attacking George Harrison. But looking back on it now, I have come to understand that I was very ill at that time, really not in control of my actions. I can only hope the Harrison family might somehow find it in their hearts to accept my apologies.

'Me and my family and the Harrisons were all failed by the system.

'At my trial, I was found not guilty on the grounds of temporary insanity. But some people, including the Harrison family, thought I had got off through a legal loophole.

'I hope now they can understand what happened to me and appreciate that it was not my fault. Physically I did it, but I was not in control of my own mind at the time.'

All Dressed Up – The Sixties And Counter-Culture

A book by Jonathan Green, published in Britain by Random House in 1998. The author claimed that George had accepted sexual favours from a young woman in exchange for a donation to charity. George took the matter to a High Court hearing and an apology and undisclosed but substantial damages were awarded to him.

The book was also withdrawn. George's solicitor Norman Chapman commented, 'The allegation is untrue and the defendants now acknowledge this to be the case.'

All Things Must Pass (album)

George began planning *All Things Must Pass* while he was still a member of the Beatles, obviously frustrated that he had so much difficulty trying to get his own numbers accepted as Beatles tracks due to the fact that priority was given to the Lennon and McCartney material.

In October 1969 he discussed his solo album. 'It's mainly just to get rid of all the songs I've got stacked up. I've got such a backlog, and at the rate of two or three an album with the group, I'm not even going to get the ones I've already done out for three or four years. I suppose I'm waiting till I've got myself a proper studio at home. And then I can just knock 'em off when I feel like it.

'In future, though, the Beatles are going to get an equal rights thing, so we'll all have as much on the album.'

He began recording on 26 May 1970 at Abbey Road Studios.

George considered three Dylan songs – 'If Not For You', which he'd recently recorded with Dylan in New York; 'I'd Have You Anytime', which he'd co-written with Dylan; and 'I Don't Want To Do It', which wasn't officially released until it was included on the *Porky's Revenge* soundtrack in the 1980s.

Other numbers included 'The Art Of Dying', about which George said he 'had been working on a song about reincarnation since 1966'.

'Isn't It A Pity' was a number from the end of 1968, also performed during jam sessions at Twickenham Studios in January 1969.

On 9 October 1970 George, Donovan and Janis Joplin were all asked by Yoko to do a special birthday song for John. Together with Eddie Klein and Mal Evans, George recorded 'It's Johnny's Birthday'. He decided to include it on the 'Apple Jam' section of the album and used the tune of 'Congratulations' for the birthday tribute. Composers Bill Martin and Phil Coulter received royalties for the track 'It's Johnny's Birthday'.

While George and the other musicians did some jam sessions, the engineers left the tapes running and several hours of instrumental recording was saved and included in a third section of the album called 'Apple Jam'.

There was so much material that George decided to issue it as a triple set, in a box with a lyric sheet and poster at double the price of a normal album.

The set entered the *Billboard* chart on 19 December 1970 and reached No. 1 on 2 January 1971, becoming a double-platinum album, eventually selling over three million copies. The album remained at the top for seven weeks (Plastic Ono Band, at the same time, only reached No. 6). In Britain it was No. 1 for eight weeks. It created a new chart record when 'My Sweet Lord' and *All Things Must Pass* topped the US and UK charts simultaneously – not even the Beatles had achieved that.

All Things Must Pass was issued in Britain and America on 27 November 1970 on Apple STCH 639. It was produced by George and Phil Spector and engineered by Ken Scott and Phil McDonald with orchestral arrangements by John Barham.

Musical credits on the album were as follows. Guitars: George Harrison, Eric Clapton, Dave Mason. Drums and percussion: Ringo Starr, Jim Gordon, Alan White. Bass guitar: Klaus Voormann, Carl Radle. Keyboard: Gary Wright, Bobby Whitlock, Billy Preston, Gary Brooker. Pedal steel guitar: Pete Drake. Tenor saxophone: Bobby Keys. Trumpet: Jim Price. Rhythm guitars and percussion: Badfinger. Tea, sympathy and tambourine: Mal Evans. Introducing the George O'Hara Smith Singers. Orchestral arrangement: John Barham. Recording engineers: Ken Scott, Philip McDonald.

Incidentally, it was the first time the quartet who became known as Derek And The Dominoes recorded together.

George also overdubbed his backing vocals several times using the name the George O'Hara Smith Singers. He missed some sessions because of health problems.

The tracks were: Record One, Side One: 'I'd Have You Anytime', 'My Sweet Lord', 'Wah-Wah', 'Isn't It A Pity (version one)'. Record One, Side Two: 'What Is Life', 'If Not For You', 'Behind That Locked Door', 'Let It Down', 'Run Of The Mill'. Record Two, Side One: 'Beware Of Darkness', 'Apple Scruffs', 'Ballad Of Sir Frankie Crisp

(Let It Roll)', 'Awaiting On You All', 'All Things Must Pass'. Record Two, Side Two: 'I Dig Love', 'Art Of Dying', 'Isn't It A Pity (version two)', 'Hear Me Lord'. Record Three ('Apple Jam') Side One: 'Out Of The Blue', 'It's Johnny's Birthday', 'Plug Me In'. Record Three, Side Two: 'I Remember Jeep', 'Thanks For The Pepperoni'.

The thirtieth anniversary double-CD set of *All Things Must Pass* was issued on Apple 72435 30475 2 8 and included a newly recorded version of 'My Sweet Lord', recorded in 2000, which was personally supervised by George, together with four previously unreleased tracks from the 1970 recording sessions. They included 'I Live For You', an outtake not used at the time, an alternative version of 'Beware Of Darkness', 'Let It Down', described as 'the original guitar and vocal from the same tape as "Beware Of Darkness" with a little overdubbing, circa 2000' and 'What Is Life', a rough mix of the backing track.

In January 2001 EMI issued an advance sampler CD on CDLRLO43 with the tracks 'My Sweet Lord', 'What Is Life', 'Isn't It A Pity', 'Ballad Of Sir Frankie Crisp (Let It Roll)', 'Wah-Wah', 'Beware Of Darkness', 'All Things Must Pass' and 'My Sweet Lord (2000)'. George said that he wanted to include the updated version of 'My Sweet Lord' 'to create something extra for the anniversary issue'.

For the anniversary release, George recorded a promotional interview called 'A Conversation With George Harrison', which was released on 15 February 2001. Chris Carter conducted the interview at Capitol Studios, Hollywood. The cover of the disc had a colourised photo of George from the original album, but altered slightly to have him holding a parasol. The number was DPRO 7087 6 15950 2 4.

This is a transcript of the interview:

Q: George, when you began the sessions for *All Things Must Pass*, did you plan to record a double album or, for that matter, a triple album?

George: Well, when I started the album I was just trying to do a record and I had so many songs that we just recorded one after the other and just kept doing backing tracks and one day I thought I better check out what's going on here and I had eighteen tracks. Also, the accountant at Abbey Road came down the stairs and said, 'Is this record going to take much longer?' So I thought, 'Well, I think that's probably enough,' and decided to put them all out at once.

Q: How have your thoughts changed regarding the production of *All Things Must Pass* since it was first recorded in 1970?

George: Well, in those days it was like the reverb was kind of used a bit more than what I would do now. In fact, I don't use reverb at all. I can't stand it. But at the time I did the record with Phil Spector, and we did it like Phil Spector would do it. You know, it's hard to go back to anything thirty years later and expect it to be how you would want it now. I dare say if I did a record today, in thirty years I'd probably want to change it. That's the only thing about the production. It was done in cinemascope and it had a lot of reverb on it compared to what I would use now, but that's how it was and at the time I really liked it.

Q: Both you and John Lennon chose to use Phil Spector as producer for your first 'proper' solo albums. How come Mr Spector?

George: Well, we knew him a little bit. He needed a job! And Phil was around. If you remember, he was brought into London by Allen Klein when we had done the record 'Get Back', or *Let It Be*, it became the *Let It Be* record. *Let It Be* was supposed to be just a live recording and we ended up doing it in the studio and nobody was happy with it. But it was troubled times. Everybody listened to it back and didn't really like it and we didn't really want to put it out.

So later on down the line Klein, this guy Allen Klein brought in Phil Spector and said, 'Well, what do you think about Phil looking at the record?' so at least John and I said, 'Yeah, let's see.' We liked Phil Spector, we loved all his records. So, let him do it, and he did what he did and then you know everybody knows the rest. And so he was around and one day I was with Phil and I was on my way to Abbey Road to do 'Instant Karma'. And so I made Phil go with me and that's how he got to do that record as well. That is how we first started working with him.

Q: Your friend Eric Clapton was originally only credited on the 'Apple Jam'. How many other tracks do you recall Eric contributing to?

George: Well, he's on nearly every track there is, like the very first note on the album is Eric, 'I'd Have You Anytime'. In those days, the record company, both my record company and his, they didn't like you to have your name on other people's records, very possessive. So if you look on the record of the last Cream record *Goodbye*, my credit is L'Angelo De Mysterioso or something. That was me. He just didn't get any credit because they said you're not allowed to. Otherwise, you've got to pay him royalties or they have to pay me royalties. You know, some silly thing like that.

Q: Let's talk briefly about a few of the songs here. 'I'd Have You Anytime' kind of sets the mood for the whole album. Tell me about writing that with Bob Dylan.

George: Well, it was just one of those simple things. I just happened to be invited to Woodstock by the Band. I spent some days with Bob and I suppose we just got round to picking up guitars and he was saying, 'Hey, show me some of those chords, those weird chords.' And that's how that came about. It's like a strange chord, really. It's called G Major 7th. It's got all these major 7th chords. You know, we just turned it into a song. So it was really nice.

Q: 'My Sweet Lord' was a worldwide hit single. What was it like being a solo chart-topper with a song that has such a positive spiritual message?

George: I can't really remember. I didn't really pay much attention to the charts. It's only now that you know people keep saying that *All Things Must Pass* was up there for seven weeks or whatever. I didn't really notice, you know. I mean, I'm not really very good at statistics or, you know, I like to just do something and let it go and then forget about it. So it was very nice, really. I mean, I got a lot of response from that record, from people. I mean, half of the Hare Krishnas joined because of that.

Q: Let's talk about a few of the new additional tracks added on to this special thirtieth anniversary release. 'My Sweet Lord (2000)', tell me about re-recording this spiritual anthem thirty years later.

George: Well, I kind of enjoyed doing it because of a few reasons. I thought the song was, you know, at the time it was so popular and it was also very controversial and the subject matter is not something that you normally hear people sing records like that, unless it's like gospel choirs or something. So I liked the idea of going back to it and especially because in this lawsuit I had about that, it was all down to these two phrases. 'Doo Doo Doo' was Phrase A and 'Doo Doo Doo Doo Doo' was Phrase B. And that constituted, you know, what they said was an infringement of copyright. So I really enjoyed singing the song again and not using those three notes in that order. And so that was one of the reasons I liked to do it, and also because it had so much response from people on a spiritual level years ago. You know, many people have written to me over the years saying thanks for doing that song because that helped me to do this or go join the Krishnas or whatever or just look into myself a bit more. So I'll see if there's a reason to reinvent the song a little bit and also maybe somebody will want to play it on the radio, give it a bit more promotion and play a better slide guitar solo. So many reasons it was fun.

Q: Another additional track, 'I Live For You', is being heard for the very first time. Tell me why this one didn't make the final cut.

George: Well, I think originally it didn't sound like we'd got it. You know, on some of those songs we recorded them and then listened to them back and said, 'Naw, I don't like it, we haven't done it right.' And that's why there are actually two versions of 'Isn't It A Pity'. And the first version, like the more up-tempo version, we did and then after doing it for a few hours, I decided I didn't like it. And then some weeks later we got round and we did it again. One of the guys in the band just started playing it and we needed to get that slow version and so then we did that. And then later I looked back at the original version and I thought, 'Oh, it's OK, so I'll use them both.' But on the one, 'I Live For You', it was just not right. Nobody had a feel for it except for the pedal steel guitar player and the rhythm guitarist. And so I didn't want to use it. I didn't think we got it and I think at the time I was thinking the song's a bit fruity, anyway. We've got enough songs, we leave it off. So I just went back and fixed it up, because people like to have bonus tracks.

Q: Okay, here's an 'Apple Jam' question. What are your memories of recording 'It's Johnny's Birthday'? Was it in honour of John Lennon's thirtieth birthday?

George: Yeah. Yoko asked us to give a recording for Johnny's birthday. So I looked in the Abbey Road tape library and I found 'Congratulations'. And I just kind of slowed it down, speeded it up, and added a few things, and made up the words. And that's what I sent to her, to Yoko. I don't know how it ended up on the jam session, but there it is.

Q: What are your favourite songs on *All Things Must Pass*, and have they changed over the years at all?

George: I think I like 'Run Of The Mill', you know it's just something about the words, what it's saying. And I like 'Isn't It A Pity'. And I like 'Awaiting On You All'. I like the same ones now as I liked then but I like them all in some way, otherwise I wouldn't have done them.

Q: So George, the album cover's been colourised now. Did you originally want a colour cover? And I see you've added some new additions to the skyline. Tell me about the artwork.

George: Well, originally no, it was black and white because it was more arty, looked more artistic, especially on the big box. But now, I thought, well, how can we, you know, if we just put it out with the same photo, first of all it needed to go back to the original photo anyway, because over the years it had gotten slightly distorted. In fact, it looked a bit like a Xerox copy. So I thought we'd better get back to the original artwork. And we did that and got the photos from the photographer, Barry Feinstein. There were colour shots taken but the colour shots, they didn't make it really. The black and white was much better. So we decided to tint it like you would an old-fashioned photograph. Somewhere down the line I turned to the art director and said, 'Maybe we should try having a flyover going through the back?' And then the whole thing evolved into gas stations and high-rise apartments, just as a little dig at the way our planet is going at the moment, or has gone over the last thirty years. It's just turning into a big concrete block. So it's a bit of a cynical joke on reality.

Q: What are your plans, if any, for the rest of your back catalogue?

George: Put them back out again. I think everything could do with remastering because originally they were done for vinyl. When CDs came in, somebody took them and digitised them. But the equipment is much better now anyways, so we can get a much more accurate sound, make a much better digital version of it. So I think to get them all back in the shops, nice and crisp and clean and fresh, that's really what we'd like to do.

Q: So, George, in closing, how would you sum up *All Things Must Pass* today?

George: I don't know, it's just something that was like my continuation from the Beatles, really. It was me sort of getting out of the Beatles and just going my own way. And so, as my first record, it was a very happy occasion. I think in some ways it stands up. The sound on some of the records are a bit old. It sounds a bit old. But I think it kind of stands up still, enough to justify what we're doing.

All Things Must Pass (song)

A track from the *All Things Must Pass* triple album, penned by George. It is 3 minutes and 45 seconds in length.

George also gave the number to Billy Preston when he co-produced Preston's Apple album *Encouraging Words*.

All Things Must Pass: The Life Of George Harrison

A book by Mark Shapiro, published in the US by St Martins Press (under the title *Behind Sad Eyes: The Life Of George Harrison*) and in the UK by Virgin in 2002.

There had been relatively few biographies of George as most biographies surrounding the ex-Beatles concentrated on John Lennon and Paul McCartney. However, with the death of George, it was inevitable that a biography would be rushed into print and this was the first of them.

Unfortunately, it contains some inaccuracies, particularly surrounding the early days. The author writes 'Skiffle was the music of the moment in London in the late 1950s,' when skiffle was, in fact, a national movement, not confined to the capital city. He writes, 'John came to rehearsals one day with the suggestion of the Beatles, taking his cue from the Crickets.' The origin of the name was not so simple and it was Stuart Sutcliffe who suggested the association with the Crickets.

Shapiro writes that George moonlighted with the Les Stewart Quartet, but George was a full-time member of the group at the time as the Quarry Men had actually ceased to function. He says that the 'Cavern offered them gigs on condition they only played jazz', which is ridiculous. They were allowed to play skiffle and were chastised for playing rock'n'roll.

The author says that Derry and the Seniors were the first of the British groups to go to Hamburg, but they were the second – the first was the London band the Jets. The author also writes, 'On 17 December 1960 the Beatles played their first post-Hamburg show at the Cavern Club.' Any basic research could have told him that the Beatles appeared at the Casbah Club, run by Pete Best's mum, on that date and that they actually made their Cavern Club debut as the Beatles on Tuesday 9 February 1961.

These are typical of the errors in the book, which also includes a detailed discography.

All Those Years Ago

A number that originally began life when Ringo Starr joined George at his FPSHOT Studio in Friar Park to record a track for Ringo's album *Can't Fight Lightning* (the LP was later issued under the title *Stop And Smell The Roses*). On Wednesday 19 November 1980 they began work on a number, laying down the basic guitar and drum tracks. This was the number that George was to develop into 'All Those Years Ago' as a tribute to the murdered John Lennon.

George was to remove Ringo's vocal from the track and sang some lyrics that he had written specially. Paul and Linda travelled from Montserrat with Denny Laine and recorded backing vocals, so the finished tribute single featuring all three surviving ex-Beatles – George, Ringo and Paul – was issued in America on Monday 11 May 1981 and in Britain on Friday 15 May.

Ringo Starr was to comment, 'An early version of "All Those Years Ago" was originally done for my album, but it didn't work for me vocally, and I really didn't like the original words. So I told George I didn't feel comfortable with it, let's forget about it. So later he put new words on it, and wound up doing it.'

George was to confirm this, saying that he originally wrote it for Ringo with slightly different words but the same chorus, and described it as having a 'more uptight kind of lyric'. He also said that after John's death, 'I changed it straight away and made it specifically about him.'

The single was co-produced by George and Ray Cooper and is 3 minutes and 43 seconds in length.

Ron Furmanek of Warner Brothers made a promotional film. There was also a 12″ promotional record, George's first such release.

The number was included on the *Somewhere In England* album and was also issued as a single in Britain on Dark Horse K 17807 with 'Writing's On The Wall', which lasted 3 minutes and 34 seconds, on the flip. The single became George's first hit in the Top 30 for eight years when it reached No. 9 in the charts.

It was issued in America on Dark Horse DRC 49725 on 11 May

1981, reaching No. 2 in the charts with a chart life of thirteen weeks – his biggest hit since 1971. Warner Brothers, who had the distribution rights to Dark Horse, also had the reissue rights and re-released the single on Dark Horse GDRC 0410 on 4 November 1981, with 'Teardrops' on the flip.

Alvin Lee 1994

George is one of the guests on this 1994 album, appearing on two of the tracks, 'Bluest Blues' and 'I Want You (She's So Heavy)' which was issued on Magnum CDTB 150.

Answer's At The End, The

A track from the 1975 album *Extra Texture (Read All About It)* lasting 5 minutes and 29 seconds. It was said to have been inspired by some writings on the wall of Friar Park by its original owner Sir Frank Crisp.

Any Road

A single from the *Brainwashed* album lasting 3 minutes and 52 seconds with George on slide and acoustic guitars, Jeff Lynne on bass guitar, piano and backing vocals, Dhani Harrison on electric guitar and backing vocals and Jim Keltner on drums.

George had originally performed this number in his VH1 special with Ravi Shankar in 1992.

A promotional video was also made with archive film of George in the studio and some concert shots.

The single was issued in Britain on 12 May 2003 as a maxi-CD with the 6-minute 12-second 'Marwa Blues' and also the promo video of 'Any Road', which was designed to play on computer screens using Quicktime.

Anything

A number by George that the Beatles began recording on Wednesday 22 February 1967, but never completed.

Apple Jam

A label designed specially for the third and last record on George's *All Things Must Pass* boxed set. The name, which is also a pun, was used partly as a description of a jam session recorded at Apple Studios. This record mainly comprised instrumentals showcasing the guitars of George and Eric Clapton.

Apple Records

When Apple Records was formed, George took an active part in the label, writing and producing for a number of artists. His participation included the following records:

Singles:
'Day After Day' by Badfinger, produced by George.
'Sweet Music' by Lon and Derreck Van Eaton, produced by George.
'I Fall Inside Your Eyes' by Jackie Lomax, produced by George.
'Try Some, Buy Some' by Ronnie Spector, written by George and co-produced with Phil Spector. He wiped off Ronnie's vocals, replaced them with his own and the track appears on his own *Living In The Material World* album.
'My Sweet Lord' by Billy Preston, produced by George and released in Britain.
'Hare Krishna Mantra' by the Radha Krishna Temple, produced by George.
'Govinda' by the Radha Krishna Temple, produced by George.
'How The Web Was Woven' by Jackie Lomax, produced by George.
'Sour Milk Sea' by Jackie Lomax. George wrote and produced and played rhythm, with Paul on bass, Ringo on drums, Eric Clapton on lead guitar and Nicky Hopkins on piano.
'Ain't That Cute' by Doris Troy, written by George and Doris Troy and produced by George.
'Jacob's Ladder' by Doris Troy, a traditional number arranged by George and Doris Troy.
'That's The Way God Planned It' by Billy Preston, produced by George.
'Joi Bangla' by Ravi Shankar, produced by George.

Albums:
Is This What You Want? by Jackie Lomax, produced by George.
That's The Way God Planned It by Billy Preston, produced by George.
Encouraging Words by Billy Preston, produced by George.
The Radha Krishna Temple, produced by George.
Raga by Ravi Shankar, produced by George.
Concert For Bangla Desh, produced by George and Phil Spector.
In Concert 1972 by Ravi Shankar and Ali Akbar Khan, produced by George, Zakir Hussein and Phil McDonald.

Apple Scruffs

A track from the *All Things Must Pass* album, penned by George and 3 minutes and 4 seconds in length.

The Apple Scruffs were a group of dedicated Beatles fans who camped outside the Beatles' Savile Row offices or Abbey Road Studios in their desire for Beatle-spotting. They even had their own magazine, *Apple Scruffs*.

One day, when they were waiting outside Abbey Road Studios, George came out and invited them into the studio. He then played them a song he'd recorded which he'd specially written for them called 'Apple Scruffs'.

The Scruffs even printed membership cards. *Saturday Evening Post* writer Al Aronovitz was to observe: 'Outside the studio door, whether it rained or not, there was always a handful of Apple Scruffs, one of them a girl all the way from Texas. Sometimes George would record from 7 p.m. to 7 a.m. and there they would be, waiting through the night, beggars for a sign of recognition on his way in or out. In the morning they'd go off to their jobs and in the evening they'd be back outside the studio door again. Their grapevine was infallible.'

The Apple Scruffs regarded themselves as an extra special group. Their members included Margo Stevens, Nancy Allen, Wendy Sutcliffe, Gill Pritchard, Carol Bedford and Sue-John, Chris, Di, Kath, Virginia, Dani and Lucy. There were also two boys, Tommy and Jimmy. The Scruffs eventually disbanded in December 1973, after the Savile Row headquarters of Apple was no longer occupied and as the members of the Beatles had gone their separate ways.

Arias, Olivia
See Harrison, Olivia

Armchair Theater
Jeff Lynne's 1990 solo debut album on which George performed. George also appeared as guest musician and vocalist on 'Every Little Thing', the first single released from the album.

12 Arnold Grove
A small terraced house in a cul-de-sac, with an alley to the rear, where Harold and Louise Harrison moved to in 1930 following their marriage. At the time they paid ten shillings a week in rent.

The property is situated in the Wavertree area of Liverpool.

It was typical of terraced houses in Liverpool at that time, as it had no bathroom or indoor toilet. There was a paved backyard with an outdoor toilet.

The Harrisons had had three previous children, Louise, Harry and Peter. Their fourth child, George, named after King George VI, was born in the house on 24 February 1943.

George Harold Harrison was to say, 'I vaguely remember tiptoeing up the stairs to see him after he was born. A tiny, squalling, miniature replica of myself.'

At bath time, baby George was originally bathed in the kitchen sink. Then, like the rest of the family, he graduated to a zinc tub, which was brought in from the yard as it was needed.

George recalled that the only heating was a single coal fire and the house was extremely cold in winter. He also remembered how he and his brothers dreaded getting up in the morning because it was literally freezing cold – and they had to make their way to the outside toilet, situated next to their father's tiny homemade hen house.

In his book *I. Me. Mine.* George wrote that the house had tiny rooms only ten feet square and 'one of those little iron cooking stoves in the back room which was the kitchen, where you had the kettle on the fire and the oven alongside'. Describing the yard, he wrote that it had 'a one-foot wide flowerbed, a toilet, a dustbin fitted into the back wall, a little henhouse where we kept cockerels'.

During the six years that George lived in the property, the rent had risen. The family had been on the housing list for eighteen years and finally packed their belongings and moved from Arnold Grove to a new council estate in Speke on 2 January 1950. George's brother Harry was to recall, 'Our little house was just two rooms up and two down, but, except for a short period when our father was away at sea, we always knew the comfort and security of a very close-knit home life.'

In his autobiography *I. Me. Mine.* George was rather more philosophical, writing, 'Try and imagine the soul entering the womb of a woman living at 12 Arnold Grove, Wavertree, Liverpool 15. There were all the barrage balloons, and the Germans bombing Liverpool. All that was going on. I sat outside the house a couple of years ago, imagining 1943, nipping through the spiritual world, the astral level, getting back into a body in that house. That really is strange when you consider the whole planet, all the planets there may be on the physical level. How do I come into that family, in that house at that time, and who am I anyway?'

Art Of Dying

A track from the *All Things Must Pass* triple album, penned by George and 3 minutes and 36 seconds in length.

The number had actually been written in 1966, but George had great difficulty in those days in trying to get his numbers recorded by the Beatles. As he was to recall, 'We'd do fourteen of theirs and maybe one of mine.' He didn't want to enter the fray of battling with John and Paul to get his numbers accepted. 'It was becoming more difficult for me because I wasn't really that into it. It became an assembly process, and for me it became a bit tiring and a bit boring.'

When he first wrote this number there was a mention of 'Mr Epstein', but this was taken out when he recorded the number four years later.

When he began recording his solo album in May 1970, Phil Spector added his usual 'overproduction' style to the number.

Aspel And Company

A London Weekend Television chat-show series hosted by Michael Aspel.

George and Ringo appeared on the show together on Saturday 5 March 1988, having recorded it on 3 March at the South Bank Studios of LWT.

The other guest on the show was the actress who portrayed Thelma Barlow on the TV soap *Coronation Street*.

George and Ringo chatted for 35 minutes and it was the first time that the two former Beatles had appeared together for an interview since the Beatles had split up.

The only other time two ex-Beatles had been together during an interview took place on 20 December 1974 when George and John Lennon were together in a hotel room following George's American tour.

Au Pair Girls

A typical example of the soft-porn movies made in Britain during the early 1970s. It starred Gabrielle Drake and Richard O'Sullivan. In January 1972, after George had arrived back at Friar Park following his trip to New York, he found the film crew filming in the grounds of his mansion. The film was issued in Britain in July of that year.

Australia

George sought a property in Australia, believing it would provide a sanctuary for him and his family against constant attention from the media and would also be ideal for his hobby of growing tropical plants. When he arrived in Australia for the first time since he'd visited with the Beatles in 1964, it was to seek some property and he bought land in Hamilton Island, and was to settle in a mansion there that actually took three years to build.

When George first arrived with Olivia and Dhani, they stayed with Bobby Jones, a racing driver, at his Gold Coast penthouse. They then stayed at the farm of a friend, tourist entrepreneur Keith William, who he'd met through a mutual friend, Jackie Stewart.

When in New South Wales, George invited the WEA staff to lunch, then went on to Melbourne in Victoria and stayed with Alan Jones, world champion racing driver, for a few days on his farm in Queensland. George visited the Melbourne Grand Prix virtually every year, but became disenchanted with his Hamilton mansion because too many people were turning up to have a glimpse at him. 'It's turning into Wallyworld,' he said, 'and there is no way I am going to live here.'

Awaiting On You All

A track from the *All Things Must Pass* triple album, penned by George, lasting 2 minutes and 45 seconds.

Baby Don't Run Away

A track from George's 1982 album *Gone Troppo*, lasting 3 minutes and 59 seconds. Billy Preston and Rodina Sloan provide backing vocals.

Badge

A George Harrison/Eric Clapton composition penned in 1968. It is 2 minutes and 45 seconds in length. The number was recorded by Cream on 2 October 1968 with George on rhythm guitar. The single was re-released as a single by RSO Records on RSO91 on 6 August 1982. There was also a 12″ version issued on RSOOX91.

A live performance of Clapton playing the number at the NEC, Birmingham in July 1986 was included as a bonus track on Clapton's single 'Bad Love' on 26 January 1990. It was issued on Duck/Warner Bros W 2644CD.

Ballad Of Sir Frankie Crisp (Let It Roll)

A track from the *All Things Must Pass* triple album, penned by George and 3 minutes and 47 seconds in length. It was inspired by the eccentric lawyer who had built Friar Park in the nineteenth century.

Baltimore Oriole

Hoagy Carmichael composed the music to this song, with lyrics by Paul Francis Webster, in 1944. Frances Langford recorded it originally and it was covered by a number of artists. George recorded it for his 1981 album *Somewhere In England* and it lasts 3 minutes and 56 seconds.

Bangla Desh

Written by George and co-produced by Phil Spector, the single was released a few days before the concert for Bangla Desh took place. It was issued in Britain on Apple R 5912 on 30 July 1971 and in America on Apple 1836 on 28 July 1971. Ringo Starr played drums and the flip-side was 'Deep Blue'. The single reached No. 23 in charts.

Barham, John

An arranger who George enlisted to help during the recording sessions at Friar Park with Ravi Shankar for the *Chants Of India* album. Barham had worked with George and Ravi previously and was mainly involved in translating Ravi's Indian compositions into western music notation.

He was initially introduced to George by Ravi in 1967 and George asked him to work on the *Wonderwall* album. He also arranged the strings, brass and choir for *All Things Must Pass*, did arrangements for Jackie Lomax's *Speak To Me* and for Badfinger's *Magic Christian* music. He worked on the Radha Krishna Temple arrangements as well as the strings and brass on George's production of Ronnie Spector's 'Try Some, Buy Some'.

Batten, Peter

The man who provided the voice of George in the *Yellow Submarine* animation film.

Batten was a lance corporal in the British army, based in Brugen, Germany. Bored, he and four other soldiers went absent without leave and travelled to London. Batten was having a drink in the Dog & Duck pub in Soho when George Dunning, producer of *Yellow Submarine*, heard his voice and cast him as the voice of George.

'It was all very strange,' recalled Batten. 'One minute I'm a soldier on the run, the next I'm meeting the Beatles and bumping into actors like Peter O'Toole. All that, and I was being paid £50 an hour. There was some whingeing from some people, because I wasn't a member of Equity, the actor's union, but overall, I felt very lucky.'

Shortly after completing the movie he was arrested at his girlfriend's flat in Islington by military policemen and then served six months of a nine-month jail sentence. He left the army in 1969 and lived for ten years in America where he got married. He and his wife then moved to Belgium where the *Daily Telegraph* traced them in 1999.

When the reissue of the film was premiered in Liverpool in 1999, Geoffrey Hughes (the voice of Paul), Paul Angelis (the voice of Ringo) and John Clive (the voice of John) all attended, but Batten couldn't be found.

The *Daily Telegraph* found him, but Batten told the newspaper that he wasn't interested in being associated with *Yellow Submarine* again. Commenting on the reissue on video and DVD he said, 'I don't understand why they are doing it. The original film was made in the hippie psychedelic days of the sixties. It was a thing of its time – there aren't many hippies around now.'

Beatle In Benton, Illinois, A – The Musical Birthplace Of The Beatles In America

A video documentary surrounding the visit George and his brother Peter made to their sister Louise at her home at 11 McCann Street, Benton, Illinois in September 1963.

Beatles Anthology, The

A project that involved George, Paul and Ringo between 1993 and 1996.

A day of interviews was conducted at George's home, and George, Paul and Ringo went into George's studio and, for the first time since 1969, they played together. Also present were director Bob Smeaton and a pair of cameramen.

Smeaton said of it: 'There's a whole load of stuff. They played some old Beatles songs, like 'Thinking Of Linking' and that sort of stuff. They did a whole load of rock'n'roll songs and we shot a load of stuff.'

George said, 'It's just some little magic that when you get certain people together it makes fire, or it makes more dynamite. Plus we had good songs. Excellent songs, and we were consistent. We were honest; we had a sense of humour and kind of looked quite good at the time. We actually had a sense of being different.'

The Beatles Anthology developed from a concept originally considered at the end of the 1960s – a television documentary of the Beatles history called *The Long And Winding Road*. Neil Aspinall had worked on it and had originally wanted it to be completed for showing at Christmas 1970, but it wasn't to be, although the idea never really faded away. It eventually resulted in a five-hour six-part television series screened in November 1995, making its debut on ABC TV in America before being sold to 110 countries. The following year *The Beatles Anthology* video set was released, an eight-volume package which ran for almost ten hours, nearly twice the length of the television series. This was followed by a series of 3 double CDs *Beatles Anthology*.

The title *Beatles Anthology* was used rather than 'The Long And Winding Road' because George objected to a series about the group being launched under the heading of a Paul McCartney composition.

To further enhance this ambitious project it was decided to release two new Beatles singles. These were to be taken from some demo records, which John Lennon had made in the 1970s. It was George who originally thought of the three surviving Beatles utilising a recording by John. George also engaged Jeff Lynne to record the numbers using 48-track technology. Two of the numbers, 'Free As A

Bird' and 'Real Love' were selected for George, Paul and Ringo, who the media now referred to as 'the Threetles' to record.

The first to be released was 'Free As A Bird', the first new Beatles single since 1970. This was followed by 'Real Love', issued in March 1996. On the recording Paul used a stand-up double bass originally used by Elvis Presley's bassist, the late Bill Black. Both Paul and George used six-string acoustic guitars to augment the electric instruments, and Ringo used a Ludwig drum kit.

Beatles, The (album)

More popularly referred to as 'the White Album', this LP featured an unprecedented four numbers by George. They were 'Savoy Truffle', 'Piggies', 'Long Long Long' and 'While My Guitar Gently Weeps'.

Beautiful Girl

A number from the *Thirty Three & 1/3* album, which is 3 minutes and 38 seconds in length.

George originally began writing the number while he was producing an album for Doris Troy in 1969. Stephen Stills was with him and George composed the first verse when he borrowed Stills' 12-string guitar. George eventually finished the song in 1976.

It's an acoustic song with Billy Preston on synthesizer and George was to comment, 'For me I can see all around beautiful girls in one way, girls who *look* good. And sometimes you see ones who don't particularly look good but have such beauty within them. And when you get a combination of both then that's fantastic. Beauty to me is something that comes from within and is not limited to the physical body, although that is helpful, that's natural, but it's really just something which is coming out of the heart, beauty like that.'

Bedford, Carol

A member of the Apple Scruffs and one of the two Scruffs to have a book published about their experiences. The other was Carolyn Lee Mitchell whose book *All Our Loving* was published in 1988. Bedford's book, *Waiting For The Beatles*, was published in 1984. While Mitchell was devoted to Paul, Bedford was devoted to George.

Carol was the member from Texas and relates how, in 1972, George came to her bedsit to see her. 'The doorbell rang, I went to the front door. When I opened it, there he was, grinning from ear to ear.

'Before I could gather my wits, George stepped into the threshold and threw his arms around me. I was shocked. I hugged him back. We stood like this for several minutes. Then he stepped back to look at me. I was wearing jeans with a soft, fluffy pink sweater. I was embarrassed. Here was George alone with me. Now what?'

Carol says that they only kissed, because George was married to Patti at the time, and it went no further. However, she goes on to relate that she had a visit from Mal Evans. He told her, 'George wants you to move to Los Angeles. He has an apartment there you could have.'

Carol asked why. 'He can't take you out places here. You know, he'd like to take you out to restaurants and places, but he's married. Reporters are everywhere. George can't get a divorce right now, so he doesn't want to be seen visiting another girl.'

Carol turned the offer down and said that she was so upset by it that she ceased being an Apple Scruff.

It doesn't actually have the ring of truth – George would be just as likely to be spotted by reporters in Los Angeles as he would in London.

Before He Was Fab

A book by Jim Kirkpatrick subtitled 'George Harrison's First American Visit'. Published by Cache River press in 2000, it detailed the three-week holiday George spent at his sister Louise's house in Benton, Illinois. He appeared on radio and also made a guest appearance on stage with a local group, the Four Vests.

Behind That Locked Door (book)

A book by Elliot J. Huntley, a musician based in Sheffield, subtitled 'George Harrison After The Break-up Of The Beatles'. Xerostar Holdings published it in Australia in January 2002. The 164-page book doesn't have any photographs and the text is the basic biography of George's life and career following the dissolution of the Beatles.

Behind That Locked Door (song)

A track from the *All Things Must Pass* triple album, penned by George, which is 3 minutes and 4 seconds in length.

Benton

A town in Illinois, 200 miles from St Louis. George's sister Louise, her husband Gordon Caldwell and their two children moved to the town on 10 March 1963 and settled in a two-storey house at 113 McCann Street.

George and his brother Peter decided to visit her there later that year on their first trip to the United States.

On 16 September George and Peter flew via New York and St Louis to stay with the Caldwell's in Benton for two weeks. They arrived on the day that 'She Loves You' was released in America.

Arriving with a day to spare they stayed overnight in New York at the Pickwick Hotel in Manhattan and took a trip to the Statue of Liberty.

When George and Peter settled into Benton, they were introduced to Gaby McCartney, a member of a local group called the Four Vests. Louise had played the group the *Please Please Me* album and Gaby and his guitarist Kenny Welch showed the brothers around the town, although he commented, 'I'd never seen any man with so much hair. Everywhere we went, people stared at him.

When the Four Vests appeared at the VFW dance in the nearby town of Eldorado, they invited George to sit in with them. McCartney was to recall, 'I thought he was going to play some of those Beatles songs, but he played Hank Williams tunes.'

A member of the audience came up to him and said that 'if you had the right handling, you could go places'.

Welch had lent George his Rickenbacker guitar and said, 'He had never seen one before and he liked it really well. He wanted to buy it.'

Since Welch didn't want to sell it, George went to a nearby town, Mount Vernon, and bought one for himself.

When he went into Benton's record store to see if they had any Beatles records, he looked through the various racks and bought some albums, one of which was James Ray's *If You Gotta Make A Fool Of Somebody*, which had the track by Ray's songwriter Rudy Clark called 'Got My Mind Set On You'.

George and Peter flew back to London on 3 October and George went straight to Abbey Road Studios where work resumed on the album *With The Beatles*.

Best Of Dark Horse 1976–1989, The

A compilation, assembled by George and dedicated to 'Friends of the Earth, Greenpeace, Parents For Safe Food, the Travelin Wilburys, Gordon Murray and anyone interested in saving our planet'.

It was issued in Britain on Dark Horse WX312 925643-1 on 23 October 1989 and in America on Dark Horse/WB 25726-2 on 17 October 1989.

The tracks were: Side One: 'Poor Little Girl', 'Blow Away', 'That's The Way It Goes', 'Cockamamie Business', 'Wake Up My Love', 'Life Itself', 'Got My Mind Set On You'. Side Two: 'Crackerbox Palace', 'Here Comes The Moon', 'Gone Troppo', 'When We Was Fab', 'Love Comes To Everyone', 'All Those Years Ago', 'Cheer Down'.

The fourteen-track compilation album was issued on a double CD and cassette, with the extra track 'Gone Troppo' and three bonus tracks: 'Cheer Down', 'Poor Little Fool' and 'Cockamamie Business', which were recorded at Friar Park between April and June 1989.

When it was issued in Italy by Warner Bros, the Italian division changed the title to *The Best Of George Harrison*, gave it a new cover design and released it in three formats – vinyl, cassette and CD.

Best Of George Harrison, The

A compilation album issued in Britain on Parlophone PAS 10011 on Saturday 20 November 1976.

As the Apple/Parlophone contract had expired, EMI/Capitol had the rights to repackage his earlier works as compilations and issued this album the day after George's new album release *Thirty Three & 1/3*.

George had suggested a title for the compilation as well as a suggested track listing, but he was completely ignored by EMI, who issued the album without his offer of co-operation. It was a strange way to treat a member of the group who had made EMI/Capitol's fortune for a decade.

George was to say, 'Well, I did have a suggestion – which I made to Capitol early in the year – as to a title and a format of songs . . . what they've done is take a lot of songs which happen to be me singing lead on my songs which were Beatles songs, when there was really a lot of good songs they could have used of me separately. Solo songs. I don't see why they didn't do that. They did that with Ringo's *Blast From Your Past* and John's *Shaved Fish*. It was just John's. It wasn't digging into Beatles records.

Obviously, following such cavalier treatment, George was very annoyed with the release and completely disowned it. He was frustrated at the fact that EMI decided to use all Beatles tracks on one side of the album while George wanted the compilation to consist purely of his solo contributions – something that EMI had allowed with their compilation albums of John Lennon and Ringo Starr. George regarded this as something of a slur, as if EMI didn't consider his solo work worthy of an entire compilation.

The design team Cream provided the cover sleeve with a photograph by Bob Cato.

The tracks were: Side One (The Beatles): 'Something', 'If I Needed Someone', 'Here Comes The Sun', 'Taxman', 'Think For Yourself', 'For You Blue', 'While My Guitar Gently Weeps'. Side Two (George Harrison): 'My Sweet Lord', 'Give Me Love (Give Me Peace On Earth)', 'You', 'Bangla Desh', 'Dark Horse', 'What Is Life'.

It was issued in America on Capitol ST 11578 on Monday 8 November 1976 where it reached No. 31 in the charts. The British release didn't enter the charts.

It was re-released as a budget album issued on EMI's 'Music For Pleasure' label on MFP 50523 on 25 November 1981. This featured a different cover from the original full-price release, utilising a photograph of George that first appeared in *The Beatles* white album.

Between The Devil And The Deep Blue Sea

The only composition not by George to be included on the *Brainwashed* album. The number was penned by Harold Arlen and Ted Koehler and the track lasts for 2 minutes and 34 seconds. It was originally recorded in 1991 with Jools Holland and Joe Brown and also featured in the TV show *Mister Roadrunner* in 1992. It was basically George's tribute to George Formby. George was on lead vocals and ukulele, Jools Holland on piano, Mark Flanagan on acoustic lead guitar, Joe Brown on acoustic rhythm guitar, Herbie Flowers on bass guitar and tuba and Ray Cooper on drums.

Beware Of Darkness

A track from the *All Things Must Pass* triple album. It was written by George and is 3 minutes and 20 seconds in length. An alternative version of the song was added to the thirtieth anniversary release of the *All Things Must Pass* double CD, which lasted 3 minutes and 46 seconds.

Billboard Century Award

George became the recipient of the very first *Billboard* Century Award at the 1992 *Billboard* Music Awards on Wednesday 9 December 1992. The event was a two-hour show, which was broadcast live from the University Amphitheatre, Los Angeles by the Fox network. Tom Petty, a fellow member of the Traveling Wilburys, presented the award to George. George commented, 'Being a Beatle was no hindrance to my career. I don't know why I got it. Somebody likes me. Bob Dylan should get one too.'

George was also interviewed about the award on *Entertainment Tonight*, which was screened the following evening.

After receiving the award he met the press backstage for a conference during which he revealed that he had been writing new material and planned to begin recording at the beginning of the following year.

As it had been announced that day that Prince Charles and Princess Diana were breaking up, he was asked his opinions on the news and said, 'I don't think they broke up. I think the press broke them up. The press have a responsibility to report fact, not just grovel around in shit. I think the British press are the worst. They should be taken out to the Tower and beheaded.'

Following Fox's televised award ceremony, there was an increase in the sale of George's solo material and the two Traveling Wilburys albums. Bob Merlis, a Warner Bros executive, commented, 'The juxtaposition of George being presented with the award by his Wilbury buddy Tom Petty captured the consumer's imaginations.'

Bit More Of You, A

An instrumental piece on George's *Extra Texture* album lasting only 45 seconds.

Black And Blue

A 1980 film featuring Heavy Metal bands such as Black Sabbath and Blue Oyster Cult in concert, which George financed.

Black, Cilla

A Liverpool singer in the same management stable as the Beatles, who was to enjoy recording success with a number of Paul McCartney compositions.

George originally wrote 'The Light That Had Lighted The World' for Cilla to record, but it ended up on his *Living In The Material World* album. He also produced a session with Cilla in August 1972 when they both recorded two songs by George in the Apple Studios. They were 'I'll Still Love You', which George later gave to Ringo for the *Rotogravure* album and 'You Got To Stay With Me'. The sessions were never completed because Cilla had been to the dentist prior to the session and the recording wasn't successful, although George kept the tapes at Friar Park. At the session, which George also produced, he played rhythm guitar, Eric Clapton played lead, Klaus Voormann bass and Ringo Starr drums.

George and Cilla bumped into each other in a vegetarian restaurant in 1982 and decided to finish a recording they began ten years earlier.

Cilla's version of the number was finally issued in 2003 when it was included on *Cilla: The Best Of 1963–78*, a 3-CD set issued to celebrate the fortieth anniversary of her recording debut.

Blackler's

A former store in Great Charlotte Street, Liverpool.

When George left Liverpool Institute he had no qualifications. He attempted to find work with Liverpool Corporation but failed to obtain a job with them. He next approached the Youth Employment Centre where he was told that a position for a window dresser at Blackler's store was available. When he applied at the store he was told the job had already been taken but was informed of a vacancy in the maintenance department who were looking for an apprentice electrician under a Mr Peet. George accepted the post and received a wage of £1.10/- per week. The year was 1960.

He was to comment, 'So I got a job cleaning all the lights with a paint brush, all those tubes to keep clean, and at Christmas I kept the grotto clean.'

When the offer came for the Silver Beetles to tour Scotland with Johnny Gentle, George handed in his notice.

The store was converted into small commercial units during the 1980s.

Blow Away

A single taken from the *George Harrison* album and issued in Britain in a picture sleeve on Dark Horse K 17327 on 2 March 1979 where it reached No. 51 in the charts. The flipside was 'Soft Touch'. It was issued in America on Dark Horse DRC 8763 on 14 February 1979 where it reached No. 16 in the charts. 'Soft-Hearted Hana' was the flip-side, a different choice from the British single.

The number, 3 minutes and 56 seconds in length, was originally written because some motor-racing friends of George asked him to pen a song.

George was to say, 'I wrote "Blow Away" on a miserable day, it was pouring with rain, and we were having a few leaks in the roof. To tell you the truth, I was a bit embarrassed by it. It was catchy and I was embarrassed to play it to anybody, it was too obvious.'

Blue Jay Way

A number composed by George, which was included on the *Magical Mystery Tour* film and soundtrack.

It was recorded at Abbey Road Studios on 6 September 1967, with overdubbing taking place on 7 September and 6 October.

Commenting on the origin of the song, George recalled that he had arrived in Los Angeles with his wife Patti on Tuesday 1 August 1967 and they'd rented a house on Blue Jay Way. It was a house belonging to a lawyer who was currently on holiday in Hawaii. Derek Taylor was due to visit them and George waited up for him. He said, 'Derek got held up. He rang to say he'd be late. I told him on the phone that the house was on Blue Jay Way. He said he could find it OK, he could always ask a cop. I waited and waited. I felt really knackered with the flight, but I didn't want to go to sleep till he came. There was a fog and it got later and later. To keep myself awake, just as a joke to fill in time, I wrote a song about waiting for him in Blue Jay Way. There was a little Hammond organ in the corner of this rented house, which I hadn't noticed. I messed around on this and the song came.'

Bob Dylan – 30th Anniversary Concert Celebration

A double album to celebrate Dylan's thirtieth anniversary, recorded at his anniversary concert on 16 October 1992 and released by Sony on 19 July 1993: the LP on 474000-1, the cassette on 474000-4 and the CD on 474000-2. George performed at the concert and is present on the track 'Absolutely Sweet Marie'. He also appears as a guitarist and vocalist on the finale 'My Back Pages'.

Boyd, Patti

George's first wife.

She was born Patricia Anne Boyd in Hampstead, London on 17 March 1945, the eldest of three sisters, the others being Paula and Helen. Helen became known as Jenny, which was the name of the Boyd's favourite doll. Due to their father's work, the entire family moved to Kenya in the 1950s and returned to London when Patti was in her late teens. In 1962 Patti (the spelling has been frequently used as either Patti or Pattie, but for this book we will dispense with the 'e') and Jenny began their modelling careers.

Director Dick Lester, who was handling an advertising campaign for Smith's Crisps, hired her to be the 'Smith's Crisps girl' and when he took over as director of the Beatles first film, *A Hard Day's Night*, he hired her for a small part as one of four schoolgirls on a train.

She arrived on the first day of filming and was to observe, 'I met them and they said hello, I couldn't believe it. They were so like how I'd imagined them to be. They were just like pictures of themselves coming to life. George hardly said hello, but the others came and chatted with us.'

Her part was cut down to a single line. When the Beatles describe that they feel like prisoners, she says, 'Prisoners?'

She recalled, 'When we started filming I could feel George looking at me and I was a bit embarrassed.'

Patti asked for the Beatles autographs, although she was too afraid of John to ask for his. When she approached George she also asked if he could sign for her two sisters. He put two kisses under the autographs for Jennie and Paula and seven kisses under the autograph for Patti.

George invited her to his trailer, but she refused. 'I was loyal, not stupid,' she says.

In fact, Patti had had a steady boyfriend for two years, Eric Swayne, a thirty-year-old photographer.

George came into the carriage where Patti was sitting with another girl, Pru, and asked her out into the corridor and then asked her to go out with him that night. She turned him down. He asked her again the following Tuesday.

She accepted George's second offer of a date and decided to drop her swain, saying, 'Eric was my boyfriend, but not any more. George is tremendous fun to be with. We want it to stay just fun without having to talk about engagements and marriages.'

By the end of the week she'd introduced George to her mother and sisters and he'd told her she reminded him of Brigitte Bardot.

George said, 'She's my kind of girl and we like each other a lot, but marriage is not on our minds. We hope to see more of each other when we can. It isn't a sin to have a girlfriend is it?'

The following week it was Easter, and the couple teamed up with John and Cynthia for a brief holiday at the Dromoland Castle Hotel in Ireland, but were hounded by the press.

George, who, more than any of the other members of the Beatles, treasured his privacy, was furious when the hotel was besieged by reporters who covered every doorway and exit, asking, 'Who's the blonde, George?' and 'What's her name?' and 'Do you love her?' The couples were left stranded in their rooms, with George saying, 'Don't we give those bastards a big enough pound of flesh every goddamn day of our lives? Why can't they just leave us alone sometimes?'

They had to be smuggled out of the hotel in a laundry van and taken directly to their airport. Then they went to Waikiki in Hawaii between 5 May and 20 May 1964. When they stopped over in Los Angeles they were spotted by photographers and George told them that Patti was 'my 29-year-old sister, my chaperone'.

George then took Patti to a bungalow he was considering buying in Esher called 'Kinfauns'. Within a month he'd bought it and they moved in together.

She then began to receive nasty letters from fans and was unprepared for the hostility, which she found frightening. She recalled, 'Hordes of wretched little girls used to lie in wait outside our gate waiting for me to go out to the shops. I was regularly kicked, bitten and even punched solely because I was George's girlfriend. "You'd better leave off our George or else," they would shout as I drove away. George attempted to talk to them about it, but every time he came round they just fell about swooning and giggling. The next morning, however, once again they'd be out in full force, screaming insults and sometimes actually threatening to murder me.'

For a time she set up a clothes stall with her sisters called 'Juniper', named after the song Donovan wrote about her sister, 'Jennifer Juniper'. She also began writing a column for the American teen magazine 16 called 'Patti's Letter From London'.

Commenting on the romance, George's father Harry said, 'When George got together with Patti, Mrs Harrison and I were delighted. Of course, to the rest of the world it might have been "Beatle Marries Model", but to those that really know them it was clear that this was a genuine modern-day love story.'

There were rumours that John Lennon had a crush on Patti at one time and he used to call her 'Batti'.

George proposed to her on Christmas Day 1964 and Patti was to say, 'We lived together for about a year before we got married. My mother knew but she never mentioned it.'

One thing that irked Patti about the proposal was that George went and asked Brian Epstein's permission. George drove to Epstein's house in Chapel Street, Belgravia and left Patti in the car while he went to see Epstein. He emerged ten minutes later to tell her, 'It's all right. Brian has said we can get married in January. Off we go!'

Patti commented, 'God has spoken!'

When John Lennon was informed, he said, 'January's a bit soon. She must be in the club.'

In September 1966 the couple flew to Bombay in India. Patti commented, 'We had really gone so George could study the sitar under Ravi Shankar. We met Ravi's guru, his spiritual guide. You can't be in India without being aware of everything. We went to a meeting at Benares, the holy city on the Ganges. Millions of people had come for a big festival that went on for three days.'

They spent five weeks in India, during which time Patti became interested in spiritual matters.

On their return she had lots of time on her hands. George, with his obsession for privacy and keeping the media at arm's length, had told Patti she had to give up all her modelling work. When she became interested in charity work, he forbade her doing that, too. Her thoughts turned to an interest in the spirituality she detected during her trip to India and she went along to Caxton Hall in London in February 1967 to listen to a lecture by the Maharishi Mahesh Yogi about his Spiritual Regeneration Movement.

She was so impressed she talked George and the other members of the Beatles into attending the Maharishi's lecture on transcendental meditation at London's Hilton Hotel in Park Lane on Thursday 24 August 1967. Those of their party in attendance were George and Patti, John and Cynthia and Paul and Jane Asher. Following his lecture, the Maharishi gave them a private audience and invited them to his seminar that weekend, which was to take place in Bangor.

That seminar was marred by the tragic news that Brian Epstein, who had intended to join them at the seminar, had been found dead.

George and Patti, together with the other members of the Beatles and their wives and girlfriends, were to join the Maharishi at his ashram in Rishikesh in India.

On 12 March 1969, the day of Paul and Linda's wedding, the police raided George and Patti's bungalow. George was to admit that there were some seeds on his coffee table, but he denied knowledge of a block of hash that Detective Sergeant Norman Pilcher alleged was found in a cupboard by a police dog.

George said, 'I'm a tidy sort of bloke – I put records in the record rack, tea in the caddy and pot in the pot box. That was the biggest block of hash I'd ever seen.'

George and Patti hadn't been invited to Paul and Linda's wedding because of the current litigation with Paul attempting to dissolve the Beatles partnership.

That day they'd been invited to a party in Chelsea. After the raid they were taken to the police station for questioning, but their solicitor Martin Poulden secured their release and they rushed home to get ready for the party.

When they arrived at the party they saw that Princess Margaret and Lord Snowdon were there, so George approached them and explained about the raid.

'Oh my, what a shame,' said Princess Margaret.

George asked her, 'Can you help us? Can you sort of use your influence to eliminate the bad news?'

The suggestion took the Princess by surprise. They were then joined by Patti's sister Paula who pulled a joint from her purse and lit it. Everyone stared at her. She assumed they wanted her to pass it around and she extended it to Princess Margaret and said, 'Here, do you want this?'

The horrified Princess and Lord Snowdon fled the party.

Pilcher was notorious for his raids on pop stars and was responsible for the bust at Keith Richards' house. He was also the one who raided John and Yoko's Montague Square flat, resulting in John's difficulties in obtaining a green card in America. Pilcher also raided the Pheasantry in March 1969 hoping to catch Eric Clapton on a drugs charge, but Eric wasn't present. The same month he raided Mick Jagger and Marianne Faithfull's Chelsea house.

Although George maintained the hash had been planted, he pleaded guilty and was fined £250. To lend weight to George's story, on Wednesday 8 November 1972 Pilcher was jailed for two years for 'conspiracy to pervert the course of justice' after being convicted of planting evidence in other cases.

Patti's life became one of frustration, with George's insistence that she didn't work. She felt isolated in the large Friar Park mansion that they had moved to in 1970, and her thoughts turned to raising a family.

Unfortunately, she seemed unable to get pregnant and eventually both George and Patti went for fertility tests. Although Patti wanted to adopt a child, George wouldn't consider it and, after six years of marriage, they began to drift apart and started to argue regularly.

Frustrated, Patti decided to take up modelling once again and agreed to take part in an Ozzie Clark fashion show. Then, during a dinner with Ringo and his wife Maureen, George declared that he was in love with Maureen.

A tearful Patti fled to the bathroom and his guests left. It was alleged that a few weeks later, when Patti returned from a shopping trip, she found George and Maureen in bed together.

When someone asked him, 'How could you, with your best friend's wife?'

An unperturbed George said, 'Incest, I guess.'

Patti then had an extramarital affair herself, with Ronnie Wood of the Faces, or rather, took part in a wife-swapping episode, which was ideal fare for the tabloids. The *News Of The World* reported that George and Ronnie Wood's wife Krissy had gone on holiday to Portugal and Switzerland while Patti and Wood were holidaying in the Bahamas. News also came out about an affair between George and actress Kathy Simmonds.

The most visible episode of the drifting relationship was the interest Eric Clapton took in George's wife.

Eric had been a friend of George from when they first met in 1964 when he was a member of the Yardbirds. Eric first met Patti in 1969 at Cream's farewell concert (although some say it was at a party at Brian Epstein's house). He recalled, 'I fell in love with her at first sight and it got heavier and heavier for me. I remember feeling a dreadful emptiness because I was certain I was never going to meet a woman quite that beautiful for myself.'

In 1969 Clapton bought a house near the Harrisons and became a frequent visitor.

He was later to say, 'What I couldn't accept was that she was out of reach for me. She was married to George and he was a mate but I had fallen in love and nobody else mattered.'

He was obsessed and began an affair with her sister, Paula, who looked a lot like Patti and had the same kind of personality.

Paula and Eric lived together for two months at Eric's mansion, Hurtwood Edge. Eric said, 'I started living with Patti's younger sister Paula because of their similarity in character and in looks. It was like a side route into Patti, that was my way of thinking.' He was to add, 'I invited Patti's sister Paula to come and hear me sing "Layla" for the first time. When she heard that vocal, she packed her bags and left my home in great distress because she realised it was about Patti and that I'd been using her.'

Patti was to realise that he was in love with her also via 'Layla', which, in his way, was a declaration of his love. He based the song on a thousand-year-old Persian book by Nizami called *Layla and Majnum*.

Eric phoned her one day in 1970 and expressed his love. Patti told him she loved George. 'I couldn't believe the situation Eric had put me in. I thought it wasn't right and I thought that our friendship was destined to end.'

Eric sent an unsigned letter saying he needed to see her, that he loved her. She took it to George, who assumed it was from a crazy person. Eric called her and confessed about the letter.

George was busy working on *All Things Must Pass*. The couple were due to see the controversial play *Oh Calcutta*. Patti went alone (some reports said she went with Eric, others that she met him there). He asked her to come to his house to listen to the Derek and The Dominoes recording and played her 'Layla'. They made love. At the after-show party, George arrived and spotted Eric and Patti hand in hand. He shouted at Eric that he was never to see his wife again and shoved Patti into the car.

The couple began to grow more and more apart and Eric still desired Patti.

George was to comment, 'Actually, Patti and I had been splitting up for years. That was the funny thing, you know. I thought that was the best thing to do, for us to split and we should have just done it much sooner. But I didn't have any problem about it. Eric had the problem. Every time I'd go and see him, he'd be really hung up about it, and I was saying, "Fuck it, man. Don't be apologising," and he didn't believe me. I was saying, "I don't care!"'

Patti said, 'I felt terrible guilt. Eric kept insisting I should leave George and go and live with him. I said I couldn't. I got cold feet. I couldn't bear it.'

Eric said, 'I told her that either she came with me or I hit the deck. I actually presented her with a packet of heroin and said, "If you don't come with me, I'm taking this for the next couple of years." I put dreadful pressure on her, but I couldn't help myself. I really could not visualise a life without her. Well, the pressure from me must have been so great that she went back and closed herself back into the house with George.'

In 1974 George went on a trip to India without Patti. She flew to Los Angeles to spend some time with her sister Jenny, who was married to Mick Fleetwood of Fleetwood Mac. Then she flew to Miami to join Eric who was recording his album *461 Ocean Boulevard* there. She claimed she did that because she thought she would manipulate Eric in order to recapture George. She then felt she'd fallen in love with Eric.

When George arrived back in London Patti told him she was going with Eric again and wouldn't be coming back.

He said, 'It's no big deal. We've separated many times but this time I don't know what will happen. In this life, there is no time to lose in an uncomfortable situation.'

At a party on the completion of *461 Ocean Boulevard*, Eric recalled, 'I went straight up to him and said, "I'm in love with your wife. What are you going to do about it?" George said, "Whatever you like, man. It doesn't worry me." He was being very spiritual about it and saying everybody should do their own thing. He then said, "You can have her and I'll have your girlfriend." I couldn't believe this. I thought he was going to chin me. Patti freaked out and ran away. Suddenly she was in limbo. George must have been very upset too. But that's crazy! If he didn't want her to leave him, he shouldn't have let me take her.'

George invited the two of them to Friar Park. Eric recalls, 'George, Patti and I were sitting in the hallway of my house. I remember George saying, "Well, I suppose I'd better divorce her." He managed to laugh it all off when I thought it was getting pretty hairy. I thought the whole situation was tense; he thought it was funny. Then he helped us all through the split-up.'

George said, 'Well, Eric didn't really run off with her because we had kind of finished with each other anyway. And, you know, for me this is what I think is the main problem. I think the fact is that I didn't get annoyed with him and I think that has always annoyed him. I think that deep down inside he wishes that it really pissed me off, but it didn't because I was happy that she went off, because we'd finished together, and it made things easier for me, you see, because otherwise we'd have had to go through all these big rows and divorces.'

George and Patti were officially divorced on 9 June 1977.

When Eric and Patti decided to get married on 27 March 1979

George and Olivia were top of the guest list, but they didn't attend. The Reverend Daniel Sanchez married the couple in Tucson, Arizona at the Apostolic Assembly of Faith in Christ Church.

Eric personally invited George and his new girlfriend Olivia to his belated wedding reception on 19 May in the garden at his home, Hurtwood Edge, in the village of Ewhurst, Surrey, 25 miles from London. George and Olivia were among the 200 guests, who included Paul McCartney, Ringo Starr, Mick Jagger, David Bowie and Lonnie Donegan. Workmen had constructed a makeshift stage for a jam session that began at 9 p.m. Jim Capaldi played drums and Paul was on bass. As the jam progressed Ginger Baker played drums. Among the various others who took to the stage were Eric Clapton and Denny Laine on guitars and Ray Cooper on keyboards. Then Paul invited Lonnie Donegan up on stage and a skiffle session began.

The next line-up saw Paul on bass, Ringo on drums and George, Clapton and Laine on guitars. Mick Jagger then jumped on stage and joined them in singing the Eddie Cochran number 'Something Else'.

With George, Paul and Ringo on the stage it was the nearest thing to a Beatles reunion!

Problems began once Eric and Patti settled in at the mansion in Hurtwood Edge. When Eric began to drink to excess, the strain was apparent. 'It was becoming very difficult. You'd look for the part of the person you knew and loved, but it was hard to find.'

Eric and Patti separated in November 1984. They were back again the following year and she joined him on his American tour. Eric said that the trouble started when he gave up drinking. 'I was very dogmatic. I was very strict, in a way that made it difficult for people to relate to me. You see, Patti likes to drink and I became very strict about that. I started to put her down and I was intolerant. Then I wouldn't take her on tour with me and we drifted apart.'

By 1985 the number of public affairs he had publicly humiliated her and the fact that he'd had two children by different women, one a son, Conor, by Lori del Santo. This was particularly hurtful as Patti was unable to have children.

After they separated she said, 'It probably took me six years to get over it, with four years of psychotherapy. My self-esteem was unbelievably low, and I found it really hard to build up relationships because I had been used to difficult people. Anybody who was sweet and nice was no challenge.'

The couple were married for seven years but finally broke up in 1986. Clapton was to say, 'We tried and tried to have a child . . . to the point where it became a pressure, an immense stumbling block to our marriage.'

Patti filed for divorce on 29 April 1988 citing Clapton's adultery with Italian TV personality Lori Santo, 29, who gave birth to Clapton's son Conor in August 1987.

Patti was to become a photographer and also involved herself in charity work. Together with Barbara Bach she co-founded SHARP in 1991, a charity to aid drug addicts and alcoholics. The same year she met property developer Rod Weston, who became her partner.

Brainwashed (album)

George's final album. It was issued posthumously in Britain on 19 November 2002 on Dark Horse/EMI CD 7243 5 43246 2 8 and in America and Canada the following day.

Produced by George, Jeff Lynne and Dhani Harrison, it contained eleven new Harrison numbers and a cover of an old standard, 'Between The Devil And The Deep Blue Sea'. Its working title was 'Portrait Of A Leg End'.

Lynne was to say, 'We started working on the album in 1999. George would come round my house and he'd always have a new song with him. He would strum them on a guitar or a ukulele. The songs just knocked me out. George talked about how he wanted the album to sound. He told Dhani a lot of things he would like to have done with the songs and left us little clues. There was always that spiritual energy that went into the lyrics as well as the music.'

George commented, 'Everybody knows they're all being brainwashed by everything. So in my music, I just sing about the eternal river that keeps flowing through this area near my home in "Pisces Fish", or I sing, "God, God, God, won't you lead us through this mess?" on "Brainwashed".'

Discussing his current music in a *Billboard* interview in 1999 George said, 'I don't listen to anything and I don't read the papers and I don't watch TV and I don't go to concerts. It doesn't matter if I did my music twenty years ago or if I did it tomorrow. It doesn't go with trends. My trousers don't get wider and tighter every six months. My music just stays what it is, and that's the way I like it.'

George played electric and acoustic guitars (including slide and dobro), ukulele, bass and keyboards. Jeff Lynne played bass, piano, guitars, keyboards and backing vocals. Dhani played electric and acoustic guitar, Wurlitzer and backing vocals. Other musicians included Jim Keltner on drums, Mike Moran and Marc Mann on keyboards and Jools Holland on piano on 'The Devil And The Deep Blue Sea'. The song 'Brainwashed' includes Bikram Ghosh on tabla, Jon Lord on piano, Sam Brown on backing vocals and Jane Lister on harp.

At the time of George's death, only one track had actually been completed in a total sense. This was 'Between The Devil And The Deep Blue Sea', which George had first recorded in the early 1990s on Jools Holland's TV show.

George realised that he would be unable to complete the album, so he asked his son Dhani and friend Jeff Lynne to complete it for him.

Dhani was to recall, 'I remember coming in from England and recording guitars with Jeff the first night. It was the most surreal thing ever. I kept turning around, looking for my dad – "Er, is that all right?" And there was no one there to tell me.

'The album was always going to be finished this way, with Jeff helping my dad and me with the final production. We just stuck to the plan, except that my dad died, which made our job more difficult.'

The numbers were: 'Any Road', 'P2 Vatican Blues (Last Saturday Night)'; 'Pisces Fish', 'Looking For My Life', 'Rising Sun', 'Marwa Blues', 'Stuck Inside A Cloud', 'Run So Far', 'Never Get Over You', 'Between The Devil And The Deep Blue Sea', 'Rocking Chair In Hawaii' and 'Brainwashed'.

Brainwashed (song)

The title track from George's posthumous album, lasting 6 minutes and 7 seconds, with George on lead vocals, slide guitar, acoustic guitar, bass guitar and background vocals. Jeff Lynne was on electric guitar, 12-string guitar, additional keyboards and background vocals with Dhani Harrison on acoustic guitar and background vocals, Jon Lord on piano, Sam Brown on background vocals, Bikram Ghosh on tabla, Jane Lister on harp, Jim Keltner on drums and Isabela Brozymowska reading from *How To Know God*.

The number was said to be about George's former manager Denis O'Brien. In a 1999 *Billboard* interview, George described it as 'a blistering anthem about social delusions in a world running down.

'I need to get that last song out of my system. To have someone sit at your table with your family every night and then betray your trust is one of the worst experiences imaginable. Sometimes songwriting is the only way I can respond to the outside world, to exorcise its demons.'

Bromberg, David

He wrote a song with George in 1972, which they called 'The Holdup'. He included it on his album *Wanted – Dead Or Alive*, released on 7 January 1974.

Brown, Joe

Born in Swarby, Lincolnshire on 13 May 1941, this singer-guitarist first found acclaim on Jack Good's *Boy Meets Girl* television series in 1959. He led his own group, Joe Brown and the Bruvvers, signed with Larry Parnes and had a string of hit singles between 1960 and 1973, including 'Darktown Strutters Ball', 'Shine', 'A Picture Of You' and 'With A Little Help From My Friends'.

Joe married Vicky Haseman, a former member of the Liverpool singing group the Vernons Girls, who became a prolific backing vocalist at recording sessions. She was able to join Joe in his country rock band Home Brew. Sadly, Vicki died from cancer in 1991.

Their daughter Sam Brown became a hit singer in her own right, and father and daughter joined forces for the first time to tour the UK in 1996.

Like George, Joe also lived in Henley-on-Thames and the two became great friends.

George wrote a fourteen-line foreword to Joe Brown's autobiography *Brown Sauce: The Life And Times Of Joe Brown*, published in Britain by Collins Willow in July 1986.

After the vicious attack George suffered in December 1999, he invited Joe and his family to spend a holiday with them in January 2000.

Brown recalled, 'I was sitting at home, the phone rang and George asked me to go to Barbados with him. It was totally unexpected, but I was pleased, because what we have in common is a love of music. Not just some music, but all music. George has no musical snobbery. When we're at his house, he'll play anything from rock to Cab Calloway or Hoagy Carmichael.

'He was a much greater influence on the Beatles than anyone ever realised because he was the quiet one and never pushed himself forward very much. I respect his privacy, so I am not going to say too much about him. He hates all that stuff. But he is really a nice man, a one-off gentleman. He's had a very nasty experience and he doesn't need all this hassle. People say, "oh, what did he expect?"

'Some fan breaks in and has a go at him, "that's the price of fame". Well, that's too high a price to pay. He can do without it.

'George struggled with the man for nearly twenty minutes before help arrived.'

George appeared on Joe Brown's Radio 2 show on 5 July 1999 discussing his favourite rock'n'roll artists – Elvis, Carl Perkins, Jerry Lee Lewis, the Coasters and Eddie Cochran. Records played included Ritchie Barrett's 'Some Other Guy' and Presley's 'I Got Stung'.

George was best man at the wedding of Joe to his second wife Manon at the Henley-on-Thames registry office at the end of 2000. At the reception in the marquee in the grounds of Joe's house, George gave a speech. Among the many other guests were Marty Wilde, Alvin Lee, Mick Jagger, Bert Weedon, Herbie Flowers and Rolf Harris.

OK magazine covered the wedding and in their December 2000 issue Joe recalled the old days. 'We were working in Liverpool and Brian Epstein booked us to do some shows, because he wanted the Beatles to go out with a main act. We did a few shows with them. They were great, even in those days. They were fantastic.

'I remember Brian introducing Paul McCartney to me as "the leader of the Beatles", and the other guys in the group all gave him a funny look. Paul was embarrassed by it.

'George is a lovely man and a good friend. We share a great interest in music. Most good musicians are not musical snobs. Our musical tastes are a much wider range than rock'n'roll. I think that's what draws George and I together as far as music is concerned. He likes the stuff that I like – George Formby, Hoagy Carmichael, Carl Perkins and Elvis Presley and all those old people. He loves music. He's not a rock'n'roller as such.

'Whenever there are a couple of guitarists around George will come over to me and play in my studio or I will go and see him. We're just good friends and play the guitar together. If he thinks of a good song for me, he will phone me up and say, "Here's a good song you can do."'

Brown, Sam

The daughter of George's friend Joe Brown. Sam was a recording artist in her own right and had enjoyed several chart hits. She also acted as a backing singer and appeared regularly on Jools Holland's BBC2 music programme *Later With Jools Holland*. When George suggested that Holland come to Switzerland and record 'A Horse To Water' with him on 1 October 2001, he also asked Jools to bring Sam with him. Sam had already acted as backing vocalist on George's 'My Sweet Lord (2000)'.

Bunbury Tails, The

A children's teatime series, which made its debut on the British TV network Channel Four at 4.55 p.m. on Wednesday 26 August 1992. Each of the episodes was five minutes in length.

The series was based on the books by David English, a former member of RSO Records, who began writing the adventures of the rabbits in 1986. It was created for television by Jan Brychta and David English and was also drawn by English.

The Bunburys are eight sporting bunny heroes who travel the world in their Bunnymobile, fighting evil powers such as the Dogfather and the Krayhound Brothers. They run, cycle, play cricket, baseball and football in events such as the Buncelona Olympics, Le Buns 24-hour race, Bunchester United Stadium and the Tour de Buns.

The Bee Gees financed the animation series as English had previously illustrated a book of their career, *Bee Gees: The Legend*.

English was to comment: 'I started writing *The Bunbury Tails* in 1986. One of the characters was called Rajbun, a little Indian rabbit. I'd known George for a long time, having met him through Eric Clapton, who'd been on RSO.

'Whilst playing cricket with George one day at Friar Park a couple of years ago, I told him about my Bunburys, as he had his Wilburys. I suggested that he might like to write a song for the cartoon series, which has been directed by Bob Godfrey, who was involved in *Yellow Submarine*.

'As I arrived back at my place in West Hampstead that night, the phone went. It was George: he'd already come up with a melody, which he played me down the telephone. It was wonderful. I went round there again the next day, and we wrote the lyrics together. George then went over to the Dorchester Hotel, I think it was where Ravi Shankar was staying, and with a little mobile tape recorder, recorded Ravi Shankar playing the sitar, right there in his hotel room, and put him on the track!

'In addition to Ravi, and other top Indian musicians, Dhani Harrison sings lead vocal. He was nine at the time. George does the back-up vocals and I sing on it as well. The whole thing, from writing, to recording, took just four days.' Ray Cooper was also percussionist on the track.

The number that George had co-written with English was called 'Ride Rajbun' and it was based on one of the characters called Rajbun, a little Indian rabbit featured in one episode, 'Rajbun Story'.

After a hurricane in Bunnybardos, a charity concert is organised at the Royal Albert Hall with Elton Bun and the Bunbury Band – with Bunny Gibb, Eric Clapbun and Hari Ison. Elton John, Eric Clapton and the Bee Gees are also featured on the soundtrack.

The number 'Ride Rajbun' was written and recorded during March 1988 and credited to 'George Harrison with Dhani Harrison and Ravi Shankar'. It became Track Five on *Bunbury Tails*, the soundtrack album issued by Polydor on Monday 5 October 1992 on Polydor CD 515 784-2 and on cassette: 515 784-4.

Bye Bye Love

A track on the 1974 *Dark Horse* album. Felice and Boudleaux Bryant composed it and it was the only number on the album not composed by George, although he did amend the lyrics. It is 4 minutes and 2 seconds in length.

George had amended the lyrics of the number to refer to his wife Patti's elopement with his best friend Eric Clapton. He refers to Patti as 'our lady' and to Eric as 'old Clapper'. Strangely enough, Eric plays guitar on the track and Patti provides the backing vocals.

Caldwell, Iris

Iris was the sister of Alan Caldwell who, under the name Rory Storm, was originally a major player in the Mersey scene. George was a regular visitor to 'Stormsville' and went out with Iris.

She recalled, 'I met George through Rory Storm. George used to rehearse in a cellar, in a house near where we lived. After a time he started inviting friends of his to 'come down and use his rehearsal room'. I remember that one of the group's who took advantage of his offer were the Quarry Men, which was John Lennon's original outfit. Later on, Rory needed another guitarist and asked George Harrison if he would join him. Everyone thought that George was a very good guitarist at the time. I think the main reason was that he was one of the very few people in Liverpool who could play "Guitar Boogie Shuffle" all the way through. Anyway, George decided that he would stick with the Quarry Men.'

The situation wasn't exactly as Iris described it as George tried to join Rory Storm's group but Rory didn't want to know because he regarded George as being too young.

(Can Only) Run So Far

A track from the *Brainwashed* album lasting 4 minutes and 5 seconds with George on lead vocals, electric guitar, acoustic guitar and background vocals. Jeff Lynne was on acoustic bass, acoustic guitar, keyboards and background vocals, Dhani Harrison on acoustic guitar and background vocals and Jim Keltner on drums.

Cancer

In July 1997 George first noticed something wrong while gardening at

Friar Park. He reached up to wipe some sweat from his neck and felt a lump. Minor surgery took place in August at Princess Margaret Hospital, Windsor when several enlarged lymph nodes were removed from his throat through an incision in his neck.

A spokesman commented, 'The operation went without a hitch and we are all confident that it's the end of the matter. George didn't want to take any risks. The procedure was routine and he is now at home and feeling fine.'

George had booked into the hospital under the name Sid Smith, to avoid any undue publicity. A hospital spokesman added, 'Afterwards, he had great difficulty talking and he was pretty grumpy because he was in pain. He could only take liquid foodstuffs on board like porridge or ice cream. And he had to write down what he wanted on paper.'

The biopsy showed that it was cancerous. George then had standard radiation therapy for two weeks at the Royal Marsden Hospital in September.

Describing this first battle against cancer, George was to say, 'I went to the Princess Margaret Hospital in Windsor to have the lump removed from my neck.

'They took it out and recommended that I have some radiation therapy, which I did, at the Royal Marsden Hospital.'

While in America in January 1998 attending the funeral of Carl Perkins, he went to see doctors at the Mayo Clinic in Rochester, Minnesota. They confirmed that there was no sign that the cancer had returned. He underwent a second series of tests in May and was given an 'all clear'.

He commented, 'I was given a clean bill of health. Sometimes, if you say the word cancer, everybody automatically thinks it will end in misery, but it's not always the case. Luckily for me, they found that this nodule was more of a warning than anything else. There are many different kinds of cancerous cells, and this was a very basic type. I was very lucky because it didn't go anywhere.

'I got it purely from smoking. I gave up cigarettes many years ago, but then started again for a while, before I stopped finally in 1997.' He added, 'It reminds you that anything can happen. Life – there's an old saying – life is like the raindrop on a lotus leaf.'

Sadly the cancer returned and in March 2001 George lost almost half a lung during a four-hour operation at St Mary's Hospital, Rochester, Minnesota, which was judged a success. He issued a statement: 'Although All Things Must Pass away, George has no plans right now and is still Living In The Material World and wishes everyone all the very best. God bless and not to worry.'

From May to late June he attended the clinic of the Sainta Giovanni Hospital in Bellinzova, Switzerland every day with Olivia. He moved there to be treated by leading cancer specialist Professor Franco

Cavalli, who worked in the clinic. It was believed that George was receiving cobalt-ray treatment for a brain tumour.

George visited Italy in May and it was while he was there that Paul dropped in to see him during his *Wingspan* promotional tour. A spokesman commented, 'Paul really wanted to see how George was and thought it was an ideal opportunity for them to get together. It was quite a moving meeting for both of them.'

In July George said that he was feeling fine after successful radiotherapy on a cancerous tumour in his brain. He issued a message saying, 'I am feeling fine and I am really sorry for the unnecessary worry which has been caused by reports appearing in today's press. Please do not worry.'

They then travelled to their home in Maui, Hawaii.

Later that month George issued another statement saying that reports that he was close to death from cancer were 'unsubstantial, untrue, insensitive and uncalled for'.

George became a patient at Staten Island University Hospital in New York, registering under the alias George Arias. He was undergoing a cancer treatment originally devised in Sweden that was known as stereotaxy or fractionated stereotactic radiosurgery. The controversial treatment involved focusing high doses of radiation on the precise location of a tumour.

Following a CT scan the patient is strapped to a body frame while a computer plans to co-ordinate a machine arm that roams over the patient, firing beams of radiation with pinpoint accuracy from hundreds of angles.

Gil Lederman, the doctor treating George, who is one of the world's leading experts on radiation oncology, explained that the method enables the patient to be treated with much higher doses of radiation than traditional therapy without endangering healthy tissue.

A source at the hospital commented that George looked frail and gaunt and said, 'The word around the hospital is that the procedure is the last chance of saving his life. George is very sick. He is nothing like the George Harrison we all remember from the Beatles.'

Incidentally, Lederman said that shortly before George died he gave Lederman's thirteen-year-old son Ariel guitar lessons. 'He played Ha-Va-Na-Gila on the guitar, then took a pen and signed the guitar to my son,' he said.

Lederman added, 'He believed death was part of life. He was not fearful of death.'

George died at 1.20 p.m. on Thursday 29 November 2001 at the age of 58. Lee Rosen, chief oncologist at UCLA Medical Center in Los Angeles, who had been treating George a few days before his death, signed the death certificate.

A family statement was issued which read: 'He left this world as he lived in it, conscious of God, fearless of death, and at peace, surrounded by family and friends. He often said, "Everything else can wait but the search for God cannot wait, and love one another."'

There was an element of confusion regarding where George actually died. It was said to be at the Beverly Hills estate, formerly owned by Courtney Love, which had been bought by Paul McCartney. When Paul had visited George in New York he suggested that George stay at the house, which was near to the UCLA Medical Center where George was to receive further cancer treatments.

Following George's death the media were informed that the house where George had died was 1971 Coldwater Canyon in the Hollywood Hills, which belonged to security consultant Gavin de Becker. This caused confusion when it was listed on the death certificate because the address turned out to be nonexistent (incidentally, 1971 was the year of the Bangla Desh concert and George's chart-topping 'My Sweet Lord').

In December, Los Angeles attorney Gloria Allred filed a complaint with the Los Angeles Police Department alleging that the integrity of public records was at stake. The police said that no one would be charged because the situation was one that was sometimes used when a celebrity had died to prevent fans besieging the address for souvenirs. They said it was not an offence to list a false address just as long as there was no intent to defraud.

When interviewed by NBC television prior to the George Harrison tribute concert at the Royal Albert Hall on 29 November 2002, Olivia said that George had never felt in control of the cancer that killed him. She commented, 'He gave his life to God a long time ago. He wasn't trying to hang on to anything. He was fine with it. Sure, nobody likes to be ill and nobody likes to be uncomfortable. But he went with what was happening.

'George dedicated a lot of his life to obtain a good ending, and I don't have any doubt that he was successful.'

Cars

George was an enthusiastic driver and was to say, 'I rate myself good behind the wheel but I'm not sure the police agree.'

In 1966 he got rid of his Aston Martin and commented, 'We never seem to get the chance to drive fast, so it seemed silly to keep them. I am getting a new Mini-Cooper, which will be all black. The suppliers are busy taking all the inside out at this moment to put in a black leather interior, with push-button windows, overdrive and a new steering wheel – so it's going to look a bit like a sports car anyway.'

George received a brand new BMW 3.0 litre CSA Coupé in July 1972. He sold it in July 1977.

George was involved in a crash on 28 February 1972. He had to appear before the magistrates in Maidenhead and told them, 'I hit a motorway interchange crash barrier because I did not see the warning sign.' He was found guilty of careless driving and fined £20. His licence was also endorsed for the second time. The first time was on Tuesday 23 February 1971.

George often found himself in trouble for speeding. On arriving in Australia for a holiday in December 1981 he was stopped for speeding and recalled, 'The policeman asked me for my driver's licence, so I opened the back of the car to get it. The cop did a double take when he saw the name, George Harrison from London. He said, studying the English licence, "You're with the Rolling Stones aren't you?"'

George was obsessed with fast cars and had his licence revoked on a number of occasions. At one time he involved Patti and himself in a serious accident. This occurred on 28 February 1972 during the return drive to Friar Park following a Ricky Nelson concert in London. George hit a roundabout at ninety miles per hour. Neither of the two was wearing a seat belt. George was thrown against the windscreen and was dazed while Patti was slumped unconscious over her seat.

A car stopped and George requested an ambulance. He required eight stitches to a cut on his scalp and had minor concussion and a bruised shoulder, but Patti was quite seriously injured. She was unconscious for some time, then remained in hospital for several days and spent a further two weeks in a nursing home. She'd suffered concussion and several broken ribs.

In 1993 George arrived at a hill-climb sports car meeting at Goodwood, Surrey driving a Rocket, which was said to be 'a little sports car designed by Gordon Murray, where the two seats are in tandem and the driver wears goggles and a flying helmet'. In addition to the Rocket, George drove a McLaren F1 sports car up and down the hill track at the site.

Among cars George owned were a Porsche Turbo and a Ferrari Dino Spyder. He drove on a ten-mile circuit near his Friar Park home.

In December 1993 he ordered a £540,000 Claren F1 Supercar, described as 'the finest driving machine yet built for the public road'.

Chants Of India

An album by Ravi Shankar, produced by George. The album is based on Vedic scriptures and the music was orchestrated by Shankar, who added several original compositions in the style of the scriptures. George also appears in the chorus and played some acoustic guitar, bass, autoharp and glockenspiel. The chants were sung in Sanskrit and were mainly prayers and mantras from religious writings such as the *Vedas* and the *Upanishads*, although Ravi also created four new chants, 'Mangalam', 'Hari Om', 'Svara Mantra' and 'Prabhujee'.

The CD was issued in America on EMI/Capitol's classic label Angel (Angel 55948-2) on 6 May 1997 and in Britain on EMI/Angel CTMCD 340 on 1 September 1997. There were sixteen tracks that were recorded in London, Madras and at George's Friar Park Studio. All the copyright to the recorded material was also in George's name.

George was interviewed by Don Heckman of the *LA Times* about the CD and mentioned his close friendship with Ravi Shankar. 'In one way, it's kind of given me a life,' he said, 'because if you don't know who you are and where you've come from and where you're going, really, what is life?

'You can have all the money in the world and all the glory. But if you don't know what is the point, then your life is empty. So, in that respect, Ravi – not just Ravi, but he was the main ingredient – patched me into the Vedic tradition. And from that I've learned all these things about yoga, about meditation, about what is, about what we are doing here, about what is the goal. I've come to understand incredible stuff, just through perusing that. Without it, I'd just be a boring old fart.'

Ravi commented, 'When we were mixing the sound, I let him lead because that is something which he has so much experience in, but composition-wise, I made all the decisions. In fact, it was my idea to utilise him, though not in a major way, just as part of the chorus, using some strums on the acoustic guitar or just a few notes on the vibraphone or autoharp.'

George had expressed his desire to appear with Ravi and perform music from the album live, but Shankar wasn't keen on the idea, saying, 'There comes the catch. If it is George, then the attraction becomes George being there, and it loses its whole approach. George doesn't want to exploit that. It's not fair to him either as a famous musician and neither is it fair to the production.'

In a 3 May 1997 interview in *Billboard* to discuss *Chants Of India*, George said, 'It's a mad world we live in and there's so much music out there that is, well, aggravating. This is our effort to achieve some semblance of balance. People everywhere are looking for something – they always have been – but maybe now more than ever ... There is something in the music that goes beyond any language, any religion. This stuff is so ancient that everything stems from it in a sense. This record may not be something you put on as background at a dinner party, but I could see it in a lot of executives' headphones.'

Shankar also discussed George in a *Billboard* interview, specifically on George's sitar playing on 'Norwegian Wood'. Ravi said, 'To tell you the truth, I had to keep my mouth shut. It was introduced to me by my nieces and nephews, who were just gaga over it. I couldn't believe it, because to me, it sounded so terrible.'

Checking Out

A HandMade film, directed by David Leland, which had George in a cameo role as a janitor. It was filmed in Los Angeles.

Cheer Down

A number that started out as an unused backing track during the *Cloud Nine* sessions. When completed, with lyrics by George and Tom Petty and music by George, it was originally offered, along with three other numbers, to Eric Clapton for his *Journeyman* album. Instead Eric, who was composing the soundtrack for *Lethal Weapon 2*, persuaded George to use George's own version of the number on the soundtrack and it is heard over the closing credits of the film.

It was also the first track on the *Lethal Weapon 2* soundtrack when the album was issued in America on 10 August 1989 on LP 1-25985, cassette 4-25985 and CD 2-25985 and in Britain by Warner Brothers on 4 September on LP 925 985-1, cassette 925 985-4 and CD 925985-2.

It was also issued as a single in America on 24 August 1989 on 7″ vinyl 7-22807 and cassette single 4-22807, although it didn't enter the charts.

Chet Atkins Picks On The Beatles

An album originally issued in 1966. George wrote the sleeve notes in which he was to comment, 'All the tracks have Chet adding harmonies and harmonics in the least expected places, and have a country feeling about them, which lend themselves to Chet's own style of picking that has inspired so many guitarists through the world (myself included, but I didn't have enough fingers at the time).' It was reissued in Japan on BMG Victory BVCP 7393 in 1996.

Children Of The Sky

A number on which George played slide guitar and provided backing vocals during a session on Saturday 26 January 1985. The number was eventually issued as a single on 7 November 1986 in Britain and on the Mike Batt album *The Hunting Of The Snark*.

Chronology

George's chronology is not as detailed as those of John and Paul, both of whom actively courted publicity. George jealously guarded his privacy, loved attending Grand Prix events, spent a great deal of his time as a gardener on his Friar Park estate, liked to spend his time with friends such as Ravi Shankar, the *Monty Python* team, 'Legs' Larry Smith and Joe Brown, and sought to conceal himself from the outside world in his other properties in Australia and Hawaii. He didn't particularly like touring and there were long periods when he didn't write or record.

1909

28 May. George's father Harold Hargreaves Harrison is born in Wavertree, Liverpool, the son of Henry Harrison and Jane Thomson.

1911

10 March. George's mother Louise French is born, the daughter of John French and Louisa Woolam.

1930
20 May. Harry and Louise are married in a civil ceremony in Liverpool.

1931
16 August. George's sister Louise is born.

1934
20 August. George's brother Harold is born.
19 September. Brian Epstein is born in Rodney Street, Liverpool.

1940
7 July. Richard Starkey (Ringo Starr) is born at home at 9 Madryn Street in Liverpool's Dingle district.
20 July. George's brother Peter is born at home in Wavertree, Liverpool.
9 October. John Winston Lennon is born at Oxford Street Maternity Home, Liverpool. No bombs fell on this night.

1942
18 June. James Paul McCartney is born in Walton Hospital, Liverpool.

1943
24 February. George is born at home at 11.42 p.m. For most of his life he believed that he'd been born on 25 February.

1945
17 March. Patricia Boyd is born.

1948
18 May. Olivia Trinidad Arias is born.

1954
3 July. George's sister Louise marries an American, Gordon Caldwell.

1957
16 January. The Cavern club opens in Liverpool.
7 September. George watches a performance by the Quarry Men.

1958
6 February. The fourteen-year-old George attends a gig for the Quarry Men at Wilson Hall, Garston at the invitation of Paul. On the bus home he plays the number 'Raunchy' on guitar for Paul and John.
12 December. George's brother Harold marries his girlfriend Irene McGann.
20 December. The Quarry Men play at the reception for the marriage of George's brother Harry to Irene McGann, which takes place at the Harrison home in Upton Green, Speke, Liverpool.

1959

1 January. George's father books the Quarry Men for a gig at Wilson Hall on behalf of his Speke Bus Depot Social Club. George's father is chairman of the club.

19 June. George leaves Liverpool Institute without completing his studies.

29 August. Opening night at the Casbah club where the Quarry Men take up their residency.

1960

18 August. The Beatles make their debut at the Indra club in Hamburg, Germany.

1 November. Bruno Koschmider gives the Beatles notice to quit.

21 November. George is deported from Hamburg for being under age. Astrid Kirchherr and Stuart Sutcliffe drive him to the station.

27 December. The Beatles, sans Stuart Sutcliffe, but with temporary bass player Chas. Newby, make a major impact at Brian Kelly's Litherland Town Hall. Among the numbers in the Beatles repertoire on which George is featured as lead vocalist are Buddy Holly's 'Crying, Waiting, Hoping', Carl Perkins' 'Glad All Over' and 'Your True Love', Elvis Presley's 'I Forgot To Remember To Forget', Eddie Fontaine's 'Nothin' Shakin' (But The Leaves On The Trees)' and the Coasters' 'Three Cool Cats' and 'Youngblood'.

1961

22 June. When the Beatles record for Bert Kaempfert in Hamburg as a backing band for Tony Sheridan, the only original Beatles number they record is 'Cry For A Shadow' penned by George, with a little help from John. Many years later, George was to recall, 'I did actually write one number, if you could call it "writing". It was in Hamburg just about the time the Shadows' "Apache" came out. Somebody asked John and myself how the tune went, and we tried to demonstrate. The result wasn't a bit like "Apache", but we liked it, and we used it in the act for a while. We even called it "Cry For A Shadow".'

20 July. The entire cover of issue No. 2 of *Mersey Beat* is devoted to the story of the Beatles recording in Hamburg. Part of the story reads, 'The Beatles recorded two further numbers for Kaempfert on their own. One side, an instrumental written by George Harrison, has not yet been named – probable titles include "Cry For A Shadow" and "Beatle Bop".' Brian Epstein ordered 144 copies of this issue.

9 November. Brian Epstein asks Bill Harry to arrange for him to visit the Cavern, where he sees the Beatles for the first time.

3 December. The Beatles meet with Brian Epstein at his office in NEMS. George makes his remark to Epstein that Paul is late due to his having a bath.

1962

1 January. At the Decca recording session, George sings 'The Sheik Of Araby'.

10 April. Stuart Sutcliffe dies in Hamburg of a brain haemorrhage due to a fall down some attic stairs.

12 April. George arrives in Hamburg, after a short illness.

6 June. At the Beatles recording audition George makes a comment to George Martin about his tie, which, arguably, endears him to their sense of humour and helps in his decision to sign up the band.

16 August. Beatles drummer Pete Best is sacked from the group.

19 August. Ringo makes his Cavern debut as a member of the Beatles. Bruno, a fan of ousted drummer Pete Best, gives George a black eye.

18 December. The Beatles begin their final season at Hamburg's Star Club. During their stay they are recorded performing and tapes of the session are released many years later. A CD release in the 1990s leads to George going to court on the Beatles' behalf.

1963

22 February. The Beatles' 'Please Please Me' tops the British charts.

28 April. George, Paul and Ringo fly to Santa Cruz, Tenerife for a brief holiday.

10 May. George is one of the judges at a beat contest at the Philharmonic Hall, Liverpool. He tells fellow judge Dick Rowe about the Rolling Stones, 'who are almost as good as our own Roadrunners', and Rowe rushes back to London to sign them up.

30 July. The Beatles record 'Roll Over Beethoven' with George on lead vocals.

23 August. George attends the wedding ceremony of John and Cynthia at Mount Pleasant in Liverpool.

12 September. The Beatles record George's song 'Don't Bother Me', with George on lead vocals.

16 September. George and his brother Peter arrive in New York on their way to visit their sister Louise in Benton, Illinois. George becomes the first member of the Beatles to set foot in the United States.

3 October. George and Peter return to London following their two-week holiday visiting their sister Louise. George says, 'America was really great. I met Tony Newley over there. He'd never heard of any of our numbers so I played him some of our records. When I left he said he wanted to record 'I Saw Her Standing There'.

4 November. The Beatles appear on the Royal Command Performance.

9 November. George signs a five-year publishing deal with Northern Songs Limited.

18 December. George, Paul and John team up with Rolf Harris to sing 'Tie Me Kangaroo Down, Sport' on his radio show, with additional lyrics by Harris. The number has since appeared on bootleg albums.

1964

5 January. George and Ringo record interviews for the BBC radio show *The Public Ear*.

12 January. *The Public Ear*, with George and Ringo's interview, is broadcast.

28 January. George flies from Paris to London to have dinner with Phil Spector and the Ronettes.

7 February. The Beatles fly to America.

8 February. George remains in the Plaza Hotel, New York with throat trouble.

9 February. George manages to appear on the *Ed Sullivan Show*, although he still hasn't fully recovered from his illness.

25 February. 60 sacks containing over 30,000 cards and presents arrive for George on his 21st birthday.

1 March. 'I'm Happy Just To Dance With You', written specially for George by John Lennon, is recorded by the Beatles with George on lead vocal.

3 March. George meets Patti Boyd for the first time on the set of *A Hard Day's Night*.

4 March. George asks Patti for a date.

20 March. George partners Hayley Mills to the premiere of *Charade* at the Regal cinema, Henley-on-Thames.

27 March. George and Patti and John and Cynthia travel to stay at Dromoland Castle in Ireland. The press discover them and they have to flee, hidden in a laundry van.

2 May. George and Patti, together with John and Cynthia, fly to Honolulu, then on to Papeete in Tahiti where they hire a yacht to sail around the islands.

26 May. George, Patti, John and Cynthia return from their holiday and George, Patti, Ringo and Hayley Mills go to a party at the Pickwick Club, London hosted by Joan Collins and Anthony Newley, who have returned to Britain from America.

27 May. George and John attend Cilla Black's 21st birthday party at Brian Epstein's flat.

17 June. In Australia with the Beatles George, together with tour organiser Lloyd Ravenscroft, sets out for a drive into the Dandenong Mountains.

2 July. On the Beatles' return from Australia George is charged £30 duty on a Pentax camera he bought in Hong Kong.

12 July. On his way to a gig at the Hippodrome Theatre, Brighton, George is involved in a motoring accident in his E-Type Jaguar in the King's Road, London.

25 July. George appears as a panellist on the TV show *Juke Box Jury*. He shares the panel with Alexandra Bastedo, Reg Varney and Carole Ann Ford. The records include a cover version of 'I Should Have Known Better' by the Naturals and 'How Can I Tell Her?' by the Fourmost.

25 August. George and Paul visit Burt Lancaster's house to watch a screening of the Peter Sellers film *A Shot In The Dark*.

11 September. George forms his own music publishing company. Initially it is called Mornyork Ltd and is later changed to Harrisongs.

8 December. George visits Ringo in University Hospital where he'd had his tonsils removed.

9 December. George and Patti fly to the Bahamas for a short break.

19 December. George and Patti return from Nassau.

24 December. The Beatles appear in 'Another Beatles Christmas Show' at the Odeon, Hammersmith, London.

1965

15 January. George, along with Ringo, attends a party given by Bob Dawbarn, a journalist with *Melody Maker*.

27 January. George acts as best man at the wedding of his brother Peter to his girlfriend Pauline.

28 January. George and Patti fly off on holiday to Europe.

11 February. George attends Ringo and Maureen's wedding.

17 February. The Beatles begin recording George's composition 'You Like Me Too Much' at Abbey Road Studios.

5 April. While filming inside an Indian restaurant during the making of the film *Help!* George becomes interested in the sitar being played by a member of the Indian group.

16 April. Cathy McGowan interviews George and John at the Wembley studios of *Ready Steady Go!*

20 April. Brian Epstein is appointed a director of George's company Harrisongs Ltd.

9 May. The Beatles attend the Bob Dylan concert at the Royal Festival Hall, London.

3 June. George and Patti and John and Cynthia attend Alan Ginsberg's 39th birthday party. They make a quick retreat when Ginsberg cavorts around naked. 'You don't do that in front of the birds,' snaps John.

7 July. George and Patti and Paul and Jane Asher attend a Moody Blues party in Roehampton.

17 July. George and Patti, John and Cynthia, and Ringo and Maureen attend a Bastille Night party at the Scotch of St James club.

8 August. George and Patti and John and Cynthia attend the Richmond Jazz Festival, primarily to see Eric Burdon and the Animals, but have to leave after they are mobbed.

9 August. John Lennon produces the Silkie performing 'You've Got To Hide Your Love Away', with Paul on guitar and George on tambourine.

15 August. Bob Dylan visits the Beatles at the Warwick Hotel following their concert at Shea Stadium and they engage in their first experience with marijuana.

21 August. George is presented with a Rickenbacker 12-string guitar by Ron Butwin and Randy Resnick of the music store B-Sharp Music in Minneapolis, Minnesota.

25 September. The King Features animated series *The Beatles* is screened on US TV, with Paul Frees providing the voices for George and John.

7 October. *Beatles Monthly* arrive at Kinfauns to undertake a photo shoot of George at home.

26 October. The Beatles receive their MBEs at Buckingham Palace. Another myth was born when John told the French *L'Express* magazine that they'd smoked pot in the Palace loo. It wasn't true.

8 November. The Beatles begin recording George's composition 'Think For Yourself' at Abbey Road.

2 December. On the way to a gig at Berwick-on-Tweed George's guitar falls off the back of his car and is smashed by oncoming traffic.

23 December. George proposes to Patti Boyd on their way to a party at Brian Epstein's house.

26 December. George visits his mum and dad at their new bungalow and stays overnight.

1966

8 January. George and Patti, John and Ringo attend a party at Mick Jagger's house at 13a Bryanston Mews East, London.

13 January. George and Patti and Mick Jagger and Chrissie Shrimpton spend the evening at Dolly's nightclub in London.

21 January. George and Patti are married at Epsom Register office. Patti wears a short red fox-fur coat given to her by George as a wedding present. Paul McCartney is the only other Beatle in attendance. Paul acts as joint best man with Brian Epstein.

22 January. George organises a press conference to announce that he is now married.

31 January. George and Patti and Paul and Jane Asher see the play *How's The World Treating You?* at the Wyndham Theatre, London.

4 February. George and Patti go to see the play *Little Malcom And His Struggle Against The Eunuchs*, starring John Hurt, at the Garrick Theatre, London.

8 February. George and Patti fly to Barbados on their honeymoon.

12 February. Photographers catch up with George and Patti on their honeymoon.

26 February. George and Patti return from Barbados.

24 March. George and Patti, Paul and Jane Asher and Cilla Black attend the premiere of the film *Alfie* at the Plaza cinema, the Haymarket, London.

27 March. George and Ringo visit Roy Orbison backstage at the Granada, Walthamstow.

11 April. The Beatles record George's 'Love You To'.

13 April. The overdubs to 'Love You To' are carried out at Abbey Road Studios.

18 April. George, Eric Clapton and John Lennon go to see the Lovin' Spoonful at the Marquee Club, Wardour Street, London.

20 April. The Beatles begin recording George's number 'Taxman' at Abbey Road Studios.

5 May. George records his guitar solo for 'I'm Only Sleeping'.

16 May. The recording of 'Taxman' is completed at Abbey Road Studios.

27 May. George and John attend the Bob Dylan concert at the Royal Albert Hall. This was the tour in which Dylan was backed by the Band and introduced electric instruments into his act, resulting in the audience booing them. A furious George told the hecklers to shut up.

1 June. George attends the Ravi Shankar performance at the Royal Albert Hall. For the rest of his life George regularly attended concerts by Ravi.

2 June. The Beatles record George's number 'I Want To Tell You'.

7 June. The Beatles rehearse at George's Kinfauns bungalow.

23 June. Sibylla's nightclub opens in London. George has a 10% share in the venture.

30 June. George is officially made a director of Kevin McDonald Associated Limited, the company running Sibylla's nightclub.

8 July. The Beatles are in New Delhi where George buys a sitar.

11 July. A cover version of 'If I Needed Someone' by Stained Glass is issued in America.

2 August. George and Patti visit Patti's mother Diana Jones in Devon.

29 August. The Beatles appear in their final American concert at Candlestick Park, San Francisco. George, who hated touring, is relieved and says, 'I'm not a Beatle anymore.'

14 September. George and Patti fly to India where George meets up with Ravi Shankar to begin training on the sitar.

15 September. George begins his sitar lessons, taking daily lessons from Shambu Das.

19 September. George conducts a press conference at the Hahal Hotel because the media have discovered he is in India. They have also discovered the fact that he and Patti had booked into their hotel under the name Mr & Mrs Sam Wells.

21 October. Donald Milnor interviews George for BBC Bombay.

22 October. George and Patti return to London.

26 October. George and Patti go to Heathrow Airport to meet Ravi Shankar.

31 October. Donovan begins a week's visit as a guest of George and Patti at Kinfauns.

20 November. George and John attend a party for the Four Tops, held by Brian Epstein at his house in Chapel Street, London.

11 December. An interview George recorded in Bombay, India in

October is broadcast on the BBC Home Service programme *The Lively Arts*.

31 December. George, Paul, Brian Epstein and Eric Clapton are refused entrance at Annabel's club because George is not wearing a tie. He turns down the offer of one from the doorman and the group then went to the nearby Lyons Corner House in Coventry Street to see the New Year in.

1967

15 January. George and Paul watch a concert by Donovan at the Royal Albert Hall.

21 January. George gives Donovan a sitar lesson.

28 January. George and John attend the Four Tops concert at the Royal Albert Hall.

13 February. The Beatles record George's composition 'It's Only A Northern Song'.

15 March. The Beatles record George's composition 'Within You, Without You'.

20 March. George and Patti and John and Cynthia are invited to tea by Ringo and Maureen at their Sunny Heights home in Weybridge.

25 March. The Beatles record George's composition 'It's All Too Much'.

3 April. George is at Abbey Road Studios completing his composition 'Within You, Without You'.

19 April. George, John, Paul and Ringo sign a business agreement setting up 'The Beatles & Co.'

24 April. George, John, Paul and Ringo attend a Donovan concert at the Royal Albert Hall.

4 June. George and Patti and Paul and Jane Asher watch the Jimi Hendrix Experience at the Saville Theatre.

14 June. George plays the violin on a recording of 'All You Need Is Love', although this version is not used.

28 June. George is fined £6 for speeding in his black Mini-Cooper.

2 July. Patti Harrison is introduced to Eric Clapton at a party at Brian Epstein's house in Chapel Street, London.

20 July. George and Patti, together with Neil Aspinall, visit Alexis Mardas in Athens.

29 July. George and Patti return to London.

1 August. George and Patti, accompanied by Mal Evans and Alexis Mardas, fly to Los Angeles. They travel as Mr & Mrs Weiss and are met at the airport by Brian Epstein's American lawyer Nat Weiss. They stay at Blue Jay Way and, while waiting for the arrival of Derek and Joan Taylor, George writes a song of that title.

2 August. George and Patti visit Ravi Shankar's music school where there were 50 pupils aged between 16 and 30. Alla Rakah, the tabla drummer, gives the lesson. They then go for a meal with Ravi Shankar on Sunset Strip.

3 August. George, along with Mal Evans and Alexis Mardas, goes along to Ravi Shankar's music school once again. George and Ravi hold a press conference at Ravi's Hollywood Bowl concert. In the meantime, Patti goes sightseeing with her sister Jenny. They attend an evening lecture by Shankar on Indian music and then go to the Mamas & Papas recording session with Derek Taylor.

4 August. George and Patti attend the four-hour Ravi Shankar Hollywood Bowl concert. Bismillah Khan plays the Indian flute – shehnal, while Ali Akbar Khan and his son Ashish play sarods. Ravi then performs for an hour on sitar with tabla player Alla Rakah.

5 August. George attends an Alla Rakah recording session and agrees to write the sleeve notes for a record by Ali's son Ashish. In the evening he dines at a Mexican restaurant in Alvera Street with Derek Taylor and his family.

6 August. George visits Ali Akbar's son and in the evening dines at Ravi Shankar's home.

7 August. George and Patti, together with Derek Taylor, visit the Haight-Ashbury district of San Francisco to see the hippies. He is disillusioned and comes away describing them as 'Bowery bums'.

9 August. George and Patti return to London.

24 August. George, John and Paul attend a lecture on Transcendental Meditation by the Maharishi Mahesh Yogi at the Hilton Hotel, London.

26 August. George and Patti, John and Cynthia, Ringo and Maureen, Paul and Jane Asher and Mick Jagger and Marianne Faithfull are formally initiated into the Maharishi's International Meditation society in Bangor, North Wales.

27 August. Brian Epstein is found dead from an accidental overdose. The Beatles are shocked to hear the news and George was to comment, 'There is no such thing as death.'

6 September. The Beatles begin recording George's composition 'Blue Jay Way'.

13 September. George and John direct a scene in the *Magical Mystery Tour* film and Miranda Ward interviews George for the BBC programme *Scene And Heard*.

29 September. David Frost discusses Transcendental Meditation and the Maharishi Mahesh Yogi with George and John on Rediffusion's *The Frost Programme*.

30 September. The first part of George's interview for *Scene And Heard* is aired.

4 October. George and John return to *The Frost Programme* to discuss spiritual interests and Brian Epstein with David Frost.

7 October. The second part of George's interview for *Scene And Heard* is aired.

19 October. George and Ringo travel to Sweden to visit the Maharishi Mahesh Yogi at his Transcendental Meditation Centre.

1 November. George and John attend a reception for the group Family at Sibylla's club in London.

3 November. The 'Blue Jay Way' sequence for *Magical Mystery Tour* is filmed at Ringo's place in Weybridge.

22 November. George is at Abbey Road Studios working on *Wonderwall*.

5 December. George and John attend a party at the Apple boutique at 94 Baker Street.

10 December. George and Ravi Shankar appear on a broadcast, which they tape at United Nations buildings in New York and London.

11 December. George begins his recordings for the film soundtrack *Wonderwall*.

15 December. Joe Massott begins filming *Wonderwall*.

16 December. George and Patti are in Paris to attend the UNICEF Gala at the Palais de Chailly with the Maharishi Mahesh Yogi.

17 December. George and John arrange a party for Beatles fan club secretaries.

20 December. George continues recording *Wonderwall* at Abbey Road Studios.

21 December. A special fancy dress party for *Magical Mystery Tour* takes place at the Royal Lancaster Hotel in London. George is dressed as a Cavalier, complete with sword, and Patti dresses as a belly dancer. Great embarrassment is caused all round when a tipsy John Lennon, dressed as a teddy boy, tries to become too familiar!

31 December. George resumes his recording sessions at Abbey Road.

1968

7 January. George flies to Bombay, India to commence work on recording tracks for the *Wonderwall* album as he wishes to record with Indian musicians. The flight takes nineteen hours with stops at Paris, Frankfurt and Tehran. Neil Aspinall, Mal Evans and Alexis Mardas accompany him. They are greeted by Shambhu Das, who runs Ravi's Bombay school, and are taken to the Airways Hotel.

9 January. After moving into the Taj Mahal Hotel, George begins recording at EMI's studio in Bombay. Stereo equipment had to be brought specially from Calcutta. He said, 'It was fantastic really. The studio is on the top of the offices but there's no soundproofing, so if you listen closely to some of the Indian tracks on the LP you can hear taxis going by.'

10 January. During his recordings for *Wonderwall* in Bombay George also observed, 'Every time the office knocked off at five-thirty we had to stop recording because you could just hear everybody stomping down the stairs. They only had a big EMI mono machine. I mixed everything as we did it there, and that was nice enough because you get spoiled working on eight and sixteen tracks.'

12 January. George records the instrumental track for 'The Inner Light'.

18 January. George returns to London.

25 January. George and John Lennon attend a Quorum fashion show at the Revolution Club in Bruton Place, London where Patti is modelling clothes by Ossie Clarke and Alice Pollock.

30 January. George completes recording his *Wonderwall* soundtrack at Abbey Road Studios.

6 February. George records the vocal for 'The Inner Light'.

16 February. George and Patti and John and Cynthia fly to India to attend the Maharishi's ashram for advance training in Transcendental Meditation.

15 March. The 'Lady Madonna' single is released in Britain. The flip-side is George's composition 'The Inner Light', the first time he has had one of his numbers included on a Beatles single.

18 March. The 'Lady Madonna'/'The Inner Light' single is released in America.

12 April. George and Patti, John and Cynthia and Alexis Mardas leave Rishikesh after rumours that the Maharishi has been paying undue attention to some female members at the ashram.

14 April. George and Patti travel to Madras to visit Ravi Shankar.

17 April. George is filmed with Ravi Shankar for a documentary.

21 April. George and Patti return to London.

25 April. George discusses his trip to India with the British press.

17 May. The world premiere of *Wonderwall* takes place at the Cannes Film Festival. George, Patti, Ringo and Maureen are in attendance.

19 May. George and Patti return to London.

22 May. George and John attend the opening of Apple Tailoring in Chelsea, which is run by designer John Crittle.

26 May. The Beatles assemble at George's bungalow to make demo recordings of the many numbers they composed in Rishikesh in preparation for *The Beatles* white album.

7 June. George, Patti, Ringo, Maureen and Mal Evans fly to California where George is to make a cameo appearance in a film *The Messenger From The East*, produced by himself and Ravi Shankar. The film is eventually released under the title *Raga*.

8 June. George and Ringo visit Joan Baez in Carmel, California.

9 June. George and Ringo play golf in Monterey.

10 June. George is filmed with Ravi Shankar for the documentary *Raga*.

11 June. George completes his film for the documentary on Ravi.

12 June. George, Ringo and party move to Los Angeles.

13 June. George and Ringo meet up with Peter Tork of the Monkees and David Crosby of the Byrds and they all take part in a jam session.

16 June. George, Patti, Ringo and Maureen fly to New York.

18 June. George, Patti, Ringo and Maureen fly back to London.

24 June. George begins producing Jackie Lomax, beginning with George's composition 'Sour Milk Sea' on which George also plays guitar.

26 June. George completes the Jackie Lomax recordings.

7 July. Patti opens her boutique in Chelsea Market with her sister Jennifer. They call it Juniper after the song 'Jennifer Juniper' which Donovan wrote about Jenny.

25 July. George records an acoustic version of 'While My Guitar Gently Weeps'.

2 August. George and Patti leave for Los Angeles.

6 August. Patti and John Lennon attend a fashion show and are interviewed by BBC radio's *Late Night Show*.

7 August. The Beatles begin recording George's 'Not Guilty', originally intended for *The Beatles* white album.

8 August. After over a hundred takes, it is decided not to include George's 'Not Guilty' on *The Beatles* double album and it is to surface many years later on the *George Harrison* album.

14 August. George accompanies John Lennon on the recording of 'What's The New Mary Jane'.

17 August. George and Patti set off on a short break to Greece, accompanied by Mal Evans.

21 August. George and Patti return from Greece.

5 September. George records the lead vocal for his composition 'While My Guitar Gently Weeps'.

6 September. Eric Clapton performs his guitar solo on 'While My Guitar Gently Weeps'.

18 September. George records an interview with Alan Smith for BBC Radio One's *Scene And Heard*.

19 September. The Beatles begin to record George's composition 'Piggies'.

28 September. George's interview with Alan Smith for *Scene And Heard* is aired.

2 October. George records 'Badge' with Cream, the song he co-wrote with Eric Clapton.

3 October. The Beatles record George's composition 'Savoy Truffle'.

7 October. The Beatles record George's composition 'Long, Long, Long'.

10 October. George forms a new music publishing company, Singalong Limited.

16 October. George arrives in Los Angeles on a seven-week visit, primarily to record the Jackie Lomax album *Is This What You Want?*

20 October. George produces a session for Jackie Lomax in Los Angeles.

21 October. George continues recording in Los Angeles.

1 November. George's first solo album, *Wonderwall Music*, is released in Britain.

3 November. While in Los Angeles George records the synthesizer track 'No Time Or Space'.

8 November. The news is finally released that George's contract with Northern Songs expired in March and is now renewed.

15 November. George has a walk-on part in a recording of *The Smothers Brothers Comedy Hour*, recorded at the CBS TV studio in Sunset Boulevard, Hollywood, in front of a live audience.

17 November. *The Smothers Brothers Comedy Hour*, with George's cameo appearance, is broadcast.

2 December. George's movie soundtrack *Wonderwall* is released in the States on Apple ST 3350.

4 December. George informs the Apple staff that members of California's Hell's Angels are due to visit the offices.

19 December. George returns from his trip to America.

1969

2 January. Work begins on the 'Get Back' project, which ends up being called *Let It Be*. Billy Preston joins the Beatles in the studio.

5 January. On the set at Twickenham Studios, where the Beatles are recording their 'Get Back' sessions, there is a dispute when Paul attempts to tell George how he should play his guitar. George says, 'All right, I'll play whatever you want me to play, or I won't play at all if you don't want me to play,' an incident which is filmed and included in their *Let It Be* movie.

6 January. Apple announces George and Derek Taylor are to write a Broadway musical about Apple. They actually make a demo of a number they have written for it called 'Hey Man', but the project is abandoned.

8 January. John Lennon makes sarcastic remarks about George's number 'I. Me. Mine.' on the set of the 'Get Back' sessions.

10 January. George walks out of the *Let It Be* set after disagreements with the other members of the group. He said, 'Paul and I were trying to have an argument and the crew carried on filming and recording us. Anyway, after one of those first mornings, I couldn't stand it – I decided, this is it – it's not fun anymore; it's very unhappy being in this band; it's a lot of crap. Thank you, I'm leaving.' And he left.

12 January. George attends the London premiere of *Wonderwall*.

15 January. George rejoins the Beatles at Twickenham Studios after an agreement that they will drop the idea of the Beatles appearing in a concert.

21 January. George receives a £100 fine for an assault on a French photographer, which took place the previous spring.

25 January. The Beatles record George's composition 'George's Blues', which is the working title of 'For You Blue'.

7 February. George enters University Hospital, London to have his tonsils removed.

8 February. George's tonsils are removed.

15 February. George leaves hospital after accepting an offer of a grisly souvenir – his tonsils in a jar, which he takes home with him!

25 February. George is at Abbey Road recording demos for 'Old Brown Shoe', 'All Things Must Pass' and 'Something'.

28 February. George arrives in Ottowa, Ontario, Canada with some Apple Records personnel to see folk singer Eric Anderson, with the intention of signing him up when his current contract lapses. Cream's *Goodbye* album is issued in Britain with the track 'Badge', co-written by George.

12 March. George and Patti's home in Esher is raided by the London drug squad led by Detective Sgt Norman Pilcher, aided by twelve police cars and a police van. They were released on bail of £500. Although the couple were to plead guilty and receive a fine, they were to say that they didn't have drugs in the house when the raid took place. (Pilcher was later arrested and convicted of planting drugs on people he arrested.)

31 March. George and Patti are fined £250 after admitting possession of drugs, which their counsel has advised them to do.

3 April. In an interview with Sue MacGregor for Radio One's *World At One* programme, George discusses Ravi Shankar.

7 April. George announces in a London newspaper that he will never keep drugs in his house again.

16 April. George begins to record 'Something'.

9 May. Apple launch their experimental label Zapple with two releases, one of which is from George's *Electronic Music* album.

11 May. George takes part in a Jack Bruce recording session, playing on the number 'Never Tell Your Mother She's Out Of Tune'.

20 May. George and John Lennon attend a meeting at their merchant bankers Ansbachers to discuss their attempts to buy Northern Songs Limited.

30 May. 'The Ballad Of John And Yoko' is released in Britain, with George's composition 'Old Brown Shoe' on the flip.

1 June. George and Patti fly to Sardinia on a holiday.

4 June. 'The Ballad Of John And Yoko'/'Old Brown Shoe' is released in America.

23 June. George and Patti return from their holiday in Sardinia.

7 July. Recording begins on George's composition 'Here Comes The Sun'.

8 July. Overdubbing takes place on 'Here Comes The Sun'.

11 July. George records the lead vocal on 'Something'.

26 July. In a series of radio advertisements paid for by Apple, George promotes the Hare Krishna movements Rathayatra Festival.

4 August. George makes rough mixes of 'Something' and 'Here Comes The Sun'.

5 August. George plays Moog synthesizer on the recording of 'Because'.

8 August. Following the photo session for the famous cover of *Abbey Road*, George and Mal Evans visit London Zoo.

19 August. George records a Moog synthesizer part in the recording of 'Here Comes The Sun'.

22 August. The Radha Krishna Temple's debut disc 'The Hare Krishna Mantra' is issued in America.

26 August. George and Mal Evans drive to Portsmouth to meet Bob Dylan.

28 August. George writes the press release for the 'Hare Krishna Mantra' single.

29 August. The Radha Krishna Temple's single 'Hare Krishna Mantra' is issued in Britain on Apple 15. Jack Bruce's debut album *Songs For A Tailor* is released in Britain on Polydor 583 058 with a contribution by George on the track 'Never Tell Your Mother She's Out Of Tune'. George, John and Ringo arrive in the Isle of Wight and join Bob Dylan at Forelands Farm.

31 August. George, John and Ringo watch Bob Dylan perform in concert at the Isle of Wight Festival.

1 September. George leaves the Isle of Wight and travels to London by helicopter.

2 September. George begins recording on Leon Russell's 'Delta Lady'.

3 September. George completes his guitar guest spot on Leon Russell's 'Delta Lady'.

5 September. George and John resign from the board of Hayling Supermarkets.

14 September. George visits A.C. Bhaktivedanta Swami Prabhupada at John Lennon's estate, Tittenhurst Park in Ascot. A transcript of the interview with the Swami and John and George is later published in book form as *Lennon '69: Search For Liberation*.

20 September. George visits his mother, who is seriously ill, in Cheshire.

6 October. The Beatles' 'Something' c/w 'Come Together' is released in America. It is George's first and only composition to appear on the A side of a Beatles single.

7 October. George records with Blind Faith on the numbers 'Exchange And Mart' and 'Spending All My Days'.

8 October. George records an interview with *Daily Express* writer David Wigg for the Radio One show *Scene And Heard*.

12 October. The first part of George's *Scene And Heard* interview is broadcast.

19 October. The second and final part of George's *Scene And Heard* interview is broadcast.

20 October. George and Patti attend a Ravi Shankar concert at the Royal Albert Hall.

31 October. 'Something' c/w 'Come Together' is released in Britain.

1 December. George and Patti and Ringo and Maureen attend the

'Delaney And Bonnie And Friends' concert at the Royal Albert Hall. George asks if he can join the tour.

2 December. George appears in his first concert with Delaney And Bonnie And Friends.

3 December. George continues his appearance on tour, at the Town Hall, Birmingham. His last appearance at the venue had been when the Beatles toured with Roy Orbison in 1963.

4 December. George continues his appearance on tour at the City Hall, Sheffield.

5 December. George continues his appearance on tour at the City Hall, Newcastle upon Tyne.

6 December. George continues his appearance on tour, this time returning to his home town for a concert at the Empire Theatre, Liverpool.

7 December. The concert this evening at the Fairfield Hall, Croydon, is recorded for the album *Delaney And Bonnie On Tour With Eric Clapton*. The album is released in Britain on 29 May 1970.

10 December. The tour moves to the Falkoner Theatre, Copenhagen, Denmark.

12 December. In another concert at the Falkoner Theatre, George makes his last appearance with Delaney and Bonnie.

15 December. George joins the Plastic Ono Band on stage at the Lyceum, London, for a UNICEF benefit. This was the first time George and John had shared a British stage since 1 May 1966.

31 December. George and Patti and Paul and Linda attend Ringo and Maureen's New Year's Eve party at their new home in Highgate.

1970
4 January. Recordings begin at Abbey Road Studios of George's composition 'I. Me. Mine.' with George, Paul and Ringo.

8 January. George records a vocal overdub for 'For You Blue', to be included on the *Let It Be* album.

14 January. George buys Friar Park, a huge mansion in Henley-on-Thames.

18 January. George continues to produce Doris Troy's first Apple album.

25 January. George begins work on Billy Preston's Apple album.

27 January. George plays lead guitar on the recording of John Lennon's 'Instant Karma'.

28 January. Billy Preston's single 'All That I've Got', which was produced by George, is issued in Britain.

18 February. George plays acoustic guitar on 'It Don't Come Easy' a number he co-wrote with Ringo.

5 March. George and Ringo are interviewed by the *New Musical Express*.

8 March. George and Ringo complete the recording of 'It Don't Come Easy'.

11 March. George is interviewed by Johnny Moran for a 'The Beatles Today' special on Radio One's *Scene And Heard* programme.

12 March. George and Patti move into their new home, the impressive Friar Park estate, originally built in the nineteenth century by Sir Frank Crisp.

15 March. George promotes the 'Govinda' single on French radio and television. Excerpts from his interview with Johnny Moran are aired.

17 March. George holds a party at Friar Park for Patti's birthday. Guests include Ringo and Maureen. Doris Troy's 'Ain't That Cute'/'Vay Con Dios' is issued in America on Apple 1820. The A side was produced by George and the song co-written by George and Doris.

23 March. George begins attending Phil Spector's sessions at Abbey Road where he attempts to provide a definitive soundtrack for *Let It Be*.

24 March. 'Govinda' by the Radha Krishna Temple is issued in America on Apple 1821.

30 March. The complete Johnny Moran interview with George is heard on the Radio One programme *Scene And Heard*.

31 March. George writes the press release for the 'Hare Krishna Mantra' single.

10 April. George is at the Savile Row offices of Apple where he is interviewed for a BBC1 religious programme *Fact Or Fantasy? Prayer And Meditation*. The show is screened on Sunday 26 April and repeated on Monday 27 April.

23 April. Together with his wife Patti and Derek Taylor, George flies to New York where he is to begin producing a Billy Preston album *Encouraging Words*.

28 April. George visits the Apple offices, which are situated at 1700 Broadway. While there Howard Smith of WPLJ Radio, interviews him.

29 April. George, in the company of Derek Taylor, visits Bob Dylan at his townhouse in MacDougal Street, Greenwich Village, New York.

30 April. At Dylan's house, George joins Dylan in a jam session, which is recorded on Dylan's home recording equipment. They perform the numbers 'When Everybody Comes To Town' and 'I'd Have You Anytime'.

1 May. George, in the company of Derek Taylor, is invited to a Bob Dylan recording session at CBS Studios in New York. George and Dylan record enough tracks for an album, but it is never officially released.

3 May. George tells the media in New York that the Beatles split is not permanent.

5 May. George, accompanied by Derek Taylor, flies back to London.

11 May. 'The Long And Winding Road' single is released in America, with George's composition 'For You Blue' on the flipside.

24 May. George begins working on his solo album *All Things Must Pass* at Abbey Road.

7 June. George completes work on Doris Troy's Apple album.

14 June. George is at Abbey Road Studios with Phil Spector and Eric Clapton's new band Derek And The Dominoes.

17 June. The album *Delaney And Bonnie On Tour* is issued in Britain on Atco 2400 013, featuring George on guitar.

18 June. George records 'Roll It' with Eric Clapton.

19 June. Apple releases the Doris Troy album 'Ain't That Cute', which George produced. George and Ringo also play on the album.

4 July. George's number 'Something' is awarded the Ivor Novello award for 'Best Song musically and lyrically of the Year'. George also breaks off his recording of the *All Things Must Pass* sessions to rush to Liverpool to see his mother, who is dying.

7 July. George attends his mother's bedside in a Liverpool hospital, where she dies of cancer.

10 July. George attends his mother's funeral when Louise Harrison is cremated in Liverpool.

12 July. George resumes work on his solo album.

12 August. George completes the recording of his first solo album.

16 August. George begins the mixing of his solo album.

4 September. Billy Preston's 'My Sweet Lord' c/w 'Long As I Got My Baby' is issued on Apple 29.

6 September. George has a meeting at Apple to discuss promotion.

7 September. George attends a meeting at EMI.

14 September. The Derek And The Dominoes single 'Tell The Truth' c/w 'Roll It Over' is released in America on Atco 6780. George plays guitar on both tracks.

17 September. George attends the rehearsals for the Festival Of Arts Of India at the Royal Albert Hall, where Ravi Shankar is to perform.

20 September. George attends the opening night of the Festival Of Arts Of India at the Royal Albert Hall.

21 September. Doris Troy's 'Jacob's Ladder' c/w 'Get Back', produced by George, is released in the States on Apple 1824.

28 September. The album *Ashton Gardner & Dyke* is issued on Capitol ST 563, with George playing guitar on one of the tracks.

15 October. George and Phil Spector begin work on the final mixing of the *All Things Must Pass* album.

23 October. George announces he will release 'Isn't It A Pity' as a single on 30 October.

24 October. George attends the Lyceum, London to watch the Incredible Stone Ground.

25 October. George cancels the release of his solo single.

26 October. George makes an announcement saying that 'My Sweet Lord' will not be his next single release after all.

28 October. George and Patti, together with Phil Spector, arrive in New York with the master tapes of *All Things Must Pass* to complete their mixing.

23 November. Despite his announcement on 26 October, the new single by George is 'My Sweet Lord', issued in America with 'Isn't It A Pity' on the flip.

25 November. George and Patti fly to New York where George introduces the Apple signing Badfinger to the press.

27 November. George's triple album *All Things Must Pass* is issued in America on Apple SRTCH 639.

30 November. *All Things Must Pass* is issued in Britain.

10 December. Brief excerpts from George's *All Things Must Pass* are featured on *Top Of The Pops*.

26 December. George's debut solo single 'My Sweet Lord' tops the *Billboard* chart and remains in the No. 1 position for four weeks.

27 December. George and Patti are the guests at the wedding of Tony Ashton of Ashton, Gardner & Dyke.

31 December. Paul McCartney files a suit to dissolve the Beatles.

1971

2 January. George's solo album *All Things Must Pass* tops the American album charts. He has created a record as he also tops the singles charts with 'My Sweet Lord'.

4 January. George attends the premiere of Mick Jagger's film *Performance*.

15 January. 'My Sweet Lord'/'What Is Life' is issued as a single in Britain on Apple R 5884.

18 January. George and Ringo meet to discuss the court action that Paul has brought to dissolve the Beatles.

25 January. George attends Wells Street Magistrates' Court, London to plead guilty to 'driving without reasonable consideration'. Sentencing is postponed until 23 February.

30 January. *All Things Must Pass* tops the British album chart and 'My Sweet Lord' tops the British singles chart.

7 February. George begins work with Phil Spector on producing a single for Ronnie Spector.

9 February. George produces the rehearsals for Ronnie Spector to cover his composition 'You'.

15 February. George's single 'What Is Life' c/w 'Apple Scruffs' is issued in America on Apple 1828.

21 February. George and Phil Spector complete Ronnie Spector's recording.

23 February. George is banned from driving for one year.

6 March. 'My Sweet Lord' reaches No. 1 in the *Melody Maker* chart.

10 March. The copyright holders of 'He's So Fine' begin their initial proceedings against George claiming that his 'My Sweet Lord' breached their copyright.

9 April. Ringo Starr's single 'It Don't Come Easy', produced by George, is released in Britain.

3 June. George plays lead guitar on Badfinger's recording of 'Day After Day'.

3 July. George attends a New York television station to watch an Ike and Tina Turner special.

4 July. George and Patti attend a concert by Leon Russell at the Inglewood Forum.

5 July. George begins recording 'Bangla Desh', which is to be his next single.

9 July. George and Patti visit Ike and Tina Turner at the Schaeffer Music Festival in Central Park.

12 July. George and Patti return to England where George holds a meeting at Apple to state that he is organising a concert for Bangla Desh.

13 July. George and Patti return to New York where George asks John Lennon if he will appear at the concert.

26 July. Rehearsals for the Concert For Bangla Desh begin at Nola Studios in New York.

27 July. George publicly announces his plan for a concert in aid of Bangla Desh.

28 July. George's single 'Bangla Desh' c/w 'Deep Blue' is released in America.

29 July. George tells John he would like him to appear at the Bangla Desh concert, but does not wish Yoko to take part. There is a fierce row between John and Yoko. When George goes to John's hotel to see if he will come to rehearsals, he finds that John has flown to Paris.

30 July. George's single 'Bangla Desh' c/w 'Deep Blue' is released in Britain.

31 July. The final rehearsals for the Bangla Desh concert take place.

1 August. The Concert For Bangla Desh takes place in Madison Square Garden, New York with an all-star cast which includes Ringo Starr, Eric Clapton, Bob Dylan, Ravi Shankar, Badfinger, Leon Russell and Billy Preston.

2 August. George begins to write the number 'The Day The World Gets 'Round'. He also begins a series of late-night sessions with Phil Spector to prepare the *Bangla Desh* album.

7 August. 'The Concert For Bangla Desh' is described by the *New Musical Express* as 'The Greatest Rock Spectacle Of The Decade'.

23 August. The release of the *Bangla Desh* album is delayed due to legal problems.

11 September. George's single 'Bangla Desh' reaches No. 10 in the British charts.

22 September. George and Patti return to Britain on the *QE2*.

30 September. George attends the opening of the new Apple Recording Studio in Savile Row.

1 October. George has a meeting with Patrick Jenkins, the Chancellor of the Exchequer, to see if he will allow copies of the *Bangla Desh* album to be tax-free. Jenkins refuses.

2 October. George and Patti sail to New York on the SS *France*.

22 November. The Apple film *Raga* receives a press screening at the Carnegie Hall Cinema, New York. George and Patti and John and Yoko are in attendance.

23 November. George appears on *The Dick Cavett Show*, performing 'Two-Faced Man' with Gary Wright. *Raga* receives its public premiere at the Carnegie Hall Cinema.

3 December. George and Ravi Shankar appear on the American *The David Frost Show*, which was recorded on 24 November. George performs 'The Holdup' with David Bromberg, a number he co-wrote with the singer at the house of journalist Al Aronowitz in New Jersey at Thanksgiving. George and Ravi also plugged *Raga*.

20 December. The *Concert For Bangla Desh* album is released in America.

1972

10 January. The *Concert For Bangla Desh* album is released in Britain.

12 January. George works on completing the *Bangla Desh* film at Friar Park.

20 January. George travels to Felixstowe in Suffolk to record interviews for the BBC Radio One series *The Beatles Story*.

8 February. The Official Beatles Fan Club closes.

28 February. George and Patti are involved in an accident on the M4 motorway near Maidenhead, on their way back to Friar Park from London. They are taken to Maidenhead Hospital and treated in the casualty department. Patti has sustained the worse injuries and has concussion.

22 March. The *Concert For Bangla Desh* film is previewed at the DeMille Theater in New York. Members of the audience include John and Yoko and singer Nino Tempo.

23 March. Apple's *Concert For Bangla Desh* film officially opens in New York.

5 June. George arrives in New York and is presented with a 'Child Is Father To The Man' award, along with Ravi Shankar and Allen Klein. The occasion is the annual luncheon of UNICEF and the award is in honour of the fundraising efforts for the people of Bangla Desh.

7 June. The *Concert For Bangla Desh* film is premiered in Sweden.

9 June. George visits Elvis Presley backstage at Madison Square Garden.

26 June. George takes delivery of his BMW 3.0 litre CSA coupé. He later sells it to a dealer in Suffolk in July 1977.

28 June. George receives two awards for 'My Sweet Lord' at the Ivor Novello Awards.

12 July. George has his licence endorsed for a second time and is fined £20 for careless driving at Maidenhead Magistrates' Court.

26 July. A preview screening of the *Concert For Bangla Desh* film takes place at the Rialto Cinema, Coventry Street, London.

27 July. The *Concert For Bangla Desh* film opens to the public at the Rialto, London.

11 August. George hires a small cinema in London for the screening of the *Raga* film.

17 August. George travels to Liverpool to see Ravi Shankar perform at the Philharmonic Hall.

23 September. George's Material World Foundation Trust sponsors Ravi's Music Festival From India at the Royal Albert Hall.

12 November. George discovers that he needs to drill 200ft deep holes in his estate grounds to find enough water to cater for his ornamental lakes.

22 November. George begins drilling for water at Friar Park. He needs vast quantities to fill his ornamental lakes, around 500,000 gallons.

28 December. George appears on the *David Frost Show* in America.

1973

13 January. George and Ringo attend an Eric Clapton concert at the Rainbow Theatre, London.

22 January. Ravi Shankar's album *In Concert 1972* is released in America. George produced the album from tapes of the concert which took place at the Philharmonic Hall, New York in October 1972.

5 February. *Little Malcolm And His Battle Against The Eunuchs*, the film produced by George, begins filming in Lancashire.

9 February. *Brother*, the Apple album by Lon and Derrek Van Eaton, is released containing the track 'Sweet Music', which George produced.

3 March. *Concert For Bangla Desh* receives a Grammy as 'Album Of The Year For 1972'.

9 March. George flies to Los Angeles.

10 March. George attends Ringo's recording session at Sunset Sound Studios and listens to some of the tracks that have been completed.

12 March. George provides some backing vocals for Ringo's session at the Sunset Sound Studios in Los Angeles.

13 March. John Lennon turns up at Sunset Sound Studios and George and Ringo join him to record John's number 'I'm The Greatest'.

23 March. Filming ends on *Little Malcolm And His Battle Against The Eunuchs*.

7 April. George, John and Ringo attend a fundraising event at Universal Studios in aid of the Pentagon Papers Legal Defence Fund.

13 April. Ravi Shankar's album *In Celebration 1972*, produced by George, is released in Britain.

23 April. Nicky Hopkins' album *The Tin Man Was A Dreamer* is released in America. It contains four tracks by George using the name George O'Hara: 'Waiting For The Band', 'Edward', 'Speed On' and 'Banana Anna'.

26 April. George officially founds his charity, the Material World Charitable Foundation, which is to receive a portion of his royalties from publishing and recordings.

29 April. George is in Los Angeles recording a Ravi Shankar album and takes time off, accompanied by Patti, to attend a Columbia Records 'A Week To Remember' party.

7 May. 'Give Me Love (Give Me Peace On Earth)' c/w 'Miss O'Dell' is released in America. It's George's first single in almost two years and tops the American charts.

25 May. 'Give Me Love (Give Me Peace On Earth)' is released in Britain. It reaches the position of No. 8.

28 May. *Radio One Club* on Radio One broadcasts a series of prerecorded interviews with George over the next three days. In America, 'Speed On', the track featuring George from Nicky Hopkins' album *The Tin Man Was A Dreamer* is released as a single.

30 May. The *Living In The Material World* album is issued in America.

31 May. Both George and Patti, fully dressed, are thrown into the swimming pool at a party for Led Zeppelin drummer John Bonham in Los Angeles.

11 June. Prerecorded musical sessions with George are broadcast on Radio One's *David Hamilton Show* today and until 15 June.

18 June. Prerecorded tapes of interviews with George for Radio One are broadcast on *Radio One Club* until 21 June. George's musical tapes are also repeated on the *David Hamilton Show* today and until 22 June.

22 June. The *Living In The Material World* album is issued in Britain and reaches No. 2 in the charts.

23 June. *Living In The Material World* tops the American charts.

25 June. Further prerecorded tapes of George are broadcast on *Radio One Club* today and until 28 June.

30 June. The single 'Give Me Love (Give Me Peace On Earth)' tops the American charts.

7 July. George travels to Heathrow Airport to welcome A.C. Bhaktivedanta Swami. The *Alan Freeman Show* on Radio One plays an alternative prerecorded tape of 'Give Me Love (Give Me Peace On Earth)'.

8 July. George takes part in a religious procession from Marble Arch to Piccadilly with A.C. Bhaktivedanta Swami.

9 July. Further prerecorded tapes of George are broadcast on *Radio One Club*, including an alternative version of 'Give Me Love (Give Me Peace On Earth)'. Musical tapes by George are also repeated on the *David Hamilton Show* today and until 13 July.

25 July. George is angry at the British taxman's insistence on collecting tax for the charity album *Concert For Bangla Desh*, but writes out a personal cheque for them for £1 million.

10 August. The Nicky Hopkins single 'Speed On', featuring George on guitar, is released in Britain.

20 August. Cheech and Chong's single 'Basketball Jones', on which George was a session guitarist, is released in America.

27 August. Cheech and Chong's album *Los Cochinos*, with the 'Basketball Jones' track, is released in America.

24 September. Ringo's single 'Photograph', which was co-written by George and Ringo, is released in America. The flipside is 'Down And Out', which was written by Ringo and co-produced with George. It reached No. 1 in the American charts for one week.

19 October. Ringo's single 'Photograph'/'Down And Out' is released in Britain. It reached No. 8 in the charts.

2 November. George, John and Ringo sue Allen Klein over payments that are due to the Beatles. Klein counter-sues. The album *On The Road To Freedom* by Alvin Lee and Mylon LeFevre is released in Britain. It contains the track 'So Sad (No Love Of His Own)', written by George and on which he plays guitar and bass guitar and provides backing vocals.

26 November. Ronnie Wood issues a statement regarding a liaison he has had with Patti. George denies that the affair happened.

27 November. The newspapers begin to suggest that George and Patti may soon split up.

17 December. 'So Sad', the track from the Alvin Lee/Mylon LeFevre album *On The Road To Freedom* is issued as a single in America.

1974

7 January. David Bromberg's album *Wanted – Dead Or Alive* includes the track 'Holdup', a song he wrote with George in 1972.

1 March. While in New York George publicly announces that he will be touring America in the autumn.

4 March. Apple officially announces that George will be touring America.

5 March. London's *Evening Standard* newspaper mistakenly reports that 'George and Ringo are to join forces for a giant tour of America this year'.

11 March. George issues a statement: 'Although I have been considering a US tour for the autumn of 1974, and although several promoters have been approached on my behalf with regard to a possible tour, no decisions have been taken either with respect to the tour itself, the promoters or the band.'

28 March. George registers a new company, Oops Publishing Ltd.

19 April. The Alvin Lee and Mylon LeFevre song 'So Sad (No Love Of His Own)', written by George, is released as a UK single.

6 May. George and Ringo attend a party held in honour of record producer Richard Perry.

25 May. George announces the launch of his own record label, Dark Horse Records.

11 July. George invests £5,000 in designer Ossie Clarke's new fashion venture.

15 August. George attends the premiere of the Willy Russell play *John, Paul, George, Ringo and Bert* in which his childhood friend George Kelly appears as Bert.

6 September. George holds a press conference to announce his Dark Horse record label and the appointment of Jonathan Clyde as a director of the company.

13 September. George launches Dark Horse Records in Britain via A&M Records with two singles, 'I Am Missing You' c/w 'Lust' by Ravi Shankar, Family & Friends and 'Costafine Town' by Splinter, both produced by George.

16 September. George's proposed tour with Ravi Shankar is officially announced.

20 September. In Britain, Dark Horse releases the Splinter album *The Place I Love* and the Ravi Shankar album *Shankar, Family & Friends*.

23 September. George's Material World Charitable Foundation sponsors Ravi Shankar's Music Festival From India at the Royal Albert Hall in London and films it on behalf of Dark Horse Records, although the film is never released. George also records the event.

25 September. Splinter's album *The Place I Love* is released in America.

7 October. The Dark Horse album *Shankar, Family & Friends* is released in America.

23 October. George holds a press conference at the Beverly Wilshire Hotel in Los Angeles to discuss his American tour.

24 October. George holds a press conference in New York to discuss his American tour.

28 October. George, John and Ringo win their court case against Allen Klein.

2 November. George appears on the first date of his solo tour at the Pacific Coliseum, Vancouver. Olivia accompanies him on the tour.

4 November. George appears at the Seattle Center Coliseum, Washington

6 November. George appears at the Cow Palace, San Francisco. Ravi Shankar's Dark Horse single 'I Am Missing You' c/w 'Lust' is released in America.

7 November. George appears at the Cow Palace, San Francisco. He arranges for a large box to be placed in the lobby of the theatre with a sign reading 'Put In Here All Your Loose, Dirty And Filthy Money'. $66,000 is raised, which is presented to the Ashbury Free Medical Clinic.

10 November. George appears at the Long Beach Arena. Splinter's Dark Horse single 'Costafine Town' is released in America.

11 November. George appears at the Forum, Los Angeles.

12 November. George appears at the Forum, Los Angeles.

14 November. George appears at the Tucson Community Center, Arizona.

16 November. George appears at the Salt Palace, Salt Lake City.

18 November. George appears at Denver Coliseum. His single 'Dark Horse' c/w 'I Don't Care Any More' is issued in America.

20 November. George appears at the St Louis Arena.

21 November. George appears at the Tulsa Assembly Center, Oklahoma.

22 November. George appears in Fort Worth, Texas.

24 November. George appears at the Hofheinz Pavilion, Houston.

25 November. George appears on radio station KLOL-FM in Houston discussing *Monty Python* and the legal dispute with Paul.

26 November. George appears in Baton Rouge, Louisiana.

27 November. George appears at the Mid-South Coliseum, Memphis.

28 November. George appears at the Omni, Atlanta.

30 November. George appears in Chicago, Illinois. Ravi Shankar is rushed to hospital with a suspected heart attack, which turns out to be a bad bout of indigestion. He doesn't return to the tour until 19 December.

4 December. George appears at the Olympia Stadium, Detroit.

6 December. George appears at Maple Leaf Gardens, Toronto, Canada. His single 'Ding Dong Ding Dong' c/w 'I Don't Care Any More' is issued in Britain. An interview with George is broadcast in Britain on *Rockspeak*, an FM stereo programme.

8 December. George appears at the Forum, Montreal, Canada.

9 December. George's album *Dark Horse* is issued in Britain.

10 December. George appears at the Boston Garden.

11 December. George appears at the Providence Civic Center, Rhode Island.

13 December. George appears at the Capitol Center, Largo, Maryland. Also on this day George, together with his father, Olivia, Ravi Shankar and Billy Preston, is invited to the White House where they meet President Ford.

14 December. George and Olivia Arias meet John Lennon and May Pang in New York.

15 December. George appears at the Nassau Coliseum, Uniondale, Long Island. John Lennon and May Pang attend the concert.

16 December. George appears at the Spectrum Bowl, Philadelphia. His album *Dark Horse* receives a Gold Disc.

17 December. George appears at the Spectrum Bowl, Philadelphia.

19 December. During the day George records a version of 'Dark Horse' at the NBC TV studios. George appears at Madison Square Garden, New York. Paul and Linda McCartney, Julian Lennon and Ringo Starr's manager Hilary Gerrard are among the audience.

20 December. George completes his North American tour in Madison Square Garden.

He holds an end of tour party at the Hippopotamus club, New York, attended by John Lennon and May Pang. George's album *Dark Horse* is issued in America.

23 December. George's single 'Ding Dong Ding Dong' c/w 'Hari's On Tour (Express)' is released in America. George shoots a 16mm promo for the number in which he dresses in different garb representing different points in the Beatles career such as the collarless jacket and Sgt Pepper uniform.

25 December. George and Olivia spend Christmas in Hawaii.

1975

5 February. George's former personal assistant, Terry Doran, resigns from Oops Publishing Ltd, one of George's companies.

7 February. 'Drink All Day (Got To Find Your Own Way)' c/w 'Haven't' by Splinter, which was produced by George, is released in Britain on Dark Horse Records.

8 February. George flies from London to Los Angeles.

10 February. Bright Tunes Music Corps begins its legal action alleging 'My Sweet Lord' plagiarised their copyright song 'He's So Fine'.

21 February. Dark Horse Records releases another Splinter single, produced by George, only weeks after their previous one. It is 'China Light' c/w 'Drink All Day (Got To Find Your Own Way)'.

28 February. George's single 'Dark Horse' c/w 'Hari's On Tour' is issued in Britain.

24 March. George is among the 200 guests at Paul McCartney's *Queen Mary* party in Long Beach, California, to celebrate the completion of recordings for the *Venus And Mars* album.

19 April. At his home in Los Angeles George records a two-hour interview with Dave Herman, a disc jockey with the New York station WNEW, which is later syndicated. The topics include a discussion on Apple, the future of Dark Horse Records and George's musical roots, highlighted by recordings by Lonnie Donegan and Slim Whitman. There were also musical cuts from the Splinter and Ravi Shankar albums and information on Jiva, Dark Horse's first American group.

24 May. The DIR syndication network in America transmits George's radio interview with Herman.

9 June. George signs Jiva to his Dark Horse label. A prerecorded interview with Paul Gambaccini is broadcast on *Rockweek*.

17 August. George's 19 April radio interview is featured in the *King Biscuit Flower Hour* radio show.

25 August. While in Los Angeles, George plays slide guitar on 'Appolonia (Frostrata)' for Tom Scott's album *New York Connection*.

6 September. An interview with George appears in the *Melody Maker*.

12 September. 'You' c/w 'World Of Stone' is issued in Britain. George makes a live appearance on Nick Horne's Capital Radio Show *Your Mother Wouldn't Like It*.

15 September. 'You' c/w 'World Of Stone' is issued in America.

17 September. George is interviewed in Los Angeles, again by American disc jockey Dave Herman.

22 September. George's album *Extra Texture (Read All About It)* is issued in America.

26 September. Island Records issues Peter Skellern's album *Hard Times*. George is featured playing guitar on the track 'Make Love Not War'.

3 October. George's album *Extra Texture (Read All About It)* is released in England.

6 October. The Splinter album *Harder To Live*, produced by George and Tom Scott, is released in America.

1 November. George's single 'You' reaches the No. 38 position in the British charts and reaches No. 20 in America.

11 November. George's album *Extra Texture (Read All About It)* achieves Gold Disc status in America.

14 November. 'The Lumberjack Song', the *Monty Python* single produced by George, is released in Britain on Charisma Records.

16 November. George and Olivia attend a dinner party at Chasen's on Hollywood Boulevard to celebrate a distribution deal with Warner Bros Records.

8 December. 'This Guitar (Can't Keep From Crying)' c/w 'Maya Love' is released in America.

13 December. George films a guest appearance in *Rutland Weekend Television* at the BBC Television Centre.

26 December. The Boxing Day special of *Rutland Weekend Television* that features George as Pirate Bob singing 'The Pirate Song' is broadcast on BBC 2.

1976

26 January. George is at the Midem Festival in Cannes, France, announcing the launch of his own label Dark Horse.

27 January. As the Beatles' nine-year contract with EMI has ended, George officially signs to his own label Dark Horse, to be distributed by A&M Records.

28 January. George is at the Carlton Hotel, Cannes, where reporters interview him regarding his signing with Dark Horse.

6 February. 'This Guitar (Can't Keep From Crying)' c/w 'Maya Love' is released in Britain.

20 April. During the *Monty Python* season at the City Center, New York, George dresses up as a Royal Canadian Mounted Policeman and joins the comedy team on stage for 'The Lumberjack Song'.

9 May. George and Ringo are among the audience at the Wings concert at Maple Leaf Gardens, Toronto, Canada.

24 May. George begins recording his album *Thirty Three & 1/3* at his Friar Park studios. Sessions continue, on and off, until 13 September.

26 July. George misses his deadline to complete his first solo album to be distributed by A&M Records due to his illness with hepatitis.

30 July. George and Ringo are unsuccessful in their attempt to place an injunction on the release of the Polydor double album *The Beatles Tapes*.

7 September. George is found guilty of subconscious plagiarism of 'He's So Fine'.

28 September. A&M Records sues George for $10m because he did not complete his new album to the deadline set by them due to his illness.

8 November. The album *The Best Of George Harrison* is released in America. Damages of $587,000 are awarded to Bright Tunes for 'He's So Fine'.

15 November. 'This Song' c/w 'Learning How To Love' is issued in America.

17 November. George attends a special Warner Brothers party at Chasen's restaurant on Hollywood Boulevard, Los Angeles to celebrate their world distribution deal with Dark Horse records.

19 November. 'This Song' c/w 'Learning How To Love' is issued in Britain. *Thirty Three & 1/3* is released in Britain. George records a *Saturday Night Live* show and performs several numbers with Paul Simon.

20 November. The *Saturday Night Live* show featuring George and Paul Simon is broadcast. His album *The Best Of George Harrison* is released in Britain.

30 November. George records an interview in the afternoon with Bob Harris for *The Old Grey Whistle Test*, which is broadcast by BBC 2 that evening and also features the promo films for 'This Song' and 'True Love'.

10 December. George buys copies of the *Rutland Weekend Television* videotapes in a London store.

1977
24 January. 'Crackerbox Palace' c/w 'Learning How To Love You' is released in America.

1 February. George prerecords an interview with disc jockey Anne Nightingale at Broadcasting House, London. It is to be broadcast in two parts. He then flies to Holland in the afternoon.

3 February. George films an interview with Veronica Television in Amsterdam, Holland.

5 February. The first part of George's interview with Anne Nightingale is broadcast. George is also in Germany where he appears on *Disco '77*, a ZDF TV show where he mimes to 'This Song'. He also visits the Hamburg district where the Beatles made their first German appearances.

6 February. George is in France continuing his short European promo-

tional visit to plug *Thirty Three & 1/3*. Michael Drucker interviews him on the TFI-TV show *Les Rendezvous Du Dimanche* and the promo for 'This Song' is screened.

11 February. 'True Love' c/w 'Pure Smokey' is released in Britain.

12 February. The second and final part of George's interview with Anne Nightingale is broadcast.

4 April. 'Dark Horse' c/w 'Yes' is released in America.

20 April. George and Olivia arrive in London from Los Angeles.

31 May. 'It's What You Value' c/w 'Woman Don't You Cry For Me' is released in Britain.

7 June. George appears at a children's party in Henley to celebrate the Queen's Silver Jubilee.

9 June. George and Patti are divorced in a London court.

28 June. George and Olivia attend a luncheon at the Savoy Hotel, London to bid farewell to Derek Taylor, who is leaving Britain to take up a post in America with Warner Brothers Records.

30 June. At the High Court in London, Mr Justice Slade listens to both 'My Sweet Lord' and 'He's So Fine'. He is informed that both parties have agreed on a settlement.

15 July. George is at Silverstone racetrack to watch the British Grand Prix.

17 July. George is still watching the races at Silverstone.

31 July. George is in New York where he is interviewed for the radio station WNEW.

2 August. George films his appearance for *The Rutles* TV project in which he appears as a television reporter.

13 November. An interview with George appears in the *News Of The World*.

18 November. His Divine Grace A.C. Bhaktivedanta Swami Prabhupada dies at the age of 81.

20 November. George pens the lyrics to 'Faster' at Friar Park.

17 December. George makes an unannounced performance at the Row Barge pub in Henley, a small country pub close to his Friar Park estate. It's his first public performance in Britain since 1969.

18 December. George and Olivia are on their way to Hawaii to spend Christmas there.

1978

1 January. George is on holiday in Hawaii where he begins composing again, writing 'Blow Away'. He also co-writes 'If You Believe' with Gary Wright.

25 January. George makes an appearance at Thames Television studios in London and pays tribute to motorcyclist Barry Sheene, who is the subject of *This Is Your Life*.

26 January. George and Olivia fly to Los Angeles prior to a nine-week holiday in Hawaii.

26 February. George composes 'Dark Sweet Lady', inspired by his girl-friend Olivia.

22 March. *All You Need Is Cash*, the Rutles film in which George appears as a reporter, is broadcast in America on NBC TV.

27 March. *All You Need Is Cash* is screened in Britain.

3 April. George is at the Long Beach Grand Prix in California.

4 April. George and Olivia return to England.

11 April. George begins working on songs for his *George Harrison* album.

2 June. George, along with his pregnant girlfriend Olivia, leaves for a three-day holiday in Madrid, Spain.

5 June. George and Olivia return from their Spanish holiday.

1 August. George and Olivia's first child Dhani is born at the Princess Christian Nursing Home in Windsor. He weighs five and a half pounds.

25 August. Following Olivia's childbirth, George takes her on a brief holiday to Amsterdam.

2 September. George and Olivia are married at a civil ceremony in Henley, four weeks after the birth of Dhani. Olivia's parents are in attendance.

3 September. George announces to the press that he has married Olivia. The couple leave for a honeymoon in Tunisia.

8 September. At FPSHOT, George begins work on tapes for *The Life Of Brian*.

15 September. George buys Brundon Mill, a house near Sudbury, for his friend Derek Taylor.

20 October. George flies to Tunisia to view the progress of the film *The Life Of Brian*. While there he is talked into making a cameo appearance in the film as Mr Papadopoulos.

26 October. George and Olivia return to England.

7 December. George visits the Guildford Civic Hall to watch a concert with Eric Clapton and Elton John and is asked to join them on stage where he performs 'Further On Up The Road'.

15 December. George and Ringo travel to Hamburg, Germany to attend the relaunch of the Star Club by their friend Horst Fascher.

1979

31 January. George and Olivia, accompanied by their friend Gary Wright, fly to Rio de Janeiro to watch the Brazilian Grand Prix at Sao Paulo's Interlagos circuit.

8 February. George and Olivia fly back into London where George is to prepare for a series of radio interviews.

9 February. George, together with Michael Jackson, appears on the Radio One show *Roundtable*. The show's host is Kid Jenson.

14 February. The album *George Harrison* is released in America, as is the single 'Blow Away' c/w 'Soft-Hearted Hana'.

15 February. George is interviewed by Peter Clements for BBC Wolverhampton.

16 February. The album *George Harrison* is released in Britain, as is the single 'Blow Away' c/w 'Soft-Hearted Hana'.

19 February. George is interviewed by Nicky Horne for *Nicky Horne's Music Scene*, screened that evening during ITV's *Thames at Six*. On his return to Friar Park, George is involved in an accident while driving his tractor and injures his foot. He is taken to Reading hospital for treatment.

23 February. George makes a live appearance on Capital Radio's *Your Mother Wouldn't Like It*, hosted by Nicky Horne.

6 March. The promotional video for 'Blow Away' receives its British TV debut on the ITV children's programme *Pop Gospel*.

27 March. Eric Clapton marries George's ex-wife Patti in Tucson, Arizona.

6 April. The promo of 'Blow Away' makes its American TV debut on *Midnight Special*.

20 April. George's single 'Love Comes To Everyone' c/w 'Soft-Hearted Hana' is released in Britain.

4 May. George's 'My Sweet Lord' is included as one of the tracks on the compilation album *Monument To British Rock*.

6 May. Capitol Radio broadcasts an interview with George.

11 May. George is interviewed on Capital Radio. His single 'Love Comes To Everyone' c/w 'Soft-Hearted Hana' is released in America.

19 May. George, Paul and Ringo perform during an impromptu session in the garden of Eric Clapton's house in Ewehurst, Surrey following Eric's recent marriage to George's first wife Patti.

24 May. George and Olivia fly to Nice in France.

26 May. George and Ringo meet at the Monaco Grand Prix and are interviewed for the American TV show *Wide World Of Sport* along with Jackie Stewart.

28 May. George and Olivia leave Nice for London.

14 July. George attends the Silverstone Grand Prix and is interviewed for ITV's *World Of Sport*. Later that day he drives Stirling Moss's car around the Donnington Park racetrack.

30 July. George's single 'Faster' c/w 'Your Love Is Forever' is released in Britain.

1 August. George, Olivia and Dhani set off for a holiday in Athens, Greece.

17 August. George, Olivia and Dhani return from their holiday in Greece.

18 August. George's promo for 'Faster' is screened in the ITV show *World Of Sport*.

22 August. The leather-bound limited edition of George's book *I. Me. Mine.* is published by Genesis.

3 September. George flies to the States for business meetings concerning Apple.

5 September. George returns to London.

13 September. George has to return to America again for urgent business meetings relating to Apple.

15 September. George returns to London.

5 October. The Clerk of Justices in Witham, Essex requests George's driving licence, as he has recently been banned from driving.

8 October. The soundtrack of *The Life Of Brian* movie is released in America. It contains the track 'Always Look On The Bright Side Of Life', which was mixed by George with the help of Phil MacDonald.

9 October. George's secretary Cherrie Cowell sends off George's driving licence to Essex.

15 October. Cherrie Cowell sends off a Christmas card signed by George to the Reverend Fraser Smith, who wishes to display it during his Christmas carol service in Nottingham.

20 October. George continues his yo-yo visits to New York on Apple business.

21 October. George returns to London.

30 October. George begins recording tracks for his *Somewhere In England* album in his Friar Park Studios.

9 November. The *Life Of Brian* movie soundtrack is released in Britain.

6 December. George and Olivia attend the Springfield Boys Club Christmas Show in northwest London.

1980

11 January. ITV screens a documentary *Brian Moore Meets Nicki Lauda*, which includes clip of George at the 1979 Silverstone Grand Prix.

14 January. *The Life Of Brian* goes on general release in Britain.

21 January. George and Olivia send a telegram to Paul and Linda following their drug bust for possessing marijuana.

22 January. George's secretary Cherrie Cowell writes to Thames Television explaining that George would be unable to attend a *This Is Your Life* on George Martin because 'he is just leaving the country for a holiday and, in fact, will not be back in the country again until the middle of March'.

11 February. George, Olivia and Dhani fly off to St Barthelemy via New York in Maurice Gibb's private jet.

19 February. Attempts are made to contact George to let him know that his house in Beverly Green, Malibu is in danger of breaking away from its hillside position.

7 March. George, Olivia and Dhani stop off in New York overnight on their return to England.

8 March. George, Olivia and Dhani arrive in London.

16 March. Musicians Willie Weeks, Neil Larsen and Andy Newmark arrive at Friar Park for the recording sessions due to begin the next day.

29 March. George and Olivia take part in the anti-nuclear march through London, organised by Friends of the Earth.

14 April. George, Olivia and Dhani visit Cornwall as they consider buying a house there.

20 May. George and Olivia visit the Chelsea Flower Show in London.

12 July. George and Olivia visit Brands Hatch by helicopter to watch the British Grand Prix.

1 August. George and Denis O'Brien officially form HandMade Films (Productions) Limited.

8 August. George, Olivia and Dhani set off on a holiday.

13 August. George phones John Lennon at the Dakota Building, but John is in a pique and refuses to answer because he is still upset that George didn't give him more prominence in the *I. Me. Mine.* book.

18 August. George, Olivia and Dhani return from their holiday and the recording of *Somewhere In England* continues.

23 September. George completes his recording for the *Somewhere In England* album.

26 September. George sets off for Los Angeles, stopping off in Montreal, Canada.

28 September. George meets up with Derek Taylor for the *Monty Python* appearance at the Hollywood Bowl. John and Yoko also join him.

1 October. Olivia and Dhani join George in Los Angeles.

5 October. George puts in writing the dispersal of his assets in the case of his death. The beneficiaries are his son Dhani, Eric Idle and Derek Taylor and his family. The balance, together with future funding, is to go to the Self-Realisation Foundation, founded by Paramahansa Yogananda.

15 October. George forms HandMade Films.

24 October. George, Olivia and Dhani return to London.

2 November. This is the date originally scheduled for the release of *Somewhere In England*. It is postponed because Warner Bros executives insist on four numbers being replaced: 'Lay His Head', 'Flying Hour', 'Sat Singing' and 'Tears Of The World'.

4 November. George has a copy of the movie *Singing In The Rain* delivered to Friar Park and returns it on 10 November.

10 November. Ringo Starr contacts George to ask him if he would appear on his next album. George says yes.

12 November. George buys a musical box from Asprey & Company of Bond Street, London for £295, which plays his composition 'Here Comes The Sun'.

18 November. George attends a meeting with the solicitors representing Apple Corps.

19 November. Ringo arrives at Friar Park to begin recording a track for his proposed album *Can't Fight Lightning* with George. The number will later form the basis for 'All Those Years Ago'.

7 December. George begins recording 'Dream Away', intended as a track for the closing titles of the *Time Bandits* movie. The track will also appear on his *Gone Troppo* album.

8 December. John Lennon is murdered in New York.

9 December. George is the first ex-Beatle to be informed of the shooting when his sister Louise phones him from America. Under the impression that John only received a flesh wound he goes back to bed. When he wakes up, on hearing that John is dead, he makes the statement: 'After all we went through together I had and still have great love and respect for him. I am shocked and stunned. To rob life is the ultimate robbery in life. This perpetual encroachment on other people's space is taken to the limit with the use of a gun. It is an outrage that people can take other people's lives when they obviously haven't got their own lives in order.'

1981

16 January. George completes the recording of *Somewhere In England* and has replaced the rejected numbers with four other songs.

26 February. George is ordered to pay $587,000 to Bright Tunes by a New York judge. Allen Klein is now the owner of the company that owns 'He's So Fine', which they alleged was copied by George in 'My Sweet Lord', but because of vested interests he only receives what he paid for the company.

16 March. George and Olivia begin the first day of a three-day stay at the Birmingham Metropole & Warwick NEC Hotel.

21 March. George, Olivia and Dhani fly to Copenhagen.

22 March. George, Olivia and Dhani return from Copenhagen.

30 March. George, Olivia and Dhani fly to Rome, staying at the Ergife Palace Hotel.

31 March. George, Olivia and Dhani return to England.

27 April. George and Olivia and Paul and Linda attend the wedding of Ringo and Barbara Bach. The wedding reception takes place at Rags club.

7 May. George receives an invitation to appear on a tribute series *Legends Within The UK*, but declines.

11 May. George's single 'All Those Years Ago' c/w 'Writing's On The Wall' is released in America. It contains a contribution from Paul and Ringo.

15 May. 'All Those Years Ago' c/w 'Writing's On The Wall' is released in Britain.

19 May. George and Olivia attend the Chelsea Flower Show in London.

31 May. George and Olivia turn down an invitation to attend the wedding of disc jockey Dave Herman.

1 June. George's album *Somewhere In England* is issued in America, where it reached No. 11 in the charts.

5 June. *Somewhere In England* is issued in Britain where it reaches No. 13 in the charts.

21 July. 'Teardrops' c/w 'Save The World' is released in America.

31 July. 'Teardrops' c/w 'Save The World' is released in Britain.

24 August. George places a deposit of £700 to pay for a replica model of Friar Park.

16 October. George appears by satellite link from London on the ABC TV Show *Good Morning America* to promote *Time Bandits*.

20 October. *Good Morning America* broadcasts another excerpt from George's interview.

4 November. 'All Those Years Ago' c/w 'Teardrops' is released in America.

6 November. *Time Bandits* premieres in America.

10 November. George buys a property in Maui, Hawaii.

27 November. Streets open in Liverpool, named after the individual Beatles. They include a George Harrison Close.

1982

9 February. George receives a UNICEF Award in Los Angeles for his charity work with the concert for Bangla Desh in 1971.

10 February. George's UNICEF Award ceremony is screened on *Good Morning America*.

11 February. George's UNICEF Award ceremony is screened on *Entertainment Tonight*, a syndicated American TV show, where he presented Hugh Downs of UNICEF with a cheque for $100,000 from the concert for Bangla Desh and was himself the recipient of a special citation.

15 February. George and Olivia book into the Los Angeles L'Ermitage Hotel in Beverly Hills under the alias Mr & Mrs Jack Lumber.

18 February. George and Olivia book out of L'Ermitage Hotel and fly back to London.

18 March. A paperback edition of George's *I. Me. Mine.* is published in Britain.

19 March. George joins Elton John on stage in Sydney, Australia to perform 'Empty Garden', Elton's tribute to John Lennon.

19 April. George appears on *Good Morning Australia* each morning until 23 April in a lengthy interview originally recorded the previous December. He is interviewed by Kerri-Anne Wright and discusses a number of subjects, including John's death, his friendship with Julian Lennon – whom he regards as being more like his mother than his father in temperament – and how the Beatles had transformed the music industry. He also has several complimentary things to say about Australia and its people.

5 May. George begins recording his *Gone Troppo* album at his Friar Park Studios.

1 August. George visits Barry Sheene at the Northampton General Hospital, following Sheene's involvement in a motorbike accident.

4 September. George is interviewed by Mukunda Goswami and discusses his spiritual beliefs and how they are reflected in his music. The complete interview is transcribed for the book *Chant And Be Happy*, published by ISKON.

10 October. The *Los Angeles Daily News* reports that George has bought a new home in the city.

16 October. George discusses *Time Bandits* and *Monty Python* in a satellite interview for *Good Morning America*.

20 October. *Good Morning America* includes a taped interview with George in which he discusses his days with the Beatles.

27 October. George's album *Gone Troppo* is released in America, along with the single 'Wake Up My Love' c/w 'Greece'.

8 November. *Gone Troppo* is issued in Britain, along with the single 'Wake Up My Love' c/w 'Greece'.

28 October. George, Olivia and Dhani fly to Washington and book into the Watergate Hotel as Mr and Mrs Tannerhill.

29 October. George and his family fly to Los Angeles.

13 December. George declines to play a benefit for the British Medical Aid For Poland Fund, but sends a cheque for several thousand pounds.

1983

23 January. An interview with George appears in the *Sunday Times*. He is still abroad at the time.

24 January. George, Olivia and Dhani fly from Calcutta to Singapore, staying overnight at the Mandarine Hotel.

26 January. George, Olivia and Dhani arrive in Perth, Australia.

27 January. The *Sun* newspaper publishes an excerpt from the interview originally published days earlier in the *Sunday Times* entitled 'I'm George, Not A Beatle'. George once again shows his distaste for the fascination with his Beatle days, commenting, 'They're not interested in me as a human being, they are only interested in the Beatles, what guitar I played on *Sgt Pepper* and all that crap. I'm almost forty and I was in the Beatles when it was a popular recording group for eight years. Yet that eight years is all that anybody wants to know about. I can understand that, but I am not the Beatles.'

7 February. The single 'I Really Love You' c/w 'Circles' is released in America.

26 March. George is in Long Beach to watch the Grand Prix. He says, 'Most musicians want to be athletic stars of some sort. My fantasy is to be a race-car driver.'

27 March. George spends his second day at the Long Beach Grand Prix.

19 April. Representatives from the Victoria & Albert Museum approach George enquiring if they could purchase a Burne-Jones window they had seen at Friar Park during a visit.

6 June. The Soviet newspaper *Sovietskaya Rossiya* praises George for his work for the Third World and for the concert for Bangla Desh.

25 July. George, Paul and Ringo meet at the Gore Hotel in London's Kensington.

13 August. In Hawaii a judge rules on a decision regarding a right-of-way path on George's property, deciding it should only be moved to 125 feet from his house, which upsets George tremendously.

9 September. The *Sun* newspaper reports that George is willing to pay out £50,000 at auction for a 1902 greenhouse. It was originally owned by a South African diamond millionaire.

12 September. George appears on the BBC2 TV show *Film '83* to discuss the latest HandMade Films release *Bullshot*.

1 December. George, Paul and Ringo meet up with Yoko Ono at the Dorchester Hotel, London to discuss Apple business.

1984

4 February. London Weekend Television presents the first of a series of late-night episodes of the American NBC TV series *Saturday Night Live*. The George Harrison appearance from 20 November 1976 is screened and two of his videos 'Crackerbox Palace' and 'This Song', both directed by Eric Osle, are shown, together with his performances of 'Here Comes The Sun' and 'Homeward Bound' with Paul Simon. George also appears in a comedy sketch with Lorne Michaels, the producer who had once offered $3,000 for the Beatles to get back together again.

24 February. George is in Hawaii at the time of his 41st birthday.

1 March. An American newspaper, the *Dallas Morning News,* announces that George and Ringo will be accepting the Liverpool Freedom Of The City Award.

6 March. An interview with George, conducted by Margaret Minxman, is published in the *Daily Mail*.

8 March. The *Daily Express* reports that George will accept Liverpool's offer of a Freedom Of The City award.

12 March. The European editions of the American publication *Newsweek* publish an interview with George.

21 May. George attends the Chelsea Flower Show in London.

30 October. George announces that he has now declined Liverpool's Freedom Of The City Award.

14 November. George leaves Los Angeles on a flight to Australia.

27 November. George travels to Auckland, New Zealand.

28 November. George attends a press conference in Auckland with Derek Taylor to promote Derek's autobiography *Fifty Years Adrift*.

29 November. George flies to Sydney, Australia.

30 November. George attends a literary party in Sydney, Australia in the company of Derek Taylor to promote Derek's autobiography *Fifty Years Adrift*.

2 December. George and Derek Taylor attend another press conference for Derek's book, this time at the Sydney Opera House.

14 December. George appears as a surprise guest on stage with Deep Purple in Sydney, Australia, during one of the group's concerts. Lead singer Ian Gillan introduces him as 'Arnold Grove from Liverpool'.

1985

18 January. The HandMade film *Water* is premiered at the Odeon, Leicester Square.

26 January. George provides backing vocal and slide guitar on the number 'Children Of The Sky', which is later released on Mike Batt's concert album *The Hunting Of The Snark*.

1 February. A prerecorded interview with George conducted by Robin Denselow is screened on BBC2's *Newsnight*. George discusses his fear of safety following John Lennon's murder.

25 February. George, Ringo and Yoko file a lawsuit against Paul for breach of contract at New York's State Supreme Court.

3 March. *The Rutles*, in which George appears as an aged reporter, is screened on BBC2.

14 March. The soundtrack to the movie *Porky's Revenge* is released in America. It includes George's recording of the Bob Dylan song 'I Don't Want To Do It'.

4 June. The compilation album *Greenpeace* is released in Britain with George's recording of 'Save The World'.

1 July. The *Porky's Revenge* movie soundtrack album is released in Britain with George's recording of Dylan's 'I Don't Want To Do It'.

5 July. The movie *Porky's Revenge* opens in Britain.

19 August. The compilation album *Greenpeace* is released in America with George's recording of 'Save The World'.

19 October. Following rehearsals with Carl Perkins, George invites Carl and the other musicians to Friar Park, where they all have a party and jam.

21 October. George and Ringo take part in the taping of the Carl Perkins special *A Rockabilly Session With Carl Perkins And Friends* at Limehouse Studios in London.

22 October. George and Ringo are interviewed on the BBC Radio One programme *Newsbeat* discussing the Carl Perkins special.

5 November. Olivia Harrison and Ringo and Barbara are among the audience at the 'Fashion Aid' evening at the Royal Albert Hall.

1986

26 January. George receives an award for HandMade Films at the *Evening Standard* Film Awards at the Savoy Hotel, London and is given a kiss on the cheek from the Duchess of Kent.

6 March. In an effort to halt the bad publicity surrounding *Shanghai Surprise*, George holds a press conference with Madonna at Shepperton Film Studios.

7 March. The TV show *The Tube* shows a four-minute prerecorded interview with George discussing the problems he has with the press regarding the *Shanghai Surprise* film. The interviewer is Paula Yates.

15 March. George appears in the 'Heartbeat '86' charity concert at the NEC in Birmingham. He takes to the stage to sing 'Money' and 'Johnny B Goode' with Robert Plant and Denny Laine.

14 April. The American morning show *Today* begins the first of a four-part feature, running from today until 18 April, based on a lengthy interview with George conducted at Friar Park.

22 April. George, together with Ringo, makes a brief appearance on BBC1's *Film '86* discussing the latest HandMade film *Mona Lisa*.

27 April. George appears on the New York radio show *Ticket To Ride*, hosted by Scott Muni.

28 May. George attends Abbey Road Studios for a soundtrack recording session for the film *Shanghai Surprise*.

12 June. *Mona Lisa* is premiered in New York.

13 June. George, Eric Clapton and Patti and Elton John attend the Worcestershire vs Leicestershire cricket match at Worcester.

15 June. Olivia teams up with Mary Hopkin to protest over the proposed closing of the local cinema in Henley.

19 June. George attends an anti-nuclear rally in Trafalgar Square, London.

20 June. The home video of *Carl Perkins And Friends – A Rockabilly Session* is released in Britain on Virgin Video.

25 June. George is interviewed in the *Daily Express* for his views regarding the Regal Cinema in Henley.

10 July. Joe Brown's autobiography *Brown Sauce – The Life And Times Of Joe Brown* is published with a foreword by George.

18 July. George has a letter published in the *Henley Standard* taking local councillors to task for approving a plan to demolish the local cinema to make way for a supermarket. At Friar Park he records an instrumental track 'Zig Zag' for the *Shanghai Surprise* film and also 'Hottest Gong In Town', the latter not released until 1992.

2 August. The charity show 'Heartbeat '86', in which George appears, is screened on BBC1, showing an excerpt of George performing 'Johnny B Goode' with Robert Plant and Denny Laine.

11 August. George's first guitar, which his mum bought for him for £3 in 1956 and was later bought by the son of a friend of George's father, is placed in Sotheby's auction with authentication and sells for £3,600.

29 August. *Shanghai Surprise* receives its world premiere in New York.

7 October. The documentary *Handmade In Hong Kong* is screened by Channel 4, featuring an interview with George and clips of him recording the soundtrack for *Shanghai Surprise*.

17 October. *Shanghai Surprise* opens in Britain.

4 December. George continues his fight to save the Regal Cinema in Henley and discovers that he has won.

10 December. The 'Heartbeat '86' show, with a guest appearance by George, is screened on American television.

24 December. *Blue Suede Shoes – Carl Perkins And Friends* is re-shown on Channel 4.

1987

5 January. George begins work on his *Cloud Nine* album at Friar Park by recording 'Vatican P2 Blues', although the number isn't used.

16 February. George, Olivia and Dhani fly to America for a business meeting.

19 February. George takes part in a jam session with Bob Dylan, Taj Mahal and John Fogarty at the Palomino Club, Hollywood, California, following two sets by Taj Mahal. During the two-hour jam, they play numbers such as 'Proud Mary', 'Dizzy Miss Lizzy' and 'I Heard It Through The Grapevine'. George recalled, 'Bob rang me up and said did I want to come out for the evening and see Taj Mahal, who was playing at the Palomino. So we went there and had a few of these Mexican beers – and had a few more. And Jesse Ed Davis is in the audience and Bob says, "Hey, why don't we all get up and play and you can sing!" Every time I get near the microphone, Dylan comes up and just starts singing this rubbish in my ear, trying to throw me.'

15 March. George and Olivia attend the BAFTA Awards at the Grosvenor Hotel in London.

27 March. George and Olivia and Ringo and Barbara attend Elton John's birthday party.

30 March. George donates money to 21-year-old Canadian Steve Fonyo, who had lost his leg to cancer and was walking from Scotland to London in aid of Cancer Research. Steve was invited to George's house for tea.

18 May. CDs of *All Things Must Pass* and *The Best Of George Harrison* are released in Britain.

5 June. George appears at the Prince's Trust Concert, performing with Ben E. King and Ringo Starr on 'Stand By Me'.

6 June. George appears for a second concert for the Prince's Trust at Wembley Arena, performing 'While My Guitar Gently Weeps' and 'Here Comes The Sun' with Ringo and Eric Clapton, and backs Ringo on 'With A Little Help From My Friends'.

20 June. The Prince's Trust concert is screened by ITV.

31 July. George is present at Brentford Magistrates' Court to answer speeding charges.

13 September. In America HBO screens the Prince's Trust Concert, which features George and Ringo. They show it again on 16, 19, 21 and 25 September.

30 September. The programme *Entertainment Tonight* screens a prerecorded interview with George.

5 October. George records a promotional interview at Warner Bros Records in Burbank, California to promote his *Cloud Nine* album.

12 October. 'Got My Mind Set On You' c/w 'Lay His Head', the first single from the *Cloud Nine* album, is released in Britain.

16 October. 'Got My Mind Set On You' c/w 'Lay His Head' is released in America. The first of a three-part interview with George promoting his *Cloud Nine* album is broadcast on Radio One. George also appears on Channel 4's *The Last Resort With Jonathan Ross* that evening.

17 October. George attends Bob Dylan's concert at Wembley Arena and is encouraged to go on stage and join Dylan on 'Rainy Day Women'. He recalled, 'It was really funny because I got pushed on stage at Wembley and sang a bit of "Rainy Day Women". I couldn't remember the words and just made up this stuff.' It is Dylan's third Wembley Arena appearance of the year. George attended all four Dylan concerts at the Arena.

19 October. The first part of a two-part interview with George promoting his *Cloud Nine* album is broadcast on the BBC programme *Breakfast Time*.

20 October. The second part of George's *Breakfast Time* interview is broadcast. He is also featured in a prerecorded interview on the Italian RAI UNO programme *TGI*. George is also featured as 'Man Of The Week' on ITV's *After Nine* programme. An interview with George, conducted by Rona Elliot, is screened in America on NBC TV's *Today* show.

21 October. The second part of a feature on George as 'Man Of the Week' is screened on *After Nine*, while the second part of another interview is screened in America on the *Today* show. George and Ringo visit Paul at his Cavendish Avenue home and enjoy dinner together while discussing their plans for a Beatles television history.

22 October. George is featured on the cover of *Rolling Stone* magazine, which includes a feature entitled 'The Return Of George Harrison'.

24 October. A prerecorded interview with George is screened in America on *Week In Rock*, an MTV programme.

29 October. The second part of an interview with George promoting *Cloud Nine* is broadcast on Radio One.

31 October. The third and final part of George's *Cloud Nine* interview is broadcast by Radio One.

2 November. George's album *Cloud Nine* is issued simultaneously in Britain and America.

6 November. A prerecorded interview with George, conducted by Geraldo Rivera, is featured on the American programme *Entertainment Tonight*, which ends the show with the promo of 'Got My Mind Set On You'.

8 November. An interview with George is broadcast on New York's WNEW Radio. Another prerecorded interview with George is featured on *Entertainment Tonight*.

17 November. A prerecorded interview with George is screened on the Dutch television show *Tros*.

18 November. A prerecorded interview with George, conducted by Mark Sheerer, is screened on ABC TV's *Good Morning America*.

20 November. A prerecorded interview with George is screened on CNN's *Showbiz Today* programme.

22 November. George is featured in a cover story in the *Observer* colour supplement, promoting *Cloud Nine*.

27 November. The second part of a prerecorded interview with George is broadcast on CNN's *Showbiz Today*.

2 December. Excerpts from George's *Cloud Nine* promotional interview, recorded on 5 October, are included on the programme *Track Record* on the European Super Channel station.

12 December. An interview with George, conducted by Selina Scott, appears on the American television programme *West 57th Street*. The CNN programme *Showbiz Today* broadcasts a profile of George.

18 December. A promotional video of George's 'When We Was Fab', directed by Kevin Godley, is filmed at Greenford Studios, Greenwich, London with George, Ringo Starr and Elton John.

22 December. An interview with George is aired on Radio One.

27 December. George features in a 60-minute Radio One special *On Cloud Nine*.

28 December. George and Olivia fly out to Los Angeles where George will promote the *Cloud Nine* album.

30 December. George appears on the Los Angeles radio station KLOS-FM on their *Rockstars* programme.

1988

1 January. Radio One broadcasts a special on the 1987 Prince's Trust Concert in which George appeared with Ringo Starr.

10 January. George is featured on the American CBS TV programme *Entertainment This Week*.

11 January. George appears on VH-I.

16 January. 'Got My Mind Set On You' tops the American charts.

20 January. George, Ringo, Julian Lennon and Yoko and Sean Lennon attend the Beatles induction into the Rock 'n' Roll Hall of Fame in New York. George performs 'All Along The Watchtower' with Bob Dylan.

24 January. MTV premieres George's promo of 'When We Was Fab'.

25 January. 'When We Was Fab' c/w 'Zig Zag' is released simultaneously in Britain and America.

7 February. George attends Eric Clapton's end-of-tour party at Clapton's Surrey house.

8 February. George flies to Los Angeles.

10 February. George, together with Jeff Lynne, appears on the syndicated show *Rockline*, a weekly radio show that is transmitted to 200 stations across the States.

11 February. Via satellite, George appears on an eight-minute spot on BBC1's *Wogan*, at the end of which the promo for 'When We Was Fab' is screened.

15 February. Genesis publishes *The Songs Of George Harrison*. George and Olivia arrive in London from Los Angeles to promote the book. A prerecorded interview with George is broadcast on CNN's *Showbiz Today*.

17 February. *Na Siekske*, a programme on the German ZDF channel, screens a prerecorded interview with George.

18 February. A brief prerecorded interview with George is transmitted on *Programa De Domingo*, a Brazilian TV channel.

20 February. A prerecorded interview with George is transmitted on the American VH-1 channel.

22 February. The *All Things Must Pass* album is issued in America on CD. George flies to Holland to record for the television show *Countdown*. A prerecorded interview with George is transmitted on the *This Morning* show in America in which the promo for 'When We Was Fab' is screened. George was to comment on the business problems the Beatles had: 'We always had a deal together that the Beatles were us four, and that if any one of us wasn't in the band, the Beatles wouldn't exist. It can't really exist just with the three of us, but at the same time, we could all be on stage together, I suppose, like we could have done at the Rock 'n' Roll Hall of Fame.'

23 February. George travels to Italy.

24 February. George's nineteen-minute appearance on the *Countdown* show is transmitted on NED 1.

25 February. George visits Eric Idle and Terry Gilliam on the set of the movie *The Adventures of Baron Munchausen*.

27 February. George is presented with an award of 'Video Of The Year' for 'When We Was Fab' at the San Remo Music Festival in Italy. The Italian station RAI UNO also interviews him. George also visits the town where Ferraris are built and, together with Olivia and Dhani, spends some time at the seaside near Genoa.

1 March. George and Olivia attend a birthday party for Renata John at Brown's in Covent Garden, London.

2 March. A prerecorded interview with George is featured on the CNN programme *Showbiz Today*.

3 March. George and Ringo are guests on the London Weekend Television show *Aspel And Company*.

5 March. The George and Ringo appearance on *Aspel And Company* is transmitted.

George plays slide guitar on Sylvia Griffin's 'Love's A State Of Mind' at FPSHOT.

8 March. The interview with George, recorded at the San Remo Music Festival, is transmitted on *Il Caso Rai*, a programme on the Italian TV station RAI UNO.

19 March. George is interviewed on the programme *Champs Elysees*, screened on the Annette 2 television channel in France.

22 March. *The Best Of George Harrison* is released on CD in America.

27 March. George flies to Los Angeles, stopping over in Toronto, Canada.

28 March. While in Toronto, George holds a press conference. He is also interviewed by the TV programmes *Global News* and *Canada AM*. He also gives a lengthy interview to the programme *MuchMusic Live Interview*.

29 March. George is in Los Angeles to film a cameo appearance in a HandMade film and is then off to Hawaii for a six-week holiday at his home there.

4 April. American radio stations transmit *Classic Cuts*, a syndicated programme of George's music.

23 April. George is featured in a prerecorded interview on the history of the Rickenbacker guitar in the Radio One documentary *A Concise History Of The Frying Pan*.

26 April. *A Concise History Of The Frying Pan* is repeated on Radio One.

2 May. George's single 'This Is Love' c/w 'Breath Away From Heaven' is released in America.

14 May. A prerecorded interview with George is featured on Norway's NRK programme *Pa Hengende Haret*.

25 May. George participates in Del Shannon's recording of 'Hot Love'.

27 May. Sylvia Griffin's single 'Love's A State Of Mind' is issued in Britain by Rocket Records. It features George on slide guitar.

7 June. George gives an after-dinner speech at the Savoy Hotel, London in tribute to Eric Clapton, who is celebrating his 25th anniversary as a performing musician at a dinner for family and friends.

13 June. George's single 'This Is Love' c/w 'Breath Away From Heaven' is released in Britain.

14 June. A home video of the 1987 Prince's Trust Concert, which includes George's performance, is released in Britain.

21 June. George attends the Royal Festival Hall in London to see the Bulgarian musicians Balkana.

13 July. A prerecorded interview with George is broadcast on the *Top Pop Special* show on the Norwegian channel NRK.

2 September. The National Film Theatre begins a five-week festival of HandMade films to celebrate the company's tenth anniversary.

22 September. *The Life Of Brian*, *Time Bandits* and *The Long Good Friday* are all released in America on home video.

1 October. The tenth anniversary of HandMade films is celebrated at a party in Shepperton Studios. George gives a speech and performs 'Honey Don't' and 'That's Alright (Mama)'.

7 October. George had hoped to attend the 'HandMade On Parade'

lecture at the National Film Theatre in London, but was delayed in Los Angeles shooting the 'Handle With Care' promo for the Traveling Wilburys.

10 October. The Westwood One one-hour special on George in the *Star Trak Profile* series is syndicated across America.

17 October. The Traveling Wilburys' debut single 'Handle With Care' c/w 'Margarita', is released simultaneously in Britain and America.

18 October. *The Traveling Wilburys Volume One* is released in America.

21 October. George, Paul and Ringo dine together.

24 October. *The Traveling Wilburys Volume One* is released in Britain.

30 October. The syndicated American radio show *Power Cuts* reports on the Traveling Wilburys.

4 November. The first of a two-part interview with George and Jeff Lynne discussing the Traveling Wilburys is screened by TV AM in Britain.

5 November. An interview with George is featured in the *Guardian* newspaper. The BBC Radio One show *Saturday Sequence* features a prerecorded interview of George discussing the Traveling Wilburys.

7 November. The second part of the two-part interview with George and Jeff Lynne is screened on TV AM.

11 November. An interview with George, conducted by Gill Pringle, is featured in the *Daily Mirror* newspaper. Among the topics discussed are Hare Krishna, Kylie Minogue, Margaret Thatcher and Bob Dylan.

6 December. Roy Orbison dies of a heart attack.

10 December. The Traveling Wilburys shoot a promo for the number 'End Of The Line' as a tribute to Roy Oribson who died a few days earlier, an empty chair was placed where he would have been sitting on the clip.

1989

8 January. The ITV network screens the Granada documentary *The Movie Life Of George*.

20 January. The promo for the Traveling Wilburys 'End Of The Line' receives a worldwide premiere.

23 January. The Traveling Wilburys single 'End Of The Line' c/w 'Congratulations' is released in America.

10 February. HandMade Films instigate a lawsuit against the distribution company Cannon Group for breach of contract.

20 February. The Traveling Wilburys single 'End Of The Line' c/w 'Congratulations' is released in Britain.

23 February. George is in Los Angeles and attends the premiere of the HandMade flm *Pow Wow Highway* at the Director's Guild Theater.

18 March. George and Olivia and Ringo and Barbara attend the London premiere of *The Adventures Of Baron Munchausen*.

21 March. The HandMade film *Checking Out* is issued in America. It features George in a cameo role and the Traveling Wilburys number 'End Of The Line' on the soundtrack.

22 March. George and Ringo are at Pinewood Studios in Buckinghamshire to join Tom Petty in the shoot of the Petty promo of the number 'I Won't Back Down'.

23 March. Shooting continues on the 'I Won't Back Down' promo.

16 April. George and Tom Petty visit the Grand Prix in Long Beach, California.

1 May. The home video of *Rock 'n' Roll – the Greatest Years 1971* includes 'My Sweet Lord' without permission and George has its release stopped.

17 May. George attends a celebrity lunch at Bill Wyman's Sticky Fingers restaurant in London, along with Tina Turner, Jim Capaldi and Steve Winwood.

31 May. Tom Petty's home video compilation *A Bunch Of Videos And Some Other Stuff* is released in America. It includes the promo of 'I Won't Back Down' in which George and Ringo appear.

7 July. George, Ringo, Eric Clapton and Jeff Lynne attend the Bob Dylan concert at the NEC, Birmingham.

25 July. George and Olivia attend the preview of the HandMade film *How To Get Ahead In Advertising* at the Lumiere Cinema, London.

26 July. George gives a radio interview to promote a peace march in Hyde Park, London.

29 July. The *Daily Express* features an interview with George and Olivia in which they discuss environmental issues.

3 August. The home video of *Porky's Revenge* is released in Britain.

10 August. The soundtrack album *Lethal Weapon 2* is released in America. It includes George's number 'Cheer Down'.

11 August. The Tom Petty video compilation *A Bunch Of Videos And Some Other Stuff* is released in Britain.

21 August. George's single 'Cheer Down' c/w 'That's What It Takes' is released in America.

2 September. A tribute to Ravi Shankar is featured on the BBC 2 programme *Network East* and includes an interview with George.

4 September. The soundtrack album *Lethal Weapon 2* is released in Britain.

10 October. The film *Wonderwall*, for which George composed the soundtrack, is issued on home video in America.

16 October. The album *The Best Of Dark Horse: 1976–1989* is released in America.

23 October. The album *The Best Of Dark Horse: 1976–1989* is released in Britain.

3 November. The home videos of the HandMade films *Water* and *A Private Function* are released in Britain. The former includes George and Ringo performing 'Freedom'.

18 November. George introduces Eric Clapton on stage at the Royal Albert Hall during the charity concert for 'Parents For Safe Foods'.

28 November. The Single 'Cheer Down' c/w 'Poor Little Girl' is released in Britain. George gives out a press statement following Paul McCartney's press conference the previous day in which Paul said he hoped to team up with George and Ringo again. George commented, 'As far as I'm concerned there won't be a Beatles reunion as long as John Lennon remains dead. What good are three Beatles without John? It's too far in the past. Let sleeping dogs lie.'

19 December. George puts his mansion on Hamilton Island, Australia up for auction, although the top bid of $3.5 million does not reach the reserve price. George has tired of the place due to noisy neighbours.

1990

8 February. *Lethal Weapon 2*, with George's 'Cheer Down' on the soundtrack, is released in America on home video.

10 February. The Radio One series *Classic Albums* features *The Traveling Wilburys Volume One*.

21 February. At the 32nd Grammy Awards *The Traveling Wilburys Volume One* and *Full Moon Fever*, the Tom Petty album, which also features George, are both nominated in the 'Album Of The Year' category.

25 February. The Discovery Channel screens the American premiere of *The Movie Life Of George*.

14 March. George and Olivia attend Michael Caine's 57th birthday party.

16 March. *Lethal Weapon 2*, with George's 'Cheer Down' on the soundtrack, is released in Britain on home video. The last HandMade film, *Nuns On The Run*, opens in Britain.

26 March. The members of the Traveling Wilburys begin writing material for their next album in Los Angeles.

31 March. The *Network East* tribute to Ravi Shankar, which features an interview with George, is repeated on BBC2.

1 April. The *Network East* Ravi Shankar tribute is screened on BBC1.

9 April. Olivia Harrison discusses her Romanian orphan appeal in the *Daily Mail* newspaper.

12 April. Warner reissues the home video of the *Concert For Bangla Desh* in Britain. Four asteroids are named after George, John, Paul and Ringo.

16 April. George records for Jim Capaldi's promo of 'Oh Lord, Why Lord'.

20 April. George and Olivia appear on Simon Bates' Radio One programme before flying to America.

27 April. The Traveling Wilburys begin to record their second album in Bel Air.

1 May. George makes a guest appearance on stage during Eric Clapton's concert at the Forum, Los Angeles, playing guitar on the numbers 'Crossroads' and 'Sunshine Of Your Love'.

2 May. The *Daily Mirror* newspaper reports that a man suspected of sending death threats to George at Friar Park has been arrested.

15 May. The Traveling Wilburys complete their recordings for *The Traveling Wilburys Volume 3*.

21 May. An interview with George appears in *USA Today*.

31 May. Olivia arrives home from Romania, where she has been involved in volunteer work for Romanian orphans.

7 June. The HandMade film *Checking Out*, in which George makes a brief appearance, is issued on home video in Britain.

18 June. 'Nobody's Child', the Traveling Wilburys single, is issued in Britain.

20 June. George and Olivia are guests on *Wogan*, which is recorded at the BBC TV Centre in Wood Lane, London. They discuss the Romanian Angel Appeal and a promo of 'Nobody's Child' is shown.

22 June. The *Wogan* show with George and Olivia's appearance is screened on BBC1.

18 July. A special luncheon in aid of the Romanian Angel Appeal is held at the Hyde Park Hotel, London with George and Olivia and Ringo and Barbara in attendance.

23 July. The album *Nobody's Child: Romanian Angel Appeal* is released in Britain.

24 July. The album *Nobody's Child: Romanian Angel Appeal* is released in America.

1 August. A one-hour documentary on the Romanian Angel Appeal includes a prerecorded interview with George.

17 September. George is a guest on Bob Dylan's album *Under The Red Sky*, released in Britain on CBS Records.

25 October. Radio One presents a forty-minute special on the forthcoming Traveling Wilburys album.

29 October. *The Traveling Wilburys Volume 3* is released in Britain.

30 October. *The Traveling Wilburys Volume 3* is released in America

5 November. The Traveling Wilburys single 'She's My Baby' c/w 'New Blue Moon' is released in Britain on 12″ single. There is also a CD version with the bonus track 'Runaway'. The 'My Sweet Lord'/'He's So Fine' dispute finally ends when Judge Owen in the New York Federal Court makes the decision that George will own the titles in Britain, the United States and Canada and Allen Klein's company ABKCO will own them in the rest of the world.

6 November. The Traveling Wilburys single 'She's My Baby' c/w 'New Blue Moon' is released in America.

11 November. George promotes the Traveling Wilburys album in a prerecorded interview on the Gloria Hunniford London Weekend television show *Sunday Sunday*.

18 November. The Royal Albert Hall is the setting for a gala concert in aid of the Parents For Safe Food Campaign, of which George's wife Olivia was an active member. George went on stage to introduce Eric Clapton.

5 December. George promotes the Traveling Wilburys' new album in a prerecorded interview for the BBC2 programme *Rapido*.

10 December. The BBC2 programme *Rapido*, with George's prerecorded interview, is repeated.

1991

7 January. In Maui two of George's neighbours, Scott Howard Whitney and Steven Philip Gold, file a civil complaint regarding the path by George's property, saying they were obstructed.

19 January. A prerecorded interview with George, in which he discusses the Gulf War, is screened on the MTV programme *Week In Rock* in America.

22 January. The *All Things Must Pass* reissue box set is issued in Britain.

23 January. The reissue of *All Things Must Pass* as a double CD with bonus tracks is released in America by Capitol.

17 February. George attends Bob Dylan's concert at the Odeon, Hammersmith, London, but declines to perform on stage. He attends the series of eight Dylan concerts at the venue.

2 March. George attends the George Formby Convention at the Winter Gardens, Blackpool. He joins actor Jimmy Nail and various ukulele players in a sing-along on stage.

3 March. At the George Formby Convention at the Winter Gardens, Blackpool, George goes on stage to perform 'In My Little Snapshot Album'. He is also interviewed for a radio tribute to Formby, *The Emperor Of Lancashire*.

18 March. The *Daily Mail* reports that George and Olivia will adopt a deaf seven-year-old Romanian orphan boy.

25 March. The Traveling Wilburys single 'Wilbury Twist' c/w 'New Blue Moon' is released simultaneously in Britain and America. There is only a cassette version in America and some of the British formats contain the bonus track 'Cool Dry Place'.

28 March. George attends the funeral of Eric Clapton's four-year-old son Conor, who died from a fall from a high building.

26 May. The George Formby radio tribute *The Emperor Of Lancashire* is broadcast, with a prerecorded interview with George.

11 June. *Somewhere In England* and *Gone Troppo* are released on CD in America.

25 June. *Thirty Three & 1/3* and *George Harrison* are released on CD in America.

30 July. *Concert For Bangla Desh* is released on CD in America.

1 August. While in America, George records an interview at Capitol

Records' Hollywood headquarters, to promote the release of *Concert For Bangla Desh* CD.

19 August. *Concert For Bangla Desh* is released on CD in Britain.

28 September. Julian Lennon's album *Help Yourself* is released with the number 'Saltwater', on which George played slide guitar. The HandMade film *Shanghai Surprise* is screened by ITV.

15 October. News of George's forthcoming tour of Japan with Eric Clapton is released.

2 November. Paul Gambaccini discusses George's musical career in the Radio One programme *Appreciation*.

4 November. George and Eric Clapton begin rehearsals for the forthcoming tour of Japan at Bray Film Studios. Clapton says, 'Japan's a bit out of the way. George can go on stage and get over his stage fright without being right in the international spotlight. If he came to the US and saw one bad review, he'd go straight home.'

12 November. A Japanese crew from NHK TV visit George at rehearsals to make a short feature for the *Subarasiji Nakamatati* show. George comments, 'It'll be special for me, because it'll be the tour which will decide whether I want to do any more touring or not, you see. This could be my first and last tour or it could just be something that begins a new period for me.'

15 November. An interview with George appears in the Japanese paper *Sports Nippon*. The interview had taken place on 28 October 1991 near Windsor where George had been rehearsing for his tour. (He continued to rehearse for five hours a day until 22 November.) He said that he'd be including early Beatles numbers such as 'If I Needed Someone' in the repertoire in a show which would last around two hours and include between fourteen and sixteen songs. He also said that if the tour was a flop he'd retire from show business and move to the Himalayas.

24 November. The feature of George, recorded on 12 November is screened by NHK TV on the *Subarasiji Nakamatati* (the name means 'Beautiful Comradeship') programme in Japan.

28 November. George and Eric Clapton arrive in Japan. It was the first time George had been there in 25 years and his flight JAL 402 touched down at Narita Airport at 3.48 p.m. George comments, 'It was really foggy and rainy. And I've been on the plane for twelve hours, so now I'm really sleepy. I should have come on a different flight.'

29 November. George and Eric hold a press conference at one o'clock in the Red Pearl Room at the Capitol Tokyo Hotel. This was formerly the Tokyo Hilton Hotel, where the Beatles stayed when they came to Japan in 1966.

30 November. George, Eric and the band rehearse at the Yokohama Arena.

1 December. The tour opens at the Yokohama Arena before an audience of 13,000 and George introduces 'All Those Years Ago' by saying,

'Hello! I hope many of you can speak much better English than I can – and I certainly can't speak very much Japanese – but this is a song which I wrote to an old friend of ours, whose name is John Lennon.' George played a guitar he obtained specially for the tour, a Roy Buchanan Bluesmaster.

2 December. At the Osaka Castle Hall, before 12,000 fans, George introduced the number 'Taxman' by saying, 'This next song is a very old song written in 1873!' George cut down his repertoire from 21 to 20 songs by cutting out 'Love Comes To Everyone'.

3 December. George appears at the Osaka Castle Hall. George further cuts his repertoire down to nineteen songs by cutting out 'Fish On The Sand'.

4 December. During his day off from the tour, George goes shopping in Osaka.

5 December. George appears at the International Exhibition Centre in Nagoya before an audience of 10,000. *Living In The Material World*, *Dark Horse* and *Extra Texture* are issued on CD in Japan to tie in with the tour.

6 December. George appears at the Hiroshima Sun Plaza Hall, Hiroshima.

7 December. On his second day off from the tour, George visits the Hiroshima Peace Park.

8 December. Eric Clapton accompanies George on a sightseeing trip around Fukouka.

9 December. George appears at the Fukouka Kokusai International Centre Hall.

10 December. Recordings of the concert at the Osaka Castle Hall take place. George introduces his number 'Cheer Down' as a song from *South Pacific*.

11 December. Another performance takes place at the Osaka Castle Hall.

12 December. George has a cold and prior to his concert at the Osaka Castle hall he is taken to the Tanaka clinic. The show brings an audience of 12,000 and George is interviewed backstage for the Japanese TV programme *Super Time*.

13 December. The *Super Time* interview with George is broadcast on Fuji TV.

14 December. George appears at the Dome Stadium, Tokyo.

15 December. The second concert at the Dome Stadium, Tokyo takes place.

16 December. George has another free day and shops at the International Market in Tokyo.

17 December. The final concert of the tour takes place at the Dome Stadium, Tokyo. George's son Dhani joins George, Eric and the group on stage during a performance of 'While My Guitar Gently Weeps' and 'Roll Over Beethoven'.

18 December. George, Olivia, Dhani and Eric fly back to England on flight JAL 401.
19 December. CNN reports from Japan on George's concert in their *Showbiz Today* programme. It includes an interview in which George says that the main reason for the tour was to help him give up smoking.

1992

22 January. *Living In The Material World*, *Extra Texture* and *Dark Horse* are released on CD in Britain and America.
1 February. Jim Keltner tells *Billboard* that there are rumours of a possible Harrison tour.
11 February. *Appreciation*, the Radio One programme in which Paul Gambaccini discusses George, is repeated.
2 March. George appears at a press conference held by Tom Petty at the Mayfair Hotel, London and the two later attend a party at the Hard Rock Café.
11 March. George files a complaint to prevent the neighbours in Hawaii using the path near his property.
17 March. George travels to Berlin with Tom Petty, who is giving a concert there.
1 April. *This Morning America* reports on George's forthcoming concert at the Royal Albert Hall.
2 April. Tickets for George's Royal Albert Hall concert go on sale.
5 April. George rehearses at the Royal Albert Hall. He is interviewed for the BBC and says, 'I will be recording a new studio album in the summer and will be touring with it upon its release.'
6 April. The Royal Albert Hall concert, in aid of the Natural Law Party, takes place.
12 April. George films an interview at George Martin's home for the forthcoming TV documentary *The Making Of Sgt Pepper*.
21 April. The George Formby radio tribute *The Emperor Of Lancashire* is repeated.
26 May. Among the Apple re-releases is George's *Wonderwall*.
6 June. The Channel 4 documentary *Mister Roadrunner*, hosted by Jools Holland, features a 1991 clip of George playing the ukulele and singing 'Between The Devil And The Deep Blue Sea'.
14 June. The TV special *The Making of Sgt Pepper* is screened.
15 June. George turns up at Carl Perkins' concert at the Hard Rock Café in London and performs 'Everybody's Trying To Be My Baby', 'Blue Suede Shoes' and 'Honey Don't' with him.
20 June. The Hard Rock performance of 'Blue Suede Shoes' with George and Carl Perkins is shown on MTV Europe's *Week In Rock*.
13 July. The double album *Live In Japan* from George's recent tour is released in Britain.
14 July. The double album *Live In Japan* is released in America.

24 August. George travels to Los Angeles from his Hawaii home and appears on some radio and TV spots, including the LA show *Rockline*.
11 September. ABC TV screens *In Concert '92* which features clips of 'Taxman' and 'Piggies' from George's Japanese tour, plus an interview.
22 September. Geoffrey Giuliano, author of an unauthorised biography of George, calls George an eccentric recluse in an interview in the *Guardian* newspaper.
27 September. *The Making Of Sgt Pepper* receives its American premiere on the Disney Channel.
5 October. George attends a concert for Gary Moore at the Royal Albert Hall and joins him on stage. The album *Bunbury Tales*, containing George's track 'Ride Rajbun', is released in Britain. A letter appears in the *Guardian* from Olivia Harrison regarding Geoffrey Giuliano's interview. 'I'm sick of this guy,' she writes.
8 October. George, Paul and Ringo meet at Paul's MPL offices.
14 October. George and Olivia fly to New York.
16 October. George and Olivia attend the Bob Dylan concert at Madison Square Garden, billed as 'Columbia Records Celebrates The Music Of Bob Dylan'. The show sold out in 72 minutes and guests include Tom Petty, Jim Keltner, Eric Clapton, Roger McGuinn, Neil Young, John Mellencamp, Willie Nelson, Johnny Cash, Roseanne Cash, Sinead O'Connor, Kris Kristofferson, the O'Jays and Ron Wood. George gets on stage and performs 'If Not For You' and 'Absolutely Sweet Marie'. He also joins in the jam session for 'My Back Pages' and 'Knockin' On Heaven's Door'. The concert is recorded for the album *Bob Dylan – 30th Anniversary Concert Celebration*.
20 October. George and Olivia set off for London on Concorde, but the flight returns to Kennedy Airport due to a warning light in the cockpit. While the aircraft is checked, George entertains passengers by playing George Formby numbers. Also present is Norman Schwarzkopf, commander in the Gulf War.
25 October. The *Sun* newspaper reports that on this night, to celebrate Gary Moore's birthday, George and Moore held a jam session in the Crooked Billet, a local pub in Henley that they frequented. When neighbours complained of the noise, the pub landlord said that George and Gary were not present, that there was a private party with entertainment provided by Cockney duo Chas & Dave.
8 November. Footage of George appearing at the George Formby Convention in Blackpool in March 1991 is cut from a programme about George Formby in *The South Bank Show*, at the request of George.
5 December. A *Billboard* interview with George, who is also its cover star, reveals that his true birthday is 24 February.
9 December. Tom Petty presents George with a special 'Century Award' from *Billboard* magazine for 'distinguished creative achievement'.

10 December. George and Paul meet up in California. George appears on *Entertainment Tonight,* a Paramount Television show.

14 December. George jams on stage with Eddie Van Halen and various other musicians in a benefit concert for the children of Toto drummer Jeff Porcaro in Los Angeles.

1993

20 February. BBC Radio Merseyside broadcasts a tribute show to George in honour of his fiftieth birthday.

25 February. George and Olivia hold a private party at the Town & Country Club, Kentish Town, London to celebrate George's birthday.

28 February. To celebrate George's fiftieth birthday ITV screens both *A Hard Day's Night* and *Help!*

6 March. PBS airs an October tribute to Bob Dylan, which features George.

8 March. The Bob Dylan tribute is repeated by PBS.

9 April. George attends the British premiere of Eric Idle's film *Splitting Heirs*.

12 April. The Traveling Wilburys are featured in the syndicated American radio series *In The Studio*.

9 May. George visits the 37th Spanish Grand Prix in Barcelona.

19 July. The *Bob Dylan – 30th Anniversary Concert Celebration* album, which includes George's performance of 'Absolutely Sweet Marie', is issued in Britain.

21 July. The *Honolulu Advertiser* has a quote from George regarding his dispute over the path close to his house: 'Have you ever been raped? I'm being raped by all these people. My privacy is being violated.'

11 August. Two of George's Maui neighbours file a lawsuit in the Hawaiian District Court regarding the path near George's house.

24 August. The *Bob Dylan – 30th Anniversary Concert Celebration* album, which includes George's performance of 'Absolutely Sweet Marie', is issued in America.

30 September. The episode of *The Simpsons* featuring George's voice-over to an animation of him debuts on the Fox TV Network in America.

3 October. The episode of *The Simpsons* featuring an animated George makes its British debut on the Sky One channel.

6 October. The two Maui neighbours dismiss their federal action against George, without prejudice – meaning they could start it up again.

7 October. George appears in a prerecorded interview on the BBC2 show *Top Gear*.

1 November. Interviews with George and Paul McCartney are included on the numerous programmes about the Beatles screened by MTV on their 'Beatles Day'.

7 November. While at the Adelaide Grand Prix George gives an interview to Channel 9, a TV news channel.

12 December. George appears in *Curves, Contours And Body Horns,* a profile of the Fender Stratocaster guitar on the ITV network.

27 December. The BBC2 programme *An Evening With Vic And Bob* includes George's appearance from *Rutland Weekend Television* in which he performs 'The Pirate Song'.

1994

11 January. George has a 96-track console fitted into his FPSHOT Studio, replacing the 48-track console that he has recorded on for the past twenty years.

31 January. In an interview in *Newsweek* magazine Paul McCartney says that he and George occasionally get on each other's nerves.

11 February. George, Paul and Ringo begin recording 'Free As A Bird' at Paul's The Mill Studios in Sussex, based on a home demo recording by John Lennon. Yoko has given it to the remaining Beatles to use as a new release to celebrate their forthcoming project *The Beatles Anthology.* George commented on the demo tape, 'Because it was only a demo, he was just plodding along and in some places he'd quicken up and in some places he'd slow down.'

10 April. George is in Phoenix, Arizona for the Slick 50 200 at Phoenix International Raceway. Racing driver Emerson Fittipaldi joins him for a meal. The *Sunday Times* publishes its Rich List, assessing George's fortune at £25 million.

17 April. George is seen with Nigel Mansell at the Long Beach Grand Prix in California.

26 April. George spends two and a half hours at Jackson's Rare Guitars in Sydney, Australia, during which he plays numerous guitars in the shop and buys two of them.

5 May. George, Paul and Ringo get together again to discuss their *Anthology* project.

18 May. George sells his HandMade Films catalogue to the Paragon Entertainment Corporation.

22 May. George goes to Pasadena City College to see Ravi Shankar. He'd earlier visited the Pink Floyd backstage at their Pasadena concert.

8 June. George, Paul and Ringo get together again to discuss their recordings based on John's demo tapes.

22 June. Jeff Lynne becomes producer when George, Paul and Ringo gather at The Mill Studios in Sussex to attempt to turn John's home demo of 'Now And Then' into a single. It is not a success and the attempt is abandoned.

23 June. The recording session with George, Paul and Ringo now takes place at George's FPSHOT Studio during which the three perform several numbers including 'Thinking Of Linking', 'Ain't She Sweet', 'Love Me Do', 'I Saw Her Standing There' and 'Blue Moon Of Kentucky'.

30 July. George is present at a motorcycle race at Donnington Park.

30 October. A prerecorded interview with George is featured on *Angel 2 – Beyond The Light* on the NBC TV network in America.

17 November. George is once again in attendance at the Adelaide Grand Prix in Australia and stays to watch the racing until 20 November.

20 December. A six-CD boxed set *Mo's Blues* is issued in a limited edition to Warner Brothers Records staff to celebrate the retirement of Mo Ostin, their chief executive. Among the tracks is one written by George entitled 'Mo'.

1995

6 February. George, Paul and Ringo resume recording at Paul's studio, The Mill.

7 February. George, Paul and Ringo continue recording from John Lennon's demo tape of 'Real Love', a number that George prefers to 'Free As A Bird'.

25 February. A prerecorded interview with George is included in the third part of *The Peter Sellers Story* on BBC2.

20 March. George, Paul and Ringo gather at The Mill to try again to produce a viable single from John's home demo of 'Now And Then', but once again are unsuccessful.

29 March. George, Paul and Ringo view early screening of their *Anthology* project in viewing rooms in Wendell Road, Chiswick.

15 May. George, Paul and Ringo gather at Paul's studio for further work on 'Real Love'.

16 May. George, Paul and Ringo complete the recording of 'Real Love' and George makes it plain that he doesn't want to be involved in any other Beatles reunion recording sessions.

18 May. George, Paul and Ringo are interviewed together in London.

22 May. George, Paul and Ringo join George Martin at Abbey Road Studios for the mixing of tracks for their CD in the *Anthology* series.

15 July. George attends Ravi Shankar's 75th birthday concert at the Barbican, London. Sporting a beard and ponytail, he sits in the front row.

19 July. George and Olivia attend the Rolling Stones concert at the Brixton Academy and then visit Ronnie Wood and his family in Richmond. In Hawaii, two of George's neighbours file a suit against him complaining of oral and written defamation, causing them actual distress.

11 November. George attends the Australian Grand Prix in Adelaide and gives driver Damon Hill a preview of the 'Free As A Bird' video. Frank Pengello also interviews him for the TV programme *Today Tonight*. Commenting on the Beatles, he says, 'The Beatles, for me, are a bit like a suit or a shirt I once wore and unfortunately, I don't mean this in a bitter way, a lot of people look at that suit and think it's me. The reality is that I'm this soul in the body. The Beatles were this thing

we did for a few years and it was such a big thing. It's amazing that people keep going on about it.'

1996

10 January. George is awarded $11.6 million in his suit against Denis O'Brien, although winning the case does not mean he will get the money from O'Brien, who is to appeal.

3 February. *Billboard* features details of George's legal battle with O'Brien.

9 March. George is interviewed in *Billboard* about the Beatles *Anthology*.

13 March. Long lost documents regarding George's involvement with ISKCON (International Society For Krishna Consciousness) are found.

16 May. George receives a summons regarding his Maui neighbours' action against him.

18 June. George begins recording 'Distance Makes No Difference With Love' with Carl Perkins at his FPSHOT Studio at Friar Park.

19 June. George continues the recording with Carl Perkins.

22 June. George and Perkins finish recording 'Distance Makes No Difference With Love'.

7 July. George continues his recording of Ravi Shankar for the *Chants Of India* project, which he began recording in India in January, at his Friar Park studio.

11 July. A group of Indian musicians join George and Ravi on the *Chants Of India* recordings. They record every day for a week, with the musicians finishing their work on 18 July.

19 July. George and Ravi continue their recordings for the *Chants Of India* until 26 July.

1 August. George and Olivia appear in a one-hour Radio One documentary *Nobody's Child*, which had been prerecorded while they had been at Broadcasting House on 20 June recording for Simon Bates' radio show.

12 August. Together with arranger John Barnham, George works on *Chants Of India* at his Friar Park Studio. More work is done on 13, 16 and 22 August.

12 September. The Hawaiian court throws out the defamation case against George.

31 October. A prerecorded interview with George is broadcast on the Brazilian television programme *Gente Que Brilha*, a documentary about Formula One champion Fittipaldi.

14 November. Denis O'Brien is in court in America to answer questions from attorneys seeking to collect damages O'Brien owes to George. On the same day the Circuit Court in Hawaii files an order stating that George's remarks in the Honolulu newspaper were 'non-defamatory, constitutionally protected rhetorical hyperbole'. The

plaintiffs' attorney is ordered to pay George's attorney's fees and costs amounting to $12,504.48.

16 December. George requests an investigation into the death threats he has been receiving for six years.

1997

8 March. George is in Melbourne for the Australian Grand Prix at Albert Park.

11 March. During a visit to the Melbourne Crown Casino, George spots a piano and proceeds to entertain the guests for two hours.

7 April. George is in New York on business relating to Apple.

3 May. George discusses *Chants Of India* in a *Billboard* interview.

6 May. The Ravi Shankar CD *Chants Of India*, produced by George, is issued in America. The CD was recorded in Friar Park, London and Madras in India and George played acoustic guitar, bass guitar, autoharp and glockenspiel on the recording.

14 May. In New York to promote *Chants Of India*, George and Ravi Shankar are interviewed by John Fugelsang at the VH-I studio for the programme *George And Ravi – Yin And Yang*.

15 May. George and Ravi record a number of interviews at the Plaza Hotel. They include the TV programmes *Access Hollywood* and *Showbiz Today*, the radio show *All Things Considered* and *People* magazine. The *All Things Considered* interview is conducted by Robert Siegel for National Public Radio and is broadcast that evening.

16 May. Continuing their promotion from the Plaza Hotel, George and Ravi are interviewed for the TV programme *CBS This Morning* and for radio interviews with Westwood One and WNEW. Reuters and Associated Press also interview them.

22 May. The CNN programme *Showbiz Today* transmits the prerecorded interview with George and Ravi discussing *Chants Of India*.

12 June. The prerecorded interview with George and Ravi is broadcast on CBS's *This Morning*.

27 June. George attends a Ravi Shankar concert at the Barbican Centre in London.

24 July. The VHI channel broadcasts *Yin And Yang*, a special featuring George and Ravi Shankar.

25 July. George and his son Dhani attend the Womad Festival in Reading, Berkshire to watch Ravi Shankar perform.

2 August. Sky News reports that George has undergone surgery for suspected throat cancer. *The Times* newspaper also prints the news.

18 August. In their *Classic Albums* series, Radio One covers the album *The Band* and includes a short interview with George.

2 August. George and Olivia attend the wedding of George's niece.

27 August. The French newspaper *Le Figaro* prints George's interview in which he slags off the current British pop scene.

1 September. Ravi Shankar's CD *Chants Of India* is released in Britain.

7 September. Derek Taylor dies. Dhani enters Brown University in Long Island where he begins the course 'Computers And Music: Introduction To Music Technology'.

12 September. George is the only ex-Beatle to attend the funeral of his friend Derek Taylor.

1998

6 January. A report in the *Sun* newspaper states that two ten-foot bronze statues of monks have been stolen from the Friar Park Estate. The monks, with an estimated value of £50,000, were sawn off their stone pillars.

19 January. Carl Perkins dies in Nashville.

23 January. George attends Carl Perkins' funeral. At the ninety-minute service, Wynona Judd asks, 'George, do you have anything to add?' George replies, 'Your True Love', do you know that one?' 'I think I could follow it, do you want to sing it?' says Judd. 'Sure,' says George, and performs an acoustic version, saying, 'I think somebody out there must know this. It's from Carl's first album.'

16 February. The Court of Appeal grants $10.9 million in George's favour in his case against Denis O'Brien.

4 March. The film *Everest*, which features five compositions by George on the soundtrack, receives its premiere at the Museum Of Science, Boston.

6 March. The documentary *Everest* goes on general release in America.

7 March. George attends the Formula One Grand Prix in Melbourne, Australia. Along with his friend Barry Sheene, he attends the Grand Prix Ball, which features a Beatles tribute band.

17 April. Paul McCartney's wife Linda dies. George was to say, 'Linda will be missed not only by Paul, her children and brother John, but by all of us who knew and loved her. She was a dear person with a passionate love of nature and its creatures and, in her passing, has earned the peace she sought in life. May God bless her.'

6 May. George turns up at the High Court in London to give evidence in Apple's suits against Lingasong, who were intending to release *The Beatles Star Club* recordings on CD.

7 May. The British newspapers report on George's court appearance.

8 May. Mr Justice Neuberger judges in favour of the Beatles, commenting, 'George's evidence is convincing while Edward Taylor's comments to the court have been confused and inconsistent.'

7 June. The *Cambridge Evening News* reports that George has made a donation of £500 to Addenbrooke Hospital's baby unit.

8 June. George and Olivia attend the London memorial service for Linda McCartney.

27 June. Dennis Rice, a reporter from the *News Of the World*, interviews George at Friar Park while George is watching the World Cup match between Italy and Norway.

28 June. The feature on George appears in the *News Of The World* under the heading 'Beatle George: My Fight Against Cancer'.

29 June. George gives a statement to the press: 'The cancerous lump is entirely down to smoking. This is more of a warning than anything else.'

9 July. George attends Ravi Shankar's concert at the Barbican, London.

11 July. George, together with his son Dhani, visits the British Grand Prix at Silverstone where he is seen speaking with fellow artists Chris de Burgh and Leo Sayer, also fans of Formula One racing.

22 July. George attends a Wembley Arena concert of rock legends including Chuck Berry, Jerry Lee Lewis and Little Richard.

2 August. George appears on a BBC Radio 2 programme discussing Blues records.

30 September. George sues Random House for libel following publication of the book *All Dressed Up: The Sixties And The Counter Culture*.

23 October. George visits Pete's Guitars in St Paul, Minnesota and buys a Hawaiian ukulele, a Fender Telecaster and an amp.

1 November. George was the cover star of the new issue of *The Guitarist* magazine, which also contained features on George, his guitar collection and also a CD, which contained tuition and backing tracks of 'Taxman', and other Beatles numbers. There was also a solo intro and backing track of 'My Sweet Lord'.

7 November. The 1992 Bob Dylan tribute concert, on which George appeared, is featured on VH1's 'Legends' weekend. An item in the *News Of The World* reads: 'George stands to make a fortune by selling the car he was sitting in when he proposed to his first wife Patti Boyd. The E-type Jaguar, which cost £2,300 when purchased new back in 1964, has his name on the log book and now boasts, experts believe, a six-figure price tag.'

2 December. George attends a concert in New York where Dave Mason and Jim Capaldi are appearing. Capaldi introduces 'You Got A Hold On Me', a song he said he'd written for George's new album. He announced, 'This is something special for someone in the audience tonight. I want him to hear it live so I could get his reaction. He is one of the greatest influences of my life. This one is for you George.'

6 December. George is spotted at the Bottom Line in Manhatten, New York.

1999

11 January. George appears on the BBC's *This Is Your Life* honouring racing driver Damon Hill, where he reveals that he had helped Damon with guitar lessons.

12 January. George wins his libel case against Random House and receives an apology, damages and costs.

1 February. *Total Guitar* features a lengthy interview with George, originally conducted by Vic Garbarini seven years earlier. In the seven-

page feature he said, 'There were lots of influences on my playing, but it would be precocious to compare myself to incredible musicians like Ravi Shankar' and 'I don't remember much at all about *Sgt Pepper*, I was in my own little world.'

21 February. At the end of the screening of *Mr Holland's Opus* on ABC TV, George makes the appeal, 'I'm George Harrison. Music can make a world of difference in the life of a child, as it did mine. To find out about Mr Holland's Opus Foundation, and to put musical instruments into the hands of children, call toll free 1-877-Mr Holland. Help keep music alive in our schools.'

6 March. George is in Australia again for the Melbourne Grand Prix and is seen with his friend, Formula One driver Mika Hakkinen.

28 March. A remastered version of the *Wonderwall* film is screened at the Gantry Cinema, Southampton. The soundtrack now includes a song by George, 'In The First Place', originally recorded for the soundtrack, but not initially included.

15 April. George arrives in America to make his regular visit to the Long Beach Grand Prix.

18 April. George attends the Long Beach Grand Prix in California.

23 April. George plays as a guest on a track of Bill Wyman's new album *Double Bill*, released today.

24 May. George and Olivia and Ringo and Barbara attend the Chelsea Flower Show in London.

2 June. George and Olivia turn up at a private party at Christie's London auction house to celebrate the forthcoming auction of a hundred of Eric Clapton's guitars in New York at the end of the month.

4 June. An announcement is made that there will be a third Traveling Wilburys album, using Carl Perkins' voice. His son Stan said he would be handing over four unreleased songs by his father which could be utilised in the same way George, Paul and Ringo used John Lennon's demos for 'Free As A Bird' and 'Real Love'. The plan never comes off.

6 June. George refuses to allow members of Henley Town Council to visit Friar Park. They want to look at the estate because George had said that he wants to add a swimming pool and a subtropical rain forest to the estate.

19 June. An interview with George, conducted by Timothy White at Friar Park, appears in *Billboard* magazine. George says, 'It's hard to think of leaving the privacy and quiet of the happy life I have here.' George mentions that his Dark Horse solo catalogue and the two Traveling Wilburys albums have reverted back to him. He mentioned that Apple bought the Beatles TV cartoons, saying, 'I always kind of liked them – they were so bad or silly they were good, if you know what I mean. And I think the passage of time might make them more fun now, in terms of being more watchable now than they really were back then. But we don't have any plans for them at the moment.'

26 June. The film *Wonderwall* is screened at Grauman's Egyptian Theatre on Hollywood Boulevard in Los Angeles as part of the 'Groovy Movies Of The Shag-A-Delic Sixties' film festival. It is the American premiere – 31 years after the film was made!

27 June. A report in the *Sunday Mirror* states that a piece of half-eaten toast, said to be a leftover from George, had sold for thousands of pounds! George is incredulous and says, 'Well I never authenticated it! That's total bullshit. I really dislike that. I ate all my toast, I never left any. The madness is the people selling it, and the people actually buying it. It's *Monty Python* time: how much would they pay for a piece of sweat? Or a piece of ear wax!'

5 July. George appears on Joe Brown's BBC Radio 2 show discussing the Beatles and his all-time favourite rock'n'roll numbers.

9 July. George, Olivia and Dhani attend a Ravi Shankar concert at the Barbican Centre in London. The Harrisons were jostled by fans as they tried to get in the stage door and Dhani physically cleared a way for his father.

10 July. In a live ITV broadcast from the Grand Prix at Silverstone, George is seen chatting to Jackie Stewart.

1 August. Neighbours in Henley complain of the fireworks display that George had organised at Friar Park to celebrate Dhani's 21st birthday.

19 August. The Rosewood Fender Telecaster which George gave to Delaney Bramlett in 1969 is put up for auction by Bramlett at Bonham's, but is withdrawn when it doesn't reach its reserve price of £200,000. It is the guitar George played on the roof of the Apple building in *Let It Be*.

21 August. Another of George's former guitars, this one signed by all four members of the Beatles, is sold at auction by satellite TV for $18,500.

19 September. A *Sunday Telegraph* article reveals they have traced Peter Batten, who provided the voice of George for the *Yellow Submarine* animated movie.

23 September. *The Times* newspaper prints the 100 Best British films of all time as voted for by members of the British film industry. Three of them are HandMade Films: *The Life Of Brian*, *Withnail And I* and *Mona Lisa*.

30 September. George's 1962 Rickenbacker 425 is auctioned at Christies in London and sells for £56,500. It was the guitar he played on *Ready, Steady, Go!* on 4 October 1963.

9 October. George, Olivia and Dhani attend a Ravi Shankar concert at the Barbican in London.

18 October. The Hawaii Supreme Court rules against George and says he must allow access to the path near to his house. George files an appeal.

25 October. George arrives in Los Angeles.

23 December. Cristin Keleher breaks into the Harrison's house in Maui, Hawaii where she eats a pizza, uses the phone and washes her clothes. George's sister-in-law spots her and calls the police. Keleher is later released on bail. The woman says she has a psychic connection to George.

30 December. George and Olivia are attacked by Michael Abram in their home at Friar Park. The heroism of them both saves their lives. In Hawaii Keleher is charged with burglary and theft.

31 December. Michael Abram is charged with attempted murder.

2000

1 January. George is allowed home from hospital and is visited by his friend Eric Idle, who says, 'He's much better.' Eric decides to stay for a few days to see that George is all right.

2 January. Paul and Ringo are asked to remain on the alert in case there are any copycat attacks.

4 January. It is claimed that George is under 24-hour guard by two former SAS men who are on 12-hour shifts at a cost of £1000 per day. Eric Idle has remained at Friar Park while George and Olivia recuperate from the attack.

7 January. The *Sun* newspaper reports that the SAS guards George has employed do not carry arms, although they are able to kill with their bare hands.

9 January. The *Daily Mirror* reports that a security group with guard dogs now patrols Friar Park, although they are only employed when George and Olivia are not present at the estate.

12 January. In Hawaii Cristin Keleher pleads not guilty, but remains in custody.

16 January. George and Olivia are at Ronnie and Jo Wood's home in Ireland. A photograph of George and Olivia during their brief holiday in Ireland is taken, to be distributed with a statement from George in which he says, 'Olivia and I are overwhelmed by the concern expressed by so many people. We thank everyone for their prayers and kindness.'

20 January. Olivia and Dhani attend a Ravi Shankar concert at the Barbican, London.

25 January. An article in the *Sun* newspaper headed 'Getting Better All The Time' reports that George was recuperating in Barbados. There are colour photos of George, Olivia, Dhani and Joe Brown and three bodyguards. They were staying at a $50,000-a-week villa.

26 January. In Hawaii Cristin Keleher's bail is reduced from $10,000 to $1,100 when her lawyer reveals that she is homeless.

30 January. Disturbed by the attack on George and Olivia, Yoko Ono told the *Independent On Sunday* newspaper that she now feared for the safety of Julian and Sean.

1 February. The Hawaiian Supreme Court upholds a 1993 decision that neighbours can use a path on George's land to reach views of the

ocean. George had already stated that if the decision went against him, he would sell the property.

3 February. Alla Rakah Khan dies of a heart attack two days after the death of his daughter.

7 February. Rod Stewart and his girlfriend Penny Lancaster join George and his family in Barbados.

9 February. Ravi Shankar is named a Commander of French Legion and Honour, the highest award a civilian can be given. He receives his award at the French Embassy in New Delhi, India.

11 February. Michael Abram is remanded to a psychiatric unit, the Scott Clinic on Merseyside, for a further eight weeks.

15 February. The American tabloid the *Globe* features photographs from George's holiday in Barbados, which had previously appeared in Britain's *Sun* newspaper. They comment, 'He appears to be healing quickly and he has no obvious scars on his body. If you look real close, you can see a red mark where the wound was.'

11 March. George is at the Australian Grand Prix in Melbourne.

12 March. While at the Australian Grand Prix at Albert Park, Melbourne, George is interviewed and comments, 'As you can see, I'm fit again. I came very close, but I'm doing OK, and I'd like to thank everybody who sent me messages. It was overwhelming and it really helped me a lot to recover.'

25 March. Emerson Fittipaldi has invited George to be the start man at Rio 2000 in Brazil.

7 April. Michael Abram is charged with the attempted murder of George and Olivia and with causing grievous bodily harm to George and unlawfully wounding Olivia.

6 June. At Oxford Crown Court Michael Abram pleads not guilty to attempted murder, grievous bodily harm and aggravated burglary. A trial is set for 14 November.

17 June. George attends the Montreal Formula One Grand Prix, where he is seen with drivers David Coulthard and Emerson Fittipaldi. George said, 'I find it easier to watch the races at home on television. With all the different camera angles you get now, it's fantastic coverage. I get to know everything that's happening.'

20 June. Ravi Shankar and his daughter Anoushka are in concert at the Barbican, London. Olivia, Dhani and his girlfriend Beth Earl and Mary McCartney are in attendance. A clip of George performing with Carl Perkins at the Hard Rock Café is shown on MTV's *Week In Rock*.

25 June. George, Olivia and Dhani with his girlfriend Beth Earl, daughter of Robert Earl of Planet Hollywood, are at the Goodwood Festival of Speed.

27 June. George and Ray Cooper attend Ravi Shankar's Barbican concert along with Olivia, Dhani and Beth Earl. Stella McCartney is in the seat behind him.

4 July. Michael Abram is granted conditional release from the Scott Clinic. Olivia and Dhani hadn't been informed. When they find out, Dhani makes the statement: 'We certainly wish Mr Abram no ill, but to be presented with this as a fact after the event is deeply upsetting and insulting and we feel again completely let down by the system. It remains the case in this country that the victim simply has no voice. The law must be changed.'

7 August. *ESPN* magazine reports that Dhani has invited skateboard champion Tony Hawk to dinner at Friar Park where he met George and Tom Petty.

25 August. In Hawaii Cristin Keleher is placed on one year's probation. She says, 'I thank God George did not press charges against me. I learned a lesson.'

22 September. George attends the Formula One races in Indianapolis, staying until 24 September.

29 September. In the British magazine *Total Film*, *The Life Of Brian* is voted the funniest film of all time. *Withnail And I* is at No. 2 and *Monty Python And The Holy Grail* at No. 5.

14 November. The first day of the Michael Abram trial.

15 November. On the second day of the trial Michael Abram is found not guilty by reason of insanity. His solicitor reads out a letter by Abram expressing remorse for his attack.

19 November. The *Sunday People* publish statements from Olivia and Dhani expressing their rage at a legal system that offers little protection for the victims of crime.

22 November. Dhani crashes his Audi 53 in Oxfordshire.

26 November. George plays George Formby songs on his ukulele at Terry Gilliam's party. Michael Palin and Terry Jones accompany him on spoons.

27 November. George and Ringo attend the Who's charity concert at the Royal Albert Hall.

1 December. The *Henley Standard* reports that Jack Straw, the Home Secretary, has assured George and Olivia that they will be informed if their attacker Michael Abram is to be released from a mental hospital.

16 December. George and Ringo attend a performance of the Cirque de Soleil in London.

17 December. George and Olivia write to the *Independent* newspaper criticising the weakness of planned government reforms to protect victims from attacks by mentally ill people.

18 December. George is interviewed by the German news agency DPA.

20 December. George tells the Reuters' press agency that he is considering calling his next album *Your Planet Is Dying, Volume One*.

22 December. The *Billboard* magazine website interviews George about the reissue of *All Things Must Pass*.

31 December. One year after their horrendous attack, George and Olivia write to the *Sunday People* describing how devastating the experience was.

2001

25 January. The French television channel Jimmy screens a TV special about George. It includes an interview with Paul McCartney.

15 February. George conducts his first Internet chats on both Yahoo and MSN.

18 February. George and a group of friends attend a Cirque de Soleil performance in Las Vegas.

22 February. *Top Of The Pops* 2 on BBC 2 celebrates George's birthday by playing the promotional film of 'Ticket To Ride', 'Let It Be' from the film and 'Yesterday' from *Blackpool Night Out*.

3 March. George discusses his interest in Formula One racing in an interview published in *The Times* newspaper.

21 March. George enters St Mary's Hospital in Rochester, Minnesota.

22 March. George undergoes a four-hour operation on his left lung.

25 March. Mark Abram alarms the residents of Rainhill on Merseyside when he is allowed to walk around the village accompanied only by a single warden.

27 March. On behalf of Queen Elizabeth II, the British High Commission in Delhi honours Ravi Shankar with the award of an Honorary Knight Commander of the Order of the British Empire.

1 April. The *Sunday People* reports that George is still in fear of the person who knifed him. He says, 'We find this absolutely incredible and horrifying. Perhaps only a fatality will awaken the psychiatrists to the dangers posed by a man like him. We've hardly begun to recover from our ordeal. Is the clinic already preparing him for integration back into the community? He has often been seen walking, escorted by just one warden, around Rainhill, near the Scott Clinic on Merseyside. The clinic said their procedures were reviewed regularly and would not be in place unless they had confidence in them.'

2 April. George is discharged from St Mary's Hospital.

7 April. There are rumours in the media that George intends to sell Friar Park.

28 April. A letter George sent to a fan in 1963 realises £3,290 at auction.

3 May. George and Olivia travel to Tuscany in Italy.

12 May. Paul McCartney visits George in Milan. They chat for an hour.

7 June. The long-running dispute regarding the path in George's Maui property is finally settled in a confidential agreement that is said to be satisfactory to all parties.

9 July. George is resting in his Maui home, but in response to rumours about his health in the media issues a statement. 'I am feeling fine. And I am really sorry for the unnecessary worry, which has been caused by the reports in today's press. Please do not worry.'

22 July. A report in the *Sunday Mirror* alleges that George Martin has said, 'George has an indomitable spirit but he knows that he is going to die soon and he is accepting of that.' The article also states that

Shyamasundara Dasa is coaching George in preparation for Hare Krishna rites of death.

23 July. George and Olivia, upset by the *Sunday Mirror* story, issue a statement. 'We are disappointed and disgusted by the report. It was unsubstantiated, untrue and totally uncalled for, when in fact Mr Harrison is active and feeling very well.' A spokesman for George Martin states that he did not make the comment attributed to him. James Desborough, editor of the British entertainment news service WENN resigns due to reports that he tampered with the quotes attributed to Martin.

8 August. The German press reports that George and Olivia have bought a four-storey villa in Switzerland.

29 August. George's lawyers seek a review and new judge in the O'Brien bankruptcy case. The previous judge had allowed O'Brien to seek bankruptcy purely because George was unable to attend because he was ill. That judge's decision was to be overturned.

1 October. The number 'A Horse To Water', written by George and Dhani, is recorded in Switzerland with Jools Holland and Sam Brown. George has the number published under RIP Ltd 2001.

30 October. George is admitted to the Staten Island University Hospital in New York City where Dr Gil Lederman is to treat George's brain tumour with fractimated stereotactic radiosurgery.

10 November. George is released from Staten Island University Hospital, but remains in the area to be treated as an outpatient.

11 November. George resigns as a director of his publishing company Harrisongs and Olivia takes his place.

12 November. Paul and Ringo spend several hours with George at Staten Island University Hospital where he is having treatment for his cancer. A spokesman said, 'Paul was tearful and sad about seeing George sick. George's passing would be a major blow to all of these. There are very few people who shared what these men shared while they were making music together.'

15 November. George leaves Staten Island University Hospital and travels to Los Angeles by private jet where he is to be treated by chemotherapy at UCLA Medical Center.

19 November. Jools Holland's album *Small World Big Band*, with George and Dhani's track 'A Horse To Water', is released in Britain.

29 November. George dies peacefully in Los Angeles at 1.20 p.m. chanting the Hare Krishna mantra. With him are Olivia, Dhani, Ravi, Sukanya and Anoushka Shankar, Shyamasunder Das and Mukunda Goswami. Ravi says, 'George looked so peaceful, surrounded by love. He was a brave, beautiful soul, full of love, childlike humour and a deep spirituality.' Cremation Specialists of Los Angeles cremated his remains within hours of his death.

30 November. Carl Roles, ex-husband of Olivia's sister, announces he is selling memorabilia relating to George. These are items he stole from

Olivia's home in the late 1970s. In the Strawberry Fields area of Central Park in New York, fans gather and sing 'Here Comes The Sun'.

1 December. Jim Keltner reports that the album George had been working on was near completion.

2 December. Michael Abram claims that he feels guilty because his actions may have helped in causing George's death.

3 December. Olivia and Dhani hold a memorial service at a chapel in Pacific Palisades, California attended by Tom Petty and Yoko Ono.

27 December. The BBC cancels a documentary on George at the request of his family.

2002

12 January. Olivia begins a lawsuit against Carl Roles, who is attempting to sell the memorabilia he stole from her house.

14 January. 'My Sweet Lord' is re-released as a single in America. Royalties in the United States will go to the Self Realisation Fellowship and royalties from the rest of the world will go to the Material World Charitable Foundation to be distributed to various charities.

28 January. Simon & Schuster republish George's book *I. Me. Mine*.

1 February. A photographic exhibition 'George Harrison 1943–2001' opens at the Govinda Gallery in Washington DC. The tribute to George contains photographs by Harry Benson, William Coupon, Barry Feinstein, Astrid Kirchherr, Gered Mankowitz, Linda McCartney, Max Scheler, Mark Seliger, Jurgen Vollmer, Robert Whitaker and Baron Wolman. It ran until 2 March 2002.

21 February. *All Things Must Pass*, a biography of George by Marc Shapiro, is published in Britain by Virgin Books.

23 February. Radio 2 broadcast *The Inner Light*, a radio documentary featuring archive interviews with George.

1 March. The latest issue of *Guitar Player* magazine features George as a cover star with the banner 'George Harrison, The Fab Life Of Rock's Most Influential Guitarist'.

13 April. Ravi Shankar and his daughter Anoushka perform a self-written tribute to George at Carnegie Hall, New York. This is part of a tribute concert for George organised by the Rainforest Foundation and called 'Carnegie Hall Benefit Concert: Give Me Love, Give Me Peace On Earth'. A number of performers played compositions by George, including Jeff Beck, Elton John, Patti LaBelle, Smokey Robinson, Nina Simone, Sting and James Taylor. Olivia and Dhana are in attendance.

18 October. Dhani Harrison appears on *Good Morning America* to promote George's final album, *Brainwashed*.

30 October. George receives a posthumous award at the British Independent Film Awards at the Pacha Club in London for his contribution to the British film industry with HandMade Films. Olivia and Dhani pick up the award.

2 November. A *Daily Mail* feature on stars whose children bear a striking resemblance to them publishes a photo of George and Dhani to show their incredible likeness.

4 November. George's book *I. Me. Mine* is republished.

20 November. A concert at the Royal Albert Hall is organised by Olivia Harrison and Eric Clapton. Among the artists who appear are Paul McCartney, Ringo Starr, Eric Clapton, Ravi Shankar, Joe Brown, Jools Holland, Jeff Lynne, Tom Petty, Jim Keltner and members of *Monty Python*. The proceeds are in aid of the Material World Charitable Trust, which George founded in 1973. The concert was televised in the New Year.

27 November. Olivia appears on NBC Television in an interview conducted by Katie Courice. It is her first interview since George's death.

29 November. A George Harrison Flower Vigil is held at the Beatles star on the Hollywood Walk Of Fame. A tribute also takes place at the Beatles Experience in Liverpool. A George Harrison postage stamp is launched in Montevideo, Uruguay.

3 December. George's performance of 'My Sweet Lord' from *The Concert For Bangla Desh* is screened on *Top Of The Pops 2*.

2003

27 January. Olivia attends the London premiere of the film *Catch Me If You Can*.

25 April. Capitol Records announce a promo of the *Brainwashed* track 'Any Road' will include previously unreleased footage from George's life. It will be the first new George Harrison music video since 'This Is Love' from *Cloud Nine* in 1988.

Circles

A track from George's 1982 album *Gone Troppo*, lasting 3 minutes and 44 seconds. Billy Preston played organ and piano on the track and Jon Lord played synthesizer.

Clapton, Eric

The closest relationship George had with a musician friend was the one he had with Eric Clapton. It was closer even than his relationship with his fellow Beatles, although some regard it as a love-hate relationship, particularly as Eric ran off with George's wife.

He was born Eric Clapp in Ripley, Surrey on 30 March 1945. His first group was called the Roosters and he next joined Casey Jones and the Engineers. In 1963 he became a member of the Yardbirds.

Eric recalled their first meeting. 'I was in the Yardbirds, and we were playing a thing called the Beatles Show at the Hammersmith Odeon in London. The Yardbirds were at the bottom of the bill, but all of the acts in between us and the Beatles were sort of music hall, English rock-'n'roll groups. And the Yardbirds were an R&B band, or even a blues band, so there was a bit of, like, "What's this all about?" George was checking me out, and I was checking him out to see if he was a real guitar player. And I realised he was. But we come from different sides of the tracks. I grew up loving black music, and he grew up with the Carl Perkins side of things, so it was blues versus rockabilly. That rockabilly style always attracted me, but I never wanted to take it up. And I think it's the same for him. The blues scene attracted him, but it evades him somehow. He's much more comfortable with the finger-picking style of guitar.'

They had become good friends since the meeting in 1964 and George even asked Eric to come over to India and lay down some licks for his *Wonderwall* movie soundtrack. When he was in Cream, Eric asked George's help in a composition he was writing and they worked on the number 'Badge' together.

In 1969, when Blind Faith disbanded, Eric bought a home near to George and became a frequent visitor to Friar Park. When Eric became part of the Delaney And Bonnie And Friends tour, George joined him on it.

They became so close that George invited him to participate in a Beatles recording session. It was a short time before he recorded 'While My Guitar Gently Weeps'. Eric was giving George a lift in his car from Surrey when suddenly George suggested that he play on the number. Eric was amazed and reluctant to do it because no other rock musician had ever been invited to play on a Beatles recording. 'No one plays on Beatles sessions,' he said. George said, 'So what. It's my song,' and told him he wanted him to be on it. The track was to appear on *The Beatles* double album and although George had recorded several versions of the number, it was the one with Eric's impressive electric guitar solo that appeared on the album, while George and John played acoustic guitars.

When George appeared at the Prince's Trust charity concert at Wembley Stadium, Eric introduced George and Ringo on stage and joined in the performance, trading lead guitar licks on 'While My Guitar Gently Weeps'.

The two used to spend a lot of their leisure time together and in July 1969, while relaxing in Eric's garden, George wrote 'Here Comes The Sun', which was to appear on the *Abbey Road* album. George recalled, 'One day I stayed off and went to Eric's house because it's nice, with trees and things. The song came right out.'

That year Eric had paid £40,000 for Hurtwood Edge, a twenty-room mansion in Surrey that he'd seen in *Country Life* magazine. He moved in there with his sixteen-year-old girlfriend Alice Ormsby Gore, the daughter of Lord Harlech, the former British Ambassador to Washington.

It was soon after this period, in 1970, that Eric became hooked on hard drugs.

When George began to organise the Concert For Bangla Desh, he naturally invited Eric to take part in it. Eric was now a drug addict and had ceased performing the year before. However, being George's friend, he agreed to appear, although his addiction to hard drugs posed a problem.

When he travelled to New York to appear on the concert he sent Alice out on to the streets to locate heroin for him. She recalled, 'I remember when we went to New York in 1971 for George Harrison's Bangla Desh concert, I was desperately running around that city trying to score some heroin for Eric. And I remember thinking how stupid it was for me, even then. I did that for him, and for myself, for three years.'

He was terribly ill and didn't attend the rehearsals. Jesse Ed Davis was ready and prepared to take his place, but Allen Klein arranged for Dr William Zahn to treat Eric and he was able to appear on stage on the day of the concert.

Eric had also gotten Alice onto hard drugs and the two were taking so much that it was costing Eric £1,500 a week. He was having to sell off his precious guitars to pay for the drugs.

Alice and Eric were together for five years. Eric remembers, 'Three of those were spent under the influence of heroin and we never communicated at all – only to have an argument. And although we had some good times, I'd never describe it as head-over-heels love. All the time I was with Alice, I was mentally with Patti. My love for Patti began almost the first day I saw her and grew in leaps and bounds.'

When Eric began his two-month affair with Patti's sister, Alice moved out. But she and Eric were reunited in March 1970. She said, 'I was in love with him, most definitely.'

Talking about Eric's obsession with George's wife Patti, Alice said, 'When he first fell in love with Patti, he was very open to me about it, but as the years went by he was very quiet on the subject.'

When George and Patti visited Eric and Alice in Wales, Eric told both of them that he was in love with Patti and wanted her as his partner.

Eric left Alice and she was found dead in a squalid bedsit in a rundown area of Bournemouth in April 1995. A needle was stuck in her arm.

Ian Dallas, the person who had introduced Eric to Alice, had also given Eric a book by the Persian writer Nizami called *The Story Of Layla And Majnum*. It was the tale of a man who fell helplessly in love with a girl who was unavailable to him and was driven to madness. Eric identified with Majnum and wrote the song 'Layla' for Patti.

He was to say, 'Patti was just trying to get George's attention, get him jealous, and so she used me. The problem was that I soon fell madly in love with her. He'd been into meditation for so long and yet couldn't keep his wife. All she wanted was for him to say, "I love you." and all he was doing was meditating.'

George, in a 1977 *Crawdaddy* interview, said: 'We both loved Eric, still do, but there were a few funny things. I pulled *his* chick once. That's happened, and now you'd think he was trying to get his own back on me. Patti and he got together after we'd really split. And actually we'd been splitting up for years. That was a funny thing, you know. I thought that was the best thing to do, for us to split, and we should've done it much sooner. I didn't have any problems about it, Eric had the problem. Every time I'd go and see him he'd really be hung up about it, and I'd be saying, "Fuck it, man, don't be apologising," and he didn't believe me. I was saying, "I don't care."'

After Alice had left Eric, Patti went to America to see her sister Jenny in San Francisco and then travelled to Florida to join Eric, who was recording his *461 Ocean Boulevard* album. She moved in with him and travelled round America with him on his tour. She recalled, 'We were not good for each other on the road on that tour.' Yet she made the decision to leave George and live with Eric. However, both of them began to drink heavily. 'Neither of us was a support to each other,' she was to say. Although he had kicked the heroin habit, Eric had become a drunk and remained so for seven years, often drinking two bottles of brandy a day.

George and Patti were divorced on 9 June 1977 and Eric and Patti were married on 27 March 1979. George and his new love Olivia were invited to the wedding, but chose not to attend, although they did turn up to the wedding reception some weeks later on 19 March at Eric's home.

Actor John Hurt was present at Friar Park one night when George invited Eric and Patti to visit him. When they arrived, George had lain out two guitars and amplifiers and invited Eric to play along with him. The guitarists improvised for two hours and Hurt recalled, 'To start with it might have been intended as a friendly gesture or a game by George. But it certainly wasn't when they were playing. It was an extraordinary duel to witness. The air was electric. Nobody dared say anything.'

Commenting on the duel, Eric said, 'I know exactly how to play in a situation like that. If someone makes the mistake of exaggerating or being a bit too flamboyant, you win by being simple. Let them also overdo it.' He added, 'Every meeting I've had with George Harrison, on any level, has been competitive. He's the kind of person who puts you on the spot and insists on having the last word. In musical situations, he's the same. My rule is always: let your opponent make the first mistake.'

In 1980 Eric described himself as a full-blown, practising alcoholic. 'Everyone used to walk around me on eggshells, they didn't know if I was going to be angry or whatever. When I'd come back from the pub I could come back happy or I could come back and smash the place up. There were times when I just took sex with my wife by force and thought that was my entitlement.' Eric and Patti were divorced in 1988.

George, Eric and Ringo appeared in a cameo scene in the HandMade film *Water*. When George joined the all-star line-up for Carl Perkins on 21 October 1985, Eric was also one of the guests.

Early in 1991 Eric's four-year-old son Conor fell to his death from the open window of an apartment. As if to seek some consolation he suggested joining George on a tour of Japan. Eric offered to head a backup band. It was Eric's insistence that finally persuaded him. George hadn't toured since 1974. He said, 'It's a good band. It's fun to be in any band. It's fun after not doing it for so long. It was good of Eric to suggest that we do it.'

Following the Japanese tour there were rumours of a rift between George and Eric, which put paid to any possibility of a further Harrison/Clapton tour. Clapton was to comment, 'Ours is a jostling relationship. He's a year or two older than me, and because he was there first, there's a bit of a swagger that never goes away. I love him dearly, but we're always testing each other.'

George also appeared again with Eric at a charity concert in April 1992.

Cloud Nine

An album released in America on Dark Horse 1-25643 on 11 November 1987 and in Britain on Dark Horse WX 123 on the same day. It was George's first album in five years, following the disappointing sales of *Gone Troppo*. The fact that a track from the album, 'Got My Mind Set On You', had been prereleased as a single, leaping into the charts and reaching No. 2, was a positive sign.

Cloud Nine was co-produced by George and Jeff Lynne and recorded mainly at FPSHOT, with some work in Australia. George had prepared a total of seventeen new tracks for consideration and he and Jeff chose eleven tracks from these. With the exception of the cover version of Rudy Clark's 'Got My Mind Set On You', George had penned all the tracks, although 'That's What It Takes' was co-written by George, Jeff Lynne and Gary Wright.

The tracks were: Side One: 'Cloud 9', 'That's What It Takes', 'Fish In The Sand', 'Just For Today', 'This Is Love' and 'When We Was Fab'. Side Two: 'Devil's Radio' 'Someplace Else', 'Wreck Of The Hesperus', 'Breath Away From Heaven', 'Got My Mind Set On You'.

Interestingly, although the album title was *Cloud Nine*, the first track included a numeral and became 'Cloud 9'. Eric Clapton is also on the track, as is saxophonist Jim Horn. Ringo Starr appears on 'When We Was Fab'.

To promote the album George recorded a 37-minute interview at Warner Brothers Records in Burbank, California on Monday 5 October 1987.

He also discussed the album during a press conference at the Sutton Place Hotel, Toronto, Canada during his promotion of the *Cloud Nine* album. Here is a transcript:

Question: You've said that you aren't especially taken in with today's music, and that the spirit doesn't seem to be there as it was in earlier years. When you were getting ready to record *Cloud Nine*, what did you do to get away from that?

George: Well, I set out not to use drum computers and midi-keyboards for a start, because most things these days are done like that. I wanted to make records like in the past, basically, and just have things a bit more human.

Q: George, how did you and Jeff Lynne meet and come to work together on this project?

George: I thought that he'd make a good producer for me, and Dave Edmunds, who was a neighbour of mine, had worked with him before, so I asked if he ever saw Jeff to tell him I'd like to meet. That was back in about 1985. So then he came over and had dinner and we just kept in touch and by the end of '86 I said, 'Well, I'm going to make a record soon, do you want to do it?'

Q: Were you familiar with his work with the Electric Light Orchestra?

George: Oh yeah, that's why I wanted to call him up and meet him. I thought he'd be perfect for me, which he was.

Q: George, I had a dream last night that you and everybody on your new record decided to go on tour. Is there any chance that dream is going to come true?

George: Possibly. But I don't fancy being the star of the show. I wouldn't mind being a part of a show doing some of my tunes, but I wouldn't like the responsibility of being out there all on my own. If I'm going to do anything at all I had better do it pretty soon, otherwise I'll be on crutches or something.

Q: You've said that you weren't that crazy about doing a big video, but 'Got My Mind Set On You', I think, is hilarious. I wondered how much of your own sense of humour was actually a part of that, and do you feel better now about the possibility of doing more videos?

George: You mean the video where I did the back flip? Well, you know, my humour is such that I have to be able to have something funny happening around me so I can be deadpan, as I'm not really into acting. I think that works very well for me. The director was a guy called Gary Weiss, who incidentally directed *The Rutles*, so he's a very funny fellow himself. He thought of having a simple setting like that room and making it move so I could just sing straight, play straight and everything else would be the joke.

Q: What gave you the idea to do the video for 'When We was Fab'?

George: Well, basically I just thought it would be nice to write a song with the sound of the '67 to '68 period. It was just a whim, really. Especially since at that time I was with Jeff Lynne in Australia and I know how much he likes the old stuff, so I started out to write it. I didn't have any lyrics at the time, so it was tentatively called 'Aussie Fab' because it was reminiscent of the Fabs and written in Australia. So it was purely a trip down memory lane.

Q: I read where your song 'Just For Today' came to being after you saw a pamphlet from Alcoholics Anonymous, which is kind of a different way of getting a song, isn't it?

George: Well, really, if you're into the songwriting mood, then anything can trigger it. I had these three friends who were all in AA in my house one night back in 1983, and this guy showed me a brochure that was called 'Just for Today'. It seemed so nice, you know, a nice idea, to try and live through this day only. I mean, it's not just for alcoholism. It's good for everybody to remember that we can only live today and that the only thing that really exists is now. The past is gone, the future we don't know about. So it's like an extension of the 'be here now' idea. I thought it would make a nice song, so I wrote it. But it's good also for AA, I think. Maybe we could make it into a TV commercial.

Q: George, at one time you considered calling your latest album 'Fab' and then you changed it to *Cloud Nine*. Why?

George: If you know about the connotations of the past, of the sixties and the Fab Four and all those things, then it's a good little joke. But if you don't know about all that, it sounds a bit pretentious. Also, when I looked at the photograph on the album sleeve with me and all these clouds, it looked more like Cloud Nine.

Q: Now that you're a solo performer, how different is it for you?

George: Well, it's totally different, really. In those days, it was the four of us. We just went into the studios and made some records, went out on tour, then went back into the studio to make some more records. That was it, really. Nowadays, it's a big business and it has to be co-ordinated. With the Beatles, after around 1964, we just had to put the records out and people rushed out to buy them. It's not like that these days. You have to work with the record labels and co-ordinate releases and do a lot of promotion work. I'm on my own, whereas in the past I had three other smartasses with me all cracking jokes.

Q: Do you miss that?

George: I miss that side of it, yes. We used to have good fun at press conferences. They used to be really great because there would always be somebody with a wisecrack. I do miss that side of the Fab Four, I admit.

Q: George, do people treat you as some sort of religious icon these days?

George: No, not really. I think people seem to give me some respect, however, which is quite nice.

Q: The last couple of years you seem to have had some reservations about getting too involved with the record business.

George: Yeah, I got a bit tired of it back around about 1980. I just felt there was no point. The way the music was going, I couldn't relate to it. I just thought, 'Well, I've got a lot of other things to do so I might as well have a rest.' Nowadays, I never consider that I'm going to be out there with this record and people may not buy it or whatever. I didn't even think about that. I mean, if you have a flop, it's a flop. I think you have to just make something that you enjoy yourself and see what happens. And I've had enough success in my life that if I fail, it's OK.'

Q: What's more difficult, being a Beatle or an ex-Beatle?

George: I think being one was much more difficult. I mean, it was fun for a long time, but there was so much pressure on us. It became really tiresome and it was good, in a way, to dissipate that energy that there was with the four of us together. You know, let it go away so that we could have some semblance of a life. Otherwise, it would have just been madness continually.

Q: Has your attitude about today's music changed?

George: Yeah. I think the main reason for the problem, you know, was the recession. It went through all kinds of businesses, through radio, the music industry, and people didn't seem to know what was happening. They were confused about what was supposed to be good. I think they lost all direction, and I just didn't want to be a part of that. Maybe the only change was that I've changed, and I just felt it would be fun to do an album and see what happens.

Q: Do you hear anything today that you like, any artists that capture your imagination?

George: Bob Dylan. I do, but unfortunately not so much in pop music or top forty. My favourite music at the moment is this Bulgarian choir. It's called the 'Mysterious Voices Of Bulgaria' and it's the most brilliant vocals, it's quite beautiful.

Q: How did you get involved with *Monty Python* in the first place?

George: Well, I've just been friendly with them for a long time and when they were beginning *The Life Of Brian* the original film company backed out as they were right into preproduction. A friend of mine asked if I could think of any way to help. I asked my business manager and he thought about it for a few days, then he came back and said, 'Yeah, OK, we'll be the producers.' So we borrowed the money from the bank and formed HandMade Films. I did it because I wanted to see the film. I couldn't stand the idea of it never being made.

Q: Could you tell me what a typical day in the life of George Harrison is like?

George: It's different all the time. Like last week I've just been getting up, going for a run around my garden, eat a bowl of Scott's porridge oats, and then right into the recording studio. Go out for dinner, finished off what I was doing, and going to bed. That kind of thing. Or get up, go to London to the office. Varied things, you know. There's no typical day, really. Get on the Concorde and fly to New York!

Q: Paul McCartney is currently working with Elvis Costello. When I heard the news I was very surprised and I thought, what a combination, to have the intelligence of a Costello with a great pop songwriter like McCartney. Do you think that Paul was in a bit of a rut and was looking for someone, I dare say, to work with similar to John Lennon?

George: I wouldn't say that Elvis Costello is like John Lennon at all. Personally, I don't think he is. I don't think he even comes close, anywhere near John. I mean, Elvis Costello is pretty good, but . . .

Q: I just meant that he was a very thoughtful writer.

George: Well, he wears glasses! But I think Paul definitely was in a rut. In a 'Rutle'. And yeah, I think it's good. He should work with various people and hopefully he'll find somebody who will actually tell him something because most people who work with Paul are afraid to say anything to him. And I think that's no good. You need to have somebody you can work with who'll tell you you're no good when you're no good. Otherwise, it's no help at all. So I look forward to hearing what they come up with. It may be good, I don't know.

Q: That brings us to the inevitable question. I read something a couple of weeks ago where you said that there was a possibility that you, Paul and Ringo might do some work together.

George: Yeah, well, Paul has asked, you know. Suggested maybe the chance of me and him writing something together and, I mean, it's pretty funny really because I've only been there about thirty years in Paul's life and now he wants to write with me. But I think it's maybe quite interesting sometime to do that. For the last few years I've spoken my mind to him. Whenever I felt something, like *Broad Street*, which I thought was a big mistake. Not making the film, because I quite enjoyed it myself, but the idea of trying to write and do everything yourself. That's the mistake. I think the only barrier between us now is our astrological signs. Some of the time we get on pretty well and the rest of the time I find that I don't really have anything in common with him.

Q: Does that surprise you, after all these years together?

George: Well, I think if you have a relationship with somebody else, you have to be able to trust each other, and to do that you have to be able to talk to each other straight. The thing with Paul is one minute he says one thing and he's really charming, and the next minute, you know, he's all uptight. Now we all go through that, good and bad stuff, but I think by now that we've got to find somewhere in the centre. Anyway, he's getting better. *Broad Street*, I think, humbled him a bit. You know, he's going to be OK.

Q: What about pop's so-called new social conscience?

George: I haven't heard it yet.

Q: Like Live Aid . . .

George: Oh, yeah, well all that's good. I like anything like that. Sometimes I feel it's a shame that it's down to musicians to go around saving the world, however. I think some of the politicians should get their fingers out occasionally.

Q: Could you tell us about your son, Dhani? Is he a budding musician?

George: Yeah, he's nine and a half and he's got a pretty good ear for music. He enjoys all kinds of music. From Mozart to Ravi Shankar to Little Richard and Chuck Berry. He's playing the piano a little bit and I think he's going to be OK. I'm not saying that's what he's going to be in his life, but he's hopefully got a good musical ability for his age.

Q: Does he understand that his father was a Beatle?

George: Now he does. You can't turn on the television without seeing something to do with the Beatles, can you? As I was just saying to somebody earlier, kids pick up on the Beatles through the old movie *Yellow Submarine*. See, I made a point of not saying anything about them to him. But by the time he was five he wanted to know how the piano part of 'Hey Bulldog' went, which completely threw me because I didn't understand where he'd heard a song like that. I haven't heard that myself really. Then I realised it was in *Yellow Submarine*.

Q: If you did go on tour, how much of a consideration would your feelings about being out in public bother you?

George: I'm not really worried about being in public. I'm not crazy about being in crowds, though. This is even just walking in an airport or being in a football match or something. It's nothing to do with people looking at me or threatening me. I just don't like crowds. I don't like traffic jams either. I don't like that situation. I prefer peace and quiet. But I don't really worry about anything like that. The only time is if you get a mob of people who know you're going to be somewhere. I mean, there's always fanatics at rock concerts. But to do a tour wouldn't be any trouble because you have all the security and you know the way in and the way out and it's no bother, really. I don't fear for my life like some people try to suggest. They've said, since John Lennon got killed, I would go and hide and I've had a big fence put around my property. I had a fence around my property back in 1965, so there's no change, really.

Q: So you don't have any bodyguards?

George: No. Absolutely, on my honour. I don't even have a roadie!

Q: When you have jam sessions at your home studio, do you do Beatle tunes and do you remember all the words?

George: No, I don't know *any* of the words. Occasionally I can remember one or two, but we don't do Beatle tunes. More likely to do Everly Brothers or Chuck Berry tunes.

Q: You've proven yourself to be an astute businessman away from the music business. Do you feel that you have rounded out your life more at this point in your career? Do you feel satisfied with what you've done?

George: Having done the film company and the various things we're talking about, I think they impress everybody else more, so their *concept of me* is now more rounded out. They all think, 'He's smarter than we thought,' but it doesn't impress me.

Q: I'd like to know about your religious philosophy. Are you still promoting it or do you keep it to yourself these days?

George: Well, I keep it to myself unless somebody asks me about it. But I still feel the same as I felt back in the sixties. I lost touch with the Krishnas when Prabhupada died, maybe ten years ago or something. I know one or two of them, but I don't really hang out with them anymore. I used to go and see the old master, you know, A.C. Bhaktivedanta, quite a lot. He was real good. I'm still involved but it's something which is more like a thing you do inside yourself. You don't actually do it in the road. It's a way of just trying to get in touch with yourself. I still write songs with it in there in little bits and pieces, but lots of songs that are unfinished say various things but maybe I say it in different ways now. There's a song on this album which is straight out of Yogananda, 'Fish On The Sand' it's called.

Q: Do you think that you were underused during the Beatle years?

George: Yeah, possibly, but the Beatle producer, George Martin, said recently how he always felt sorry because he concentrated more on them and he should have paid more attention to me. He said, 'I hope you'll forgive me.' But I'm quite happy with my role in the Beatles. You know, it split up because of all those problems, there were too many songs. Because we got too close to each other, but I'm quite happy with the way things went. I feel that whatever I am now, I always have been that, you know. Maybe different things have taken longer to reach the surface or whatever, but I'm who I am and I am not really that much different to how I was then. Maybe I'm more able to express it or maybe people are more interested now in what I have to say. Because in the sixties and the early seventies they thought I was a loony. Because I just went to India, did all that bit.

Q: George, you seem like such a modest person despite the incredible events of your life.

George: I'm not a fanatical person. About astrology or anything, really. I don't want you to get me wrong, but I'm a Pisces, and Pisces is like that. One half going where the other half's just been. I tend to be more withdrawn or whatever. If you look at Pisces, they're the spiritual ones who often get pushed around, but these days it's really mostly clear sailing.

Concert For Bangla Desh, The

In March 1971, following political problems and strife between the various regions in Bangla Desh, in the eastern half of Pakistan, Pakistan's ruling general sent in the army to deal with any opposition. Then, in December 1971, a cyclone swept across the region, causing immense devastation.

There was a complete breakdown throughout the country with no clean water, no food, no adequate shelter and, in addition to the fear of military suppression, hunger and disease were rife in the country.

Ravi Shankar had family and friends in Bangla Desh and was aware of the intense suffering of the people there.

In June 1971, while in Los Angeles, he decided to try to raise some money, perhaps a few thousand dollars, to help the people of Bangla Desh. At the time he was completing the film *Messenger From The East* with George and he asked George if he would help him with a benefit show, perhaps acting as a compere for the night.

Ravi gave George some magazines with articles about the famine and George decided that a small-scale concert wasn't good enough. As he was to remark later, 'The Beatles had been trained to the view that if you're going to do it, you might as well do it big.'

George approached Allen Klein and instructed him to book the 20,000-seater Madison Square Garden in New York. As soon as news of the concert was announced, the seats sold out and a further show was arranged for the same night, Sunday 1 August, which also sold out almost immediately. Both shows had sold out within six hours.

George also contacted Apple's A&R head, Phil Spector, with instructions to record the concert and he approached Apple Films to document the event.

A number of George's immediate musician friends became involved

– Badfinger, Billy Preston, Jesse Ed Davis, Carl Radle, Klaus Voormann and Jim Keltner.

The most obvious musicians who would attract the most spectacular publicity were clearly the ex-Beatles. Realising that there could be no agreement for the four Beatles to perform together again as the Beatles due to the court case which Paul had brought to dissolve the group, George believed that they could still appear, performing individual solo spots.

He immediately contacted Ringo, who took time off from filming the Western *Blindman* to travel to New York for rehearsals. John and Yoko had been planning to travel to New York to complete their recording of an album in July, so John agreed to appear. Even Paul gave a tentative approval of the project and seemed willing to appear. However, it seems that he wanted some of the different business difficulties resolved first, which couldn't be done at the time, so he pulled out.

When John arrived with the omnipresent Yoko, George had to explain that he only wanted John to appear on the show and not Yoko. She was furious and created such a violent argument that John's glasses were broken. John was so upset he immediately left and took the first plane to Europe, ending up in Paris!

It's a pity that posterity was denied John's appearance at this highly important concert due to Yoko's determination to cling like a limpet to everything John did, proving that he was unable to carry on a solo career like the other ex-members as Yoko insisted on being involved in all his records and concerts.

Leon Russell agreed to appear – as did Bob Dylan.

Dylan's appearance was kept secret until he actually walked on stage, which created an absolute sensation, as everyone had believed he'd retired from the music scene.

This coup hadn't been easy for George to arrange as Dylan had been missing rehearsals, then phoning George to say he couldn't handle the pressure and wouldn't appear after all.

George also had difficulties regarding Eric Clapton's participation. Like Dylan, Clapton hadn't made any appearances for a year and he was hooked on drugs. In fact, as soon as he arrived in New York he sent his girlfriend Alice Ormsby-Gore out onto the streets to score some heroin for him. He was so ill he was unable to attend rehearsals the night before the concert and Jesse Ed Davis was on stand-by as his replacement.

Fortunately, both Dylan (George was on tenterhooks because even at the start of the concert he wasn't sure whether Dylan would turn up) and Clapton (who had treatment by Doctor William Zahm earlier that day) were able to perform.

The concert began with George introducing Ravi Shankar for a set of Indian music. Ravi played sitar and his other musicians were Ali Akbar

Khan on sarod, Alla Rakah on tabla and Kamala Chakravarty on tamboura.

The next to appear was George, who opened his set with 'Wah-Wah'. His backing musicians were Eric Clapton on guitar, Ringo Starr and Jim Keltner on drums, Leon Russell on piano, Billy Preston on keyboards, Jesse Ed Davis on electric guitar, Jim Horn leading a brass section, Klaus Voormann on bass, Claudia Linnear leading a nine-piece gospel choral and three members of Badfinger on acoustic guitars.

They performed 'My Sweet Lord', 'Awaiting On You All', 'Beware Of Darkness', 'That's The Way God Planned It' (a Billy Preston show-piece), 'It Don't Come Easy' (a Ringo Starr showpiece), 'While My Guitar Gently Weeps' (with Eric Clapton's classic solo), 'Something' and 'Here Comes The Sun'.

George then introduced Dylan, saying, 'I'd like to bring on a friend of us all – Mister Bob Dylan.'

A bearded Dylan, dressed in denim jacket and jeans, opened with 'A Hard Rain's Gonna Fall'. He next performed 'Mr Tambourine Man', 'Blowin' In The Wind', 'It Takes A Lot To Laugh, It Takes A Train To Cry' and 'Just Like A Woman'.

On the last number he was joined by George on guitar, Ringo on tambourine and Leon Russell on bass.

Following the two shows there was a celebration party. The following morning, when George read the positive reviews in the local papers, he sat down and wrote the song 'The Day The World Gets 'Round'.

The full listing of artists was: Rock performers: George Harrison, Eric Clapton, Jesse Ed Davis and Don Preston on guitars; Pete Ham, Tom Evans and Joey Molland of Badfinger on acoustic guitars; Mike Gibbins of Badfinger on percussion; Billy Preston on organ; Leon Russell on piano and bass; Carl Radle and Klaus Voormann on bass; Ringo Starr on drums and tambourine; Jim Keltner on drums; Bob Dylan on harmonica and acoustic guitar; Jim Horn, Chuck Findley and Ollie Mitchell on horns; George Harrison, Billy Preston, Ringo Starr, Leon Russell, Don Preston and Bob Dylan on vocals; Alan Beutler, Marlin Green, Jeanie Green, Jo Green, Dolores Hall, Jackie Kelso, Claudia Linnear, Lou McCreary and Don Nix on backing vocals. Indian music section: Ravi Shankar on sitar, Ali Akbar Khan on sarod, Alla Rakah on tabla and Kamala Chakravarty on tamboura.

A particularly disappointing aspect was that although all the artists were donating their services to aid the poor and starving people of Bangla Desh, the tax inspectors of both Britain and America wanted their pound of flesh. They demanded the full tax from all the proceedings, uninterested in the fact that this was literally taking the food out of the mouths of a starved and battered people. The idealistic George was disillusioned by this intransigence from the tax authorities, but he signed a personal cheque to cover the demands.

The concert itself brought in a quarter of a million dollars and the album and film generated millions, yet there seemed to be some problems regarding these funds. An article in *New York* magazine implied that Allen Klein had absconded with some of the money and Klein responded with a multi-million-dollar lawsuit, which he then dropped. There was a lot of red tape involved before the people of Bangla Desh began to receive the money.

The Concert For Bangla Desh (it was spelt as two words on the concert, album and film, although the name was to become a single word) was the template for all the great charity rock shows to follow, such as Live Aid. Considering the impact and influence of the event, and also all the other charity work George was involved with, it's difficult to equate the fact that he was never recommended for any honours apart from his MBE, the lowest order of knighthood. Bob Geldof, for instance, received a knighthood for Live Aid and comedians, pop singers and numerous other people in the music business have been awarded CBEs, OBEs and even knighthoods, but George, a vital member of the most celebrated music group of all time, a great charity donor, someone who has brought prestige and honour to Britain, in addition to the wealth, plus the fact that he virtually revived the British film industry with HandMade Films, was never considered for anything following the 1966 MBE honour, which shows the lack of foresight of those who recommend the awards.

Recalling the event, George was to say, 'The Concert For Bangla Desh' happened because of my relationship with Ravi. He is such a humble person. He said, "I am going to do this show. Maybe, if you or Peter Sellers or both of you can come on and do something or announce something, maybe we can make $25,000 and do something about this terrible war."

'I said, "If you want me to be involved, I think I'd better be really involved," so I started recruiting all these people. It was difficult at first, but once it got closer to the show I had commitments from so many people that some had to be turned down.

'Everybody wanted to be in it.

'Mainly the concert was to attract attention to the situation that was happening at one time. The money we raised was secondary, and although we had some problems because Allen Klein had not been handling it right, they still got plenty of money, even though it was a drop in the ocean. The main thing was, we spread the word and helped get the war ended. Little Bengali waiters in Indian restaurants still come up to me and say, "When we were fighting in the jungle, it was so great to know there was someone out there supporting us."

'The Concert for Bangladesh was just a moral stance. These kinds of things have grown over the years, but what we did showed that musicians and people are more humane than politicians. Today people accept the commitment rock'n'roll musicians have when they perform for a charity. When I did it, they said things like, "He's only doing this to be nice."'

Concert For Bangla Desh (album)

George asked Phil Spector to record the concert and Spector brought in a 16-track mobile unit and placed 44 microphones around the hall.

The album was issued in America on Monday 20 December 1971 and in Britain on 10 January 1972. There had been arguments between George and Capitol Records as the company had originally refused to release the album unless they received some financial recompense. George pointed out that Phil Spector had mixed the album at no cost and that Apple had supplied the booklet and album at no cost and that other record companies had allowed their artists to appear on the album. He felt that Capitol had to give something and threatened to take the album to CBS if they didn't. His arguments paid off and Capitol gave an advance payment of $3,750,000.

Record One, Side One: Introductions by George Harrison and Ravi Shankar, 'Bangla Dhun'. Record One, Side Two: 'Wah-Wah', 'My Sweet Lord', 'Awaiting On You All', 'That's The Way God Planned It'. Record Two, Side One: 'It Don't Come Easy', 'Beware Of Darkness', Introduction of the band by George, 'While My Guitar Gently Weeps'. Record Two, Side Two: 'Jumpin' Jack Flash'/'Youngblood', 'Here Comes The Sun'. Record Three, Side One: 'A Hard Rain's Gonna Fall', 'It Takes A Lot To Laugh, It Takes A Train To Cry', 'Blowin' In The Wind', 'Mr Tambourine Man', 'Just Like A Woman'. Record Three, Side Two: 'Something', 'Bangla Desh'.

On 1 August 1991, the twentieth anniversary of the concert, George was able to discuss it at a press call at Capitol Records headquarters in Los Angeles to promote the re-release of the album on CD (Capitol/Apple CDP 7 93265 2):

Q: Have you kept up with the events in Bangladesh over the years?

George: Only inasmuch as probably most other people would by seeing it in the newspapers or on the television news. And there's been plenty of that recently.

Q: How will Bangladesh benefit from the new CD release of *Concert For Bangla Desh*?

George: Well, inasmuch as the portion of the money, I'm not exactly sure at this stage exactly how much of the cost of the record goes to the UNICEF fund, but through UNICEF they will have the money that this record makes as did the old film and the original record. And they will benefit inasmuch as, I think it's only really for the children of Bangladesh, unfortunately, but that was how it was prescribed back twenty years ago, so it's through medical aid and food and suchlike for the children there.

Q: What were the most memorable moments about the Concert For Bangla Desh?

George: I think the most memorable thing, really, was the fact that it came off and that it worked, because there was very little time preceding the concert to organise it. The concert happened to be on August the first because that was the only day Madison Square Garden was available, so it's pure coincidence. And all the people that were assembled with very short notice or very little rehearsal – some cases there was no rehearsal. I managed to do a little bit with the horn players and with the rhythm section, but that was the main thing, that it actually worked.

Q: How did you assemble the band?

George: It was a question of phoning, really, just the friends that I knew and see who was available to turn up . . . so telephone calls, really. I spent one month, I think the month of June into half of July, just telephoning people. So that's how it happened.

Q: What do you think were the concert's short-term benefits?

George: Well, the main objective at that point in time for the concert was not so much to try and raise a lot of money, I mean, that was a secondary kind of thing. The most important thing was to point out the fact that, at that stage, Pakistan was having a war with Bengal and that these people were getting killed and wiped out. And there were a lot of countries supporting Pakistan with armaments and stuff. And that, really, was to bring world attention to the fact that the Bengalis were being treated very poorly and then, secondly maybe, to raise people's awareness and hopefully get some money that may help in some way, that situation.

Q: What were the concert's long-term benefits?

George: Well, the same as the short-term benefits, really. To make people aware of what was happening and to try to change that situation that was going on, the politics of that situation, and then bring some kind of aid to the people who were suffering.

Q: How much money was raised for the children of Bangladesh?

George: Well, to date, $13.5 million have come directly from the concert and from the record and film that was our original twenty years ago. I know that isn't very much these days – $13.5 million is very little compared to some of these things like Band Aid and stuff. But you have to remember, that was at a time when nobody was really aware of this kind of benefit concert, certainly there hadn't been anything like that, and of course, $13.5 million back then was probably much more than it's worth now. But, hopefully, this CD coming out has the ability to maybe make another $5–10 million, who knows . . . if you all go out and buy it.

Concert For Bangla Desh (film)

In addition to the album, a CBS TV broadcast of the Bangla Desh concert took place and a film was also made, directed by Paul Swimmer and distributed by 20th Century Fox. This was premiered the following year on 23 March 1972 in New York. This version was in 70mm film with six-track sound. George had worked with the director on the film, putting together the best excerpts from both shows.

Discussing the film, George said, 'I put all the expense to Apple at the time, and the only way Apple could break even was if the film came out any good. And the film wasn't that good! The cameramen were crazy and it took Dylan and I months to try to make it into something decent.

'All the cameras had cables hanging in front of them, and another camera was out of focus all the way through so we couldn't use that one. The film finally shows what the concert was about. I said to the artists, "Look, we are recording and filming it, but if it turns out lousy, I promise you we are not going to put it out. I want you to see it and hopefully you will agree to let us do it."

'Bob came down to the editing of the film, but he didn't really want to, I mean if you look at Bob's section, there is one single camera shot all the way through. Which, in a way, you can get into. It is funny, once you realise it is not changing camera angles and it is all grainy. But that was because Bob wanted it like that, he's a bit of a funny little fellow! But he wanted it like that, so I am not going to argue. It was great to have him in it at all.'

The film received a special preview screening at the Rialto Cinema, Coventry Street, London on Wednesday 26 July 1972 and opened to the public the following day.

One disappointment was the fact that while all the artists concerned were happy to perform without a fee for such a deserving cause, and also to waive any payment for the use of their performances on film and on the soundtrack album, the record companies concerned weren't so generous. At first Capitol Records refused to distribute the album unless they received some financial reward from it. George threatened to take it to CBS if Capitol didn't give way. Capitol eventually released it and paid an advance payment on sales to Apple of $3,750,000.

Concert For George, The

A tribute concert, with profits in aid of the Material World Charitable Foundation, that took place at the Royal Albert Hall on Friday 29 November 2002 on the first anniversary of George's death. It was organised by Olivia Harrison and Eric Clapton and Olivia was to say, 'The tribute for George will resound not only within the Albert Hall but will hopefully reach the spirit of the man who was so loved by his friends who will be performing and attending.'

On stage George's 12-string Rickenbacker was propped up on a stand. Eric Clapton then announced that the first half of the concert would comprise traditional Indian music, followed by Western music in the second.

Ravi Shankar and his daughter Anoushka began the Indian section with a prayer, with Jeff Lynne taking over on vocals for 'The Inner Light', which was followed by 'Jairaj', a piece written for George by Ravi. As he'd written in the programme: 'George was like a son to me and my Indian name for him was "Jairaj". This is a song for my dear George. George loved Krishna, whose name was also Hari.' Anoushka then continued her performance with Ravi and Olivia sitting by the side of the stage. The first half was completed by a medley of Indian classical and folk music.

Opening the second half were the members of *Monty Python's Flying Circus*, with the exception of John Cleese, who performed 'Sit On My Face (And Tell Me That You Love Me)', followed by 'The Lumberjack Song' – George had produced their record of the number.

Various artists then performed some of George's memorable compositions: 'I Want To Tell You', Jeff Lynne; 'If I Needed Someone', Eric Clapton and Jeff Lynne; 'Old Brown Shoe', Eric Clapton and Gary Brooker; 'Give Me Love (Give Me Peace On Earth)', Jeff Lynne; 'Beware Of Darkness', Eric Clapton; 'Here Comes The Sun', Joe Brown; 'That's The Way It Goes', Joe Brown; 'A Horse To Water', Sam Brown and Jools Holland; 'Taxman', Tom Petty & the Heartbreakers; 'I Need You', Tom Petty & the Heartbreakers; 'Handle With Care', Tom Petty and Jeff Lynne; 'Isn't It A Pity', Eric Clapton and Billy Preston; 'Photograph', Ringo Starr; 'Honey Don't', Ringo Starr; 'For You Blue', Paul McCartney; 'Something', Eric Clapton and Paul McCartney; 'All Things Must Pass', Paul McCartney; 'While My Guitar Gently Weeps', Eric Clapton; 'My Sweet Lord', Billy Preston; 'Wah Wah', Eric Clapton and Jeff Lynne; 'I'll See You In My Dreams', Joe Brown and all the other performers.

George's son Dhani had been on stage throughout the concert playing one of his father's acoustic guitars. Olivia told Paul McCartney: 'Seeing Dhani up there on stage with you all makes it look like George stayed young and you all got old!'

Concert For George Harrison, The

A tribute concert held at the Empire Theatre, Liverpool on 24 February 2002.

It was a joint promotion between Liverpool Council, *Liverpool Echo*, Radio City, Radio Merseyside and Cavern City Tours, with the proceeds being donated to cancer charities.

Among the artists who appeared were Chris De Burgh, Ian Gillan, Steve Harley, Jools Holland, Paul Weller and Richard Ashcroft.

Mike Storey, leader of Liverpool council was to say, 'When George Harrison died Liverpool lost one of its most talented musicians. He was one of the most influential figures in the music industry over the past forty years, both through his work with the Beatles and then later as a solo writer, performer and successful film maker.

'He was also a great ambassador for the city and popular culture. A true man of peace whose life was summed up by his final words, which were to 'love one another'. Everything will go to charities and not a penny will go on administration costs or bureaucracy, so this community concert will make a real difference to a really worthy cause. I am sure George would have approved.'

Paul McCartney was a surprise guest and said, 'I thought I should just come on and say how much George would have loved this.' He then talked about his early friendship with George and announced, 'This is for George,' before singing an a cappella 'Yesterday' in which he altered the lyrics to 'Why *he* had to go, I don't know, *he* wouldn't say.'

Olivia and Dhani said they were touched by the idea of the concert.

Cooper, Ray

A noted percussionist, born in Hertfordshire in 1947 and raised in London.

He studied classical piano for twelve years, but then decided to become a percussionist and found fame as an in-demand session musician, contributing to albums by numerous major artists including the Beatles, the Rolling Stones, Elton John and Harry Nilsson.

Cooper worked frequently with George and performed on the *Concert For Bangla Desh*. He was a member of the Singing Rebel Band, along with George, in the HandMade film *Water*. He appeared on the albums *George Harrison*, *Somewhere In England*, *Cloud Nine* and *Live In Japan*, also co-producing the first with George. He also appeared with George on the TV special *Carl Perkins & Friends* and, following George's death, was one of the musicians who appeared in 'The Concert For George' on 29 November 2002.

Countdown

A Dutch television series. George flew out to Holland on Monday 22 February 1988 and recorded for the programme at the Con Cordia TV Studios in Bussum. It was transmitted on Wednesday 24 February 1988. George introduced promotional videos of 'Got My Mind Set On You' and 'When We Was Fab'. He also read out the current Dutch Top 10. His appearance lasted nineteen minutes.

Crackerbox Palace

A track on the 1976 album *Thirty Three & 1/3* lasting 3 minutes and 55 seconds.

It wasn't issued as a single in Britain but it was released in America on Dark Horse DRC 8313 on 25 January 1977, with 'Learning How To Love You' on the flip. This was the second time George had used the number as a B side as it had previously appeared as the flip of 'This Song'.

George recalled, 'In the song when I say I met someone called Mr Grief, it isn't just a clever rhyme with *life* as most people would think. There is a real person, and I met him in southern France. He was talking to me, and the way he was talking really struck me. So I told him, "I don't know if this is an insult or not, but you remind me of Lord Buckley. He's my favourite comedian." He's dead now, but he was one of the first real hip comics. And the guy nearly fell over. He said, "Hey, I managed him for eighteen years!"

'So we were talking about Lord Buckley, and Mr Grief said he lived in a little shack, which he called Crackerbox Palace, because with Lord Buckley everything was "Milord, Milady and gentlemen and the Royal Court," everything was beautiful and "up" and everybody was royal with Buckley. And so he lived in this little place Crackerbox Palace. I loved it and I just wrote on the back of my cigarette packet "Crackerbox Palace". I loved it, just the way it sounded. I loved the whole idea of it, so I wrote a song and turned it from that shack into a phrase for the physical world. The world is very serious and at times such a very sad place. But at the same time, it's such a joke. It's *all* Crackerbox Palace.'

A promo for the film was shot at Friar Park with Eric Idle directing.

Cry For A Shadow

The only original Beatles composition the group recorded at their Bert Kaempfert sessions as a backing band to Tony Sheridan in May 1961.

George had originally composed the instrumental when Liverpool singer Rory Storm challenged him to write a Shadows-style number. The working title was 'Beatle Bop'.

After recording some numbers backing Sheridan, the Beatles asked Kaempfert if they could record a few numbers on their own, which included 'Ain't She Sweet'. When asked if they had any original compositions, they played numbers written by John and Paul, but Kaempfert decided on recording George's instrumental instead, which became the first Beatles composition to be recorded professionally. It was also issued on a French EP on April 1962, along with 'Why (Can't You Love Me Again)', 'My Bonnie' and 'The Saints'. The EP was also issued in Spain and Argentina later that year.

It was issued as a single in Germany and news of its recording originally appeared on the cover of *Mersey Beat* issue No. 2 in July 1961.

The single 'Cry For A Shadow' c/w 'Why' was also released in America on MGM K 13227 on 27 March 1964 and was included on the Beatles *Anthology 1* CDs.

Dark Horse (album)

An album recorded and produced at George's home recording studio FPSHOT and A&M Studios in Los Angeles between September and October 1974.

It was issued in America on Apple SMAS 3418 on 9 December 1974 and reached No. 4 in the *Billboard* charts. It was issued in Britain on Apple PAS 10008 on 20 December 1974 but failed to make any impact on the British charts.

George had hastened the production of the album in order to have it released in time for his upcoming American tour in November and December of that year. Unfortunately, at the time he was suffering from laryngitis, a fact that is apparent on some of the tracks.

During the recording, George used a large and various gathering of musicians. They were: Ruben Ford, a guitarist on the tracks 'Hari's On Tour', 'Simply Shady' and 'Dark Horse'; Eric Clapton, guitarist on 'Bye Bye Love'; Mick Jones, guitarist on 'Ding Dong'; Alvin Lee, guitarist on 'Ding Dong'; Ron Wood, guitarist on 'Ding Dong'; Max Bennett, bass on 'Hari's On Tour'; Willie Weeks, bass on 'So Sad', 'Maya Love', 'Dark Horse', 'Far East Man' and 'It Is He'; Klaus Voormann, bass on 'Ding Dong'; John Guerin, drums on 'Hari's On Tour' and 'Simply Shady'; Ringo Starr, drums on 'So Sad' and 'Ding Dong'; Jim Keltner, drums on 'So Sad' and 'Ding Dong' and hi-hat on 'Dark Horse'; Andy Newmark, drums on 'Maya Love', 'Dark Horse', 'Far East Man' and 'It Is He'; Roger Kennaway, piano on 'Hari's On Tour' and 'Simply Shady'; Nicky Hopkins, piano on 'So Sad'; Billy Preston, piano on 'Maya Love', 'Dark Horse' and 'Far East Man'; Chuck Findlay, Jim Horn and Tom Scott, flutes on 'Dark Horse' and 'It Is He'; Emil Richards, wobble board on 'It Is He' and crochet on 'Dark Horse'.

Backing vocals were by Patti Harrison on 'Bye Bye Love' and Lon and Derrek Van Eaton on 'Dark Horse'.

The gatefold was designed by Tom Wilkes and featured photography by Terry Doran.

The tracks were: Side One: 'Hari's On Tour (Express)', 'Simply Shady', 'So Sad', 'Bye Bye Love', 'Maya Love'. Side Two: 'Ding Dong', 'Dark Horse', 'Far East Man', 'It Is He'.

EMI decided to re-release it on a budget label and it was issued in Britain on Music For Pleasure MFP 50510 on 27 November 1980. It was also re-released in America on Capitol SN-16055 in October 1980.

Dark Horse (single)

A single lasting 3 minutes and 51 seconds that was issued in Britain on Apple R 6001 on 28 February 1975 with 'Hari's On Tour (Express)' on the flip. It was issued in America on Apple 1877 on 18 November 1974. The flipside was 'I Don't Care Anymore'. The American single reached No. 15 in the charts, but the British single made no impact.

Dark Horse Radio Special

A 12″ promotional record released in 1974. George had formed his own label, Dark Horse Records Ltd, that year. The first two acts he signed were Ravi Shankar and Splinter. George produced the first two albums on the label, Splinter's *The Place I Love* on which George performed on every track, and *Shankar, Family & Friends* on which both George and Ringo performed.

In order to promote the albums and the new label, George had an interview recorded with DJ Nicky Horne, which was distributed to radio stations under the title 'Dark Horse Radio Special'.

It also included excerpts from the two albums.

Horne asked George: 'I'd like to talk about the Dark Horse label and Splinter, and of course, Ravi Shankar. How did you get the label together in the first place? Why didn't you go through Apple?'

George told him, 'Because, as Newton said, "All Apples must fall." I mean, Apple was just going through such chaos, from a business point of view anyway, and at that time John and Paul really didn't want to know. They were getting ready to sweep Apple Records underneath the carpet. And Ringo and I were planning to try and keep it going and there was so much problem just from old contracts that it seemed simpler just to start afresh.'

Horne said, 'Splinter were discovered by the loveable Mal Evans, weren't they?'

'You could say that,' answered George. 'They were in a band years ago called Half-Breed and Mal Evans, who's been with the Beatles for years, brought a tape and tried to get them on Apple. I remember listening and saying, "Well, that's not bad you know, I don't think it's that good." He said, "Well, just listen. It's the singer really."

'So we didn't do anything with him but when John Lennon made a record to help in *Oz*'s defence, the *Oz* people couldn't sing so good so he got Bill Elliott to sing. They split up from that band and then about a year ago I was making a film called *Little Malcolm And His Struggle Against The Eunuchs*. And in this film we needed somebody in a nightclub scene, just in the background. So Mal Evans brought along those two guys and they did this song, which really fitted well.

'The film is not the sort of film that's easy to sell, so I thought, if I can make a hit then maybe the film people would be more interested in the movie. Then I heard the rest of the songs and they were so good I got involved in making the album. And the song from *Little Malcolm* still isn't out yet because we did too many songs.'

Horne asked, 'Is the film actually going to be released now?'

George replied, 'Yes, it's fantastic. It doesn't have distribution at the moment, but we put it in the Berlin Film Festival and it won a silver award. John Hurt, the actor who plays the part of Little Malcolm, won the award and I just found out yesterday that we won the golden award at the Atlanta Film Festival.'

Horne continued, 'You produced the album, and most of it was recorded in your home studio, wasn't it?'

George said, 'It was recorded in David Niven's fridge actually, at Henley-on-Thames! No, we built a little studio at home to save the drive up and down the M4, and the studio is really very nice, a little plug for Eddy Veal of AudioTec, 'cause he did a fantastic job and it sounds really nice.

'I learned from John Lennon's studio when he built an eight-track in Ascot, which this guy Eddy had worked on. After the studio got going, John recorded the *Imagine* album there, and when he started recording he found that there were certain things about it. He started off just wanting a simple little eight-track studio, but actually, when we got down to it, it was with Phil Spector. He wanted tape echo on everything, 49 guitar players, and there just weren't enough facilities. In normal studios you ask the engineer, "Well, I want to do this," and in EMI they'd phone up some guy and he'd come in in a white coat about eight hours later pushing a trolley and it's all a big deal. So I wanted that built-in as standard equipment. Consequently the studio at Henley is five years ahead of all the studios in London.'

Horne then asked, 'Going back to Splinter, lots of famous musos played on it. They had a lot of help . . .'

George said, 'Not really, I mean . . .'

Horne interrupted, 'Klaus Voormann . . .'

George said, 'Well, yes, but everybody I know is famous. I don't know anybody who isn't famous so it's not really that we're putting famous people on, it's just that my friends . . .'

Horne interjected, 'The best.'

George continued, 'In some way. And even if they were un-famous when I first met them, like Klaus Voormann, nobody had ever heard of him, but now he's famous.'

Horne said, 'George, I'd like to bring in one point – that obviously I've never met you before and the image that I had of you by reading all the pop papers, and all the things about you, that you were terribly into mysticism and pretty far out and all that.'

George said, 'Misrepresentation, you see.'

Horne continued, 'You're very down to earth now that we actually meet.'

George said, 'I'm very practical.'

Horne mentioned, 'The press paint a very different picture of you.'

George said, 'Yes, because the press are such dummies, generally speaking. I mean, there are some great writers and great articles in papers and they in some way do a useful job. Their whole thing is to just sell a paper with some stupid headline, so they tend to misrepresent what's happening. My image has come across like I'm some weird old mystical ex-Beatle, the gentle giant of pop. You know. What's all that? It's stupid.'

Horne said, 'People obviously think that because the four of you went to India, and then you come back from India and you're the only one that sort of got anything concrete out of it, that you're really into the sort of mysticism thing.'

George answered, 'Well, I think the others did get a little. I would really be disappointed to think that Ringo and Paul and John didn't get anything out of it. But it's the way we viewed it. First of all I got into Indian music and Ravi Shankar, who had helped me have an alternate point of view on music, on life, on cultures and on the origin of where we're all coming from. And through him, I had a feel for India before I went there with John, Paul and Ringo.'

Horne then said, 'Can I quickly continue that discussion we were having before, because it brings us on to the Material World Foundation. Could you explain that, because a lot of what you do is for the Material World Foundation, isn't it?'

George explained, 'Yes, OK. I mean, there's so many things it's hard just to précis everything into a few minutes. When we came back from India, we thought we'd start our own company 'cause Brian Epstein had died; we decided to go on our own. We wanted to try and be nice, except it backfired because of our lack of experience. So Apple turned into a seething pit of people, freeloaders and people wanting everything.

'People always think that the Beatles money is just pouring out of their ears so it's nothing just to give a fiver or a tenner or twenty quid or a thousand pounds or even a hundred thousand pounds. But with the British government, I have to earn a hundred or a hundred and fifty quid to spend ten pounds. So if I go round giving people tenners out me pocket all the time, it's really I'm giving them a hundred quid.

'So at Apple we thought of the idea of a Foundation. But like so many other good ideas, they got lost in the chaos. When the Bangla Desh situation occurred, if I'd have had a foundation then we could have sponsored the concert and the money could have gone there as quick as possible without any problems. So we set up the Foundation. It took three years and then you need money to give away. So I thought the easiest way to do it is to give the copyrights of my songs and when I make a record, if it sells then the money goes to the receiver for the performance and the money that the publishers and songwriters would normally get goes to the Foundation. So if the Red Cross says, "Give us a pound," I can give them a pound. I don't have to earn ten.'

Horne asked, 'Is that the same sort of thing with Dark Horse, your new record label?'

George replied, 'No. Dark Horse is just a label. It is purely just like an outlet. Whatever I produce now, it goes to Dark Horse and they in turn have a deal with A&M. Most of the stuff will be what I produce, although I can still rent other producers. Splinter's record I produced, but I don't necessarily have to produce all of Splinter's.'

Horne then said, 'Tell me about Ravi Shankar.'

George explained, 'Basically I'm just a Liverpudlian rock'n'roller, so I can understand why people in the West don't understand Indian music or don't want to. I first heard this music in 1966, not just Ravi and sitar but lots of different instruments put together like an orchestra. It was so fantastic I knew that was the way people in the West would suddenly realise there's more to it than what they think. Because there is a tendency for them to think, "Oh yeah, Indians, they lie on nails and they don't eat cows and they're all starving and they can play any notes they like in their music." You know, that's the impression the West has been given.

'Every piece of music can be written and sung. Even down to the drums. They can play the drum rhythms, they can write then down and they can say them. They have a language. It's so complex, Indian classical music. It's like light years ahead of anything in the West and the nearest anyone's come to it, I suppose, is certain jazz musicians. And they're usually the ones who'll acknowledge that Indian music is far out. Even John Coltrane, he's studied with Ravi. Ravi's spent time with lots of musicians just giving them ideas on various rhythms.

'Ravi Shankar has been well received by people who like classical Indian music, but he spent fifteen years touring the world doing one-night stands staying in Howard Johnson's. The Beatles gave up touring after three years. And now he's got an audience for classical music and he's earned it. But then that in itself had pigeonholed him into the hole of being a classical sitar Indian musician. Whereas actually that's only the surface of that man. He's so fantastic as a composer that this is just a hint.

'His album is so refreshing musically if people can listen to it with an open mind. I tell you, Ravi Shankar will knock spots off Tchaikovsky and the lot of them. And all Tchaikovsky's fans and Bach and Beethoven, OK they were great but they're all dead. Who's there now? Who's writing anything good now? Stravinsky's probably dead too. Then you've got all the other guys who are ripping off Stravinsky and all them, and all the symphony orchestras who are trying to copy the last copy of the copy of the copy of Bach. But who's actually composing really good fresh music now? Well, I dunno, but I know Ravi is. And people need to realise that he's not just in a pigeonhole of being a sitar player, he's a composer and, you know, he's something else. God bless him.'

Dark Horse Records

Originally founded by George in Britain in May 1974, initially to be distributed by A&M Records. George completed the five-year deal with A&M's Jerry Moss in which A&M had the distribution rights to the new label and George was to provide four solo albums and also to personally participate in the production of other Dark Horse artists.

The first two acts signed to the new label were Ravi Shankar and Splinter. The label enjoyed its first hit with Splinter's 'Costafine Town'.

George was to sign himself to the label on Tuesday 27 January 1976 when the Beatles recording contract with EMI Records had expired. His first thought was to record an album for the label and he explained his thoughts on the project to *Melody Maker*, saying, 'I'd like someone to produce me, either that or a co-producer or just a friend working with me. I've found there's no way that you can judge your own work. It's always useful to have a friend around. Maybe I should get Ry Cooder to produce me. I've always liked his work. But the nearest I've got to him was waving to him when we were watching Bob Marley and the Wailers.'

George began recording his next album *Thirty Three & 1/3* on Monday 24 May 1976 and the sessions lasted until mid-September of that year. However, on Tuesday 28 September 1976, A&M Records claimed that he hadn't finished the album by 26 July and therefore hadn't complied with the terms of his contract with them. They stated that not only did he not complete the album by that date but also failed to return an advance of £588,000. In Los Angeles they sued him for $10 million and also sought an injunction to prevent him making any more records until the case was heard.

After negotiations, both parties agreed to terminate the contract and George arranged for Warner Brothers to distribute the Dark Horse label, signing with them in November 1976.

He was to comment on the affair: 'When you hear about somebody getting sued for something, all it gets down to is the first press release seems to be the good guy. And that's the case, as it happened. It came in the papers about A&M suing me because I didn't deliver an album, but it goes much deeper than that. What happened was, we had a deal for Dark Horse and I had a deal for myself, which didn't happen until this year because I was with EMI and Capitol. They were trying to get together over the two years to finalise the details. The attorney who was with them when they made the deal was not the one with them when they were filling in the details. He read the deal and he said they were going to use my money to offset Dark Horse. We said, "No. No. It's in the contract. It has been there for two years. You don't cross-collateralise me and Dark Horse." And the attorney said, "I can't believe the other attorney did this to you." So, in effect, what happened was they realised they had not made themselves such a good deal.

'Instead of phoning me up and saying, "Now look, George, we have made ourselves a bad deal, let's talk about it and work it out," they found the only legal grounds they had was that I had hepatitis, so my album was two months delayed. We had, in the original contract, that I would give it to them around the 25th of July. And so they picked on that legal point and said, "OK, we'll get him on that." I arrived in LA with my album under my arm, all happy, and I was given this letter saying, "Give us back the million dollars," which was an advance, "and give us the album, and when you give us the album, you don't get the million back."

'Now I turned down a great deal from Capitol and EMI which was of more value, from the money point of view and guarantees, than what I took with A&M. But I took that because of the relationship we were, supposedly, going to have, which turned out we never did. And that was it. I couldn't live with that sort of situation, so I left. We backed the truck up to the office and filled it with our stuff and we went off. But, almost overnight, me and Dark Horse Records were transferred from A&M on one side of the Hollywood Hills to Warner Brothers on the other, and a new album *Thirty Three & 1/3*, was soon in the racks in the record stores.'

Warner Brothers held a special reception to celebrate their world-wide distribution deal for Dark Horse at Chasen's, Hollywood Boulevard, Los Angeles. Prior to entering the restaurant, George answered some questions for reporters.

Q: Are you going to expand the Dark Horse roster?

George: No. I'm not interested in signing a lot. I made up my mind over the last year what we've got, and basically I'll keep it at that and see how it goes. I don't want to get into a big deal. It's too time consuming. But if we do well we'll see how things go. If we don't do well I'll just keep it small.

Q: What about a tour?

George: I had some dates planned for this year but I became sick halfway through the album and had to stop. I was sick in bed for two and a half months with hepatitis so I had to cancel the dates.

It was going to be Germany, Amsterdam, London, Paris and Japan, which was the first part of the tour, so I'm going to do that next year. I'm going to India for Ravi Shankar's niece's wedding and I'll stay in India for a while and be back here around January and maybe make a new album and then go on the road next summer. It takes such a long time to organise things like that.

Q: What about a band?

George: No, not at the moment. But I'd try and keep it real simple and have to wait and see how that will evolve.

Q: What did you learn from your first solo tour?

George: I learned that I should make sure that I have plenty of rest before it. Because last time I had such a heavy work schedule that I did myself in right before the tour. I just had no throat. I learned a lot of things. Possibly I'll do a Dark Horse tour this time and take some of the other Dark Horse acts. A special show.

The artists signed to the Dark Horse label were Splinter, the Ravi Shankar Family, Attitudes, Jiva, Henry McCullough and Stairsteps.

The following Dark Horse singles were distributed by A&M Records:

'I Am Missing You' c/w 'Lust', Ravi Shankar.
'Costafine Town' c/w 'Elly-Mae', Splinter.
'China Light' c/w 'Haven't Got Time', Splinter.
'Ain't Live Enough' c/w 'The Whole World's Crazy', Attitudes.
'From Us To You' c/w 'Time', Stairsteps.
'Something's Goin' On Inside LA' c/w 'Take My Love', Jiva.
'Which Way Will I Get Home' c/w 'What Is It (If You Never Ever Tried It Yourself)', Splinter.
'Honey Don't Leave LA' c/w 'Lend A Hand', Attitudes.
'Tell Me Why' c/w 'Salaam', Stairsteps.
'After Five Years' c/w 'Halfway There', Splinter.
'Sweet Summer Music' c/w 'If We Want To', Attitudes.

The following Dark Horse singles were distributed by Warner Brothers Records:

'This Song' c/w 'Learning How To Love You', George Harrison.
'Crackerbox Palace' c/w 'Learning How To Love You', George Harrison.
'Sweet Summer Music' c/w 'Being Here With You', Attitudes.
'Round & Round' c/w 'I'll Bend For You', Splinter.
'In A Stranger's Arms' c/w 'Good News', Attitudes.
'Shuffle' c/w 'From Me To You', Keni Burke.
'Keep On Singing' c/w 'Day', Keni Burke.
'Motions Of Love' c/w 'I Need Your Love', Splinter.
'Blow Away' c/w 'Soft-Hearted Hana', George Harrison.

'All Those Years Ago' c/w 'Writing's On The Wall', George Harrison.
'Teardrops' c/w 'Save The World', George Harrison.
'All Those Years Ago' c/w 'Teardrops', George Harrison.
'I Really Love You' c/w 'Circles', George Harrison.
'Got My Mind Set On You' c/w 'Lay His Head', George Harrison.
'When We was Fab' c/w 'Zig Zag', George Harrison.

Warner also released some promotional singles, not available to the general public.

The following Dark Horse albums were distributed by A&M Records:

The Place I Love, Splinter.
Shankar, Family & Friends, Ravi Shankar.
Jiva, Jiva.
2nd Resurrection, Stairsteps.
Mind Your Own Business, Henry McCullough.
Harder To Live, Splinter.
Ravi Shankar's Music Festival From India, Ravi Shankar.
Attitudes, Attitudes.

The following Dark Horse albums were distributed by Warner Brothers Records:

Thirty Three & 1/3, George Harrison.
Good News, Attitudes.
Keni Burke, Keni Burke.
Two Man Band, Splinter.
George Harrison, George Harrison.
Somewhere In England, George Harrison.
Gone Troppo, George Harrison.
Cloud Nine, George Harrison.

Dark Sweet Lady

A number George wrote on 26 February 1978, inspired by Olivia, during their nine-week holiday in Hawaii. It was included on the 1979 album *George Harrison* and is 3 minutes and 22 seconds in length.

Davis, Ivor

The *Daily Express* journalist who ghosted a column by George on the Beatles 1964 tour of America.

He spent a total of 32 days travelling with the Beatles, writing a column three times a week chronicling the American tour.

A third of the way through the tour, George approached him and said, 'That's a load of old rubbish you're writing under my name. It's so bloody boring.'

Davis agreed, but pointed out that after the first two weeks George began to go to bed at 2 a.m. and didn't wake up until the following afternoon. As Davis's deadline for the column was 10 p.m., he had to make up the stories based on his own observations of the tour. He told George that if he got out of bed earlier and spent some time with him, then perhaps the column wouldn't be so boring.

George agreed and began to put some input into the column.

Day The World Gets 'Round, The

A number George wrote on the day following his Concert For Bangla Desh event. He included it as a track on his *Living In The Material World* album. It is 2 minutes and 48 seconds in length.

Dear One

A track from the 1976 *Thirty Three & 1/3* album, 5 minutes and 8 seconds in length.

George originally wrote the number while he was in the Virgin Islands earlier that year.

He was to say, 'I dedicate this song to Paramatsa Yogananda, who is a swami from India who left his body in 1952. As opposed to dying, he left his body. And he's been probably the greatest inspiration to me. I met a lot of really good swamis and Yogis, I like their company whenever I get the chance to spend some time with them. Yogananda I never met personally in this body, but he had such terrific influence on me for some very subtle reason, I can't quite put my finger on it. And I just dedicate this to him, because it's like . . . a lot of my feelings are the result of what he taught and is teaching still in his subtle state. And I wrote this and it's like a prayer really, and it's just a realisation of appreciation.'

Deep Blue

A song George wrote to describe his feelings as his mother's health deteriorated. She died of a terminal illness on 7 July 1970 during the *All Things Must Pass* sessions.

The track was produced by George and Phil Spector, and is 3 minutes and 40 seconds in length. It was issued as the flipside of 'Bangla Desh', which was released in Britain on Apple R 5912 on 30 July 1971.

George was to say, 'I wrote the song "Deep Blue" at home one exhausted morning with those major and minor chords. It's filled with the frustration and gloom of going to these hospitals, and the feeling of disease that permeated the atmosphere. Not being able to do anything for suffering family or loved ones is an awful experience.'

Dehra Dun

A number George wrote at the Maharishi Mahesh Yogi's ashram in India. In the Beatles *Anthology*, a version of the number recorded by

George on a ukulele on the lawn of Friar Park on 23 June 1994 is included. Dehra Dun was the name of a village 25 miles away from Rishikesh.

Delaney & Bonnie & Friends

Delaney Bramlett was a solo artist in America before meeting Bonnie Lynn. The two teamed up and also got married. They gathered a group of musicians to tour as Delaney & Bonnie & Friends and late in 1969 arrived in London for a European tour.

On 5 December 1969 Delaney & Bonnie & Friends were appearing at the Royal Albert Hall. George, Patti and the other members of the Beatles were in attendance. The outfit was on a two-month tour of England, Germany and Switzerland and among the musicians appearing were Eric Clapton, Bobby Whitlock, Billy Preston, Dave Mason, Micky Hopkins, Klaus Voormann, Rita Coolidge and Jim Gordon. The Beatles went backstage and George began to talk to Delaney Bramlett.

Bramlett was to relate to Marc Shapiro, author of *All Things Must Pass*: 'George just came backstage and we started talking and he said how much he liked the show and, all of a sudden, he asked, "Can I do the tour with you?" I said, "Sure, of course you can play." He said, "Well, can you pick me up at my house?" I said, "Sure, but does anybody know how to get there?" Well, we had Klaus Voormann, Billy Preston and a whole lot of other people in the band who knew where George lived. So I said no problem.'

The bus arrived at George's house the next morning and Bramlett says, 'We came by in our bus and there was all of George's gear sitting outside on the sidewalk. I went up to the door and there was George, all ready to go, and insisting that they immediately load up his stuff. George went back into the house to get a couple of things as Patti came to the doorway. I asked Patti if she was OK with this and she said "fine", turned round and walked back into the house. I don't think Patti was OK with it. It sure didn't seem like she liked the idea very much.'

When George joined the bus, Delaney recalled, 'It was odd. I'm just a musician and a singer. I was definitely in awe of the Beatles, but George acted like he was basically in awe of me. It was basically two musicians getting together and liking what the other did. For me, he was just like one of the gang from day one.'

The first concert with George was at the Empire Theatre, Liverpool.

George gave Delaney his 1961 Rickenbacker 425 guitar, used in the *Let It Be* sessions during the tour.

Delaney and Bonnie were to divorce late in 1972.

Derek And The Dominos

A group who were formed after the Delaney & Bonnie tour and made their recording debut on George's first post-Beatles album *All Things Must Pass*. It comprised Eric Clapton with former members of Delaney and Bonnie's group. Apart from Eric, the quartet comprised drummer Jim Gordon, bass guitarist Carl Radle and organist Bobby Whitlock. The group made their debut at the Lyceum, London on 14 June. Their double album was *Layla And Other Love Songs*, the title number being Clapton's love song to George's wife Patti.

Devil's Radio

A number from the *Cloud Nine* album that was inspired by a placard George had seen at a little church near where Dhani went to school. It read: 'Gossip – the Devil's radio – don't be a broadcaster.'

There was a 12″ promotional single issued to AOR stations in America in early 1988 on Dark Horse PRO-A 2889 entitled 'Devil's Radio (Gossip)'.

The number was recorded at FPSHOT in 1987 and was co-produced by George and Jeff Lynne.

George included the number in his repertoire during the 1991 Japanese tour.

Dick Cavett Show, The

An American ABC Television chat show on which George videotaped an appearance on Tuesday 23 November 1971.

Cavett thought he detected tension between George and other members of the Beatles and said, 'Is there a slight undercurrent of hostility between you and the other members? Are you, in any sense, in contact with each other?'

George replied, 'I saw John last night actually at the premiere of *Raga*, which is what we should talk about maybe.'

Cavett said, 'OK. But what did you say?'

'Hi. Hello,' said George.

Cavett asked, 'Do you get writers who say these sort of things? What did he come back with?'

When George said, 'Hi,' the audience laughed.

Cavett pressed him, 'Was there more?'

George said, 'You don't need boring people to talk to on your show. I'm most probably the biggest bore you've had on your show.'

Cavett replied, 'Really – you think?'

George continued, 'They asked me, "Do you want to come on *The Dick Cavett Show*,' and I said, "I've got nothing to talk about really," and they said, "Well, think of something – anything." So I thought, "OK, I'll go and talk about *Raga*."'

Cavett said, 'You mean, that's it! When we're done talking about that . . .'

George interrupted, 'Then I'll go.'

A surprised Cavett said, 'You don't like to talk, then?'

George replied, 'Well, not really. Sometimes, if there's something to say. But there's really nothing to say these days.'

However, George did broach other subjects, talking about his recordings and drugs, the American comedian Jack Benny, and he also began to comment about American television, saying, 'It's such a load of rubbish.' Then he quickly added, to the amusement of the audience, 'But not *The Dick Cavett Show*, of course.'

He continued, 'It just drives you crazy, you know. The commercials. You're just getting into something and they'd say, "Sorry, now another word from . . . and another word from . . ." They just put on commercials all the time. You don't know if it's the commercials or the show.'

After discussing some other subjects, George was joined by Ravi Shankar and the conversation turned to the Concert For Bangla Desh and the reasons why the album hadn't been released, due mainly to problems regarding the revenue. George pointed out, 'We'll get it out. I'll even get it out with CBS. Bhaskar will then have to sue me! We're going to play the sue me, sue you blues. Sue me Bhaskar.'

George was referring to Bhaskar Menon, the president of Capitol Records who, little more than a week after the broadcast, stated, 'Harrison is clearly not in possession of all the facts.'

George also performed 'Two-Faced Man' on the show, accompanied by Gary Wright and Wonder Wheel.

Ding Dong

A fourth solo single from George, released in Britain on Apple R 6002 on 6 December 1974 where it reached No. 38 in the charts. 'I Don't Care Any More', which was on the flip, possible relates to George's frustrations with the 'My Sweet Lord' lawsuit.

Engravings that George had noticed on the walls of his Friar Park mansion proved to be the inspiration behind 'Ding Dong'.

It was released in America on Apple 1879 on 23 December 1974 where it reached No. 36 in the charts. The flipside was a different track from the British release, 'Hari's On Tour (Express)'. The track also featured Ringo Starr on drums.

George was to comment, 'It's very optimistic. Instead of getting stuck in a rut, everybody should try ringing out the old and ringing in the new. I mean, they all hold hands and dance about, doing "Knees Up Mother Brown" every New Year's Eve but they never apply it. They sing about it, but they never apply it to their lives. I mean, it is comical, but at the same time it is pretty good. I was just sitting by the fire, playing the guitar and I looked up on the wall, and there it was written, carved into the wall in oak: 'Ring out the old, ring in the new" on the left, and on the right of the fire: 'Ring out the false, ring in the true.' I thought, "God, it took me five years of looking at that, before I realised it was a song." A loony, who used to own the house, he built it, and it has got all these great things written all over the place. "Yesterday, today was tomorrow," was written in the stone on a window in the garden buildings, and on the other window, "Tomorrow, today will be yesterday."'

Dirty World

A track from *The Traveling Wilburys: Volume 1*, with Bob Dylan taking over lead vocals. Apart from the Wilburys themselves, other musicians included Jim Keltner on drums, Ray Cooper on percussion and Jim Horn on horns.

Discography

This is a discography of 7″ singles and 12″ albums issued in Britain and America. It does not include the numerous other records issued as CDs, promotional albums and CDs, MC singles, tracks on 'various artists' compilations and bootlegs.

Singles:

'My Sweet Lord' c/w 'Isn't It A Pity' was issued in America on Apple 2995 on 23 November 1970.

'My Sweet Lord' c/w 'What Is Life' was issued in Britain on Apple R 5884 on 15 January 1971.

'What Is Life' c/w 'Apple Scruffs' was issued in America on Apple 1828 on 15 February 1971.

'Bangla Desh' c/w 'Deep Blue' was issued in Britain on Apple R 5912 on 30 July 1971 and in America on Apple 1836 on 28 July 1971.

'Give Me Love (Give Me Peace On Earth)' c/w 'Miss O'Dell' was issued in Britain on Apple R5988 on 25 May 1973 and in America on Apple 1862 on 7 May 1973.

'Ding Dong' c/w 'I Don't Care Any More' was issued in Britain on Apple R 6002 on 6 December 1974 and in America on Apple 1879 on 23 December 1973.

'Dark Horse' c/w 'I Don't Care Any More' was issued in America on Apple 1877 on 18 November 1974.

'Dark Horse' c/w 'Hari's On Tour (Express)' was issued in Britain on Apple R 6001 on 28 February 1975.

'You' c/w 'World Of Stone' was issued in Britain on Apple R 6007 on 12 September 1975 and in America on 15 September 1975 on Apple 1884.

'This Guitar (Can't Keep From Crying)' c/w 'Maya Love' was issued in Britain on Apple R 6012 on 6 February 1976 and in America on Apple 1885 on 8 December 1975.

'This Song' c/w 'Learning How To Love You' was issued in Britain on Dark Horse K 16856 on 19 November 1976 and in America on Dark Horse DRC 8294 on 15 November 1976.

'My Sweet Lord' c/w 'What Is Life' was issued in America on Capitol Starline on 25 December 1976.

'Crackerbox Palace' c/w 'Learning How To Love You' was issued in America on Dark Horse DRC 8313 on 24 January 1977.

'True Love' c/w 'Pure Smokey' was issued in Britain on Dark Horse K 16896 on 18 February 1977.

'Dark Horse' c/w 'You' was issued in America on Capitol Starline 6245 on 4 April 1977.

'It's What You Value' c/w 'Woman Don't You Cry For Me' was issued in Britain on Dark Horse K 16967 on 10 June 1977.

'Blow Away' c/w 'Soft Touch' was issued in Britain on Dark Horse K 17327 on 16 February 1979.

'Blow Away' c/w 'Soft-Hearted Hana' was issued in America on Dark Horse DRC 8763 on 19 February 1979.

'Love Comes To Everyone' c/w 'Soft-Hearted Hana' was issued in Britain on Dark Horse K17284 on 27 April 1979.

'Love Comes To Everyone' c/w 'Soft Touch' was issued in America on Dark Horse DRC 8844 on 14 May 1979.

'Faster' c/w 'Your Love Is Forever' was issued in Britain on Dark Horse K 17423 on 13 July 1979.

'Faster' c/w 'Your Love Is Forever' (a picture disc) was issued in Britain on Dark Horse K 17423P.

'All Those Years Ago' c/w 'Writing's On The Wall' was issued in Britain on Dark Horse K 17807 on 15 May 1981 and in America on Dark Horse DRC 49725 on 11 May 1981.

'Teardrops' c/w 'Save The World' was issued in Britain on Dark Horse K 17837 on 31 July 1981 and in America on Dark Horse DRC 49785.

'All Those Years Ago' c/w 'Teardrops' was issued in America on Dark Horse GDR CO410 on 9 November 1981.

'Wake Up My Love' c/w 'Greece' was issued in Britain on Dark Horse 9 29864-7 on 29 October 1982 and in America on Dark Horse 7-29864.

'I Really Love You' c/w 'Circles' was issued in America on Dark Horse 7-29744 on 7 February 1983.

'I Don't Want To Do It' c/w 'Queen Of The Hop' was issued in America on Columbia 38-04887 on 22 April 1985.

'Got My Mind Set On You' c/w 'Lay His Head' was issued in Britain on Dark Horse W 8178 on 12 October 1987 and in America on Dark Horse 7-28178 on 6 October 1987.

'Got My Mind Set On You' c/w 'Lay His Head' (a limited edition box) was issued in Britain on Dark Horse W 8178B on 12 October 1987.

'Got My Mind Set On You' (extended version) c/w 'Got My Mind Set On You' (single version) c/w 'Lay His Head', an extended format 12″ single release was issued in Britain on Dark Horse W 8178T on 12 October 1987.

'Got My Mind Set On You' (extended version) c/w 'Got My Mind Set On You' (single version) c/w 'Lay His Head', an extended format 12″ picture disc release was issued in Britain on Dark Horse W 8178T on 12 October 1987.

'When We Was Fab' c/w 'Zig Zag' was issued in Britain on Dark Horse W 8131 on 25 January 1988 and in America on Dark Horse 7-28131 on 26 January 1988.

'When We Was Fab' c/w 'Zig Zag' (a limited edition box set) was issued in Britain on Dark Horse W 8131B on 1 February 1988.

'This Is Love' c/w 'Breath Away From Heaven' was issued in Britain on Dark Horse W 7913 on 16 May 1988 and in America on Dark Horse 7-27913 on 10 May 1988.

'Handle With Care' c/w 'Margarita' by the Traveling Wilburys was issued in Britain on Wilbury W 7732 on 17 October 1988 and in America on Wilbury 7-27732 on 11 October 1988.

'Handle With Care' c/w 'Margarita' (a limited edition box set) by the Traveling Wilburys was issued in Britain on Wilbury W 7732W on 17 October 1988.

'End Of The Line' c/w 'Congratulations' by the Traveling Wilburys was issued in Britain on Wilbury W 7637 on 20 February 1989 and in America on Wilbury 7-27637 on 23 January 1989.

'Got My Mind Set On You' c/w 'When We Was Fab' was issued in America on WB Back-to-Back Hits on 1 July 1989.

'Handle With Care' c/w 'End Of The Line' was issued in America on WB Back-to-Back Hits on 1 July 1989.

'Cheer Down' c/w 'Poor Little Girl' was issued in Britain on Dark Horse W 2696 on 27 November 1989.

'Cheer Down' c/w 'That's What It Takes' was issued in America on Warner Bros 7-22807 on 22 August 1989.

'Handle With Care' c/w 'End Of The Line' by the Traveling Wilburys was issued in America on Warner Bros on 12 April 1990.

'Nobody's Child' c/w 'Lumiere – Dave Stewart & The Spiritual Cowboys' by the Traveling Wilburys was issued in Britain on Wilbury W 9773 on 18 June 1990.

'She's My Baby' c/w 'New Blue Moon' (instrumental version) by the Traveling Wilburys was issued in Britain on Wilbury W 9523 on 5 November 1990.

'Wilbury Twist' c/w 'New Blue Moon' (instrumental version) by the Traveling Wilburys was issued in Britain on Wilbury W 0018 on 25 March 1991 and in America on Wilbury Warner Bros on the same day.

'Wilbury Twist' c/w 'New Blue Moon' (instrumental version) (a special limited edition) by the Traveling Wilburys was issued in Britain on Wilbury W 0018W on 25 March 1991.

'My Sweet Lord' c/w 'Give Me Love (Give Me Peace On Earth)' was issued in Britain on 11 May 1997 and in America on 11 March 1997.

'Any Road' was issued in Britain on 12 March 2003.

Albums:

Wonderwall Music was issued in Britain on Apple Apcor 1 on 1 November 1968 in a mono version and on Apple Sapcor 1 on the same day in a stereo version. It was issued in America on 2 December 1968. *Electronic Sound* was issued in Britain on Zapple 01 on 9 May 1969. It was issued in America on 26 May 1969.

All Things Must Pass was issued in Britain on Apple STCH 639 on 30 November 1970. It was issued in America on 27 November 1970.

The Concert For Bangla Desh was issued in Britain on Apple STC 3385 on 1 January 1972. It was issued in America on 20 December 1971.

Living In The Material World was issued in Britain on Apple PAS 10006 on 22 June 1973. It was issued in America on 29 May 1973.

Dark Horse was issued in Britain on Apple PAS 1000 on 20 December 1974. It was issued in America on 9 December 1974.

Extra Texture (Read All About It) was issued in Britain on Apple PAS 10009 on 3 October 1975. It was issued in America on 22 September 1975.

Thirty Three & 1/3 was issued in Britain on Dark Horse K56319 on 19 November 1976. It was issued in America on 22 November 1976.

The Best Of George Harrison was issued in Britain on Parlophone PAS 10011 on 20 November 1976. It was issued in America on 8 November 1976.

George Harrison was issued in Britain on Dark Horse K 56562 on 16 February 1979. It was issued in America on 20 February 1979.

Dark Horse was issued in Britain on Music For Pleasure MFP 50510 on 17 November 1980.

Thirty Three & 1/3 was issued in Britain on Dark Horse K 56319 on 1 January 1981.

Somewhere In England was issued in Britain on Dark Horse K 56870 on 5 June 1981. It was issued in America on 1 June 1981.

The Best Of George Harrison was issued in Britain on Music For Pleasure MFP 50523 on 25 November 1981.

Gone Troppo was issued in Britain on Dark Horse 023 743-1 on 8 November 1982. It was issued in America on 8 November 1982

Cloud Nine was issued in Britain on Dark Horse WX 123 on 2 November 1987. It was issued in America on 3 November 1987.

The Traveling Wilburys Volume 1 was issued in Britain on Wilbury WX 353 on 24 October 1988. It was issued in America on 25 October 1988.

Best Of Dark Horse 1976–1989 was issued in Britain on Dark Horse WX 312 on 23 October 1989. It was issued in America on 17 October 1989.

Nobody's Child was issued in Britain on Wilbury WX 353 on 23 July 1990.

The Traveling Wilburys Volume 3 was issued in Britain on Wilbury WX 384. It was issued in America on 6 November 1990.

Live In Japan was issued in Britain on Dark Horse 7599 26964-1 on 13 July 1992. It was issued in America on 14 July 1992.

All Things Must Pass, a re-release with bonus tracks, was issued in Britain on GN 7243 530474-1 on 19 February 2001.

Brainwashed was issued in Britain on 19 November 2002.

Distance Makes No Difference

A number George recorded with Carl Perkins at FPSHOT on 18, 19 and 21 June 1996. George produced and the engineer was John Etchells.

The number was penned by Perkins, who wrote it for his wife Valda the night before he was due to record with George. He arrived at Friar Park with four or five songs for George to choose from, but as soon as he played the number to George, George loved it. 'I hadn't even written the lyrics down yet,' said Perkins.

Carl played lead guitar and vocal, George played a slide guitar solo, bass guitar and background vocals. Jim Capaldi was on drums.

It was included on Perkins' album *Go Cat Go!* released on 15 October 1996.

Do You Want To Know A Secret?

A number penned by John Lennon, which was recorded at Abbey Road on 11 February 1963 with George on lead vocal. George said that the number had been inspired by an R&B hit by the Stereos in 1961 called 'I Really Love You'. It was included on the Beatles' debut album *Please Please Me* and was also covered in Britain by Billy J. Kramer, who topped the charts with the single.

Don't Bother Me

The first composition by George to appear on a Beatles album. It was recorded at Abbey Road Studios on 11 and 12 September 1963 and was included on the *With The Beatles* album in Britain and the *Meet The Beatles* album in America.

Bill Harry met George frequently in Liverpool clubs and wanted to know why all the original Beatles compositions were by Lennon and McCartney when the first-ever mention in print of an original Beatles composition was that of George's 'Cry For A Shadow', which appeared on the cover of issue No. 2 of *Mersey Beat*. At first Harry suggested that George team up with Ringo. George actually tried that and told Harry, 'I almost did a number with Ringo. He was playing my guitar and I had the tape on, so we tried something. We played it back fast and we had a song.'

However, the partnership with Ringo didn't happen and Harry kept pressing George to write songs. George told him, 'I can't write lyrics. If I could write lyrics as easy as I could write melodies I would be churning them out like Paul and John.'

When Harry bumped into George in the Cabin club in Wood Street he took him back to the *Mersey Beat* office nearby and had another chat about George songwriting. That was the last time he mentioned it.

Then, when Harry visited the Beatles at the ABC, Blackpool on Sunday 19 July 1963, George took him aside and thanked him. When Harry asked what he was thanking him for, George told him that he'd been going out to a club one night and realised he might bump into him and then be badgered about writing songs. Since he thought he'd be bothered again he got the inspiration to write 'Don't Bother Me'. He thanked Harry again, saying he'd already received more than £7,000 in royalties.

Oddly enough, George didn't mention this in his book *I. Me. Mine*. saying he'd written the number in a hotel in Bournemouth. Maybe that's where he completed the song, but the origin and the title were conceived in Liverpool.

Donegan, Lonnie

A seminal influence on George, known as 'the King of Skiffle'.

Born Anthony Donegan in Glasgow on 29 April 1933, he enjoyed a number of hits, including 'Rock Island Line', which set off what became known as 'the skiffle boom' in Britain.

George's brother Harry, whose girlfriend and eventual wife Irene took George to see Donegan at the Empire Theatre, Liverpool recalled, 'In 1958 Lonnie Donegan was appearing at the Empire and of course George just had to go. In fact, he borrowed the money from our parents so that he could see every single show!

'Anyway, he found out where Lonnie was staying, which happened to be a house in Speke, so George went round and hammered on the door until he came out and gave George his autograph. Of course, he immediately raced home to show everyone.'

Donegan was one of the guests at Eric and Patti Clapton's wedding reception.

Donovan

A singer/songwriter, born Donovan Phillip Leitch in Glasgow, Scotland on 10 May 1946.

He first met the Beatles in 1965 and struck up a close relationship with George. He was one of several celebrities who were with them in Rishikesh when they were studying meditation at the ashram of the Maharishi Mahesh Yogi.

George gave Donovan a book by Yogananda, the autobiography of a yogi, and Donovan gave George the 'Diamond Sutra'.

It was George who was to give credit to Donovan's input on the Beatles songs written at Rishikesh which were used on *The Beatles* white album.

Donovan accompanied George to Dehra Dun, a village in the lower Himalayas and recalls that the two of them wrote a number 'Derradoon', which was never recorded, although George sang a few lines of the number in the Beatles *Anthology* video.

Whilst at Rishikesh George also contributed to Donovan's song 'Hurdy Gurdy Man', writing a third verse for the song.

When Donovan was recording the number in London, the musicians at the 'Hurdy Gurdy Man' session were Jimmy Page on guitar, John

Bonham on drums and John Paul Jones on bass guitar – prior to the formation of Led Zeppelin. When they were recording the number, Page played a guitar part that was considered so extraordinary that producer Mickie Most said they didn't have time to include the third verse, so George's lyrics weren't included on the original release. However, in 1990 the number was included on the CD *The Classics Live* and George's third verse was included on 'Hurdy Gurdy Man'.

Dovedale Primary School

A school situated in Herondale Road, Liverpool 18.

George was two years below John Lennon when he entered the school, but the two never met there. In John's class were George's brother Peter and Jimmy Tarbuck. Normally, entrance to the school was at the age of five, but George had to wait until he was six years old because local schools at that time were overcrowded due to the 'bulge' (the amount of babies born immediately at the end of the Second World War).

George and Peter hadn't been able to enrol at Alderwood Junior School almost opposite where they lived because it was full. They had to travel five miles, back to the Wavertree area and Dovedale School in Herondale Road.

George was to recall: 'When I was eight or nine years old, my teacher Mr Lyons caned me and got me on the wrist. It was swollen and when I got home, I tried to hide it but my father saw it and then next day he came down to the school and Mr Lyons was called out of the class and my dad stuck one on him.'

He was to say, 'I was sad leaving Dovedale. The headmaster told us that we might feel smart big boys now, but at the next school we'd be the little boys once again. It seemed such a waste after all that hustling to be one of the big lads.'

Drake, Peter

American country musician, noted for his expertise on pedal steel guitar. Based in Nashville, he played a major role in Bob Dylan's *Nashville Skyline* album. Dylan recommended him to George, who brought him in to play on his debut solo album *All Things Must Pass* at a cost of $10,000.

Drake was also to coax Ringo Starr to Nashville to work on a country album.

He died in 1988.

Dream Away

A track on George's 1982 album *Gone Troppo*. George originally wrote the number for the *Time Bandits* film. He was originally going to write a complete soundtrack for the movie, but never got around to it. Dave Mattacks plays drums on the track.

Dylan, Bob

Bob Dylan, born Robert Allen Zimmerman on 24 May 1941 wasn't an original influence on the Beatles. Al Aronowitz of the *Saturday Evening Post* originally brought him to their attention in 1963.

It was Aronowitz who introduced them to the folk singer in 1964 and later that year he visited them at the Delmonico Hotel, where he introduced them to marijuana.

Initially, it was John Lennon who seemed to be the big Dylan fan and there was no doubt that the Dylan influence contributed to his writing, but it was later George who became the close friend of the American singer/songwriter.

The Beatles attended Bob Dylan's concert at the Royal Albert Hall on 9 May 1965. This was the occasion when Dylan had decided to abandon acoustic and 'go electric', resulting in members of the audience booing him. 'Leave him alone . . . shut up!' George shouted at the hecklers. George said, 'It was all still pure Dylan, and he has to find out his own directions. If he felt he wanted electrification, that's the way he had to do it.'

George and Patti visited Dylan at his home in Bearsville, Woodstock in November 1968, around the time of Thanksgiving, after completing some recordings with Jackie Lomax in Los Angeles, and spent two weeks with him.

In his book *I. Me. Mine.* George mentions the visit, saying that the number 'I'd Have You Anytime' was started in Woodstock He mentions that Dylan had been out of commission for some time after breaking his neck in a motorcycle accident. George said he spent time hanging around the house with Dylan's kids, but felt that Bob seemed nervous and uncomfortable, even though he was in his own home. He loosened up on the third day when they got the guitars out and began to play.

When Dylan was appearing at the Isle of Wight festival, George arranged to meet him at Heathrow. However, Dylan's plane arrived early and he was whisked away. On Tuesday 26 August 1969 George drove down to see him and stayed with Bob at Forehands Farm in Bembridge, before returning home on the Thursday.

George, in the company of Derek Taylor, also visited Dylan in May 1970 in New York. They arrived on 28 April and George phoned Dylan to make an appointment to see him. On 29 April George and Taylor dropped round to Dylan's apartment and Dylan played them some tunes on his piano. The next day George and Dylan jammed together and on 1 May, when Dylan renewed his recording of the album *New Morning*, George turned up at the sessions.

George also invited Dylan to appear on the Concert For Bangla Desh.

In addition to appearing on stage with him at various concerts in Britain, George also recorded the Dylan number for the *Porky's*

Revenge soundtrack. On a visit to Los Angeles in 1986 he accompanied Dylan to the Palomino club to see Jesse Ed Davis and they joined him on stage, along with John Fogerty and Taj Mahal.

When the Beatles were inducted into the Rock'n'Roll Hall of Fame on 20 January 1988, George and Dylan performed 'All Along The Watchtower' together.

George was to say, 'Dylan is so brilliant. To me, he makes William Shakespeare look like Billy Joel.'

In the spring of 1988, while in Los Angeles putting together a track for a 12″ single from *Cloud Nine*, George needed an extra track for the B side and asked Jeff Lynne to help him on the session. They then rang Bob Dylan, who had a garage studio and Lynne also brought Roy Orbison along for the ride.

Together with Tom Petty, all five musicians were at Dylan's house and started to throw in ideas while George and Jeff worked on lyrics. George said, 'I thought of the first line, then everyone was writing words, with Dylan saying some hysterical things.

'Then we thought, "If Roy Orbison's coming along, we might as well have a lonely bit from him."'

The finished track was called 'Handle With Care' after the instructions on a cardboard box in Dylan's garage. The track was deemed too good to be wasted on a B side, and the concept of the five musicians was also a dream team, so they decided to continue recording, calling themselves the Traveling Wilburys.

Eddy, Duane

A New York musician, noted for his 'twangy guitar' playing, who was an early influence on George. It was said that George was able to join the Quarry Men after playing the Eddy number 'Ramrod' to John Lennon.

At one time George was to say, 'I'd like to play as well as Duane Eddy or Chet Atkins.'

Eddy's eponymous album was first issued in June 1987. It was reissued in December 1994 on the See For Miles label SEECD 417, retitled *His Twangy Guitar And The Rebels.* George is featured on the tracks 'Theme For Something Really Important' and 'The Trembler'.

Eddy played on two tracks of George's album when he visited George at his home studio. George then played on two tracks of Eddy's album. George dropped into Eddy's Los Angeles recording session in February 1987.

Electronic Sound

Following *Wonderwall*, George's second solo album also failed to make any impact on the British charts following its release on Zapple 02, Apple's experimental label, on 9 May 1969. It only reached No. 191 in the American charts following its release there on Zapple ST 3358 26 May 1969.

Side One (lasting 18 minutes and 37 seconds) was called 'Under The Mersey Wall', the title being a twist on 'Over The Mersey Wall', a column in the *Liverpool Echo* by a journalist called George Harrison. This was recorded at George's house in Esher, Surrey in February 1969.

Side Two (lasting 25 minutes and 3 seconds) was 'No Time Or Space', recorded in California in the summer of 1968.

The Zapple press release on 'Under The Mersey Wall', penned by Apple's 'house hippy' press officer Richard DiLello, read: 'In February 1969, in a mounting vortex of decibels, there came to pass a wrecked chord of environmental sound that went beyond the genre of hashish cocktail music. The bass line has been milked through the Moog machine and, lo and high, we behold electronic music . . . that becomes sounds that floor the mind, not to forget the soul, o solo mio.'

The release for 'No Time No Space' read: 'In California, through the machine gun of his mind, George thought aloud to himself and in his composure he has exposed the thought patterns beating on his brow, and dramatically opposed, he has exposed, through the medium of the Moog, a pottage of space music. And on and on we go . . . George Harrison versus Godzilla and King Kong in space.'

The inner-sleeve notes also contained a quote from an Arthur Wax (George): 'There are a lot of people around, making a lot of noise, here's some more.'

George also included two of his own paintings on the sleeve.

George said, 'All I did was get that very first Moog synthesizer, with the big patch unit and the keyboards that you could never tune, and I put a microphone into a tape machine. I recorded whatever came out.'

Zapple, as Apple's experimental label, was the right home for *Electronic Sound*. George had recently acquired a Moog synthesizer, which had been developed by Dr Robert Moog during 1963 and 1964.

Californian electronic composer Bernie Krause helped George a lot on this album and was originally given a prominent credit on the album cover, although when it was released his name was erased by silver paint. Krause was later to claim that he had created the music as a demonstration tape for the synthesizer and that George had taken his tapes. This seems unlikely, as Krause didn't press the matter.

The sleeve design is credited to George as it features two paintings by him.

It was reissued as a CD in Britain in 1997 on Zapple 7243 8 55239 2 2. George turned down a 1,000-word essay for the CD booklet and simply wrote, 'It could be called avant-garde, but a more apt description would be (in the words of my old friend Alvin) "Avant-garde clue!"'

Alvin referred to guitarist Alvin Lee, one of George's friends.

Epsom Register Office

The Surrey venue where George and Patti were married.

George had wanted to keep the actual details of the wedding secret because he didn't want journalists and photographers 'intruding' – he was a great protector of his own privacy. However, he informed press officer Tony Barrow that following the actual ceremony Tony could make a statement to the press and that he, George, together with Patti, would then be willing to participate in a press conference about the wedding on the day following the event.

The couple had been living together for almost two years when George approached Brian Epstein in December 1965 to ask permission for him to get married. He'd left Patti outside in their car while he went into Brian's house in Chapel Street, London, to discuss it with him. Ten minutes later he returned and told Patti, 'It's all right, Brian has said we can get married in January. Off we go!'

Patti replied, 'God has spoken!'

Only close friends and associates were informed, with the plea that they keep it to themselves. John Lennon said, 'January's a bit soon, she must be in the club.'

Rumours of the impending nuptials still circulated and on the eve of the wedding, a journalist called Mike Housego spent most of Thursday 20 January parked outside George's house. By the evening he had managed to talk George into having a word with him on his doorstep. 'Is it true that you and Patti are getting married tomorrow morning?' he asked.

'No,' said George.

George and Patti asked Paul McCartney to be best man and he agreed. Brian Epstein assumed that he would automatically receive the invitation to be best man, so to avoid embarrassment there were two best men at the wedding – Paul and Brian.

John Lennon and Ringo Starr were on holiday in Trinidad at the time, but they sent flowers and greetings.

The wedding took place on Friday morning, 21 January 1966 at 11 o'clock. Also in attendance were George and Patti's parents, plus Neil Aspinall and Mal Evans.

Following the ceremony there was a small, intimate wedding lunch at the couple's bungalow, 'Kinfauns'.

George's mother Louise told a friend: 'I felt as if I had lost everything. Quite silly, really. As we were in the car with them returning from the ceremony, George took my hand and said, "It doesn't mean because I'm married I don't need you anymore, Mum. We need you more now." He's such a lovable son, and cares about how people feel.'

That evening Brian Epstein hosted a dinner party at his home for the married couple. George and Judy Martin and members of NEMS staff were among the guests.

George and Patti stayed at Kinfauns on their wedding night and Neil and Mal were houseguests. The couple had decided not to go on their honeymoon immediately as, having kept the news away from the press, they thought they'd then announce the details at a press conference the next day.

On Saturday 22 January George and Patti held their press conference at NEMS' offices in Argyll Street and then flew off on their honeymoon to Barbados.

At the conference a journalist asked, 'How on earth did you manage to keep it secret?'

'Simple,' said George. 'We didn't tell anyone.'

Epstein, Brian

The Beatles' first manager was born in a private nursing home in Rodney Street, Liverpool on 19 September 1934.

While managing his family's store, NEMS (North End Music Stores), he began stocking copies of *Mersey Beat* in July 1961, learning of the Beatles and the amazing local music scene. He asked *Mersey Beat* founder Bill Harry to arrange for him to visit the Cavern to see the Beatles and decided to manage them. After having a brief chat with them in the dressing room he left a message with George asking if they could arrange to meet him at NEMS.

Paul was ten minutes late for the meeting. The punctilious Epstein was quite annoyed when Paul hadn't turned up on time.

'Sorry, Mr Epstein,' said George. 'He's just been having a bath.'

Brian was still angry and said, 'This is disgraceful. He is going to be very late.'

'Late,' said George, 'but very clean.'

By 1967 their association with Epstein was becoming tenuous. They no longer toured and didn't need him in the recording studios. There were even rumours that they would not be re-signing with him as his contract was due to terminate.

Then, on 27 August 1967, his body was found in his bed at his Chapel Street, London home.

At the time the Beatles were in Bangor studying transcendental meditation with the Maharishi Mahesh Yogi.

They were shocked to hear the news. A reporter asked George, 'Have you spoken to Brian since you've been here with the Maharishi this weekend?' George replied, 'I spoke to him on Wednesday evening. The evening before we first saw the Maharishi's lecture. He was in great spirits.' The reporter asked, 'And when did he tell you that he would like to become initiated?' George said, 'Well, when we arrived here on Friday I got a telephone call later that day to say that Brian would follow us up and be here Monday.' George was then asked, 'Has the Maharishi ever met Brian Epstein?' John Lennon said, 'No, but he was looking forward to it,' and George said, 'There is no such thing as death, only in the physical sense. We know that he is OK now. He will return because he was striving for happiness and desired bliss so much.'

Brian was only 32 years old. His body was buried at the Jewish Cemetery in Long Lane, Aintree, Liverpool.

Eric Clapton And His Rolling Hotel

A 70-minute film, released to limited screening in 1980 by Angle films. The movie is about Eric's 1978 tour of Germany on which Eric's group and crew travelled on a train called the Rolling Hotel – a reference to a train that Hermann Goering had built. The film includes George performing 'Further On Up The Road' on stage at the Civic Hall, Guildford on Thursday 7 December 1978 when he'd attended the theatre to watch Eric and Elton John in concert and had been invited up onto the stage.

Evans, Mal

The Beatles' road manager. Mal had been a telecommunications engineer when he decided to drop into the Cavern club one lunch time. The Cavern fascinated him and he became a regular, during which time he and George became friends.

He invited George to his house one day to listen to his records and George suggested that he become a 'bouncer' at the Cavern and even introduced him to Cavern owner Ray McFall. Mal then began working at the Cavern and three months later Brian Epstein offered him the job as road manager of the Beatles, working under Neil Aspinall. He later became a personal assistant to the Beatles and then an executive at Apple.

Mal documented his travels with the Beatles and even filmed them during their period at Rishikesh.

In 1968 he reported his travels to America with George in *Beatles Monthly* magazine He recalled that on Friday 7 June he picked up George's Jumbo acoustic guitar from Abbey Road Studios and took it to Heathrow airport where he joined George and Patti and Ringo and Maureen on their trip to America. They flew nonstop to Los Angeles and caught a privately chartered Lear Jet to San Francisco. They then had to go to Monterey where George was filming with Ravi Shankar.

They were met by Nat Weiss, their American attorney, and booked into the country club Del Monte Lodge, where Bing Crosby was staying. On Saturday 8 June they went shopping in Carmel and in the afternoon visited Joan Baez. On Sunday George practised on his sitar and then suggested that they play golf.

On Monday 9 June they met up with Ravi Shankar, who taught George a new raga he'd never heard before. They then filmed George. This was the film with the original working title 'East Meets West', but ended up as *Raga*. They then returned to the lodge and did some more filming the next day. On Wednesday 20 June they left for Los Angeles and visited Peter Tork. Dave Crosby had also dropped in and there was a jam session with George, Tork, Crosby, Peter Asher and Ringo.

Mal was killed on Sunday 4 January 1976 when Fran Hughes, a girl he was living with in Los Angeles called the police and said, 'My old man has a gun and has taken valium and is really screwed up.'

When the police arrived at the venue, Mal still held a gun and the police shot him.

Everest

A special wide-screen, high-definition film documentary about the world's highest mountain made for showing at IMAX cinemas.

The soundtrack featured orchestral versions of five of George's numbers: 'All Things Must Pass', 'Life Itself', 'This Is Love', 'Give Me Love (Give Me Peace On Earth)' and 'Here Comes The Sun'. The last song was actually performed by George and was taken from his *Live In Japan* tour.

The film received its premiere at the Museum of Science in Boston on Wednesday 4 March 1998 and went on general release in America two days later. It opened at the IMAX Cinema in the Trocadero, London the following month.

Extra Texture (Read All About It)

An album issued in Britain on Apple PAS 10000 on 9 September 1975. George produced the album mainly at the A&M Studios in Los Angeles in May and June 1975, with Norman Kinney as engineer.

George composed all ten tracks and engaged a wide range of musicians to participate. They included Jim Gordon on drums on 'You' and Andy Newmark on drums on 'His Name Is Legs'. Jim Keltner provided percussion on all tracks with the exception of 'His Name Is Legs'. Carl Radle played bass on 'You', Paul Stallworth played bass on 'The Answer's At The End' and 'Tired Of Midnight Blue' and also provided backing vocals on 'Can't Stop Thinking About You'. Klaus Voormann played bass on 'Ooh Baby', 'World Of Stone' and 'Can't Stop Thinking About You'. Willie Weeks played bass on 'His Name Is Legs'. Leon Russell played keyboards on 'You' and 'Tired Of Midnight Blue'. David Foster played piano on 'The Answer's At The End', 'This Guitar (Can't Keep From Crying)', 'World Of Stone', 'Grey Cloudy Lies' and 'His Name Is Legs' and also electric piano on 'Can't Stop Thinking About You' and organ on 'You'. Nicky Hopkins played piano on 'Can't Stop Thinking About You'. Billy Preston played piano on 'His Name Is Legs'. Gary Wright played electric piano on 'You' and 'Ooh Baby' and organ on 'The Answer's At The End' and 'World Of Stone'. Jim Horn played saxophone on 'You' and, together with Chuck Findlay on 'Ooh Baby' and 'His Name Is Legs'. Jesse Ed Davis played guitar on 'This Guitar', 'Ooh Baby', 'World Of Stone', 'Can't Stop Thinking About You' and 'Grey Cloudy Lies'.

Among the variety of instruments George played were guitar on all tracks, plus acoustic guitar on 'This Guitar (Can't Keep From Crying)', ARP bass on 'This Guitar (Can't Keep From Crying)', ARP on 'Grey Cloudy Lies' and piano on 'His Name Is Legs'.

The tracks were: Side One: 'You', 'The Answer's At The End', 'This Guitar (Can't Keep From Crying)', 'Ooh Baby (You Know That I Love You)', 'World Of Stone'. Side Two: 'A Bit More Of You', 'Can't Stop

Thinking About You', 'Tired Of Midnight Blue', 'Grey Cloudy Lies', 'His Name Is Legs (Ladies And Gentlemen)'.

It was George's final album issued on the Apple label and reached No. 25 in the British charts and No. 8 in the American.

Far East Man

A number George recorded at FPSHOT in October 1973 when he'd invited Ronnie Wood and his wife Chrissie to stay at Friar Park for a month. He was inspired by the T-shirt worn by Chrissie, which she'd obtained during the Faces recent tour of the Far East. Musicians on the track included Mick Taylor on bass, Jean Rousell and Ian McLagan on piano/keyboards and Andy Newmark on drums.

George wrote the lyrics and collaborated on the music with Wood.

The number, lasting 5 minutes and 48 seconds, was to appear on Ronnie Wood's album *I've Got My Own Album To Do*, which was issued in America by Warner Brothers on 23 September and in Britain on 27 September 1974.

George altered the lyrics and re-recorded the number during his sessions for the *Dark Horse* album.

Faster

A single issued in Britain on Monday 30 July 1979 on Dark Horse K 17423 with 'Your Love Is Forever' on the flip. It was also issued as a limited edition picture disc on Dark Horse K17 423P, the first picture disc from any ex-Beatle.

The number, 4 minutes and 39 seconds in length, was a track from the *George Harrison* album.

Royalties from the record were donated to the Gunnar Nilsson Cancer Fund. The Swedish-born Nilsson was a Formula One driver who had died from cancer in 1978.

George said that various drivers, including Jackie Stewart and Niki Lauda, inspired the number. *Faster* had been the title of Jackie Stewart's book and George paid tribute to the courage of Lauda following a serious crash. He also paid tribute to Ronnie Peterson, a driver who was killed in Milan in September 1978. George dedicated the record to the 'Entire Formula One Circus' and the picture disc sported photographs of Jackie Stewart, Niki Lauda, Jody Scheckter, Jochen Rindt, Jim Clark, Graham Hill, Emerson Fittipaldi, Stirling Moss and Juan Manuel Fangio.

The record begins with the sound of racing cars, recorded at the British Grand Prix in 1978.

While he was in Nice attending the Monaco Grand Prix, George persuaded racing driver Jackie Stewart to appear in the promo for 'Faster', filming him on Monday 28 May 1979. Stewart is seen driving George around the racetrack while George sings the song in the rear seat.

Ffrench, Darby

George's great-grandfather, born in County Wexford, Ireland in 1825. The ancestors of his, and therefore George's, family could be traced to the French Norman knights in the thirteenth century who settled in southern Ireland.

They built a castle in County Wexford and the local peasants called them Ffrench, a name that they adopted. They thrived for the next four centuries until Oliver Cromwell took over as Lord Protector. As the Ffrench family refused to renounce their Catholicism they were stripped of their wealth and had to work the land for the next 300 years.

Darby ran a small two-acre farm in Corah, County Wexford and married Ellen Whelan, George's great-grandmother, who was born in 1831.

Their rent was £1.4s.6d, but it was a struggle to find the money to pay it. The couple also had five children to support.

James died in 1906 at the age of 81 and Ellen died two months later at the age of 75. Their children, dropping the first 'f' from their name, spent four years attempting to run the farm, but when the eldest daughter Elizabeth died in 1911, they decided to sell it off and divide the proceeds between them.

Fifty Years Adrift (In An Open-Necked Shirt)

Derek Taylor's autobiography, published in a limited edition by Genesis Publications in 1985, which George edited. George also aided in the promotion down under by flying to New Zealand and taking part in a literary lunch for 300 people with Derek at the Hyatt Hotel, Auckland on 28 November 1984. He then joined Derek on 30 November at the Sydney Opera House in Australia for another literary lunch with an audience of 200 people.

Filmography

George is the former Beatle most associated with the film industry due to his connection with HandMade Films. His film work has been quite extensive, appearing as himself, in acting roles, as a composer, producer, director and miscellaneous crew member, in addition to his numerous guest appearances on television.

His first stint as an actor was in *A Hard Day's Night*, where scriptwriter Alun Owen wrote him into a solo scene.

Paul and George split up in search of Ringo and George wanders into a building opposite the theatre they are appearing in.

He peers through a glass door where a young woman is typing. He goes in, about to ask her if she had seen Ringo and she says, 'Oh, there you are.'

'I'm sorry, I must have made a mistake,' says George.

'You haven't, you're just late,' she says. She looks George over and remarks, 'Oh, yes, he's going to be very pleased with you.'

'Is he?' asks a puzzled George.

'Yes, you're quite a feather in the cap.' She picks up the phone on her desk. 'I've got one ... Oh, I think so ... Oh, yes, he *can* talk. Well ... I think you ought to see him.'

She crosses to a door behind her desk that has gilt lettering with the words 'Simon Marshall' on it and jerks her head at George.

'Well, come in.'

George apologises and follows her into the room.

There is a man in the room, with some assistants. Behind him is a poster stating: 'WAY OUT. Your Own TV Special With Susan Campey. Director, Simon Marshall.'

The secretary indicates George and says, 'Will this do, Simon?'

He looks George up and down, then nods and says, 'Not bad, dolly, not really bad.' Flicking his hand at George he says, 'Turn around, chicky baby.'

George does a little turn.

'Oh, yes, a definite poss. He'll look good alongside Susan,' he says.

Then turning to George again he says, 'All right, Sunny Jim, this is all going to be quite painless.'

One of the assistants suddenly seems to recognise George and turns to Marshall.

An irritated Marshall says, 'Don't breathe on me, Adrian.'

Adrian tries to talk, 'But ...'

Then George comments, 'Look, I'm terribly sorry but I'm afraid there's been some sort of misunderstanding.'

Marshall says, 'Oh, you can come off it with us. You don't have to do the old adenoidal glottal stop and carry on for our benefit.'

'I'm afraid you don't understand,' George says.

'Oh my God – he's a natural,' says Marshall.

The secretary, looking slightly worried, says, 'Well, I did tell them not to send us any more real ones.'

Marshall nods. 'They ought to know by now that the phonies are much easier to handle. Still, he's a good type.'

He then turns to George and says, 'We want you to give us your opinion on some clothes for teenagers.'

'Oh, by all means. I'd be quite prepared for that eventuality,' says George.

'Well, not your real opinion, naturally,' says Marshall, 'It'll be written out and you'll learn it.' He glances nervously at his secretary and says, 'Can he read?'

'Of course I can,' says George.

'I mean lines, ducky – can you read lines?'

'I'll have a bash,' says George.

A pleased Marshall says, 'Good. Sweetie, get him whatever it is they drink . . . a cokearama?'

'Ta,' says George.

Marshall says, 'Well, at least he's polite, Tony, show him the shirts.'

One of the aides begins to lay out some shirts in front of George.

Marshall oozes, 'You'll like these. You'll really "dig" them. They're "fab" . . . and all the other pimply hyperboles.'

George looks at the shirts, frowns, then comments, 'I wouldn't be seen dead in them. They're dead grotty.'

Marshall is taken aback. 'Grotty?'

'Yeah, grotesque,' says George.

Marshall turns to his secretary, 'Make a note of that word and give it to Susan.'

Then he muses, 'I think it's rather touching, really. Here's this kid trying to give me his utterly valueless opinion when I know for a fact that within four weeks he'll be suffering from a violent inferiority complex and loss of status if he isn't wearing one of these nasty things. Of course they're grotty, you wretched nit. That's why they were designed . . . but that's what you'll want.'

'But I won't,' says George.

Marshall begins to get upset, 'You can be replaced, you know, chicky baby.'

'I don't care,' says George.

Marshall continues, 'And that pose is out too, Sunny Jim. The new thing is to care passionately, and be right wing. Anyway, you won't meet Susan if you don't co-operate.'

'And who's this Susan when she's at home?' asks George. Then he remembers, 'You mean that posh bird who gets everything wrong?'

'I beg your pardon,' says Marshall.

'Oh, yes,' says George, 'the lads frequently gather round the set to watch her for a giggle. Once we even all sat down and wrote those letters saying how gear she was and all that rubbish . . .'

'She's a trendsetter. It's her profession!' says Marshall.

'She's a drag,' says George. 'A well-known drag. We turn the sound down on her . . .'

Marshall is furious. 'Get him out of here,' he storms.

'Have I said something amiss?' George asks.

Tony and Adrian hustle George to the door. He shrugs them off, turns to Marshall and says, 'Sorry about the shirts.'

'Get him out,' screams Marshall, then looks worried and turns to his secretary. 'You don't think he's a new phenomenon, do you?'

'You mean an early clue to the new direction,' she says.

Marshall rummages in his desk, saying, 'Where's the calendar?' then seems relieved, saying, 'No, he's just a troublemaker. The change isn't due for three weeks. All the same . . . make a note not to extend Susan's contract. Let's not take any unnecessary chances.'

Along with Ringo's main scene, this was the best acting scene of a Beatle in the movie. Paul's scene ended up on the cutting floor and there were only short scenes for John and not one written around him.

As a producer, George was executive producer of all the HandMade films. He was also producer of *Black And Blue* in 1980, *Privates On Parade* in 1982 and *Little Malcolm* in 1974. He was also producer of 1972's *Concert For Bangla Desh* film and is down as producer, with the other members of the Beatles, of *Let It Be* and *Magical Mystery Tour*.

His composing credits began in 1964 with *A Hard Day's Night* for the song 'Don't Bother Me'. He also receives his credits for the compositions that appeared in the Beatles films *Help! Yellow Submarine* and *Let It Be*.

His first film soundtrack was *Wonderwall* in 1969 and his song 'Here Comes The Sun' was included in the 1978 film *Sgt Pepper's Lonely Hearts Club Band*. The same year saw some of his songs included in the film *I Wanna Hold Your Hand*. He composed songs and additional material for 1981's *Time Bandits* and songs for *Shanghai Surprise* in 1986 and *Lethal Weapon 2* in 1989. His song 'What Is Life' was in the soundtrack of *Goodfellas* in 1990 and the 1999 movie *Big Daddy*. His song 'Here Comes The Sun' was included on the 1993 *Point Of No Return* soundtrack and he had a number of his songs in the 1995 television miniseries *The Beatles Anthology*. The Imax film *Everest* in 1998 included songs by George, while his songs also appear in two films in the year 2000, *The Beatles Revolution* and *The Beatles Yellow Submarine Adventure*. He provided songs and addition material for *Ram Dass, Fierce Grace* in 2001 and his song 'While My Guitar Gently Weeps' was included in the television special 'Party At The Palace: The Queen's Concerts, Buckingham Palace' in 2002.

As an actor George appeared in *A Hard Day's Night, Help!* and *Magical Mystery Tour* and as himself in *Let It Be*. His singing voice was used in the 1965 animated series *The Beatles* and the 1968 animated feature *Yellow Submarine*. George appeared as an elderly interviewer in the 1978 spoof *The Rutles* and the same year made a guest appearance in the TV movie *Ringo*. In 1979 he portrayed Mr Papadopolous in *Life Of Brian* and was a nightclub singer in *Shanghai Surprise* in 1986.

He has also appeared as a miscellaneous crew member on two occasions, in the 1979 film *Being There* and as a guitarist on 'Leave The Light Out' in the 1990 video *Belinda Carlisle: Runaway Videos*.

George has appeared as himself in numerous television specials, videos and films, whether in a personal appearance, cameo spot or in archive footage. Here is a selection: *What's Happening! The Beatles In The USA* (1964), *Around The Beatles* (1964), *A Hard Day's Night* (1964), *Pop Gear* (1965), *Help!* (1965), *The Beatles At Shea Stadium* (1965), *Tokyo Concert* (1966), *Our World* (1967), *The Beatles Mod Odyssey* (1968), *Let It Be* (1970), *Music* (1971), *Concert For Bangla Desh* (1972), *Muhammad Ali, The Greatest* (1974), *The Beatles And Beyond* (1977), *The Day The Music Died* (1977), *I Wanna Hold Your Hand* (1978), *Eric Clapton And His Rolling Hotel* (1980), *Ready Steady Go! Volume 1* (1983), *The Compleat Beatles* (1984), *Water* (1985), *Ready Steady Go! Volume 2* (1985), *Ready Steady Go! The Beatles Live* (1985), *Rock 'n' Roll Goldmine: The Sixties* (1985), *Bye Bye Star Club* (1987), *Rolling Stone Presents Twenty Years Of Rock & Roll* (1987), *It Was 20 Years Ago Today* (1987), *Imagine: John Lennon* (1988) *The 1960s: Music, Memories And Milestones* (1988), *Michael Kamen: Concert For Saxophone* (1991), *Secrets* (1992), *Fame In The Twentieth Century* (1993), *Bob Dylan: 30th Anniversary Concert Celebration* (1993), *America Comes To Graceland* (1993), *The Beatles: The First US Visit* (1994), *The Beatles Anthology* (1995), *You Can't Do That! The Making Of A Hard Day's Night* (1995), *The History Of Rock 'n' Roll, Vol 3* (1995), *The Beatles Diary* (1996), *Alf Bicknell's Beatles Diary* (1996), *A Really Big Show: Ed Sullivan's 50th Anniversary* (1998), *Bring Me Sunshine: The Heart And Soul Of Eric Morecambe* (1988), *The Beatles Celebration* (1999), *Gimme Some Truth* (2000), *Hollywood Rocks The Movies: The Early Years (1955–1970)* (2000), *Hendrix* (2000), *The Beatles Revolution* (2000), *Jazz* (2001), *Wingspan* (2001), *Standing In The Shadows Of Motown* (2002) and *Naqoyqatsi* (2002).

George also made a number of guest appearances, either in person or via archive footage. Here is a selection: *Toast Of The Town*, 9 February 1964; *Doctor Who*, 1963; *Frost On Sunday*, 8 September 1968; *The Morecambe & Wise Show*, 1968; *Rutland Weekend Television*, 1975; *Saturday Night Live*, 1975; *The Simpsons*, 1989; *This Is Your Life: Damon Hill*, 11 January 1999; *Absolutt Underholdning*, 2001.

Fittipaldi, Emerson
Brazilian-born Formula One world champion who was a close friend of George.

The two first met at Brands Hatch in 1973. Fittipaldi recalled, 'We became great friends and we used to meet away from the races. We used to spend the holidays with our families together and every time I went to England, we used to meet.'

In 1995 Fittipaldi fractured his lower back in a plane crash in Araraguara, Brazil. On 31 October 1996 George was filmed singing 'Here Comes Emerson', a version of 'Here Comes The Sun' in which he was congratulating Fittipaldi on his recovery from the accident.

Fittipaldi last saw George in August 2001 and related, 'I spent three days in Lugano, Switzerland, with George and his wife Olivia, and we talked a lot. When I arrived I felt that he was very much depressed, but little by little he became shiny and in the last day he didn't want to let me come home. He showed me many new songs that he was recording for a new CD. Many of them talked about Christ, which made me happy 'cause I then knew he had accepted Christ in his heart and believed in eternal life. When he liked someone, he would become a big friend. He would always show great care and signs of love for his friends. His disease was depressing him, but he had always a warrior feeling and would always show an impressive love for life. His wife Olivia was always a great warrior by George's side.'

Fleetwood, Mick
The drummer with Fleetwood Mac who, at one time, was George's brother-in-law because he was married to Jennifer, the sister of George's wife Patti.

Jennifer was also the inspiration behind Donovan's song 'Jennifer Juniper', and had lived for a while in San Francisco where she took George and Patti into the Haight-Ashbury district. Mick also accompanied the Beatles when they visited the Maharishi in Bangor, Wales.

Flying
Despite the fact that he flew in aircraft numerous times, particularly between America and England during his solo years, George always had a fear of flying. He even revealed a dream he had. 'One dream that really sticks in my mind is where an aeroplane came zooming down and crashed in front of me.

'Anyway, the plane crashed with a big explosion and all the fuel flew through the air from miles away. I jumped away and lay flat on the ground to protect myself, but all this fuel was aflame and landed on my legs.

'I was sort of shouting, "Ooh, ooh, ouch," and things, jumping about all over the place like I'd sat down on a hot stove.

'All the hairs on my legs were burned off and my trouser legs were in tatters.

'But I don't know how it all ended, I think I woke up after that.'

He also recalled a real incident. 'We were taking off from Liverpool for one of our frequent flights across the country when the plane suddenly came to a halt just as it was about to leave the ground. That gave me the jitters but what was to follow will make me sympathise with Elvis Presley's fear of flying for the rest of my days.

'As we made the proper takeoff the emergency exit by which I was sitting suddenly flew open.

'I had heard stories about people being sucked out of aircraft, and I don't mind admitting I was pretty terrified. Our manager Brian Epstein, who was sitting next to me, grabbed my arm and I yelled out for the air hostess – but she thought I was fooling as we often do since we fly in this plane so frequently.'

In 1965, during the Beatles' tour of America, a chartered aircraft developed engine trouble and was replaced by an old plane that was to fly them to the West Coast. Noting the worn fittings in the interior, a worried George began to examine them. He noted a dusty coil of rope on a rack and asked the stewardess what it was.

'It's an escape ladder,' she said.

'How long is it?' asked George.

'About twelve feet, I guess,' she replied.

'I take it we shall fly to California at a steady thirteen feet all the way then,' said George.

Flying Hour

A number which George co-wrote with Mick Ralphs, former member of Mott The Hoople and Bad Company. It was originally recorded in March 1978 during the *George Harrison* album sessions, but was actually scheduled to be included on the *Somewhere In England* album. However, it was one of the four tracks rejected by Warner Brothers.

It was eventually issued on the limited edition *Songs By George Harrison* book and CD package in February 1988.

For You Blue

A number composed by George, which was included on the *Let It Be* album. It is 2 minutes and 24 seconds in length.

The inspiration was said to be George's wife Patti. The number was recorded at Apple Studios on 25 January 1969 and it is also included in the film *Let It Be*.

During the bluesy number, George says 'Dig those rhythm and blues' and 'Elmore James got nothing on this, baby.'

It was issued as a single in America on 11 May 1970, but failed to make an impact in the charts. George was to include the number in the repertoire of his 1974 *Dark Horse* tour and it was included on *The Best Of George Harrison* compilation, issued in Britain on 20 November 1976.

'For You Blue' was also issued as the flipside of 'The Long And Winding Road', which topped the charts after it was issued in America on 11 May 1970.

Formby, George

George Formby was born George Booth Jr in Lancashire in 1904. The entertainer was born blind, but later regained his sight following a coughing fit. In the 1930s and early 1940s he became the No.2 box-office star in Britain after Gracie Fields.

He starred in more than twenty films and had numerous best-selling records.

He was a favourite of both John Lennon and George Harrison, who admired his expertise on the ukulele – and a tribute to Formby is actually contained at the end of the 'Real Love' promo video.

John Lennon's mother played ukulele, influenced by Formby, and John first learned to play a stringed musical instrument using a ukulele.

George admired Formby so much that he became an honorary president of the George Formby Appreciation Society. On Sunday 3 March 1991 he turned up at the annual George Formby Convention at the Winter Gardens, Blackpool.

The compere announced him to the Formby fans. 'After some persuasion, I'd like to introduce Mr George Harrison, who says he's nervous.'

George came onto the stage and said, 'I thought I'd retired from all this years ago. You'll have to bear with me as I'm not certain I know the right chords, but you're all welcome to join in.'

He then played Formby's 'In My Little Snapshot Album', a song from Formby's 1938 film *I See Ice*, on his ukulele.

In the evening, at the convention finale, he was joined by Olivia and Dhani, Derek and Joan Taylor and Brian Roylance and he went on stage with his ukelele once again.

George also recorded an interview with BBC radio for the Formby tribute programme *The Emperor Of Lancashire*.

At the close of the 'Free As A Bird' single there is a backwards message by John Lennon saying 'turned out nice again'. That was Formby's catchphrase.

Frampton, Peter

A former member of the Herd and Humble Pie, who also starred in the feature film *Sgt Pepper's Lonely Hearts Club Band*.

A friend of his introduced him to George during the Doris Troy recording sessions for Apple at Trident Studios. When he walked into the control room, George said, 'Hello, Pete,' even though they hadn't met before, because he'd recognised him from television appearances. George then asked him, 'Do you want to play guitar on a number?'

George gave him his Les Paul and Pete thought that he was going to play rhythm, but George said, 'No, Pete, you don't understand. I want you to play the solo, the lead.'

Frampton then did the lead on the track 'Ain't That Cute'.

When George began recording *All Things Must Pass* he called Frampton and asked him if he would like to come and play acoustic guitar, as he and Badfinger would also be playing acoustic. Pete jumped at the chance.

Pete played on all of the tracks that featured the American country player Pete Drake, whom Bob Dylan had recommended to George. Then George called him again, saying he needed to do some more acoustics, and the two of them sat together in Studio 2 at Abbey Road adding and overdubbing acoustics to a number of tracks. Frampton recalled that the experience sitting there and also jamming with George on Beatles and Little Richard numbers, with Phil Spector watching from the control room, was more enjoyable for him than experiencing the success of his own hit album *Frampton Comes Alive*.

However, when the *All Things Must Pass* album came out, Frampton found that he wasn't included on the credits.

In 1997–98 he became a member of Ringo Starr's All Starr Band.

French, John

George's grandfather on his mother's side. He was born in Ireland in 1870 and later immigrated to Liverpool where he joined the police force. He was sacked, along with the rest of the police force, in a union dispute known as the Liverpool Lock Out during which policemen were locked out of their own police stations. He then became a carriage driver, ferrying guests to the White Tower Hotel. He went on to work as a street lamplighter and soon after he met and married a local Liverpool girl, Louise Wullam. They managed to save enough money to rent a terraced house at 9 Albert Grove in Wavertree. The couple then had seven children, including George's mother Louise.

Sadly, John was penniless when he died in 1937.

Friar Park

A Gothic mansion, situated in Henley-on-Thames, and built in 1896 by a solicitor, Sir Frank Crisp. Crisp designed the building himself, styling it on chateaux he had seen on holidays. He put in towers, turrets and gargoyles. He also adorned the structure with lots of gargoyles of friars and in the interior had little carved friars that switched on the lights if you twisted their noses.

A sign that Crisp had made stating 'Keep on the grass' amused George.

There are thirty acres of grounds, with gardens that were originally laid out as miniature Swiss Alps, with lakes and grottoes that were inhabited by carved spiders and monsters. The lake was divided in two in such a way that the lower lake could not be seen from the house. Crisp arranged a bridge over the lower lake in a position that anyone crossing it would appear to anyone in the house to be walking on water.

George bought the house in 1971 for £200,000. Inside the thirty acres is a complex the size of a small village with several cottages and outbuildings. The house itself has 120 rooms.

Friar Park eventually cost George £1.5m to renovate. He added a swimming pool, heliport, tennis court, a playhouse, an ornate fountain dedicated to Lord Shiva and a state-of-the-art recording studio.

He hired a chef, cleaners, and a ten-strong team of workers to care for spectacular gardens, which feature three lakes built on different levels, a series of caves filled with distorting mirrors, an Alpine rock garden and a 100-foot high replica of the Matterhorn. At one time George was said to employ 33 full-time horticulturalists. He also had signs near the front gate. There were nine flags representing the major nations and next to each was a 'no trespassing' notice in the equivalent language. The message after the American flag was 'Get Your Ass Out Of Here'.

George had the first floor converted into the world's largest private recording studio and the mansion's garages housed his collection of four black Porsches.

George's 'keep out' messages may have some relevance, not only for the privacy, which George wanted to maintain, but also due to the vulnerability of the property, despite its security systems. In 1990, following John Lennon's murder, a gunman threatened to kill George and police marksmen were sent to protect him at the mansion. The same year George and his family received further mail threatening to kill them and the police were called in to investigate. In May of that year they arrested a man who had been sending threatening letters such as 'Time you Went' and 'Goodbye George'.

In 1992 the FBI revealed that a deranged American had been prowling round Friar Park and had threatened to burn it down. At one point an intruder was seen vaulting over the walls of the grounds and there were at least two burglary attempts during the 1990s. In 1994 the alarm system was damaged during an attempted break-in and a new system was fitted at a cost of one million pounds. Despite this, Michael Abram was able to enter the mansion where he attempted to kill George.

Gente Que Brilha

A Brazilian television special (the name means 'People Who Shine'), screened on the SBT Channel on 31 October 1996. The show was in honour of Brazilian Formula One racing champion Emerson Fittipaldi. There was a brief biography, with the Beatles number 'Yesterday' playing in the background. George was interviewed and played a version of 'Here Comes The Sun' on acoustic guitar in which he'd altered the lyrics to honour his friend:

Hello Emmo, Emerson, Emerson, Emerson, Emerson Fittipaldi
    Emerson, Emerson, Emerson, Emerson Fittipaldi
    Hello Emmo, you've been through a difficult time in these last couple of months.
    Hello Emmo, so good to see you're well again. So let's go to the beach and drink twenty caipirinhas each.
    It's all right, Emerson, Emerson, Emerson, Emerson Fittipaldi, here comes the sun.
    Here comes Emerson. I say we love you Emerson, Emerson, Emerson, Emerson Fittipaldi.

George also said that he looked forward to meeting Emerson on their next holiday.

George And Ravi – Yin And Yang

A 22-minute television special on VHI, hosted by John Fugelsang, first screened on Thursday 24 July 1997. It featured George and Ravi Shankar in an interview and also performing. It was edited down from a 150-minute recording.

This is part of the transcript of the broadcast show:

Fugelsang: It's been a great year for music fans. Last year saw the release of Ravi Shankar's four-CD boxed set *In Celebration*, and this year has brought us the release of the new album *Chants Of India*, produced by George Harrison. And it's a great thrill for me to be here today with two of the greatest living artists in music, from the East and the West: Ravi Shankar and George Harrison. Thank you both for joining us.

George/Ravi: Thank you.

Fugelsang: George, how did you first come to meet Ravi and discover the music?

George: During the days when there was the mania, the Beatlemania, well I got involved with the records, you know. I bought some of Ravi's records and I listened to it, and although my intellect didn't really know what was happening, or didn't know much about the music, just the pure sound of it and what it was playing, it just appealed to me so much. It hit a spot in me very deep, and it was, you know, I just recognised it somehow. And along with that I just had a feeling that I was going to meet him. It was just one of those things and at the same time when I played the sitar, very badly, on a Beatle record, then Ravi was coming to London.

A lot of press were trying to set it up that we'd meet, but I just avoided that. You know, I didn't want it to, you know, be on the front page of a newspaper as a gimmick because it meant more to me than that. So I thought, well, I'll wait and meet him in my own time. And that arrived on an occasion, there was a society called Asian Music Circle and the fellow who ran that, who I'd got to know, he said Ravi's going to come, he was in London, he was going to come for lunch, and we met like that way. Then he came to my house and got me to learn how to hold the sitar and put me through the basic lessons of sitar.

Fugelsang: Ravi, I've always wanted to ask you, how did you feel the first time you heard 'Norwegian Wood'? What did you honestly think of George's sitar playing?

Ravi: When my niece and nephews, they made me hear this, and that was after I met George. I hadn't heard anything before that and I wasn't much impressed by it, you know. But I saw the effect on the young people, I couldn't believe it, even in India. It was not only in the West, it seemed they were just lapping it up as you say. They loved it so much.

Fugelsang: How did the other guys in the Beatles react when you started bringing this – when you brought this instrument into the studio?

George: Well, in those days, you know, we were growing very

quickly and there was a lot of influences that we were . . . I mean that was the best thing about our band. We were very open-minded to everything and we were listening to all kinds of music, you know. Like avant-garde music, later became known as 'avant-garde a clue!' and various things like that.

So, you know, they just thought, 'well, that's good,' they liked the sound of it, and on 'Norwegian Wood' it was just one of those songs that just needed that little extra and the sitar I'd bought, a very cheap one in a shop called India Craft in London, and even though it sounded bad it still fitted into the song and it gave it that little extra thing so they were quite happy about it.

I went to India with Ravi, to see India, to learn some music, and just to experience India. But I also wanted to know about the Himalayas. That is the thing that's always fascinated me about the idea that . . . I mean, it sounds like a lofty thing to say on VHI, but basically, you know, what are we doing on this planet? And I think throughout the Beatle experience that we'd had, we'd grown so many years within a short period of time. I'd experienced so many things and met so many people but I realised there was nothing actually that was giving me a buzz anymore. I wanted something better, I remember thinking, I'd love to meet somebody who will really impress me – and that's when I men Ravi. Which is funny, because he's this little fellow with this obscure instrument, from our point of view, and yet it led me into such depths. And I think that's the most important thing. It still is for me.

You know I get confused when I look around at the world and I see everybody's running around and you know, as Bob Dylan said, 'He's not busy being born, he's busy dying,' and yet nobody's trying to figure out what's the cause of death and what happens when you die. I mean that, to me, is the only thing really that's of any importance. The rest is all secondary. I believe in the thing I read years ago, which I think was in the Bible, it said, 'Knock and the door will be opened,' and it's true. If you want to know anything in this life you just have to knock on the door. Whether that be physically on somebody else's door and ask them a question or, which I was lucky to find, is meditation. You know, it's all within.

And that's really why for me this record's important, because it's another little key to open up the within. For each individual to be able to sit and turn off – 'turn off your mind, relax and float downstream' – and listen to something that has its roots in the transcendental, because really even all the words of these songs, they carry with it a very subtle spiritual vibration. And it goes beyond intellect really. So if you let yourself be free to let that have an effect on you, if can have an effect, a positive effect.

Fugelsang: Ravi, how was it for you when you first met George? What was your take on Beatlemania?

Ravi: I'm ashamed to say that I knew almost nothing about them when I first, you know, met them, excepting that they're very popular. And meeting them in parties I was so impressed by George at that time, who looked so much younger and was so inquisitive. Asking about so many different things. Mostly music, sitar and, of course, along with that certain spiritual . . . and the only thing . . . I felt that his enthusiasm was so real, you see, and I wanted to give as much as I could through my sitar of course, because that is the only thing that I know of. The rest I cannot express.

He talks so beautifully. He is used to words. He writes poems. He writes songs. I do sometimes foolishly, but I'm not that much . . . I express myself through notes, musical notes, so it's a different way of . . . but anyway.

As you said when I met him and we started off immediately after a few days, as he said earlier, to sit properly, how to hold the sitar and, you know, how to handle the finger position and all that, the basic things. And he was so interested and he was so quick in learning and then we fixed immediately for him to come to India and he came. We fixed it for six weeks but, unfortunately, it didn't happen because people recognised him after a week or so and there was such a commotion in Bombay that we had to run away to Kashmir and live in a houseboat and all that. But unfortunately, we had to leave. There was some . . .

George: I believe *Sgt Pepper* or something was getting . . .

Ravi: Then I thought, my God, I couldn't believe that any four people could create such a storm all over the world.

George: The Spice boys.

Ravi: And it was not that I was unknown or anything, you know. I was playing concerts in Carnegie Hall and different places, but as a classical Indian musician. But the moment it was known that he had become my disciple, it was like wildfire. I became so popular with the young people all of a sudden, and I was rediscovered, as they say, and then I took that role of a superstar for a number of years because of him.

'Cause, you know, the whole thing was going a bit not to my liking because of the association of drugs and things like that. So I really had a very difficult time for the next few years putting my music in the right register or right place, but because I did that is why I am here today also. Sitting with you. Otherwise I wouldn't have been here. People have really come to understand the depth and seriousness of our music along with all the, you know, enjoying part of it, the entertainment part that is there, but the true root and that's what is also projected in this particular record.

Fugelsang: I want to talk to you about the early 1970s, the concert for Bangla Desh. Now how did this all come about? Was it Ravi who set it in motion?

Ravi: Yes, it was that period when Eastern Pakistan and the Pakistan government had problems and they wanted to get separate, and they wanted to name it Bangla Desh. It was mainly the language issue. It started with that and then became a big political issue. But our concern was ... my concern was that many of my relatives were there. They came as refugees, a lot of children. So all that was very painful to me and I was at that time planning to give a benefit show and maybe raise twenty, twenty-five, thirty thousand dollars and send it, you know – and George happened to be in Los Angeles at that time and he saw how unhappy I was, and I told him. He said, 'That's nothing, let's do something big,' and immediately he, like magic, phoned up, fixed Madison Square Garden and all his friends, Eric Clapton, Bob Dylan, and it was magic, really. And he wrote that song also, 'Bangla Desh'. So overnight that name became known all over the world, you know.

George: America was actually shipping armaments to Pakistan who were, you know, just massacring everybody and the more I read about it and understood what was going on, I thought, well, we've got to do something and it had to be quick. And what we did really was only to point it out. That's what I felt.

Fugelsang: It was a very controversial thing in Bangla Desh. John Lennon used to get in trouble all the time for his activism. Did anyone tell you, you know, it's a little bit hot, don't go there? Were you discouraged at all by people for pursuing it?

George: No, not really. I think that was one of the things that I developed, just by being in the Beatles, was being bold. And I think John had a lot to do with that, you know, because John Lennon, you know, if he felt something strongly, he just did it. And you know, I picked up a lot of that by being a friend of John's. Just that attitude of, well, we'll just go for it, just do it.

Ravi: This was something unique. The whole spirit was so beautiful, Bangla Desh concert.

George: It was just pure adrenaline, and it was very lucky that it came off because all the musicians weren't there for rehearsal. We rehearsed bits and pieces with different people but we didn't have everybody all on at one time until the show itself. And we were just very lucky really that it all came together.

At this point George began strumming on a guitar.

Fugelsang: Want to try one of the Beatles tunes? Want to try 'Something'? A Bob song? A Carl Perkins song? I'll take a Rick Astley song, George. I'll take a Spice Girls medley George.

George: I'll play one of mine, if I can think of one.

Audience member shouts: 'All Things Must Pass'!
George: Really?

He plays two verses of 'All Things Must Pass'.

Fugelsang: I'd like to start off talking about the *Chants Of India* album because it's a real beautiful CD, record, whatever we call them these days. Do you think that an American audience is going to be able to relate to the music on the album?

George: I think so. It's like, first of all, it's not really like sitar music. I know Ravi's sitting here with his sitar, everybody knows him from sitar music, but it isn't really sitar music. I mean, it's basically spiritual music, spiritual songs, ancient mantras, and passages from the *Vedas*, which are the most ancient text on earth. And so it's these ancient songs which are all spiritual music, but trying to put it in a context where it doesn't change it from what it basically is but at the same time has the instrumentation to make it palatable to not only Westerners but to everybody.

Ravi: Well, I always had in mind not to make it so difficult for hearing for people who are not used to our music, for instance. But apart from the words, which are very old and they all mean almost the same thing: you know, peace, love, for equality, for trees, for nature, for human beings, body, soul, everything. About thirty, forty years ago these were absolutely not heard. You were not permitted to even . . . you had to give it only to your disciples and that also privately in the car, not loudly. But now books are all printed. Everything is out even in network. So as far as words are concerned they are open now, but the tune that I had to give, or added slight orchestration in the background, was with this very thought, that it should match this old sentiment of whole spiritual context that it has. At the same time, not be too much, or sound too ritualistic, or fundamentalistic, or anything like that. That's the main thing that I tried.

Fugelsang: Well, for a kid from Long Island I never thought I'd get to say this on TV. Please welcome, performing 'Prabhujee' from *Chants Of India*, joined by Ravi Shankar's wife Sukanya, please welcome Ravi Shankar and George Harrison.

They then performed 'Prabhujee'.
Some film excerpts were included in the programme, including a clip of Ravi and George meeting from the film *Raga* and clips from the *Concert For Bangla Desh* film.
Two other numbers from the original recording were edited out of the VH-I broadcast. They were 'If You Belong To Me' from the *Traveling Wilburys Volume 3* album and 'If You Don't Know Where You're Going, Any Road Will Take You', which was one of George's unreleased compositions.

George Harrison

An album recorded at FPSHOT between April and October 1978. George and Russ Titelman produced it. While in Hawaii in February that year he'd written some of the songs, including 'Love Comes To Everyone', 'If You Believe', 'Dark Sweet Lady', 'Soft-Hearted Hana' and 'Here Comes The Moon'.

George was also inspired to write some numbers that he thought his friends on the Formula One circuit would enjoy, with 'Faster' being one of the songs. In fact, George hadn't had an album released for two years because he'd taken a break from the songwriting and was spending his time travelling to various countries to visit the Grand Prix races. He'd also formed firm friendships with Formula One drivers and it was they who persuaded him to begin recording again. The inner sleeve included a photograph of George and Jackie Stewart, and two of the numbers, 'Blow Away' and 'Faster' were about Formula One racing. Nine of the ten songs were written by George and 'If You Believe' was co-written by George and Gary Wright.

Musicians on the album were Andy Newman on drums; Willie Weeks on bass; Neil Larson on keyboards and MiniMoog; Ray Cooper on percussion; Steve Winwood on PolyMoog, harmonium, MiniMoog and backing vocals; Emil Richards on marimba; Gayle Levant on harp; Eric Clapton on guitar and Gary Wright. The string and horn arrangements were by Del Newman.

George Harrison was released in America on 20 February 1979 on Dark Horse DHK 3255 and in Britain on 23 February 1979 on Dark Horse K 56562. It was his first album in two years and didn't enjoy any chart success

The tracks were: Side One: 'Love Comes To Everyone', 'Not Guilty', 'Here Comes The Moon', 'Soft-Hearted Hana', 'Blow Away'. Side Two: 'Faster', 'Dark Sweet Lady', 'Your Love Is Forever', 'Soft Touch', 'If You Believe'.

George Harrison (4149)

A minor planet that was named in honour of George. The planet was discovered on 9 March 1984 by B.A. Skill at the Anderson Mesa Station of the Lowell Observatory.

George Harrison And Friends

The Maharishi Mahesh Yogi launched the Natural Law Party in March 1992.

In order to raise money for the party's campaign in the British General Election, George decided to organise a concert at the Royal Albert Hall on Monday 6 April 1992, billed as 'George Harrison & Friends: Election Is A Celebration'.

On Thursday 2 April it was announced that George would be appearing on the show, which would become his first British appearance as the top-of-the-bill performer. It was also his first appearance at the venue since 15 September 1963, when he appeared there as a member of the Beatles in 'The Great Pop Prom'.

The concert began at 7.30 p.m. with Dr Jeffrey Clements, leader of the Natural Law Party, who told the audience that the party would bring 'a beautiful new sunshine to the nation'. He then introduced George who introduced Joe Walsh, former member of bands such as the James Gang and the Eagles, who began his set with a solo performance at the piano before being joined by his band, who included Ringo's son Zak Starkey. Following his twenty-minute set, the second guest Gary Moore appeared on stage. Gary, who appeared on the Traveling Wilburys' most recent album, had also been given a song penned by George for his *Still Got The Blues* album.

When it came time for George to appear, he had an impressive line-up of musicians waiting for him on stage. They included singers Tessa Niles and Katie Kissoon, Greg Phillinganes on keyboards, Andy Fairweather-Low on guitar, Steve Ferrone and Chuck Leavell on drums, Ray Cooper on percussion, Ray Cooper on bass and Mike Campbell on guitar.

They began with 'I Want To Tell You', George's track from the *Revolver* album. On the next number, 'Old Brown Shoe', George turned to rhythm guitar with Fairweather-Low playing lead. At the end of the song he seemed relieved at the reception and said, 'I didn't expect anything like this.' He then performed 'Taxman', which included a new verse pointing out the introduction of VAT (Value Added Tax, a tax which hadn't been around when George first penned the song in 1966), with Mike Campbell on lead guitar.

George then introduced the Hijack Band, which was the band he'd performed with on his Japanese tour the year previously. George played acoustic guitar and Fairweather-Low played bottleneck on 'Give Me Love (Give Me Peace On Earth)'. 'Something' was then introduced, with a laser effect to produce impact.

A brass section joined the band for 'What Is Life', followed by 'Piggies', which contained an additional verse that had been left off the version on *The Beatles* white album. Next followed 'Got My Mind Set On You', with George actually forgetting one of the verses. The next numbers were 'Cloud 9' and 'Here Comes The Sun'.

George then said, 'Feel free to sing along with this one. There's only three words in it,' and then performed 'My Sweet Lord'.

At the end of the following song, 'All Those Years Ago', he said, 'God bless John Lennon.'

'Isn't It A Pity' followed 'Cheer Down', then George said, 'Let's get rid of all those stiffs in Parliament, and we'll all be laughing,' and he played 'Devil's Radio'. The band left the stage but reappeared five minutes later following the requests for an encore, with George announcing 'a couple of friends you've already met' as they individually reappeared on stage. A huge cheer went up as Ringo Starr joined them. In an earlier radio interview, Ringo had said he wouldn't be performing that night, but he'd obviously had a change of mind after watching the show from his box. He sat behind the second drum kit and the band performed 'While My Guitar Gently Weeps'.

They next performed 'Roll Over Beethoven'. Further members of the band reappeared on stage, this time accompanied by George's son Dhani, with his electric guitar, and they played 'Roll Over Beethoven' again.

George's performance had lasted for an hour and forty minutes. Among the members of the audience were Patti Boyd, Cynthia Lennon, Julian Lennon, Mary McCartney and Neil Aspinall.

After the show George said, 'I've had a wonderful time. I must do it again. It was great to see so many old friends. I'm really overwhelmed by all the people who came to see me. It was a great high.'

George Harrison Birthday Tribute
See 'Concert For George Harrison, The'.

George Harrison Multimedia Tour
A CD-rom by Bhakti Caitanya Swami, issued by Krishna Culture in 2003. It's basically a trip through George's life using photos and narration, with some emphasis on his contributions to the Hare Krishna cause.

George Harrison: El Hombre Invisible
A 365-page Spanish-language book by Javier Tarazona and Ricardo Gil, published by Editorial Milenio in October 1999.

George Harrison: His Words, Wit And Wisdom
A book of almost 400 quotes from George compiled by Belmo and published in 2002. An exclusive bonus was the transcript of the only post-Beatles radio interview with George and John, recorded in 1974 in a New York hotel room. The book also contained over two dozen photographs, including rare pics from a Beatles concert in Cincinnati, and a very detailed discography of almost 300 recordings, including his guest appearances, production work, concert, radio, TV appearances and recordings which hadn't been released.

George's Column
The column in the *Daily Express* newspaper ghosted by Derek Taylor. Derek, together with his editor, had approached Brian Epstein with the idea of a regular column by a member of the Beatles. Epstein asked them who they would choose. Derek said he preferred George. Epstein thought that was a good choice as John and Paul were tied up with

their songwriting and Ringo was a relative newcomer to the group. Brian asked them what the pay would be and thought their offer was derisory and made them increase it.

Derek wrote the first column himself, and George didn't even see it. When he did look at the columns, he wasn't too enamoured, but decided to co-operate more and put some input into Derek's efforts.

The columns lasted almost eight months, although an early column, in which George discussed money, upset Brian Epstein.

It read: 'This year I will probably earn, gross, upwards of £50,000 for appearances on stage and in other mediums. Big though it is, this figure is not final. Money comes in from our royalties on photographs, books, magazines, sweaters, badges, wigs, chewing gum, seasonal cards and discs.

'Our manager, "Eppy", Brian Epstein, takes his percentage, which is on a sliding scale up to 25% and I don't begrudge him a penny because he is the fifth Beatle and the best friend we have. We buy our own clothes and equipment out of the earnings and probably when the taxman finishes I'm left with about £9,000 a year for spends.'

It obviously reads like journalist's copy and not the way George himself would write.

Give Me Love (Give Me Peace On Earth)

A single released in Britain on Apple R 5988 on 25 May 1973, lasting 3 minutes and 32 seconds. It was issued in America on Apple 1862 on 7 May 1973 and became George's second solo single to top the American charts. It was George's first single to be released for two years. The track was the first single issued from the *Living In The Material World* album, which was recorded during sessions between January and April 1973. It reached No. 8 in the British charts. 'Miss O'Dell' was on the flipside.

Globe, The

An American tabloid. Taking up an allegation in Geoffrey Giuliano's 1989 book *Dark Horse*, the paper asserted that George was a Nazi sympathiser who wore Nazi uniforms and had a Nazi flag flying outside Friar Park. The tabloid took Giuliano's absurd fantasy even further with the result that George filed a $200 million lawsuit against the paper. Bert Fields, George's attorney at the time, said that George was very, very upset about the libellous article and decided to sue only when the *Globe* refused to print a retraction and apology.

Field said, 'George deplores Nazism and everything that Hitler stood for.'

Go Cat Go!

Carl Perkins' last album, recorded in 1996 and issued on Dinosaur Records. It was only the second album after the 1973 *Ringo* to include contributions from all four members of the Beatles. There was a live version of John Lennon performing 'Blue Suede Shoes' from his Toronto Rock'n'Roll Revival appearance, Paul's version of 'My Old Friend', Ringo's All Starr Band version of 'Matchbox', and George and Carl duetted on George's 'Distance Makes No Difference With Love', which George produced and played on for Carl at Friar Park.

Gone Troppo (album)

An album by George issued in Britain on 5 November 1982 on Dark Horse 923734-1 and in America on 8 November 1982 on Dark Horse 1-23734.

George, Ray Cooper and Phil McDonald produced it.

The album was recorded in George's home studio during the spring and early summer of 1982 (except for the track 'Dream Away' from the *Time Bandits* film).

The tracks were: Side One: 'Wake Up My Love', 'That's The Way It Goes', 'I Really Love You', 'Greece', 'Gone Troppo'. Side Two: 'Mystical One', 'Unknown Delight', 'Baby Don't Run Away', 'Dream Away', 'Circles'.

The cover was designed by George's friend 'Legs' Larry Smith and included a photograph of George taken by photographer Terry O'Neill. Along with the song lyrics on the inner sleeve was an instruction on how to make cement!

'Troppo' is Australian slang, meaning to be mentally affected by a tropical climate.

The album failed to make much impact in America, where it only managed to reach No. 108 in the *Billboard* charts. One possible reason for its failure is that George refused to promote the album.

On the album George played guitars, bass, synthesizers, marimba, Jal-Tarang and mandolin. Ray Cooper was on percussion, Herbie Flowers played bass, Mike Moran was on keyboards, synthesizer, bass synthesizer and piano and Henry Sinetti was on drums.

Various other musicians made guest appearances on various tracks and included Gary Brooker, Joe Brown, Alan Jones, Jim Keltner, Neil Larson, Jon Lord, Dave Mattacks, Billy Preston and Willie Weeks.

Possibly disillusioned by the failure of the album, George decided not to record for a time. He commented, 'Well, I don't have to make records any longer, which is a relief . . . because I'm not really of the competitive nature. I don't want to have to go out there doing all this stuff which is necessary now. Let's face it, it's a cut-throat business and I'm not really into that, so I no longer have to make records.

'Since I don't have a commitment to the music industry, I've been writing much more music than in the past. For instance, the last couple of months I've written about 28 songs and I make demos, which are better because they can be of good quality. When you get to making a record, though, it's something serious.'

Gone Troppo (song)

The title track of George's only album of 1982, which closed the first side of the album. It was penned by George and lasts 4 minutes and 24 seconds. The backing singers were Joe and Vicki Brown, and Jim Keltner played percussion.

Good Morning Australia

While in Australia in December 1981 George was interviewed by Kerri-Anne Wright at Whitsunday Passage, off the Queensland Coast, for this TV programme. George requested that the interview not be used until he'd returned to England. The interview was then broadcast on the morning show over a period of five days from Monday 19 to Friday 23 April 1982.

At one point in the interview, which was recorded outdoors, it began to rain. Here is a transcript:

Kerri-Anne: George, how would you describe yourself today, 1982?

George: As, uh, a middle-aged ex-pop star, I think.

Kerri-Anne: Is that all?

George: I don't really . . . I dunno, it's just sort of a funny question, I suppose. Ex-pop star, peace-seeker, gardener, ex-celeb, until now again.

Kerri-Anne: Your own privacy, you obviously regard that very highly and when John Lennon was murdered, how did that affect your lifestyle, more from a safety point of view or from an emotional point of view?

George: I think from both points of view. First of all, it was obviously such a shock because assassination is something which up until that time hadn't really got down to that level. I mean, it was always presidents and leaders like that. I wouldn't think, you know, somebody who's a pop star was important enough to kill. It's a terrible thing: I don't think anybody is important enough to kill, really, but I can see why those assassinations of political leaders and stuff, just extremists. Obviously if it could happen to him it could happen to anybody, you know, who gets up on a stage or who walks out of a car. So it was a bit scary from that side. But you can't go around worrying, I mean I think it's like, say, a plane crash – there's a friend of mine who is terrified, I think we've all been through that, fear of flying. A friend of mine was terrified of flying and in the end he decided to go to a psychiatrist and instead of the psychiatrist saying to him the sort of thing you would expect, he said to him, 'It doesn't matter if you crash, you're not important,' which is true, really. It's like an ego thing if *I* am going to crash, *me*, I'm so important that I'm going to crash. Really, you know, that's another way of looking at it, you're not *that* important. And the same thing goes for assassination. I would like to think that I'm not that important.

Kerri-Anne: While he mightn't be worried about protecting himself, George has been keeping an eye on John Lennon's son Julian. As he told us about Julian, George revealed some surprising things about the character of John Lennon; things that he wouldn't like to see carried on by Julian as he launches his own career.

George: Julian happens to be very talented. He's really good. He's got a lot of good tunes. He's only just started to try and do lyrics. Apart from physically looking like John a bit, with glasses and long hair, he really isn't anything like John. He's more like his mother. He's a much gentler, softer person. John was like, very tough; I mean he had that ability to be gentle and soft and was lovely, but he was, you know, he was acid too. I mean he gave that hard edge to the Beatles.

Kerri-Anne: Why do you think that was? What gave him that tough edge?

George: Well, it may be because of the way he was, you know, a sort of an orphink – as Popeye would say! He was an orphan, you know. His father left home and, you know, you've heard the song, 'Mother, you left me, but I didn't leave you.' But, you know, John was a much harder, tougher person. Julian is gentle and so I don't think there's any comparison. And it's unfortunate that Julian is allowing himself to be interviewed or put in the newspapers and all that.

Kerri-Anne: George is a very sincere gentleman, a lot of great philosophies, a *great* sense of humour, and I didn't find him the quiet one. It's obvious even after a short meeting with George Harrison that he's a deeply religious man, far from fanatical, but living for his Lord. A year after the Australian tour he met the Indian sitar player Ravi Shankar. Thus began a close association not only with Indian music and yoga but with Eastern religions, the laws of karma and Krishna.

George: My involvement in that gave me a much better under-standing of certain things and how I see it is that the soul is in the body for a period of time, and then it leaves the body. It's like, in a way, the body is like a suit that you put on.

Kerri-Anne: Do you know? Have you any idea where it goes?

George: Yeah. Well, the soul – Christ said it in the Bible about the three cages of the bird of paradise, the soul being the bird of paradise and the three cages being the three bodies that house the soul. And there's the, they call it the causal body and then around that is the astral body and then there's the gross physical body. So death is really when the physical body falls off, but the soul's still in two of the bodies, so it's then on the astral level.

Kerri-Anne: You hear a lot about astral travel today. People are just sort of lying there and they look above themselves or look down and there they are. Have you ever astral travelled? In that sense?

George: I had a strange experience when I was in Rishikesh. I went on a meditation trip – course, I should say, not a trip – where the object was to meditate deeper and deeper and deeper for longer periods of time. The goal is really to plug into the divine energy and to raise your state of consciousness and tune in to the subtler states of consciousness. All those things like walking on water and dematerialising your body at will are just sort of the things that happen along the way.

So, it's hard to actually explain it, but it was a feeling of just the consciousness travelling, I don't know where to – it wasn't up, down, left or right, but it was just no body there, but at the same time you don't feel as if you're missing anything, you know, the consciousness is complete.

Kerri-Anne: The supernatural – do you believe in any of that supernatural phenomena?

George: I once got involved when our first manager died, Brian Epstein. I had so many spiritualists calling me up saying Brian Epstein wanted to talk to me. In fact, I think I talked to him more after he died than I did when he was alive!

Kerri-Anne: Really?

George: You know, and I just decided there's no point pursuing any of that because all they get . . .

Kerri-Anne: Do you think it's all a joke, though?

George: No. Well, part of it is a joke, but there, some people can become mediums.

Kerri-Anne: What about superstition. Do you believe in superstition?

George: I like all the odd numbers, you know. I'm not keen on 2, 4, 6 and 8.

Kerri-Anne: Do you think life is all predetermined?

George: In some respects it is, although we do have control over our actions right at this moment. I think that what we are now is the result of our past actions. What we're going to be is going to be the result of our present actions. As again, they said in the Bible, 'God is not mocked, whatsoever man soweth that shall he also reap.' That means the law of karma – action/reaction. There's certain things that maybe there's no way out, like, there's no way I wasn't going to be in the Beatles, even though I didn't know it. In retrospect I can see that's what it was – it was a set-up. At the same time, I do have control over my actions and I can do good actions or bad actions or I could try being a pop star forever and going on TV and do concerts and be a celebrity, or I can be a gardener.

Kerri-Anne: Well, it will probably come as a surprise to learn that the split-up of the Beatles had its origins as far back as their Australian tour in 1964. In an exclusive interview with *Good Morning Australia* George Harrison has revealed that touring was just too much pressure for the group. He says that is when the split-up really began. George talks nostalgically about the heady days of Beatlemania and makes some rather startling admissions about the Beatles' use of drugs. One of the most successful and talked about tours ever in Australia – but as it turns out, the Beatles really didn't enjoy this tour, or for that matter, any tour. Eighteen years later, a relaxed George Harrison talked about the phenomenon that was the Beatles.

George: Well, to the music industry it was a shot in the arm, there's no question about it. I saw the graph in the *Financial Times* in London and, you know, the record business was going along like this and it just went 'shhhh!' It's not just the music industry. After us they went ahead and signed *everybody*, especially from Liverpool, and, you know, everybody knows about what happened. It became a huge business. It was not just that, though, it was the clothes. I remember the Duke of Edinburgh once saying, 'What a great boost for British corduroy.' All those things. I mean, that's why they gave us those, the medals, because you know, it boosted fashion and Britain just generally got a shot in the arm. Now they've all gone back to being, you know, moaning again.

Kerri-Anne: It was reported also that Yoko Ono was quite instrumental in the break-up of the Beatles, the split. Is that true?

George: We were splitting long before that, really. You know, I mean, just the pressure. When we stopped touring, we only toured two years, really, like I think '65 and '66 around the world. And it was just too much pressure. At the end of '66 we just decided, that's it! We'll just go in the studio and work there. We were doomed from the beginning because we were like monkeys in a zoo. Everybody needs space in order to grow and I think that the public and the press split the Beatles probably more than Yoko or Linda McCartney.

Kerri-Anne: As it turned out, the Beatles sought an escape from the pressure. As George says, they were doomed from the beginning and it was right back then when they first tried drugs. In those days when it was super, super pressurised, the drugs and the alcohol. I mean, was it easy or difficult to rely on drugs to try and get you through those times because obviously you were very young and in a high-pressure business. Did you have to rely a lot on drugs and alcohol to make it through?

George: Well, not rely on them. It's just that they were good fun at the time. I mean, it started – I was seventeen when I first went, we went to Hamburg. We were given a job in the Reeperbahn, which is the naughtiest part of Hamburg. They booked us for eight hours a night and then the club we were in had to close down. The police shut it down so they moved us into another club where there was another band also booked for eight hours. So instead of giving us four hours each, we started at two in the afternoon and did an hour, and they did an hour, we did an hour, and we went right through, you know, till the following morning. And after we were . . . by the second week of doing that, around the sixth set when we were flagging a bit and the boss of the club, who was a gangster, brought all his gangster pals in saying, you know, wanted us to jump up and down doing 'What'd I Say' or something. So then they started slipping us these pills called Preludin, which were women's slimming pills. And we'd take them and froth at the mouth and leap up and down singing 'What'd I Say'. Then they invented marijuana and somebody just gave it to us and we smoked it, and the best thing about that was that we used to drink whisky and the moment marijuana came, we just knocked the whisky on the head. But, you know, it's just like anything, it was not bad. I always knew from when I was a kid, you know, seeing films about Chet Baker or, you know, these jazz people who OD'd on heroin. I never ever wanted to know about heroin. I didn't, I just kept away from it and a lot of my friends died and are still dying. But I think, well, I was a bit lucky. I felt I had a tilt mechanism, you know. I could get a bit loaded but then I'd always cut out: 'OK, that's enough!' – and go and get straight. And after a while, you know, it sort of gets boring.

Kerri-Anne: In 1971 George Harrison organised one of the biggest charity concerts ever held – the concert for Bangla Desh. It not only raised ten thousand dollars, it drew the world's finest musicians, at least the finest according to George. As we discovered, George has some strong feelings about which artists are good and which ones are bad.

What about the comparison to today's music? You made the statement that today's music is an example of 'ugly prancing egos'. Could you give us an example of an ugly prancing ego that we might see?

George: Well, I didn't catch any of the names too much because as soon as I'd see them I'd think, you know, those songs, bluh, bluh . . . they just shout and there's no melodies, no words worth talking about. You know, the musicianship became so bad, because . . . we were pretty naïve and we were very amateur in a way but at the same time we tried to create interesting music, saying something, you know? I mean, these people aren't saying anything and the reason why they're not saying anything is because they don't know anything. That's a pretty strong statement, but it's true. I mean, I'm talking about probably 95% of the, not just the pop or the punk or whatever, but the entire world of music. Maybe I'm just a fussy person but I want something to say something, something to enrich my experience. You know, I don't want somebody just hitting me on the head with a hammer; that can't teach me anything.

Kerri-Anne: Is there anybody who does that for you today?

George: Who enriches? Sure. Bob Dylan is the guv'nor. I mean, if all he'd ever written was 'Blowin' In The Wind', he's done much more than the average person. And there's musicians I like purely as musicians for fun, like Ry Cooder. I don't know if he's popular, he's a Warner Brothers artist and he's a great guitar player and he's, uh, you must have heard of Ry Cooder. Anyway, he's ace. And I like my old pals like Eric Clapton and, you know, out of the newer people . . . I dunno, I went gardening about six years ago.

Kerri-Anne: What about Elton John?

George: Elton is a really good entertainer. You know, he's very talented, but still, he doesn't say anything, really. You know, OK, 'Crocodile Rock' and all that. I like Elton a lot but there's a lack of depth of experience.

Kerri-Anne: George, was it your sense of humour that brought you into financing a lot of movies that you've been involved in, the *Monty Python* movies recently?

George: Yeah. I think the *Python* one in the first place, *The Life Of Brian*, was due to the fact that I was friendly mainly with Eric Idle, you know, who is 'nudge-nudge, wink-wink, say no more'; and they were doing, they started the film and the backers, who were EMI in England, Lew Grade, they backed out of it. I think they thought it was a bit too Jewish or something, and a friend of mine just asked, could you think of a way of helping them get the film made. Being a *Python* fan I just wanted to see the movie as well. I asked my business manager if he could think of a way of doing it, and he did, and we became the producers of the film and then it just went from there. We did some other things, bought another film that Lew Grade was going to get rid of called *The Long Good Friday*, which is an excellent English film, and we made a film which is out, I think, at this moment called *Time Bandits*, which was written by the American in *Monty Python*, Terry Gilliam, and Michael Palin, and it also had a part by John Cleese. I don't know if you've seen it, he plays Robin Hood. And now I'm sort of suddenly in the film industry.

Kerri-Anne: Do you like being a film producer?

George: Well, it's easy. I mean, it's a bit of a risk. It's much more risky than making records. I mean, you can spend $150,000 making an album, whereas a movie, I mean, they cost millions.

Kerri-Anne: Like so many of the world's rich and famous, ex-Beatle George Harrison has fallen in love with Australia. On his recent holiday here he told us in an exclusive interview he'd most likely be buying land, even if it's just an excuse to keep coming back. These days Harrison spends most of his time tending a huge garden at home beside the Thames in England. But we found him relaxing on Hamilton Island in Queensland's Whitsunday Passage. It was the final stop on his holiday after visiting many different areas and meeting a lot of people, some of whom, strangely enough, didn't even recognise him.

George: The Australians' attitude is good. I went in the flight deck of the Quantas 747. Now if you do that sort of situation in other places they would say, 'Oh, yes sire, hello sire,' or 'Yes, Mr Harrison' or whatever, but you just go in there and they say, 'Alright George, how ya doin'?' You know? And I like that directness, there's no what they call bullshit. I don't know if you can say that on Australian television, but you know, people are just more straightforward. I got caught for speeding the first day I got in a car . . .

Kerri-Anne: Here is Australia?

George: Yeah. And the police, when I stopped, I had to open the back of my car to get my drivers licence out to show him, and he said, you know, you look like one of the Rolling Stones. And I said, 'Oh, really?' and I said, 'Look, I'm sorry, you know, I didn't notice the sign and I only just got here,' and all that, and he says, 'Oh, well, you know, just watch out and be careful.'

Kerri-Anne: Did he look at your name on the licence?

George: Yeah, he didn't . . . unless he did know and he was being funny, saying the Rolling Stones. But you know, he was quite nice and I've said it a number of times and I'll say it again, the biggest mistake that the British made was not sending us out here and keeping all the convicts up there, because this is, you know, as far as I'm concerned this is much more fun.

Kerri-Anne: The fun he's talking about is the great Barrier Reef, the retreat which the Harrison family sought for part of their time in Australia. Harrison still spends most of his life quietly, puttering around in his garden at home by the Thames in England. Now it seems the ex-Beatle will be spending more time here and investing in property in Queensland.

George: I think it's great, the Barrier Reef and all these islands.

Kerri-Anne: Is it true you may be investing in a little unit or what?

George: Well, everywhere we go, somebody says, 'Oh, he's coming to buy,' you know, Australia or wherever you are. I must say that it would be nice to have somewhere out here, I mean, just as an excuse to keep coming back, but I didn't really come just to try and buy Australia. Lex Luthor . . .

Kerri-Anne: Would you ever consider recording in Australia?

George: Yeah. You know, there's no point in me doing it at the moment because I've got a studio, which I spent a lot of money on building, which is in my house in England. So, you know, it's much more practical. I've got everything there already and I have all the facilities that I need. But maybe sometime in the future, I wouldn't mind.

Kerri-Anne: Well, George, all I can say is thank you very much for your time, energy, inviting us to your little paradise, singing in the rain for us, talking in the rain.

George: Thank you. Good morning, Australia. And I also want to just say hello to Alan Jones because I tried calling you, Alan, if you're watching, for two and a half weeks, but I couldn't get through to you and I missed you. I would've liked to have seen you, but give us a shout if you come to England.

Goswami, Mukunda

The person who introduced George to the Hare Krishna movement in London in 1969.

The New Zealand-born Goswami struck up a close friendship with George, who co-signed the lease on the group's first temple in central London. George also supported Goswami and other Hare Krishna devotees over the years and funded the printing of various Hare Krishna books for them, in addition to lending them his home on Hamilton Island in Australia as a writing retreat. He also wrote the foreword to Goswami's book *Divine Nature*.

In December 2001, Goswami and another Krishna devotee Shyamasunder Das came to London to help ease George's path into reincarnation.

In an interview, Goswami was to say, 'He was a very spiritual person who was unafraid to die. He was a believer in God.

'Natural happiness is something everyone is looking for and reincarnation gives people a sense of progress or hope knowing there's something better and that death isn't the end of everything.

'The soul continues and death needn't be a dismal experience knowing there is a better experience waiting.'

Got My Mind Set On You

The first single released from the *Cloud Nine* album. It was issued in Britain on Monday 12 October 1987 where it reached the No. 2 position and in America on Friday 16 October where it was to top the charts. 'Lay His Head' was on the flip.

It was George's first US chart-topper since 'Give Me Love (Give Me Peace On Earth)' in 1973. It became George's biggest UK hit since 'My Sweet Lord' seventeen years previously.

There was also a 12″ extended mix of the number issued in Britain only and the single was issued in several other alternative formats.

George made two promotional videos for the number in America, only one of which was approved for broadcast. This was produced by Kathryn Ireland and directed by Gary Weiss and features George in a haunted house, singing the song while sitting in a chair with his electric guitar. He then leaps from the chair and begins disco dancing – although a double did the dance routine for him.

The second promo was apparently quite pedestrian and featured George looking into a 'what the butler saw' machine at an amusement arcade. This second video was actually screened on the *Chart Show*.

In America the number was available on 7″ vinyl on Dark Horse 7-28178 and a cassette single Dark Horse 4-28178. There was also a promotional CD of the track issued to American radio stations on PRO-CD-2846.

It was released in Britain on Dark Horse W 8178. A limited edition box of the number was also issued on the same day.

The number was a cover of a song by Rudy Clark and the only track on the *Cloud Nine* album that George didn't write himself. James Ray first covered it in the 1950s.

Greece

A number on the 1982 *Gone Troppo* album, penned by George and lasting 3 minutes and 57 seconds. Billy Preston played keyboards and synthesizer on the track.

It was also issued as the flipside of the single 'Wake Up My Love'.

Guest Appearances

George made more guest appearances on other people's albums than any of the other former Beatles.

He delighted in performing on other people's recordings, or joining them on stage, often using pseudonyms, and did so far more often than John, Paul or Ringo.

George contributed to solo projects by Jim Capaldi, Belinda Carlisle, Eric Clapton, Duane Eddy, Sylvia Griffin, Jeff Healey, Jeff Lynne, Gary Moore, Roy Orbison, Tom Petty, Ravi Shankar, Del Shannon, Gary Wright and others.

George played guitar and tambourine on the Silkie's version of 'You've Got To Hide Your Love Away' in 1965.

An early production of his was recording his Liverpool friends The Remo Four for his *Wonderwall* soundtrack and with the number 'In The First Place', originally recorded in 1967 that was only released thirty years later in 1997.

From then on George was to make a wide variety of guest appearances.

1968:
George wrote and produced the Jackie Lomax single 'Sour Milk Sea' on which he also played rhythm guitar, in addition to producing and playing guitar on Jackie's 'The Eagle Laughs At You'. When in Rishikesh, he added a verse to Donovan's song 'Hurdy Gurdy Man', which was left off the original recording but reintroduced when it was reissued in 1990.

1969:
The year saw him co-write 'Badge' with Eric Clapton and he played guitar on the recording, a number featured on Cream's album *Goodbye*, issued in March of that year. May saw George producing the Jackie Lomax album *Is This What You Want?* and he played guitar on some of the tracks. He sang harmony on the 'Carolina On My Mind' track on James Taylor's eponymous album. He also played bass guitar and remixed 'King Of Fuh', a single by the Apple band Brute Force and co-produced 'Hari Krishna Mantra' and 'Prayer To The Spiritual Masters' with Paul McCartney for the Radha Krishna Temple. He played guitar on the songs 'Exchange And Mart' and 'Spending All My Days' on the *Blind Faith* album. He also produced the Billy Preston album *That's The Way God Planned It* and played guitar on some of the tracks. In October he contributed to Jack Bruce's album *Songs For A Tailor*, playing guitar on the song 'Never Tell Your Mother She's Out Of Tune'. He produced Billy Preston's 'Everything's All Right'. On John Lennon's *Wedding Album* he played guitar on the song 'Who Has Seen The Wind?' and the single 'Cold Turkey'. He played guitar on Joe Cocker's version of 'Something'.

1970:
George produced the Billy Preston single 'All That I've Got (I'm Gonna Give It To You)', played guitar on the song 'As I Get Older' and also produced Jackie Lomax's 'How The Web Was Woven'. He played guitar and piano on John Lennon's 'Instant Karma'. He produced and was co-writer of Doris Troy's 'Ain't That Cute' and played guitar on her 'Vaja Con Dios'. He produced the next Radha Krishna Temple single 'Govinda', arranged Doris Troy's 'Jacob's Ladder' and produced and played guitar on her 'Get Back' track. He co-wrote and played guitar on Ashton, Gardner & Dyke's 'I'm Your Spiritual Breadman' and played guitar on a number of the tracks on Doris Troy's eponymous Apple album. He next co-produced Billy Preston's album *Encouraging Words* and played guitar, wrote some tracks and provided occasional backing vocals. George co-produced and co-wrote 'Tandoori Chicken' with Phil Spector, a track that wasn't released, and wrote, produced and played guitar on Ronnie Spector's 'Try Some, Buy Some' and a number of other tracks, which weren't released. He next produced the Radha Krishna Temple's

eponymous album, also playing guitar on a number of the tracks. Retaining the Eastern flavour, he produced the Ravi Shankar album *Raga*. He participated on four songs on the Badfinger album *Straight Up*, playing acoustic and Stratocaster guitars on 'I'd Die Babe' and slide guitar on 'Name Of The Game', 'Suitcase' and 'Day After Day', also producing the songs. He sang harmony on James Taylor's Apple single 'Carolina On My Mind'. Using the pseudonym Mysterioso, he played guitar on the tracks 'Coming Home', 'I Don't Want To Discuss It', 'A Little Richard Medley', 'Only You Know And I Know', 'Poor Elijah – Tribute to Johnson', 'That's What My Man Is For', 'Things Get Better' and 'Where There's A Will There's A Way' on the *Delaney & Bonnie & Friends On Tour With Eric Clapton* album. He played guitar and sang backing vocals on 'Roll It Over', the flipside of the Derek & The Dominoes single 'Tell The Truth'. He played guitar on 'Went To See The Gypsy' on Bob Dylan's *New Morning* album. Next came the *Concert For Bangla Desh* album, which he co-produced and performed on, an acclaimed venture that raised millions in aid of the children of Bangla Desh. In March of that year he was featured on several of the tracks of Leon Russell's eponymous album. George produced and played guitar on Ringo Starr's single 'It Don't Come Easy' and also produced Ravi Shankar's single 'Joi Bangla'.

1971:

George played on Gary Wright's album *Footprints* using the pseudonym George O'Hara. He played sitar on 'Greenfield Morning' on the *Yoko Ono/Plastic Ono Band* album. On Bobby Whitlock's eponymous album he played guitar on the tracks 'Stand For Our Rights' and 'Two-Faced Man'. He played dobro on 'Crippled Inside' and guitar on 'Gimme Some Truth', 'Oh My Love', 'Don't Wanna Be A Soldier', 'Mamma I Don't Want To Die' and 'How Do You Sleep?' on John Lennon's *Imagine* album. He played guitar on 'I Wrote A Simple Song' on Billy Preston's album *The Best*. He produced Badfinger's 'Day After Day' single and produced *Raga*, the movie soundtrack to the Ravi Shankar film. He co-produced Badfinger's album *Straight Up*, playing guitar on the tracks 'Day After Day', 'I'd Die Babe', 'Name Of The Game' and 'Suitcase'.

1972:

During this year he was the co-writer on the track 'The Holdup' on David Bromberg's eponymous album and also produced 'Sweet Music' on the *Brother* album by Apple artists Lon & Derek Van Eaton. His number 'Sue Me, Sue You Blues' was featured on the Jesse Ed Davis album *Ululu*. That year also saw him contributing to Harry Nilsson's album *Son Of Schmilsson*, playing guitar on the track 'You're Breakin' My Heart'. In April he contributed a guitar solo on the track 'Tell The

Truth' on the *History Of Eric Clapton* anthology, which also included 'Badge'. He produced and played guitar on Ringo Starr's 'Back Off Boogaloo' single and played guitar on 'Cold Turkey' and 'Don't Worry Kyoko' on John Lennon's *Some Time In New York City* album. He played guitar on the track 'Bootleg' on Bobby Key's eponymous album. He played guitar on 'Lovely Lady', 'Nothin' Gonna Get You Down' and 'Doing The Right Thing' and sang on 'If I Had Time' on Rudy Romero's *To The World* album.

1973:
He involved himself with Ringo Starr's album *Ringo*, co-writing and adding vocals to 'Photograph', writing, playing guitar and singing on 'Sunshine Life For Me', co-writing and playing guitar on 'You And Me Babe' and playing guitar on 'Photograph' and 'I'm The Greatest'. He was co-producer of the Ravi Shankar and Ali Akbar Khan double album *In Concert 1972* and wrote, played slide guitar, guitar, bass guitar and provided backing vocals for the track 'So Sad (No Love Of His Own)' on the Alvin Lee/Mylon Lefevre album. On the Don Nix album *Hobos Heroes And Street Corner Clowns* he played guitar on the track 'I Need You' and produced and provided vocals on 'The Train Don't Stop Here Anymore'. He was featured on guitar on the track 'If You've Got Love' on the Dave Mason album *It's Like You Never Left*, using the pseudonym 'Son of Harry'. He also contributed to Nicky Hopkins' album *The Tin Man Was A Dreamer*, playing guitar on the songs 'Banana Anna', 'Edward', 'Speed On' and 'Waiting For The Band'. He played guitar on the track 'Basketball Jones' on the album *Cheech And Chong's Greatest Hits*. The song 'Badge', which he co-wrote with Eric Clapton, he performed live on the album *Eric Clapton's Rainbow Concert*.

1974:
He contributed to David Bomberg's *Wanted Dead Or Alive* album, co-writing the song 'The Holdup' and produced the Splinter album *The Place I Love*, providing backing on each track playing a variety of instruments including guitar, harmonium, percussion, mandolin, Moog and acoustic guitar. He also produced Ravi Shankar's album *Shankar, Family And Friends*, also contributing to various tracks on vocals, autoharp and acoustic guitars. He was also songwriter and played guitar and provided backing vocals on 'Far East Man', a track from Ron Wood's album *I've Got My Own Album To Do*.

1975:
George co-produced and played the guitar on the tracks 'Lonely Man' and 'After Five Years' on Splinter's album *Harder To Live*. He also produced the *Monty Python* single 'The Lumberjack Song'. George played guitar on 'Make Love Not War', a track on Peter Skellern's

Hard Times album. He also played guitar on the track 'That's Life' on Billy Preston's album *It's My Pleasure*.

1976:
This year saw him producing Ravi Shankar's album *Ravi Shankar's Music Festival From India* and Shankar's *In Celebration*, on which he also played guitar and autoharp on 'I Am Missing You' and autoharp on 'Friar Park'. He also wrote 'I'll Still Love You' for Ringo Starr's *Rotogravure* album. He played slide guitar on Tom Scott's 'Appolonia (Frostrata)', which appears on the album *New York Connection*. He was co-producer and guitarist on a Japanese version of the Splinter single 'Lonely Man' and contributed to Larry Hosford's *Cross Words* album, playing guitar on 'Direct Me' and providing backing vocals for 'Wishing I Could'.

1977:
George was executive producer and played guitar on Splinter's single 'I'll Bend For You'. He was also executive producer and played guitar on Splinter's album *Two Man Band*.

1978:
George played slide guitar on 'The Last Time', a track on the Hall & Oates album *Along The Red Ledge*.

1979:
This year saw him acting as co-mixer on the track 'Always Look On The Bright Side Of Life' from the soundtrack of the *Monty Python* film *The Life Of Brian*.

1981:
George produced and played guitar on 'You Belong To Me' and wrote and produced 'Wrack My Brain' on the Ringo Starr album *Stop And Smell The Roses*. On Mick Fleetwood's solo album, *The Visitor*, George played 12-string and slide guitar and joined in on backing vocals on the track 'Walk A Thin Line'.

1982:
Gary Brooker received the contribution of George on guitar for the track 'Mineral Man' on his *Lead Me To The Water* album.

1983:
George acted as producer and provided backing vocals for 'Bullshot', the theme to the HandMade film of the same name.

1985:
He sang the Bob Dylan song 'I Don't Want To Do It' on the soundtrack of *Porky's Revenge*. He also contributed to the soundtrack of *Water*,

co-writing 'Focus Of Attention' and 'Celebration' and also playing guitar on the tracks. His 'Save The World' track was also included on the *Greenpeace* charity album.

1986:
George played guitar on the track 'Talk Don't Bother Me' on Alvin Lee's album *Detroit Diesel* and played guitar and sang on the tracks 'Blue Moon Of Kentucky', 'Blue Suede Shoes', 'Gone Gone Gone', 'Glad All Over', 'Night Train To Memphis', 'Amen', 'That's all Right (Mama)', 'The World Is Waiting For The Sunrise', 'Whole Lotta Shakin' Goin' On' and 'Your True Love' on the album *Blue Suede Shoes (A Rockabilly Session With Carl Perkins and Friends)*. He also played lead guitar on the track 'Children Of The Sky' on Mike Batt's concept album *The Hunting Of The Snark*.

1987:
1987 saw him producing and playing autoharp on 'Friar Park' a track on the Ravi Shankar CD *Tana Mana*. Together with Jeff Lynne he co-produced and played slide guitar on 'The Trembler' and 'Theme For Something Really Important' tracks on the album *Duane Eddy*. George's 'While My Guitar Gently Weeps' was included on the sound-track of the HandMade classic *Withnail And I*. He also performed 'While My Guitar Gently Weeps' and 'Here Comes The Sun' on the album *The Prince's Trust Concert 1987*.

1988:
Traveling Wilburys Vol 1 was released with George as co-producer and playing guitar and providing backing vocals on the tracks 'Dirty World', 'Congratulations', 'Tweeter And The Monkey Man', 'Rattled', 'Margarita', 'Last Night' and 'Not Alone Anymore'. Eric Clapton's *Crossroads* album included 'Badge' and George playing guitar and singing backing vocals on 'Roll It Over' and guitar on 'Tell The Truth'. On Sylvia Griffin's single 'Love's A State Of Mind' there was a slide guitar contribution from George. George made a guest appearance playing a slide guitar solo on '(I Don't Wanna) Hold Back', a track from the Gary Wright album *Who Am I*. He also appeared on the track 'Oh Lord, Why Lord' on Jim Capaldi's album *Some Came Running*. He produced the song 'Sweet Music' on Derrek Van Eaton's album *Give A Little Love*.

1989:
George wrote, played guitar and provided backing vocals on the track 'Run So Far' on Eric Clapton's CD *Journeyman*. He also contributed to *Songs From The Garage*, Tom Petty's solo album. Along with Ringo, George appeared on the promo of Tom Petty's 'I Won't Back Down', a track from Petty's *Full Moon Fever*, on which

he played acoustic guitar. George played guitar and sang backing vocals on the record. On Belinda Carlisle's album *Runaway Horses* he played a slide guitar solo on the single 'Leave A Light On' and played bass and 12-string on 'Deep Deep Ocean'. He played acoustic guitar on 'A Love So Beautiful', a track from Roy Orbison's *Mystery Girl* album and also provided backing vocals on the track 'You Got It'. He played and composed 'Cheer Down' on the *Lethal Weapon 2* soundtrack.

1990:
George played guitar on the track 'Take Away The Sadness' on Jim Horn's album *Work It Out*. On *Armchair Theatre*, Jeff Lynne's first solo album, George appeared as guest artist on four of the eleven tracks – he played acoustic guitar and backing vocals on 'Every Little Thing'; slide guitar, acoustic guitar, harmony vocal and backing vocals on 'Lift Me Up'; slide guitar and acoustic guitar on 'September Song'; and slide guitar and acoustic guitar on 'Stormy Weather'. His 'Blow Away' was included on the soundtrack of the *Nuns On The Run* film. He played guitar on 'Lu Le La' on Vicki Brown's album *About Love And Life*. He wrote, played guitar and provided backing vocals on 'That Kind Of Woman' on an Eric Clapton CD and the Traveling Wilburys track 'Nobody's Child' appeared on *Nobody's Child – The Romanian Angel Appeal* album. George was co-writer and co-producer and played acoustic and electric guitars, sitar, mandolins and provided backing vocals on the tracks 'If You Belonged To Me', 'Seven Deadly Sins', 'Poor House', 'You Took My Breath Away' and 'Cool Dry Place' on the *Traveling Wilburys Vol 3* CD. He was co-producer and played guitars and provided backing vocals on the Traveling Wilburys CD-single 'Runaway'. He wrote, played acoustic guitar and provided backing vocals on the Jeff Healey Band interpretation of 'While My Guitar Gently Weeps' on their album *Hell To Pay*. George wrote, played rhythm and slide guitar and provided backing vocals on the track 'That Kind Of Woman' on Gary Moore's album *Still Got The Blues*. He also played slide guitar on the title track of Bob Dylan's *Under The Red Sky* album.

1991:
George played slide guitar on 'Saltwater', a number on Julian Lennon's fourth solo album *Help Yourself* and also played guitar on 'If Not For You' on Dylan's *The Bootleg Series. Volumes 1–3* album. He sang backing vocals on 'Hot Love' on Del Shannon's album *Callin' Out My Name*.

1992:
Zoom was an album by Alvin Lee on which George is featured on slide guitar on the track 'Real Life Blues'. The same year saw *Growing Up*

In Public, an album by Jimmy Nail on which George and Gary Moore played on the track 'Real Love' (*not* the Beatles number). George also wrote and produced 'Ride Rajbun' for the *Bunbury Tails* soundtrack album.

1993:
There was another contribution to a Dylan recording when *The 30th Anniversary Concert Celebration* was released with George singing lead vocals on 'Absolutely Sweet Marie' and playing guitar and singing back up on 'Knockin' On Heaven's Door' and 'My Back Pages'.

1994:
George played guitar on 'I Want You (She's So Heavy)' and 'The Bluest Blues' tracks on Alvin Lee's *I Hear You Rockin'* album.

1995:
George provided backing vocals on 'Don't Try To Own Me' on Gary Wright's album *First Signs Of Life*.

1996:
George was producer, mixer, played guitar, bass guitar and provided backing vocals on the track 'Distance Makes No Difference' on Carl Perkins' album *Go Cat Go!* and arranged and played guitar and auto-harp on Ravi Shankar's *In Celebration (Highlights)*.

1997:
George produced Ravi Shankar's *Chants Of India* CD and also provided backing vocals and played several instruments including acoustic guitar, bass guitar, autoharp, glockenspiel, vibraphone and marimba on various tracks.

1998:
George produced Ravi's 1998 2-CD set *Raga Mala*. He played lead guitar on 'King Of Broken Hearts' and 'I'll Be Fine Everywhere' on Ringo Starr's *Vertical Man* album. The score of the film *Everest* included versions of George's numbers 'All Things Must Pass', 'Life Itself', 'This Is Love', 'Give Me Love (Give Me Peace On Earth)' and 'Here Comes The Sun'.

2000:
George played slide guitar on the 'Punchdrunk' track of the Rubyhorse album *How Far Have You Come?*

2001:
George played slide guitar on 'Love Letters', a track on Bill Wyman's double CD *Double Bill*. George also played guitar on Jim Capaldi's

single and album track 'Anna Julia'. He played slide guitar on 'A Long Time Gone' and 'All She Wanted' on the Electric Light Orchestra album *Zoom*.

2002:
'Horse To Water' by George was included on the Jools Holland album *Small World Big Band*, which was retitled *Jools Holland's Big Band Rhythm & Blues* when it was issued in the States.

Guinness Album: Hits Of The 70s, The
A double-album compilation by various artists, issued in Britain on 5 December 1980 on CBS 10020. It was the second compilation album to include George's track of 'My Sweet Lord'.

Haight-Ashbury

A district in San Francisco that, in the late 1960s, was known as a main centre for the 'hippy' movement. George became the only Beatle to visit the area during the famous 'Summer Of Love'.

George, along with Derek Taylor, Neil Aspinall, Alexis Mardas and Patti and Jenny Boyd, was visiting the district on 7 August 1967. They parked their limousine and went on walkabout. A busker thrust a guitar in his hand, literally ordering him to play. He tried a few chords of 'Baby You're A Rich Man' then thrust the guitar back and the crowd began to get restless and hostile. They returned to the car within half an hour because of the attitude of the crowds.

George said, 'I don't mind anybody dropping out of anything but it's the imposition on somebody else I don't like. I've just realised that it doesn't matter what you are as long as you work – in fact, if you drop out, you put yourself further away from the goal of life than if you were to keep on working.'

While on his brief walkabout, George turned down tabs of LSD and tokes of marijuana that the hippies were offering him.

He said that he had been looking for some enlightenment from the hippies, but 'instead it was all these spotty kid dropouts who had taken too many different drugs. Their brains were all strangled. I gave up drugs after I saw that.'

His image of Haight-Ashbury and the 'Summer of Love' was severely dented and he said, 'I'd thought it would be something like King's Road, only more. Somehow I expected them all to own their own little shops. I expected them all to be nice and clean and friendly and happy.'

George was also to recall, 'I was being treated like the Messiah. It certainly showed me what was really happening in the drug culture. It wasn't what I thought – spiritual awakenings and being artistic – it was like alcoholism, like any addiction. That was the turning point for me. That's when I really went for the meditation.'

Handle With Care
A Traveling Wilburys' single, issued in 1988. A promo was filmed in Los Angeles in October 1988, directed by David Leland, and produced by Limelight Films.

Hand Made In Hong Kong
A television documentary about the filming of *Shanghai Surprise*, directed by Geoff Wonfor. It was shown on Channel Four in Britain on 7 October 1987, although Madonna and Sean Penn unsuccessfully attempted to stop the screening.

Sean Penn, around this time, had seemed to be a very disruptive presence during the filming. Wonfer was to comment, 'Without George I think we'd have given up and gone home. There were times when I could have hit Penn. It was only George who helped me keep my cool.'

HandMade Films
In 1973 Peter Sellers introduced George to Denis O'Brien in Los Angeles. George and the American businessman, who'd been trained both as a lawyer and as an accountant, decided to go into business together.

The company eventually formed by George and O'Brien in 1978 was called HandMade Films. George explained: 'The name of the company came about as a bit of a joke. I'd been to Wooky Hole in Somerset and when you come out of the cave you go through an old paper mill, where they show you how they make old underpants into paper. So I bought a few rolls, and they had this watermark 'British HandMade Paper'. I said, "Let's call our company British HandMade Films." But when we went to register it we were told, "You can't call it British! You can only call things British if everybody is on strike the whole time and it's making huge losses." So we said, "Sod it – we'll just call it HandMade Films!"'

The opportunity for an investment came up when EMI withdrew their financial backing for a *Monty Python* film, *The Life Of Brian*, on the suggestion of Lord Delfont. George and O'Brien raised the money and the film became a success, particularly in America where it counts. George even made a guest appearance in the movie.

EMI had originally agreed to back *The Life Of Brian* to the tune of $4 million. The *Python* team had established that they would have sole artistic control of the film, but Lord Delfont demanded changes and refused to allow the EMI financing unless the team toed the line.

George and Denis then entered the picture. George said: 'When I heard about the *Python* film, because they were friends of mine (especially Eric and Michael) and because I wanted to see their movie, I had a word with Denis. "How can we help my mates?" And a little while later Denis rang me and said, "OK, I've figured a way to get it made," and he got rolling.'

The movie was directed by Terry Jones and was filmed in Tunisia. Set at the time of Christ, it concerned a baby born in a manger at the same time as Jesus. Brian's life parallels that of the Messiah and he becomes involved with the People's Liberation Front of Judea. It was considered blasphemous by some in Britain, but was one of the biggest-grossing films in America when it opened there in 1979, earning $21m at the American box office alone.

As executive producer of most of the films, George made suggestions at the scripting stage, occasionally contributed original music and made a few cameo appearances – in *The Life Of Brian*, *Water*, *Shanghai Surprise* and *Checking Out*. Original or previously released material by George or the Beatles appeared in *Time Bandits*, *Water*, *Shanghai Surprise*, *Withnail And I*, *Track 29* and *Nuns On The Run*.

Another controversial film which HandMade films were determined to rescue was *The Long Good Friday*, which EMI had decided not to release. Instead, the gritty gangster film was to be emasculated and sold directly to television. HandMade stepped in and distributed the movie, which proved to be quite successful. It was a tough, action-packed thriller about an East End gang leader about to do a deal with the Mafia who is suddenly involved in a battle with the IRA. It starred Bob Hoskins and Helen Mirren.

HandMade's next venture was to finance the 1981 release *Time Bandits*, which had been co-scripted by Michael Palin and Terry Gilliam. It concerns a group of dwarfs who have stolen a map of the universe, and it relates how they set out through gaps in the structure of time in search of treasure, accompanied by Kevin, a twentieth-century schoolboy. During their adventures they encounter King Agamemnon (Sean Connery) battling the Minotaur, Napoleon (Ian Holm) sacking Italy, and Robin Hood (John Cleese) in Sherwood Forest. There is a climactic battle between Good and Evil, enacted by Sir Ralph Richardson and David Warner.

1983 was HandMade's busiest year, with several releases, including *The Missionary*, starring Michael Palin. Directed by Richard Loncraine, the film took a swipe at the hypocrisy of Edwardian morals in the tale of a missionary, recently returned from Africa, who is sent to London's East End to convert the women of ill repute.

Another comedy was *Privates On Parade* directed by Michael Blakemore. The film starred John Cleese as Major Giles Flack and concerned an ill-assorted concert troupe in Malaya shortly after the Second World War, with a camp performance from Denis Quilley as the homosexual Captain Terry.

A more dramatic presentation was *Scrubbers*, directed by Mai Zetterling, and set in a penal institute for girls.

The other 1983 production was *Bullshot*, a satire on boys' heroes of the 1930s such as Bulldog Drummond. The film related how captain Hugh 'Bullshot' Crummond (Alan Sherman) rescued Professor Fenton from Otto Von Bruno (Ron House) and his wife (Frances Tomelty) with the help of the Professor's daughter, Rosemary. Ian Le Frenais produced the film, which was directed by Dick Clement and featured appearances by Mel Smith, Billy Connolly and 'Legs' Larry Smith.

Scenes were set in Henley, close to George's Friar Park mansion. George appeared on an edition of the BBC 2 programme *Film '83* discussing the movie on 12 September 1983 in an interview with Nicholas Shakespeare:

George: Well, I'm somebody who happens to get involved occasionally with movies like this. This is a sort of low-budget film and it's a new group of people, at least new to the big-time film industry and, you know, we do sort of smallish things, really, and I wouldn't say I was a mogul, but it's quite fun, it's interesting.

Shakespeare: Did you have any say in choosing this?

George: No. Well, I mean, I did read the script and hear about, you know . . . but it wasn't a choice that I made, if that's what you mean, but I certainly do not object to it.

Shakespeare: Might you have to bail it out if it goes wrong?

George: Well, if it goes wrong it's, yeah, I suppose so. I mean, I stand to lose money if it loses, but I mean that's the risk that you take, really. But these days I think you should be able to, with a low-budget film, be able to, you know, at least break even, if not make anything. You know, I mean, if you talk over a period of years, and there's a lot of countries, and there's television and video, but hopefully it will get a decent theatrical release and, you know, who knows?

Shakespeare: Are you sad to have lost *Monty Python*?

George: I haven't lost *Monty Python*, they're still good friends of mine. If you mean the fact that we didn't produce their last film, I'm not sad. I didn't produce the first two. It was a pleasure to be able to, at that time, bail them out of that situation and . . . I came out with a film that was funny. You know, I'm happy whichever way things turn out. I don't try to hang on, you know. I'd rather hang on to friendships than business deals.

Shakespeare: Have you got any more ideas for films, or any more projects?

George: There are a lot of things, you know. Obviously, the more films that we have made, the more scripts come in. There are a lot of scripts and there's a lot of ideas in the works and it's a

matter of sorting them out, you know. The ones which are going
to be made into films sort of evolve out of a period of time.

Although George didn't seem unduly concerned that the *Monty
Python* team had gone to someone else with *The Meaning Of Life*,
Denis O'Brien was a trifle upset that the Pythons had done a deal
directly with Universal in Hollywood without offering them the possibility of distributing the film in other territories outside the US.

George commented: 'We never had a contract with them to say that
you must stick with us forever. All we did was start the film, as a fan
and as a friend, and see it to success. If I can help someone like Gilliam,
with his eccentricities which border on genius, I will, subject to Denis
putting it on a realistic basis so that we don't go bankrupt inside six
months.'

Michael Palin intimated that the suggestion of some ambitious financial schemes, put to them by Denis, frightened them off. 'Whenever
heavy commercial pressures are put on the Pythons we always react
against it. Denis, with the best will in the world, tried to line us up with
big corporations in America to sell our material – we were offered
shares in companies and that kind of thing – and for a month it all
seemed wonderful. Then we all looked at each other and said, "This is
not our world – we're not really happy here."'

For a time, HandMade set up a distribution arm, but they were relatively unsuccessful with *Tattoo*, *The Burning* and *Venom*, and so they
decided to concentrate on funding films.

In 1984 – their sixth year of operation – HandMade announced that
they would be making between three and five movies each year and had
three planned for 1984. There was a big-budget project starring Michael
Caine called *Water*, produced by Ian Le Frenais and directed by Dick
Clement, with supporting actors Leonard Rossiter and Billy Connolly.
Michael Mowbray was to direct a comedy called *Port Royal*, set in
Britain in the 1940s, starring Michael Palin and Maggie Smith. The final
project of the year was *Travelling Men*, directed by John Mackenzie.

In their first decade the company produced twenty-two films and
only lost money on six of them.

In their tenth year they only produced one film, *Nuns On The Run*
(1990) and scaled back operations, cutting their London staff and
closing the New York office.

Harrison had met with his partner Denis O'Brien through Peter Sellers,
but George was later to discover that HandMade Films was heavily in
debt and that O'Brien, who was supposedly to share in the loans he
had encouraged George to make, had arranged it so that only George
was liable.

George split with O'Brien in 1993. The following year, on 18 May
1994, HandMade was sold to Paragon Entertainment Corporation of
Toronto, Canada for $8.5m. This gave Paragon 23 films with distribu-

tion rights and rights to the name. Group chairman Jon Slan said, 'HandMade is a quality company with tremendous assets.'

Below are listed the HandMade films made during George's time:
Monty Python's The Life Of Brian (1979)
A Sense Of Freedom (1979)
The Long Good Friday (marketed by HandMade Distribution) (1980)
The Burning (marketed by HandMade Distribution) (1980)
Time Bandits (1981)
Tattoo (marketed by HandMade Distribution) (1981)
Venom (marketed by HandMade Distribution) (1981)
Monty Python Live At The Hollywood Bowl (1983)
Scrubbers (1982)
Privates On Parade (1983)
Bullshot (1983)
The Missionary (1983)
A Private Function (1984)
Water (1985)
Shanghai Surprise (1986)
Mona Lisa (1986)
Five Corners (1987)
Bellman And True (1987)
Withnail And I (1987)
Track 29 (1987)
How To Get Ahead In Advertising (1988)
The Lonely Passion Of Judith Hearne (1988)
The Raggedy Rawney (1989)
Cold Dog Soup (1989)
Checking Out (1989)
Pow Wow Highway (1989)
Nuns On The Run (1990)

HandMade Films 10th Anniversary Album, The
A British release on AVM Records in 1989 that featured three tracks by George.

Hard Day's Night, A
The Beatles' debut film. Director Dick Lester said that he considered George to have the best acting ability of the four. He commented, 'Ringo, because his was the showy part, he was the odd one out, so he was given characteristics that were more sympathetic. John, I don't think was interested, and didn't bother. Paul was too interested and tried too hard, and George was always the one that was forgotten. So he just got on with it.'

George's role in *A Hard Day's Night* worked quite well for him. The film brought him into the limelight and also proved lucky for him as he met his first wife on the set.

George always delivered his wittiest lines in a deadpan sort of way, in contrast to John's savage, caustic wit. 'Do you like playing the guitar?' he's asked at the press reception in the film. 'Next to kissing girls, it's favourites,' he replies.

When George sets out to find the missing Ringo in the film, he wanders into an office reception area, where he's mistaken for someone else who was due for an audition and is taken into the offices of Simon Marshall. The condescending Marshall is director of a teenager's TV programme, hosted by the teen pundit Susan Campey. He asks for George's opinion 'on some clothes for teenagers'. George is shown some shirts. 'You'll like these. You'll really dig them. They're "fab" . . . and all the other pimply hyperboles,' says Marshall.

George looks at the array and comments, 'I wouldn't be seen dead in them, they're dead grotty.'

Marshall nearly has apoplexy and tells George that, despite the fact that they're 'grotty', he'll soon be wearing them.

'But I won't,' says George.

When Marshall mentions his resident teenager Susan Campey, George exclaims, 'You mean that posh bird who gets everything wrong?'

Marshall has to have George hustled out of the office, frightened that he is the herald of some new trend that his advisers have missed.

George, quite unconcerned, says, 'Sorry about the shirts.'

It was a good scene and George carried it off well.

Hare Krishna

George discovered Hare Krishna in 1966 when he met Ravi Shankar, who he came to regard as his spiritual father.

At one time George wanted to devote his full-time energies to Hare Krishna, shaving his head and living with his disciples, but was persuaded not to.

George was to say, 'I feel at home with Krishna. I think that's something that has been there from a previous birth. So it was like a door opening to me at the time, but it was also like a jigsaw puzzle and I needed all these little pieces to help me make the complete picture.'

Kripamaya Das, a spokesman for Bhaktivedanta Manor, which George bought for the movement, commented, 'Back in 1970 he decided to put the chant to music and it got to number seven of *Top Of The Pops* and all around the world.

'Then he decided he would like to move into the manor and become one of the shaven-headed members of the Hare Krishna movement.

'The founder of the movement said, no, your task is much better if you take the teaching and you put them in music.'

Das was also to comment about his visits to the manor in Letchmore Heath. 'When he came, he came as a worshipper. He was very shy and quiet but when he came he would play a little hand-pump organ that we have and he would sing and lead the singing.'

He once chanted the Hare Krishna mantra for 23 hours continuously on a drive through Europe, as he related in the book *Chant And Be Happy: The Story Of The Hare Krishna Mantra*: 'I once chanted the mantra all the way from France to Portugal nonstop. I drove for about 23 hours and chanted all the way. It gets you feeling a bit invincible. The funny thing was that I didn't even know where I was going. I had bought a map, and I knew basically which way I was aiming, but I couldn't speak French, Spanish or Portuguese. Strangely, none of that seemed to matter. Once you get chanting, things start to happen transcendentally.

'I remember once I was on an airplane that was in an electric storm. It was hit by lightning three times, and a Boeing 707 went right over the top of us, missing by inches. I thought the back end of the plane had blown off. As soon as the plane began bouncing around I started chanting Hare Krishna. The whole thing went on for about two hours with the plane dropping hundreds of feet, all the lights were out and there were all these explosions. Everybody was terrified. I ended up with my feet pressed against the seat in front yelling "Hare Krishna" at the top of my lungs.

'I knew for me the difference between making it and not making it was chanting the mantra. Peter Sellers also swore that chanting Hare Krishna had saved him from a plane crash once.'

When Michael Abram was stabbing George, trying to kill him, George was chanting the Hare Krishna mantra.

Hare Krishna Tribute To George Harrison
A second video tribute from the British Hare Krishna movement, released by ITV Productions in 2002.

There are numerous photographs of George with the Hare Krishna group and interviews about George with many of his friends from the movement including Syamasundara Dasa, Mukunda Goswami and Gurudas Dasa.

Harrison
A book published by *Rolling Stone* magazine in May 2002 in which Olivia had penned a foreword. The 242-page book contained more than a hundred photographs, including previously unseen family shots, together with news stories and features on George from *Rolling Stone* issues between 1968 and 1987.

Harrison, Dhani
George's only son, born 1 August 1978 at the Princess Christian Nursery Home in Windsor. He was named because 'dha' and 'ni' are notes of the Indian music scale and also the Sanskrit word for 'wealthy'.

He was born four weeks before his parents were married and was reared at Friar Park. He was educated in the Montesorri method at the

Dolphin School in Twyford. He then attended Shiplake College where he studied design technology. He later attended Brown University in America.

Although he said that he wanted to become a botanist and not a musician, he began to appear as a guitarist on guest tracks of his father's and even co-wrote songs with him. Dhani also appeared on stage with George at the Royal Albert Hall in 1992 at a concert for the Maharishi's political party.

Looking remarkably like his father, Dhani has also been reared in a spiritual life and meditates on a regular basis.

George and Olivia were to say, 'We can instil the right values in our son. It is his nightmare that he should grow up spoiled.'

After his first professional work on the *Brainwashed* album, he was to say, 'I don't really plan to be a pop star. I just want to be able to make music without the whole "my dad" thing hanging over me, which everyone in my position goes through.'

Harrison, Edward
George's great-grandfather on his paternal side. He was born on 13 January 1849 in Etna Street, West Derby, Liverpool, the son of Robert Harrison, a joiner, and Jane, nee Shepherd.

Harrison, Harold Hargreaves
George's father, who was born on 28 May 1909, the son of Henry and Jane (nee Thompson) Harrison of 26 Wellington Road, Wavertree.

He left school at the age of fourteen and his initial job was selling mangles, but by the age of seventeen he gave that up to go to sea and was engaged as a steward on the White Star Line.

In 1929 Harold began courting Louise French, a greengrocer's assistant and, on 20 May 1930, they were married in a civil ceremony at the Brownlow Hill Register Office and moved into 12 Arnold Grove, Wavertree.

Harold earned £8 a month while at sea and Louise took a job in a grocery store for 40 shillings a month.

Their first child, Louise, was born in 1931 and their second, Harold, was born in 1934 – a custom at the time was naming children after their parents.

In 1936 Harold left the White Star Line, seeking employment locally, which was hard to find. For 15 months the family had to live off welfare payments of 23 shillings a week, but in 1937 Harold secured a job as a bus conductor and the next year became a bus driver.

Their second son, Peter, was born in 1940 and their last child, George, was born in 1943.

Harold was a lapsed Anglican and didn't insist on his children attending church. At one time, he and his wife Louise taught ballroom dancing to beginners in their spare time.

Harold became a Union official at the Speke Depot Social Club, and was master of ceremonies at their Saturday night events. He even booked his son's new group the Quarry Men at a Union function at Wilson Hall, Garston on 1 January 1959.

In 1965, Harold was earning £10 per week and George offered to pay him £30 per week if he would retire. He then bought his parents a bungalow in Appleton, near Warrington, Cheshire for £10,000.

After the death of Louise, Harold took to visiting George regularly at Friar Park.

He died of emphysema at Friar Park in May 1978. George was to say that on the eve of his father's death he had a dream in which his father bade him farewell.

Harrison, Harry

George's elder brother and Harry and Louise's second child. Named after his father, as Louise was named after her mother, he was known as Harry Junior. His memories of the early years in Arnold Grove he says are 'wonderful' and recalls, 'Our little house was just two rooms up and down but, except for a short period when our father was away at sea, we always knew the comfort and security of a very close-knit home life.'

He once recalled a story about George's first guitar. 'He had rested it up against a wall and was talking to a mate when someone suddenly pushed back a chair right into it. Although George had it repaired, it was never the same again. What he really wanted, though, was an electric guitar, but Dad wasn't keen on him having it on hire purchase. He always said you shouldn't buy anything unless you had the money to pay for it.

'Anyhow, one night George, who was then working for Blackler's, came round to my flat. He went into a long speech about how much better an electric model would be. I realised he was working up to something, but said nothing. Then he finally came out with it. He knew Dad wouldn't let him have anything on hire purchase, so he wanted me to sign the guarantee forms. I wasn't very keen but he persuaded me to go to Hessy's, the Liverpool shop where all the groups bought their instruments. There he showed me the guitar he wanted. It was priced at £120. George fiddled with it, trying to look like an expert, but no sound came out. So the salesman pushed a button on the amplifier, and suddenly there was a tremendous blast and all the instruments on the opposite wall crashed to the floor. After that, I just had to let poor George have his guitar.'

When Harry was called up for national service, his girlfriend Irene McGann used to keep George company and even took him to see the Lonnie Donegan shows at Liverpool Empire. When Harry was demobbed, he became a mechanic and married Irene and the Quarry Men played at their wedding reception on 20 December 1959.

Once he'd established himself in Friar Park, George appointed Harry estate manager and he moved onto the grounds with his wife Irene.

Harrison, Henry
George's grandfather on his paternal side. Henry was born on 21 January 1882 at 12 Queen Street, the son of Edward Harrison, a stone-mason, and Elizabeth, the daughter of John Hargreaves, a carter. Henry became a master bricklayer and married Jane Thompson, the daughter of James Thompson, an engine driver of 3 Wellington Grove, Liverpool. The couple were married in Holy Trinity Church, Wavertree on 17 August 1902.

Harrison, Irene
The wife of George's elder brother Harry.

When she first began going out with Harry in 1956, she met George shortly after his thirteenth birthday. Harry had to complete his national service, so Irene, whose older sister had left for Canada, treated George as a younger brother.

When she married Harry, George used to visit their flat, sometimes taking Paul McCartney along with him.

Harrison, Louise (mother)
George's mother, the daughter of John French, a lamplighter, and seam-stress Louisa Wullam, was born in Liverpool on 10 March 1911. While working as a grocer's assistant she met Harold Harrison, a ship's steward, and the two were married at Brownlow Hill Register Office in Liverpool on 20 May 1930.

Louise gave up her job when her first child, Louise, was born on 16 August 1931. She then gave birth to three sons, Harold on 20 July 1934, Peter on 20 July 1940 and George Harold on 24 February 1943.

Her husband left the White Star line and, after a period of unem-ployment, later became a bus conductor. The two of them also ran ball-room dancing lessons.

When George became interested in music, Louise supported him, and when he was thirteen she bought him an acoustic guitar for £3. She also let his group the Quarry Men rehearse in her drawing room, and when the Beatles appeared at the Cavern she visited the club to show her support.

Louise and Harold were also very supportive of George's fans and often invited them into the house. She would also travel into Liverpool city centre to visit the Beatles fan club and take home all the letters addressed to George. Although they amounted to about 2,000 per month between 1963 and 1966 she would read every one of them and answer as many as it was possible for her to do.

Discussing George's early youth, Mrs Harrison was to comment,

'George was always full of fun when he was a child. He never caused any big trouble and even the neighbours liked him a lot, which is unusual with little boys.

'I was very proud of the way he liked to help old people. I have always been interested in this sort of work myself and used to take George around with me when I went visiting elderly people in our district.

'I remember one day, when I took him to the pictures with me. He was only eight years old at the time. When we came out of the cinema there was an old tramp sitting on a wall. George immediately suggested that we give him half a crown. Money meant nothing at all to him then and he could not see why I shouldn't give money to every old person we met.

'He was always fond of entertaining other people. When he was ten years old, his dad gave him some hand puppets for Christmas. From then on, whenever we had visitors, he always insisted on giving a little show kneeling behind the settee.

'The first time he ever got a big urge to play the guitar was when he was thirteen years old. His brother Peter bought one and George promptly tried to learn to play it. Eventually, he formed a small group with some friends and they went along for an audition at the Speke British Legion Hall. The main act did not turn up, so George's group played instead. They only knew two songs and once they had done both of them, they started again with the first and went on playing the same two over and over again. The audience loved it and they were given the regular artist's fee. I remember noticing, when they walked into our house afterwards, that the bass guitarist's fingers were bleeding, he'd played so hard.'

George bought his parents a bungalow in Appleton, near Warrington in 1965. Sadly, Louise was only to spend five years there as she became terribly ill with a brain tumour.

In an interview in *Musician* magazine in 1986, George told his favourite journalist Timothy White: 'She's got a tumour on the brain. But the doctor was an idiot and saying, "There's nothing wrong with her, she's having some psychological trouble." When I went up to see her, she didn't even know who I was. I had to punch the doctor out, because in England the family doctor has to be the one to get the specialist. So he got the guy to look at her and she ended up in the neurological hospital.

'The specialist said, "She could end up being a vegetable, but if it was my wife or mother, I'd do the operation." Which was a horrendous thing where they had to drill a hole in her skull. She recovered a little bit for about seven months. And during that period, my father, who'd taken care of her, had suddenly exploded with ulcers and was in the same hospital. I was pretending to both of them that the other one was OK.

'I wrote the song "Deep Blue" at home one exhausted morning with those major and minor chords. It's filled with the frustration and gloom of going to these hospitals, and the feeling of disease that permeated the atmosphere. Not being able to do anything for suffering family or loved ones is an awful experience.'

Louise was taken ill in July 1969 and died on 7 July 1970.

A group of American fans established the Louise F. Harrison Memorial Cancer Fund in her memory.

Harrison, Louise (sister)

George's elder sister and the first child of Harold and Louise Harrison.

She was born on 16 August 1931 and married an American, Gordon Caldwell, on 3 July 1954. The couple initially moved to America in April 1954. Louise had two children, Gordon (born 1 April 1957) and Leslie (29 September 1959). For a time they also lived in Canada.

Gordon was a mechanical engineer and was hired by the Freeman Coal Company. In March 1963 the family moved to Benton, Illinois, 200 miles from St Louis, moving into 113 McCann Street, where George and his brother Peter visited them later that year, arriving on Monday 16 September, the day 'She Loves You' was released in America.

George was to say, 'I've wanted to go there for years, but I could never afford it before. Also, this might be my last chance for a while, 'cause it may be ages before the Beatles can get two weeks free again.'

When the Beatles arrived in America in February 1964 to appear on the *Ed Sullivan Show*, George was taken ill with a high fever. Louise moved into the adjacent room and nursed him at the Plaza Hotel while Neil Aspinall deputised for him at the rehearsals. As a result of her care, George was able to appear on the actual television show.

Louise proved to be the most visible of the Harrison siblings. While Harold and Peter have always kept a low profile, Louise has always been keen to promote the association with her brother.

When the Beatles made their impact in 1964 Louise was busy undertaking radio broadcasts from her McCann Street house, called 'Beatle Reports'. They were broadcast to eighteen radio stations across America. To carry them out she was liaising with Brian Epstein by phone almost every day.

She was divorced in 1982 and settled in Saratoga, Florida.

By 1992 Louise (now known as Louise Kane) was appearing at Beatles festivals all over the world. In 1995 she released an album *All About The Beatles* on Redcar Records 2012.

She also developed a non-profit-making organisation 'We Care' Global Family Inc. In the 1990s Louise also produced and ran public service announcements known as 'Good Earthkeeping Tips' on radio. Each sixty-second spot featured George's song 'Save The World', with facts and tips on environmental issues.

Harrison, Olivia

George's second wife. She was born Olivia Trinidad Arias in Mexico City on 18 May 1948 to Zeke, a dry cleaner and Mary Louise Arias, a seamstress. She had a brother Peter and a sister Linda.

The family moved to California and Olivia was educated at Hawthorne High School. She became a secretary and in 1974 was working at A&M Records and was then moved to Dark Horse Records. George had spoken to her several times by phone and they first met at a party. She was 27 years old at the time. He liked her and decided to have her background checked by a friend. He was pleased with the results and asked her to join him on his 1974 American tour. The two then went on a holiday to Hawaii and then travelled to Friar Park.

In 1976 George's health began to decline and he decided that he could cure himself purely by prayer. His condition deteriorated; he had liver damage and hepatitis. Olivia made him see a doctor. She began extensive research into his illness and discovered an acupuncturist called Dr Zion Yu. Together with George she travelled to California where Dr Yu treated George. There was an immediate improvement in his condition and within a few months he had made a complete recovery.

They decided to spend the winter in Britain because George preferred the traditional cold Christmas in England rather than suffer the heat of Los Angeles, although the couple did live initially in George's $700,000 Beverly Hills mansion, which had a guest house, tennis court and swimming pool. They both found that it was far too large for them and sold it for a smaller home which they felt gave them a sense of privacy. They also stayed for a time in the Hollywood hills with Ringo Starr and his wife Barbara.

A friend observed, 'There was a serene and calming presence that George and Olivia gave off. George had fresh flowers placed in the house and there was incense burning, pictures of holy men, the smell of curried rice dishes – long-grain rice – wafting in from the kitchen. They're both health-food eaters.

'You know something is going on when they're around but it isn't something George shoves down your throat. They are both very thoughtful, and she has a great sense of humour. She is a lovely woman, far from the Hollywood-model type, far too spiritual. The harmony between them is clear and apparent to anyone around them.'

In December 1977 Olivia announced that she was pregnant and the couple decided to get married the following year. However, George's father fell ill and died in May 1978, so the wedding was postponed. Olivia then gave birth to their son Dhani at the Princess Christian Nursing Home in Windsor. The couple were married on 2 September 1978 at Henley Registry Office with Olivia's parents in attendance. The wedding was announced to the media five days later and the couple then went on their honeymoon to Tunisia.

Olivia had been used to keeping a low profile, but when she heard of the plight of Romanian orphans, she contacted the wives of the other former members of the Beatles, Barbara Bach, Linda McCartney and Yoko Ono, and enlisted their help in a campaign to help the children.

She recalled, 'It was sort of a gradual assault on my conscience. It was slowly wearing away at me and I decided that perhaps we should try to raise some money. I went to Romania and was just overwhelmed, devastated and shocked by the starvation.'

Following George's death, Olivia helped to organise a number of tributes, including one on 29 November 2002. This was a concert at the Royal Albert Hall, London to commemorate the first anniversary of George's death. Paul McCartney, Ringo Starr, Eric Clapton, Tom Petty and Jeff Lynne were among the performers. Proceeds from the concert went to cancer research and Olivia was to say, 'The tribute for George will resound, not only within the Albert Hall, but hopefully reach the spirit of the man so loved by his friends who will be performing and attending.'

Harrison, Peter

Peter was born on 20 July 1940 at the Harrison home in Arnold Grove, the same year as John Lennon. Together with their elder brother Harry, the brothers were very close. George was to recall a time when the three children each bought a hen and put them in a cage in their small back yard. Only Peter's hen survived, but the family later hired a man to wring its neck and they ate it for their Christmas dinner.

When they moved to Upton Green in Speke, Peter and George had to travel by bus all the way back to Wavertree to attend Dovedale Primary School.

The two used to play guitars together in the family sitting room. They decided to form a group and engaged Peter's friend Arthur Kelly and two other pals, called themselves the Rebels and had their one and only engagement at the British Legion Club in Speke in 1956.

On leaving school, Peter became a panel beater and welder. He still lived with his parents when the Beatles fame began to spread and he used to help his mum and dad prepare coffee and sandwiches for fans who used to visit the house.

Peter also accompanied George on his first visit to America in September 1963 to visit their elder sister Louise, who had married an American. They flew via New York and stayed in the Big Apple for a day, visiting the Statue of Liberty before flying to St Louis to spend a fortnight with Louise at her home in Benton, Illinois.

When George settled into Friar Park, he invited both his brothers and their families to come and live there and work on the estate. Peter was engaged as head gardener in charge of ten gardeners and a full-time botanist. He was to say, 'I hardly see George. When we do talk it is usually about the garden. He is a fanatic.'

Hawaii

George's first impressions of Hawaii occurred when, on 2 May 1964, George and Patti and John and Cynthia set off on holiday to Honolulu together, seeking to evade the press by travelling to Amsterdam from London and then across the North Pole from Iceland to Edmonton, Canada and then on to Hawaii.

George recalled, 'When we got to Honolulu we found that all the newspapers had been checking the hotels to find out where we were. So we made up that story about us having to leave right away – it sort of gave the impression that we were off to another part of the world.'

Because of the pressure from the press they then set off for Papeete in Tahiti where they chartered a yacht.

George said, 'I spent a lot of time just fishing off the boat with nylon lines and hooks – and a lot of hope! But there was plenty of diving and harpooning and all that sort of stuff. Marvellous. You forgot all about the Top Twenty and everything.

'John and I made our own 8mm cine films while we were over there. We put on these great black wigs and strange costumes. John wore five pairs of glasses all at the same time. We tried to make ourselves look as horrible and savage as possible.'

They returned to London on 26 May.

The experience of Hawaii eventually led to George buying a home there in 1979. He bought a house in Maui, Hawaii, which proved to be a retreat where he and his family could visit regularly to relax, and also a place to invite their friends such as Eric Idle and his wife Tania.

His home was called 'Kuppu Qulua' and was separated from the road by a two-mile stretch of ground.

This Maui home was the subject of *Gone Troppo*. A nearby town was called Hana, which George celebrated in his song 'Soft-Hearted Hana', a number that was dedicated to Bob Longhi, a local restaurateur. Kris Kristofferson and Richard Prior had houses on the island and other celebrities with property there included Dolly Parton and Tom Selleck.

When George and Olivia took up residence during the month of October 1981, they decided to help a friend, Dr Zion Yu, to celebrate the opening of his rejuvenation centre. George says, 'If I lived here I'd be in twice a week.'

There was a rumour that Sidney Altman, a Beverly Hills designer, had installed an unusual toilet in the property in 1983. The story went that it was a carved toilet that looked like a church pew. The seat was a flower-painted ceramic, with a candleholder hanging to one side and a bell on the other. The bell was to let the family know when the toilet was free. The toilet was also said to play 'Lucy In The Sky With Diamonds' when the seat was lifted.

George denied the existence of such a ridiculous toilet.

On Saturday 13 August 1983 George was sued for £26m by two

neighbours regarding a right-of-way. George screamed at reporters, 'Have you ever been raped? I'm being raped by all these people.' The path was sixty feet away from George's property and he requested that it be moved to one side of his estate, but the judge ordered that it be moved only 125 feet from George's house. George told reporters, 'Privacy is the single most important thing in my life.'

The dispute went on for many years and in 1993 Circuit Court Judge John McConnell decided that people could use a path across George's property at Nahiku, Maui, in order to view the ocean. George appealed, saying his property was being violated. The original landowner had subdivided several hundred acres to create five lots, including the 63-acre lot that George had bought in 1981.

The trail on George's land provided access to Kapukaulua Point, a rocky bluff overlooking the ocean. George had allowed residents to use the trail until he found that some of them were allowing nonresidents access to the trail so that they could see his home.

Although the neighbours claimed that easements included on their property deeds gave them the right to access the trail, George contended that his deed did not specify that the easement for the other landowners existed.

In 2000 the Hawaii Supreme Court reversed the 1993 decision by Judge McConnell and said that the dispute could go to trial.

However, the Hawaii Supreme court didn't alter the ruling that George may no longer forbid his neighbours trespassing on his property.

He's So Fine

A number by Ronald Mack (who died in 1963). The song was a hit for the Chiffons. The music publishers, Bright Tunes, brought a legal action against George claiming that his song 'My Sweet Lord' plagiarised 'He's So Fine', their copyright number. The case dragged on for ten years, during which time Allen Klein, who was Apple's business manager at the time George recorded 'My Sweet Lord', bought the Bright Tunes catalogue for his ABKCO Company.

On 5 February 1990 New York Federal Judge Richard Owen made a judgement that was accepted by both parties, leaving only the financial arrangements to be settled.

The judgement decreed that ABKCO would own 'He's So Fine' for the world, with the exception of Britain, America and Canada where George would own it, subject to a purchase price of $270,020, and that George would own 'My Sweet Lord' worldwide, although ABKCO would be entitled to a share in the composition throughout the world, with the exception of Britain, America and Canada.

George's legal representative commented, 'This is the only time I'm aware of where the defendant was found guilty of copyright infringement and wound up being awarded the song in question.'

This was probably because, in 1981, George argued that Klein should not be able to buy a song and then sue his former client.

George made an ironic tune out of the case called 'This Song' on his *Thirty Three & 1/3* album.

Hear Me Lord

A track from the *All Things Must Pass* triple album, penned by George and 5 minutes and 42 seconds in length.

It was one of the numbers performed by George at the Concert For Bangla Desh.

Hell To Pay

An album by the Jeff Healey Band, issued in America by Arista on 25 May 1990 and in Britain on 29 May 1990. George played guitar and provided vocal backing on the track 'While My Guitar Gently Weeps'.

Here Comes The Moon

A track on the 1979 *George Harrison* album lasting 4 minutes and 39 seconds. George wrote this in Hawaii, inspired by the effect of the moonlight. It also harks back to 'Here Comes The Sun'.

Here Comes The Sun

A number George penned early in 1969, which was recorded by the Beatles at Abbey Road Studios on 7 July 1969. Overdubbing was added on 8 and 16 July and 6, 11, 15 and 19 August. John Lennon didn't record on the original session but took part in the overdubbing. The number, 3 minutes and 4 seconds in length, was included on the *Abbey Road* album.

George was to comment that the number 'was written at the time when Apple was getting like school, where we had to go and be businessmen, all this signing accounts, and "sign this, sign that". Anyway, it seems as if winter in England goes on forever; by the time spring comes you really deserve it. So one day I decided – I'm going to "sag off" Apple – and I went over to Eric's [Clapton] house. I was walking in his garden. The relief of not having to go and see all those dopey accountants was wonderful, and I was walking around the garden with one of Eric's acoustic guitars and wrote "Here Comes The Sun".'

George also used his Moog on the track.

Steve Harley of Cockney Rebel covered the song some years later. His version was issued on 24 July 1976 and was a Top 30 hit in Britain.

His Name Is Legs (Ladies And Gentlemen)

A number devoted to George's friend, the eccentric 'Legs' Larry Smith, a former member of the Bonzo Dog Doo-Dah Band. The number was included on the 1975 *Extra Texture* album and featured George on guitar, Andy Newmark on drums, Willie Weeks on bass, Billy Preston and David Foster on keyboards and Legs on guest vocals.

The song is 5 minutes and 44 seconds in length.

Holland, Jools

Former member of Squeeze and host of the long-running BBC2 series *Later With Jools Holland*. He was an interviewer for both *The Beatles Anthology* and Paul McCartney's *Live At The Cavern*.

Jools had said to George in 1992 that he'd recorded a piece of music for a show called *Mr Roadrunner*, which was shown on television in America. He asked George if he would do a song for it and he recorded 'Between The Devil And The Deep Blue Sea'. Some years later Holland asked him if he could use the song and George said, 'No, I don't want you to use that. In fact, it's been bootlegged, but I've written this new song.'

George then invited him to come out to Switzerland and record the new number with him that was called 'A Horse To Water'.

Holland also used vocalist Sam Brown regularly on his shows. Sam was the daughter of George's friend Joe Brown and George told Holland, 'I've got this song, listen to the demo of it, and if you like it, come out with Sam, she can sing on a couple of things for me and then we'll do the song.'

Jools and Sam flew to Switzerland and recorded the number on 1 October 2001. George sang on the number but seemed too ill to play the guitar. It was the last recording he made.

The number appeared on the album *Jools Holland's Big Band Rhythm & Blues*, which was issued in America in October 2001 on Rhino Records.

Hong Kong Blues

A number by Hoagy Carmichael that he composed in 1938 and recorded himself on a number of occasions. A wide range of artists including George Melly, Pearl Bailey, Frank Ifield and Kenny Ball also covered it and it was included in the 1945 film *To Have And Have Not*. It was one of two Carmichael numbers that George recorded for his *Somewhere In England* album and was 2 minutes and 53 seconds in length. It was originally intended to be the opening track, but as Warner Bros required changes to the album it ended up as the fourth track on the second side.

George had first heard 'Hong Kong Blues' when he was only four years old, and liked Hoagy Carmichael all his life. Talking about when he quit the Liverpool Institute, he said, 'I had already made up my mind when I was about twelve that I was not going into the army at any cost. I liked music since I can remember. "Hong Kong Blues", that's one of the first songs I can remember, real bluesy.'

Hopkins, Nicky

One of Britain's most successful session musicians. Born in London, he studied classical piano at the Royal Academy of Music and began to play piano on many major recording sessions, including joining George and Ringo on the number 'Is This What You Want'. He also joined George and Ringo on Harry Nilsson's album *Son Of Schmilsson*.

George played guitar on four tracks of Hopkins' solo album *The Tin Man Was A Dreamer* and they both appeared on Cheech and Chong's *Basketball Jones*.

Hopkins was hired to perform on a number of George's albums and productions including *Living In The Material World*, *Dark Horse*, *Extra Texture* and *The Shankar Family & Friends*.

Nicky died in Nashville at the age of fifty on 6 September 1994.

Horn, Jim

A session musician who led the horn section on George's *Concert For Bangla Desh*. He had been recommended and introduced to George by Leon Russell – and George introduced him on stage as 'Jim Horn and the Hollywood Horns', a name that seemed to stick. Horn was also part of George's *Dark Horse* tour.

He was to play on recordings by all four ex-Beatles, but particularly on recordings by George. Among the albums he is heard on are *Cloud Nine*, *Living In The Material World*, *Dark Horse* and *Extra Texture*. He also worked on the second Traveling Wilburys album.

George returned the compliment by playing slide guitar on Horn's *Work It Out* album.

In 2000 he issued another of his own albums, *A Beatles Tribute*.

Horse To Water, A

A song George dedicated to Dhani, which he co-wrote with his son and recorded on 1 October 2001 in the Swiss villa where he was fighting against brain cancer. Also recording the number with them was Jools Holland. The number appeared on *Small World, Big Band* by Jools Holland and his Rhythm and Blues Orchestra, released on 19 November 2001.

The song was published under RIP Limited, 2001, rather than George's usual music publishing company Harrisongs – an example of George's black humour. Because of his illness he had also resigned as a director from Harrisongs and Olivia had taken his place on the board.

Holland, who travelled to Switzerland for the recording session, was to comment, 'George suggested we do a track and it was wonderful to work with one of the great, legendary artists in the world.'

I Dig Love

A track from the *All Things Must Pass* triple album, penned by George, lasting 4 minutes and 54 seconds.

I Don't Care Anymore

The flipside of 'Ding Dong', lasting 2 minutes and 36 seconds. It was issued in Britain on 6 December 1974, although it wasn't used as the B side of the American 'Ding Dong' release. It possibly refers to George's attitude to the long running 'My Sweet Lord'/'He's So Fine' lawsuit.

I Don't Want to Do It

A Bob Dylan number George recorded for the third *Porky's* film *Porky's Revenge 2,* which was included on the original motion picture soundtrack issued in America on Monday 18 March 1985 on Columbia JS 39983 and as a CD in November 1988 on Mobile Fidelity MFCD-797. The album was issued in Britain on Friday 28 June 1985 on CBS 70265. Other artists on the soundtrack included Carl Perkins, Dave Edmunds and Jeff Beck.

The song had a country music element to it and was George's first recording outing since his *Gone Troppo* album three years previously. 'I Don't Want To Do It', however, was a number he'd initially introduced during his preproduction sessions for *All Things Must Pass* in May 1970. He also made a studio demo of the number in the early 1980s.

It was Dave Edmunds who had talked George into recording for the *Porky's* soundtrack and he assembled backing musicians who included Kenny Aaronson on bass, Michael Shrieve on drums and Chuck

Leavell on keyboards. Edmunds produced and the number was recorded at the Record Plant West in Los Angeles.

Following the release of the album, Edmunds decided on releasing a remix as a single. He prepared the remix at the Maison Rouge Studios, London and it was issued in America only on Columbia 38-04887 on 22 April 1985 with the Dave Edmunds' number 'Queen Of The Hop' on the flipside. It failed to register in the charts.

I Forgot To Remember To Forget
A number that the Beatles introduced into their act in 1962, with George on lead vocals. Stanley Kesler and Charlie Feathers had written the number and Elvis Presley had recorded it in 1956.

The group performed the number on their 18 May 1964 radio show *From Us To You*. The performance with George on lead vocals that they played on their second *From Us To You* show was included on *The Beatles Live At The BBC* CDs.

I Live for You
A bonus track added to the *All Things Must Pass* double-CD reissue in 1991.

Discussing the track with *Billboard*, George commented on why it was left off the original album. 'I suddenly realised I'd got too many tracks for an album and that one track sounded like we hadn't nailed it properly, and it sounded on top of that a bit too fruity. I didn't include it because I never finished it. But coming back to it, I fixed the drums up very simply. But the main thing about it for me is the Pete Drake solo on pedal steel guitar. He died, and I often thought if his family is still around, then suddenly they'll be hearing him playing this thing that they've never heard before. I really loved his pedal steel guitar – the bagpipes of country and western.'

I Need You
A number penned by George, which the Beatles recorded for the *Help!* album. It was a song George wrote for Patti, as they were apart during the filming of *Help!* in the Bahamas. George sings lead, with Paul and John adding harmony vocals.

It was recorded on 15 February 1965 and Paul overdubbed lead guitar the following day.

I Really Love You
A number penned by Leroy Swearingen, which was a hit for the Stereos in 1961. George recorded the doo-wop number and included it on his *Gone Troppo* album. It is 2 minutes and 53 seconds in length. It was also issued as a single in America on 7 February 1983 on Dark Horse 7-29744. 'Circles' was on the flip.

Rocky Sharpe and the Replays also recently recorded the number.

I Remember Jeep

A track from the *All Things Must Pass* triple album, penned by George and 8 minutes and 5 seconds in length.

George wrote the number in honour of Eric Clapton's dog Jeep. Ginger Baker appears on drums and the other musicians are George and Eric Clapton on guitars, Billy Preston on keyboards and Klaus Voormann on bass.

I Want To Tell You

A number written by George, included on the *Revolver* album and 2 minutes and 26 seconds in length. It was recorded at Abbey Road studios on 2 June 1966. The bass was overdubbed on 3 June, which was the first bass overdub on a Beatles track.

I Won't Back Down

A single taken from the Tom Petty album *Full Moon Fever*, which was issued in Britain on MCA Records on 24 April 1969. George was a guest guitarist on the recording.

I'd Have You Anytime

The opening track from the *All Things Must Pass* triple album It was penned by George and Bob Dylan and lasts 2 minutes and 57 seconds.

I'll Still Love You

A track on Ringo's *Rotogravure* album, issued in 1976. It was the final incarnation of a song George had originally written under the title 'Whenever'. He'd recorded it himself during the May 1970 *All Things Must Pass* sessions. He'd initially intended it for Shirley Bassey and attempts to record it were also made by Ronnie Spector and Leon and Mary Russell under a new title 'When Every Song Is Sung'. Ringo, along with Eric Clapton, also played on the number when George produced a Cilla Black version. This was never released as the session was marred by Cilla's recent visit to a dentist. It's possible that, by participating in this session, Ringo may have reminded George of the number when asking for a song for his *Rotogravure* project.

I'm Happy Just To Dance With You

A number that John Lennon wrote specially for George to sing in the film *A Hard Day's Night*, although he was ungenerous enough to remark, 'I would never have sung it myself.' The Beatles recorded it on Sunday 1 March 1964, the first time they had been inside a studio on a Sunday to record.

In addition to the *A Hard Day's Night* soundtrack, the number was released as the B side of 'I'll Cry Instead', which was released in America in July 1964 and was included on Capitol's *Something New* album.

I'm Your Spiritual Breadman

A number by Ashton, Gardner & Dyke, recorded at De Lane Lee Studios in London on which George made a guest appearance. It was released in July 1970.

I. Me. Mine. (book)

Originally published by Genesis on Friday 4 July 1980 in a limited edition of 2,000 copies priced at £148 each.

It was the nearest thing to an autobiography we have had from George. Derek Taylor worked on the book with him and the initial part of the book comprises George's reminiscences about his life, with comments by Taylor in italics. This is followed by a 48-page section of photographs and then the main part of the book, 80 of George's lyrics. These are accompanied by illustrations of the handwritten manuscripts and some brief comments on each song by George.

Simon & Schuster published a paperback version of George's book in November 1981 in America and a British paperback edition was also published, which irked many of the people who had paid the premium price for the Genesis edition.

Following George's death, the book was republished in 2002 by Chronicle Books in an edition that included several new photographs and an introduction by Olivia, in which she wrote about George and Derek. 'I miss them both dreadfully along with the joy their combined humour, intelligence and affection brought into my life.'

I. Me. Mine. (song)

A number composed by George, which was included on the *Let It Be* album. It is 2 minutes and 24 seconds in length.

George said that it concerned the ego, which he became aware of after taking LSD and viewed things relative to his own ego. He also claimed to have based the music on a song performed by an American band he saw on television.

Allen Klein thought it was an Italian song because he thought the title similar to 'Cara Mia Mine'.

'I. Me. Mine.' was recorded at Abbey Road on 3 January 1969, although John Lennon isn't present on the track as he was absent at the time. Billy Preston accompanied George, Paul and Ringo on organ and there were some overdubbed strings by session musicians. Phil Spector was to overdub an orchestra on the track on 1 April that year.

In 1997, George discussed 'I. Me. Mine.', which had been included in the Beatles *Anthology*. He said, 'I kept coming across the words I, me and mine in books about yoga and stuff. I mean, you know, about the meaning of life and the difference between the ego and the soul, you know, the real you and the you that people mistake their identity to be, this bones and . . . bag of flesh and bones, and the ego, and that's really it. I, me and mine is all ego orientation. But it is something which is used all the time. People, you know: "No one's frightened of saying it, everyone's playing it, coming on strong all the time. All through your life, I me mine."'

Idle, Eric

A member of the *Monty Python* comedy team, who became one of George's close friends.

They wrote the 'Pirate Song' together for the *Rutland Weekend Television* special screened on BBC2 on Boxing Day 1975.

He was invited to induct George into the Hollywood Bowl Hall of Fame on 28 June 2002.

Eric was to comment, 'When they told me they were going to induct my friend George Harrison into the Hollywood Bowl Hall Of Fame posthumously my first thought was, "I bet he won't show up." Because, unlike some others one might mention – but won't – he really wasn't into honours. He was one of those odd people who believe that life is somehow more important than show business. Which I know is a heresy here in Hollywood, and I'm sorry to bring it up here in the very bowel of Hollywood but I can hear his voice saying, "Oh very nice, very useful, a posthumous award – where am I supposed to put it? What's next for me then? A posthumous Grammy? An ex-knighthood? An After-Life Achievement Award?" He's going to need a whole new shelf up there.

'I think he would prefer to be inducted *posthumorously* because he loved comedians – poor, sick, sad, deranged, lovable puppies that we are – because they, like him, had the ability to say the wrong thing at the right time, which is what we call humour.

'He put *Monty Python* on here at the Hollywood Bowl and he paid for the movie *The Life Of Brian*, because he wanted to see it. Still the most anybody has ever paid for a cinema ticket!

'What made George special, apart from his being the best guitarist in the Beatles, was what he did with his life after they achieved everything. He realised that this fame business was, and I'll use the technical philosophical term here, complete bullshit. And he turned to find beauty and truth and meaning in life and – more extraordinarily – found it.

'Michael Palin said George's passing was really sad but it does make the afterlife seem much more attractive. He was a gardener – he grew beauty in everything he did – in his life, in his music, in his marriage and as a father. I was on an island somewhere when a man came up to him and said, "George Harrison, oh my God, what are you doing here?" and he said, "Well, everyone's got to be somewhere."

'Well, alas, he isn't here. But we are. And that's the point. This isn't for him. This is for us, because we want to honour him. We want to remember him, we want to say, "thanks, George" for being. And we really miss you.'

In 2002 Eric's new show *Everything Or Nothing* included a tribute to George

If I Needed Someone

A composition by George that was included on the *Rubber Soul* album. It was recorded at Abbey Road Studios on 16 October 1965. It lasts 2 minutes and 15 seconds. George's lead vocal was double-tracked and he played his Rickenbacker Fireglo 360/12 and was to comment in *I. Me. Mine*. '"If I Needed Someone" is like a million other songs written around the D chord. If you move your finger about you get various little melodies. That guitar line, or variations on it, is found in many a song and it amazes me that people still find new permutations of the same notes.'

Apart from the *Rubber Soul* album, the number was included on the American release *Yesterday ... And Today* and also on *The Best Of George Harrison* albums. The Hollies covered the number, which entered the British charts in December 1965. However, George was to criticise their version publicly, saying, 'They've spoiled it. The Hollies are all right musically, but the way they do their records they sound like session men who've just got together in a studio without ever seeing each other before.'

Graham Nash of the Hollies was furious and felt that George's remarks had sabotaged the single's success. It only reached No. 20 in the charts, while their previous single had reached No. 4 and their follow-up to 'If I Needed Someone' reached No. 2.

Nash commented, 'Not only do those comments disappoint and hurt us, but we are sick of everything the Beatles say or do being taken as law. The thing that hurt us most was George Harrison's knock at us as musicians. And I would like to ask, if we have made such a disgusting mess of his brainchild song, will he give all the royalties from our record to charity?'

If Not For You

On 1 May 1970, while in New York, George played on Bob Dylan's recording of 'If Not For You'. However, when Dylan issued his album *New Morning* later that year, the version on the LP wasn't the one on which George was a guest. This version was to appear in the 1990s on the CBS *Bootleg Rarities* series, which featured a Dylan rarities box.

George took this number back to England with him and recorded it for his *All Things Must Pass* album, a track which is 3 minutes and 28 seconds in length.

Olivia Newton John was to cover 'If Not For You' based on George's version of the number and had a chart hit with it.

If You Believe

A number credited to George and Gary Wright. The two began composing it in England on New Year's Day 1978 and it was included on the *George Harrison* album. The track lasts for 2 minutes and 53 seconds.

If You Don't Know Where You're Going Any Road Will Take You There

A number by George that he performed during the recording of the VH-I programme *George Harrison And Ravi Shankar – Yin And Yang* at VH-I studios in New York on 14 May 1997. It wasn't included in the show when the programme was broadcast on 24 July 1997.

In Celebration

A four-disc boxed set of Ravi Shankar, released in the UK in 1996 on EMI CD7243 5 55577 28 to celebrate Ravi's 75th birthday. There is a written introduction by George and photos of George and Ravi in a booklet. George produced several of the tracks (some of which were co-produced with Alan Kozlowski), namely 'Jait', 'I Am Missing You', 'Dispute And Violence', 'Vandana', 'Oh Bhagawan', 'Friar Park', 'Ta Na Tom' and 'I Am Missing You'.

Angel Records and Dark Horse had joined forces to produce the set, which contained over forty tracks in five hours of playing time. The first CD featured 'Classical Sitar', the second 'Orchestral and Ensembles', the third 'East–West Collaboration' and the fourth 'Vocal And Experimental'.

On one of the pieces, 'Friar Park', Ravi was joined by Ray Cooper on marimba and George on autoharp.

Other musicians who performed on the set included Ringo Starr, Ashish Khan, Ali Akbar Khan, Alla Rakah and Zubin Mehta.

In Spite Of All The Danger

The first number ever recorded by the group who evolved into the Beatles. At the time they were performing under the name the Quarry Men and comprised John Lennon, Paul McCartney, George Harrison, Colin Hanton and John Lowe.

The group recorded two numbers at the studio of Percy Philips, which was situated at 53 Kensington, Liverpool, on 12 July 1958. The other song recorded was the Buddy Holly number 'That'll Be The Day'. 'In Spite Of All The Danger' sported the composer credit Harrison/McCartney and Paul sang the lead vocal.

This establishes the fact that George co-wrote the earliest recorded work with Paul.

The number was eventually issued on *The Beatles Anthology 1* CD.

In The First Place

In 1997, when *Wonderwall* director Joe Massott produced his 'director's cut' of the soundtrack, George had provided a reel of music cues for him, which included the track 'In The First Place', which hadn't been included in the original film soundtrack. Produced by George, this was a number by the Remo Four, with Tony Ashton providing the vocals. A single was issued in January 1999, produced by George, which included the original Abbey Road mix and also a movie mix.

Inner Light, The

A number composed by George, which was included as the flipside of 'Lady Madonna'. This was the first time a composition by George had been included on a Beatles single.

It was issued in Britain on 15 March 1968 and in America on 18 March 1968.

Juan Mascaro, the Sanskrit teacher at Cambridge University, had sent George a book called *Lamps Of Fire*. In it was a translation from the *Tao Te Ching* and George based the number on it, saying, 'It was nice, the words said everything.'

George recorded the music with Indian musicians at EMI Studios in Bombay, India on 12 January 1968 and overdubbed his lead vocal at Abbey Road Studios on 6 February, with John and Paul adding their background vocals two days later.

The tape operator, Jerry Boys, was to recall: 'George had this big thing about not wanting to sing it because he didn't feel confident that he could do the song justice. I remember Paul saying, "You must have a go, don't worry about it, it's good."'

Internet

George gave his first online chats on 15 February 2001 with a fifty-minute chat on Yahoo!Chat and a thirty-minute spell on MSN Live.

The first online chat crashed under the weight of some 300,000 participants.

George commented, 'They should call it more of a "Web type" because you don't actually chat. Somebody here at Capitol Records is doing it. I'll just answer the questions and they'll type them in. If Britney Spears or Justin Timberlake were online, I could understand the crush. But this is a 58-year-old man who's been silent musically for more than a decade and is only appearing to promote the re-release of a 30-year-old record.'

Asked about a Beatles reunion tour, he said, 'Stranger things have happened.' When asked if he and Paul were getting along he commented, 'Scan not a friend with a microscope glass. You know his faults. Then let his foibles pass. Old Victorian Proverb. I'm sure there's enough about me that pisses him off, but I think we have now grown old enough to realise that we're both pretty damn cute.' George answered the questions from the Capitol Tower in Hollywood. With tongue in cheek he said, 'I got all my ideas from the Rutles. Particularly the 12-string Rickenbackers and slide guitar styles, I got from Stig O'Hara. I met him once and he is a super chap.'

On MSN Live he was asked if he was asked to join the Beatles because he knew all the chords to 'Twenty Flight Rock'. He replied, 'No. Paul knew 'Twenty Flight Rock', but I did too.

When asked where he was spiritually when he recorded 'My Sweet Lord' he answered, 'A very famous Indian saint said, "If there is a God, we must see him. And if there is a soul, we must perceive it." In the West they still argue if God really exists. Basically, I am in the same place. The song really came from Swami Vivekananda.'

He was asked who the musicians were who he liked currently. 'Hoagy Carmichael. There are many, many, many musicians.'

Asked if there was anything he would like to do which he hadn't done before, he said, 'Dematerialise my body.'

George had also set up his own website at www.allthingsmusic-pass.com and said, 'Websites for me are still new territory. I still don't really know what they are supposed to do, but it was fun thinking of ideas and seeing them put together on the screen. I hope people enjoy it.'

Isn't It A Pity?

A number included on the *All Things Must Pass* triple album. It was penned by George and the Beatles originally rehearsed the song during their 'Get Back' (which became *Let It Be*) sessions in January 1969.

Interestingly enough, George had two versions of the number featured on his triple-album set. The recording of 'Isn't It A Pity (Version One)' began on 2 June 1970 and is on side four of the album. This was the version that almost became the first single to be issued from the album in October 1970, but it ended up as the flipside of 'My Sweet Lord' in America.

The second version, at 4 minutes and 44 seconds in length, is not as ponderous as the first, which lasts for 7 minutes and 8 seconds.

It Is He

The closing track on the 1974 *Dark Horse* album, lasting 4 minutes and 43 seconds. It was inspired by George's experiences while he was in Brindabin, India.

It's All Too Much

A number composed by George, which was included on the *Yellow Submarine* soundtrack album. It is 6 minutes and 16 seconds in length, although slightly longer in the actual film. 'It's All Too Much' was recorded at De Lane Lea Music recording studios in London on 25 May 1967, with overdubbing taking place on 26 May and 2 June.

The song was said to have been inspired by George's wife Patti and there is a lyrical reference, 'With your long blonde hair and your eyes of blue', which is a line taken from a song, 'Sorrow', which had been recorded by the Merseys.

It's Johnny's Birthday

A track from the *All Things Must Pass* triple album, lasting only 49 seconds. Yoko Ono had requested George to write a greeting for John Lennon's birthday on 9 October and George recorded a short piece based on the tune 'Congratulations', which Cliff Richard sang in the 1968 Eurovision Song Contest.

It is credited to songwriters Bill Martin and Phil Coulter because the melody is based on their song 'Congratulations'.

It's What You Value

The opening track of the 1976 *Thirty Three & 1/3* album, which is 5 minutes and 6 seconds in length. George composed the number during his 1974 American tour.

It was also released in Britain as a single on Dark Horse K 16968 on 10 June 1977 with 'Woman Don't You Cry For Me' on the flip. It failed to make any impact on the charts.

George recalled, 'There was this friend of mine – I was trying to get him to play on the tour and he wouldn't do it, and so . . . I really needed him to play . . . and so I was saying, "Come on, come on, please play." And he was saying, "OK." Finally! I bugged him to death until he agreed to play. And so he said, "OK, but look, I don't want to be paid for the tour, but I'm sick of driving that old Volkswagen bus." And I was saying, "OK, maybe I'll get you a car." So we got him a car and bought him a Mercedes 450, and then some people I later heard were saying, "Hey, how come you got a motor car, I only got . . ." So I just thought in that song, "Someone's driving a 450 and his friends are so wild, but I've found out that it's all up to what you value and to where you are." That's all. It's really . . . to some person it's a big deal, to somebody else it's just a throwaway thing.'

George was talking about his American tour of 1974 and the musician concerned was drummer Jim Keltner, who wanted to be paid with a Mercedes 450SL instead of money.

Jiva

A four-piece band from Los Angeles that became the second rock group and the first American act to be signed by George for his Dark Horse label on Monday 9 June 1975.

They comprised Michael Lanning on guitar and lead vocals, Michael Reed on drums and percussion, James Strauss on bass and vocals and Thomas Hilton on guitar and vocals. They released only one album with Dark Horse, on which Gary Wright played keyboards. This was *Jiva*, issued in America on Dark Horse SP 22003 on 6 October 1975 and in Britain on Dark Horse AMLH 2203 on 31 October 1975. There was also a single 'Something's Goin' On Inside LA' c/w 'Take My Love', issued in America on 11 February 1976 on Dark Horse DH 10006.

The group were unsuccessful and left the label in 1976.

Kelly, Arthur

Originally a friend of George's brother Peter, who brought him into George's group the Rebels, who made a single appearance at the British Legion Club in Speke. Arthur then became a very close friend of George and was in the same class at Liverpool Institute.

When the fourteen-year-old George began dating Iris Caldwell, sister of Liverpool rocker Rory Storm, they made it a foursome when Arthur began dating Iris's best friend.

Then, when George became a member of the Quarry Men after Len Garry had left them, they lacked a bass guitarist. John Lennon offered the job to Arthur, but he couldn't afford the £60 necessary to buy an instrument and possibly missed out on being a Beatle.

However, he did go on to portray Bert in the West End production of Willy Russell's *John, Paul, George, Ringo and Bert*. George came along to see Arthur in the role, but found the play painful and left before the performance ended.

Arthur enjoyed a career as an actor in various stage and television productions, including the acclaimed series *The Boys From The Black Stuff*.

Keltner, Jim

An internationally renowned session drummer. He first met George during a Gary Wright recording session in London. George told him that he liked the work he had done with Ry Cooder and after the Wright session George had him play maracas on Ringo's 'It Don't Come Easy'. He also invited him to appear on *Concert For Bangla Desh*. When Keltner appeared on George's first solo tour of America in

November 1974, he requested a Mercedes 450SL car instead of his fee. Inspired by Keltner, George wrote the song 'Its What You Value'.

Keltner said that following the attack on George in December 1999, George was still keeping busy and that he travelled to Britain to help George complete some unfinished songs.

He commented, 'He started bringing stuff out of the vaults that he wanted to actually finish. I put drums on a tremendous amount of that stuff. Some of the songs I played on were absolutely wonderful, brilliant. I can't wait to see what he does with them – I don't know whether he'll have somebody to help him produce, but I'm sure he'll come out with something cool.'

Khan, Alla Rakah
An Indian musician who was a virtuoso on the tabla. He performed on *Concert For Bangla Desh* and also on the Ravi Shankar *In Celebration* release produced by George.

His daughter died on 1 February 2000 and Allah died of a heart attack two days later.

Kinfauns
The bungalow in Claremont Road, Fair-Mile Estate, near Esher, which George and Patti moved into during July 1964. They had to take down the sign outside the house to stop fans visiting him and were still pestered by fans although there were tall hedges outside the house. One group got inside Kinfauns and stole George's pyjamas. He also woke up one morning to find two fans hiding under the bed. So he installed electronically operated gates.

The bungalow was furnished in pine. George built himself a mini-recording studio and music room by knocking down one of the walls. His musical complex was crammed with all his guitars, amplifiers and tape decks – and he was the first person in Britain to own a Moog synthesizer, and it was there that he taped his 'Under The Mersey Wall' part of his *Electronic Sounds* album. He also had a heated pool installed in the garden, and displayed one of John's cartoons of two bald-headed naked men, rendered in a mosaic of tiles on the wall overlooking the end of the pool. There were also murals on the walls painted by the Fool, the Dutch designers who were to work for Apple. There was a drugs bust at Kinfauns in March 1969 and George and Patti eventually moved out and settled in Friar Park in January 1970.

Kirchherr, Astrid
The blonde German student, born in Hamburg in 1938, who befriended the Beatles during their first trip to Hamburg.

Her boyfriend Klaus Voormann took her to see them perform at the Kaiserkeller club and she fell in love with their bass guitarist Stuart Sutcliffe. Their romance was the subject of the feature film *Backbeat*.

Tragically, Stuart died of a brain haemorrhage caused by a fall down the attic steps at Astrid's house.

George was to say, 'I always had lots of fights with Stuart, but I really liked him and we were very friendly before he died.'

Astrid took some classic photographs of the group and her individual studies, particularly of George, are among the best photographs of them ever taken.

She was to comment, 'We never thought about George's intelligence one way or another. We knew he wasn't stupid, but he was just such a lovely young boy. He was so sweet and open about everything. I got on like a house on fire with George.'

Astrid seemed very protective of George. Both she and Stuart drove him to the railway station on 21 November 1960 when he was deported from Hamburg for being under age.

The group of friends Klaus and Astrid brought to see the Beatles at the Kaiserkeller referred to George as 'the beautiful one'.

Astrid had originally given Stuart a new style of haircut. She next gave George the same style. When Jurgen Vollmer cut John and Paul's hair in the same way, the 'moptop' was born.

Remembering her impressions of George, Astrid was also to say, 'George was lovely. Wide-eyed, innocent, open and very loving and warm. He was always extremely popular with the fans and even in Hamburg had a dedicated, affectionate following. He used to tell me that he'd never met a girl like me before, and he meant it. Here I was, a photographer, with my own little car, living that sort of carefree artist's life with my friends.

'I felt protective of George. He was a long way from home and seemed to miss the attention of his family. The other boys were more grown-up and so were a little less concerned with all that.

'I know, for example, that he always looked up to John, and probably even Stu, as big-brother figures. And conversely, it was sometimes difficult for them not to see George as something of a pain for being so young. Still, in their own way, they loved him. We all did. Even when things were pretty rough they all stuck together. They often argued amongst themselves, but just let an outsider have a go at one of them and sparks would fly. At first they were close out of necessity; later it was out of love.'

Learning How To Love You

The flipside of the November 1976 single 'This Song', lasting 4 minutes and 10 seconds. It was also the final track on the *Thirty Three & 1/3* album.

George had originally written the number for Herb Alpert, but then decided to record it himself.

He commented, 'I felt, like, when the sixties thing happened, and the main thing I felt from the result of the LSD thing which was earlier on and then later getting involved with meditation, was the realisation that all the goodness and all the strength and things that can support life is coming out of love. And not just as simple as one guy saying to a chick, "I love you," like an emotional sort of thing. Just real love, which is, like, unconditional love, because so often we say, "I love you *if*, I love you *when*, I love you *but*." And that's not *real* love. Love is "I love you, even if you kick me in the head or stab me in the back".'

Lee, Alvin

A noted guitarist and leader of the group Ten Years After. Alvin became one of George's musician friends. The two met in November 1973 at their local pub, the Row Barge in Henley-on-Thames. Lee lived in Woodcote, which was only three miles away from Friar Park. George accepted an invitation to guest on Lee's album. The two later collaborated on composing the song 'Shelter In Your Love'. Lee recorded the number in 1985 and included it on his 1985 album *Detroit Diesel*.

Lennon, John

Contrary to what many books on the Beatles allege, John Lennon was not born in the middle of an air raid. When he was born at 6.30 a.m. on 9 October 1940 at Oxford Street Maternity hospital in Liverpool, the air raids had ceased for a time.

Cynthia in her book *A Twist Of Lennon* writes, 'John and I would leave college hand in hand, just happy to be in each other's company for a while, when we would be brought down to earth with a bump by a yell that could only mean one thing – George.

'He would hurriedly catch up and neither of us would have the heart to tell this thin gangly kid in school uniform to push off. Poor George. He hadn't really got on to the stage of serious girlfriends and was unaware of what it was all about. So we would spend lost afternoons as a jolly threesome.'

John was to say, 'I couldn't be bothered with him when he first came round. He was a kid who played guitar, and a friend of Paul's, which made it all easier. It took me years to come round to him, to start considering him as an equal.'

John was also to recall, 'George's relationship with me was one of a young follower and an older guy. He was like a disciple of mine when we started. He used to follow me and my first girlfriend around wherever we went. We'd come out of school and he'd be hovering around.'

George was to recollect the year 1957 and his visit to see the Quarry Men and said: 'I'd been invited to see them play several times by Paul but for some reason never got round to it before. I remember being very impressed with John's big thick sideboards and trendy teddy-boy clothes. He was a terribly sarcastic bugger right from day one, but I never dared back down from him. In a way, all that emotional rough stuff was simply a way for him to help separate the men from the boys, I think, I was never intimidated by him. Whenever he had a go at me I just gave him a little bit of his own right back.'

When they were appearing in Hamburg they often got involved in an altercation on stage. John said, 'We ended up getting real pissed off about something and George threw some food at me. I said I would smash his face in for him. We had a shouting match on stage, but that was all. I never did anything.'

Initially, John and Paul put a wall up between them to prevent George's songs being recorded, almost until the stage of *The Beatles* double album, with John saying, 'He had been left out because he had not been a songwriter until that point.'

George also didn't get much help or encouragement and it was only with reluctance that John helped him at one time. He recalled, 'I remember one day he called to ask me for help on "Taxman", one of his bigger songs. I threw in a few one-liners to help the song along because that's what he asked for. He came to me because he couldn't go to Paul because Paul wouldn't have helped him at that period. I didn't really want to help him. I thought, "Oh no, don't tell me I have to work on George's stuff." But because I loved him and didn't want to hurt him, when he called, I just sort of held my tongue and said OK.'

George and Patti and John and Cynthia went on a few holidays together, one of them in the Caribbean. When discussing it, George said, 'While we were in the Caribbean, John and I took up all sorts of weird sports that we had always wanted to try our hand at. One day we went water-skiing. I was going along quite happily towards the shore and the boatman made a normal turn out towards the open ocean – but he'd left it a bit too late, and before I'd realised what was happening, I was skimming the top of razor-sharp coral, which was almost up to the surface.

'I dread to think what would have happened if the water had been an inch shallower. It was the nastiest moment of my life.'

George and John really became estranged when Yoko appeared on the scene. George disliked her immediately, and John took exception to his attitude.

After the release of the *All Things Must Pass* album. George was to recall, 'I remember John was really negative at the time. I was away and he came round to my house and there was a friend of mine living there who was also a friend of John's. John just saw the album cover and said, "He must be fucking mad, putting three records out. And look at the picture on the front, he looks like an asthmatic Leon Russell." There was a lot of negativity going down. I just felt that whatever happened, whether it was a flop or a success, I was going to go on my own just to have a bit of peace of mind.'

When George was sued for 'My Sweet Lord' John commented, 'He walked right into it. He knew what he was doing. He must have known. He's smarter than that. He could have changed a couple of bars in that song and nobody could ever have touched him. But he just let it go and paid the price. Maybe he thought God would just sort of let him off.'

When George was organising the Concert For Bangla Desh, he invited John to appear and John accepted. However, when George said he didn't want Yoko Ono to participate there was a furious argument between Yoko and John, which ended up in John not appearing on one of the most memorable concerts in rock history.

When George published his autobiography *I. Me. Mine*. John was very upset when he read it. He said, 'I was hurt by George's book. He put a book out privately on his life that, by glaring omission, says that my influence on his life is absolutely zilch and nil. In his book, which is purportedly this clarity of vision of his influence on each song he wrote, he remembers every two-bit sax player or guitarist he met in subsequent years. I'm not in the book. It's a love-hate relationship and I think George still bears resentment towards me for being a daddy who left home. He would not agree with this but that's my feeling about it. I was just hurt. I was just left out as if I didn't exist.'

George did feel guilty about hurting John's feelings and in mid-1980 he called the Dakota, where John was living, and left a message. 'Please call George. He's very anxious to talk to you.' John was to say, 'Well, it's kind of George to call after forgetting to mention me in the book.' John didn't return the call and the two were never in contact again.

When John was killed, George was to say, 'After all we went through together I had and still have great love and respect for John Lennon. I am shocked and stunned. To rob life is the ultimate robbery in life. This perpetual encroachment on other people's space is taken to the limit with the use of a gun. It is an outrage that people can take other people's lives when they obviously haven't got their own lives in order.'

George then rewrote the lyrics to a song he'd composed 'Can't Fight Lightning' and recorded it in January 1981 as 'All Those Years Ago' as a tribute to John. Paul and Ringo were also featured on the track, which was issued as a single in May 1981.

Les Stewart Quartet, The

A group George joined between January 1959 and August 1959. The Quarry Men had virtually disbanded and John and Paul had actually ceased performing and were writing songs together. Skiffle music was on the wane and Liverpool bands were turning to rock'n'roll.

George was on guitar and vocals, with leader Les Stewart on guitar and vocals, Ken Brown on guitar and vocals and Geoff Skinner on drums.

It was in August of that year that the change came about. George might have remained with the Quartet and John and Paul might have continued writing and given up performing altogether if Les Stewart, in a pique, decided not to take up the residency offered by Mrs Mona Best for the Casbah, a new club opening in Hayman's Green, West Derby, Liverpool. The Les Stewart Quartet appeared regularly at Lowlands, which was in the same street as the Casbah, but because he was annoyed that Brown was missing rehearsals to help prepare the Casbah for its opening night, Stewart turned down the residency.

Brown suggested to George that they form another group and take up the Casbah offer. George than contacted John and Paul and the four made their debut at the new club on 29 August 1958 – and the rest is history.

After George and Ken left him, Stewart then went on to play with various other Liverpool bands including Lee Castle & The Barons, The Kansas City Five and The Long & The Tall & The Short.

Let It Be (film)

The final Beatles film, originally known as 'Get Back', which George was originally reluctant to have anything to do with.

George showed his unhappiness and frustration with the project when he walked out on 10 January 1969. He felt that Paul had been patronising to him during the filming – at one point he said to George, 'I always seem to be annoying you.'

At another point, Paul began to make suggestions as to how George should play his guitar! George replied, 'All right, I'll play whatever you want me to play. Or I won't play at all if you don't want me to play.'

George returned to the sessions on 22 January bringing Billy Preston with him, hoping that with the participation of another musician, tensions might be lessened.

George was to comment, 'The Beatles' film is just pure documentary of us slogging and working on the album really. We were thinking of how to do a TV show, but really, it was much easier just to make it into a film. It's very informative, but it's not really nice for me, I can't stand seeing it, but for other people who don't know really what we're about, who like to go in and see our warts, it's very good. You can see us talk, you can hear us playing, you can hear us coughing, it's the recordings, you know, the balance and everything is just right, the silence in between tracks, well, this is not really like that. There's a nice song of Paul's, which is one of those that probably hundreds of people will record. Somebody's gonna have a hit with it. It's called "The Long And Winding Road", it's one of those ballad, standard sort of things.'

Commenting on the film in the *Morning Star*, critic Nina Hibbin wrote, 'George Harrison, with his strong-boned face and shut-in expression, looks as if he could fit into any tough and isolated position – as a shepherd in Bulgaria or the manager of a suburban post office.'

Let It Down

A track from the *All Things Must Pass* triple album, penned by George and 4 minutes and 54 seconds in length.

Let It Rock

A BBC2 radio show hosted by Joe Brown. The show featured a guest who selected their favourite rock'n'roll records. Brown introduced George, a good friend of his, on the 5 July 1999 show. The first record selected was 'Whole Lotta Shakin'' by Jerry Lee Lewis, which George said was 'one of the greatest records of all time – it just pounds'. He then picked 'Heartbreak Hotel' by Elvis Presley saying that he was riding a bike when he was fourteen years old and heard someone playing the number. It was the first time he became aware of rock'n'roll and said, 'It changed the course of my life. What a sound, what a record.' His next pick was another Elvis record 'Milk Cow Blues' followed by the B side of a Chuck Berry record, 'Deep Feeling'. Next was 'Yackety Yak' by the Coasters, followed by Ritchie Barret's version of 'Some Other Guy'. 'Your True Love' by Carl Perkins, which George had performed at Perkins' funeral was next followed by 'Lonesome Tears In My Eyes' by Dorsey and Johnny Burnette. Roy Orbison's 'California Blue' was next and the final selection was Eddie Cochran's 'C'mon Everybody'.

Life Of Brian, The
See HandMade Films.

Light That Has Lighted The World, The
George originally wrote this as the flipside to Cilla Black's 'When Every Song Is Sung', but the record wasn't completed and George recorded it for his own *Living In The Material World* album. It is 3 minutes and 26 seconds in length.

Little Malcolm And His Struggle Against The Eunuchs (aka Little Malcolm)
Although George's contributions to the film industry are recognised via his involvement with HandMade Films, George was actually already executive producer of a movie before the *Monty Python* team approached him regarding help in financing *The Life Of Brian*.

George financed and was executive producer of the film *Little Malcolm And His Struggle Against The Eunuchs* in 1973.

George had first seen the stage version of the play, in the company of Mal Evans, in London in 1966. David Halliwell wrote the play and John Hurt starred in both stage and film versions.

Hurt played art student Malcolm Scrawdyke, who is expelled from his school due to his rebellious nature. His revenge is to trick the headmaster, Dennis Charles Nipple (David Warner), into destroying a valuable stolen painting. He then persuades two other students, Wick Blagdon (John McEnery) and Irwin Ingham (Raymond Platt) to quit school. They start a revolutionary 'Party Of Dynamic Erection'.

The film was released in July 1974 and had its world premiere at the Berlin Film Festival, where it was to receive the Silver Bear Award. It also received the Gold Medal Award at the Atlanta Film Festival. Its commercial premiere took place in London's West End in February 1975, with George and Olivia attending the first screening.

The film had a running time of 110 minutes, and was an Apple films/George Harrison presentation, directed by Stuart Cooper with music by Stanley Myers.

The International Film Guide in 1976 was to observe, 'The sexual and artistic frustration often to be found lurking behind the bombast of the student revolutionary has no greater admirer than former Beatle George Harrison, who entirely financed this film version.'

Live In Japan
A lavish 274-page leather-bound book that includes 500 photographs from George's tour of Japan in 1991.

It was published by Genesis Books in July 1993 in a limited edition of 3,500 copies, with a prepublication price of £275, each copy personally signed by George. It also contained text from members of the band, the road crew and George himself. Additional material included a double-CD set, four guitar plectrums and a replica backstage pass to the Japanese concerts and after-gig receptions.

Live In Japan. George Harrison With Eric Clapton And His Band

The live album of George's tour of Japan issued in America on 14 July 1992. The British release was on 13 July on Dark Horse 7599 26964-1. There was also a five-track promotional sampler sent to American radio stations.

The album bears the legend, 'Produced by Spike and Nelson Wilbury.'

George had originally planned an album of his first American tour in 1974 but, due to the savage reviews, the idea was dropped. However, with the success of the Japanese tour, the double-CD was approved.

There were all kinds of rumours surrounding the tour, intimating that the relationship between George and Eric had become strained and that a possible further tour of them together again would never take place – which it didn't. It's also interesting to note that this 84-minute double set, which includes versions of every song performed during the Japanese shows, doesn't include any of the Clapton numbers that he performed without George. This could actually be due to contractual problems as George was signed to Dark Horse Records (distributed by Warner Bros) while Eric was signed to Duck Records.

The tracks on the two-CD set were: CD One: 'I Want To Tell You', 'Old Brown Shoe', 'Taxman', 'Give Me Love (Give Me Peace On Earth)', 'If I Needed Someone', 'Something', 'What Is Life', 'Dark Horse', 'Piggies', 'Got My Mind Set On You'. CD Two: 'Cloud 9', 'Here Comes The Sun', 'My Sweet Lord', 'All Those Years Ago', 'Cheer Down', 'Devil's Radio', 'Isn't It A Pity', 'While My Guitar Gently Weeps', 'Roll Over Beethoven'.

To coincide with the release, Warner Brothers issued a press release under the heading: 'Stardom, Slagging And Smoking: A Talk With George Harrison.'

It read:

'I knew that eventually I'd have to try it again, and I thought I'd better do it soon before I got too old to take the trouble. Besides, I wanted to stop smoking and having to sing every night was the best motivation I could think of.'

So says George Harrison, with famous deference, on the subject of his return to live performing after a seventeen-year absence from the concert stage. And while the stated reasons for his long-delayed return to the boards should be taken with a few grains of salt, the result, as chronicled on *Live In Japan*, his latest Warner Bros/Dark Horse Records release, is certain to be embraced wholeheartedly.

Featuring a world-class backing band, formed and fronted by long-time friend and collaborator Eric Clapton, *Live In Japan* highlights nineteen choice cuts on two discs, covering the entire range of Harrison's career – from his earliest Beatles classics to his recent, resounding solo hits. Mixing unabashed nostalgia with the unvarnished joy of live performing, it's a collection that serves as a satisfying bookend for the artist's career to date, as well as an intriguing signpost to future forays.

It was 1974 when Harrison last braved the limelight on a barn-storming North American tour, but during that time this particular quarter of the Fab Four has been anything but resting on his laurels. The formation of Dark Horse Records and his movie production company, HandMade Films, are only two of the milestones along the way. A fistful of solo albums, including *Dark Horse*, *Thirty Three & 1/3* and *Somewhere In England* yielded to a well-deserved respite from the music business in the mid-1980s. 1989 marked a spectacular return to form with *Cloud Nine*, his aptly titled ninth solo album, spotlighting the smash hit (and *Live in Japan* showstopper) 'Got My Mind Set On You'. A pair of platinum-plus albums with the most engaging mystery band of all time, the Traveling Wilburys, rounded out one decade and launched him into a new. The 90s found Harrison's worldwide fan following primed for the next move from an artist famed for following his musical instincts . . . wherever they might lead.

The direction, as it turned out, was due east, thanks largely to the urging of Eric Clapton. 'It was Eric who encouraged me to give performing a go again,' Harrison explains. 'He made it very easy by offering to let me step into the band he'd be working with.'

The band in question, featured in various combinations on a number of Clapton's recent releases, included drummer Steve Ferrone, percussionist Ray Cooper, keyboard wizards Greg Phillinganes and Chuck Leavell, bassist Nathan East, backing vocalists Tessa Niles and Katie Kissoon, along with guitarist/vocalist Andy Fairweather-Low and, of course, Clapton himself on guitar and backing vocals. 'It was a great line-up,' enthuses Harrison, 'and again, very encouraging for me to discover how much we all enjoyed working together.'

'Eric also thought that Japan would be a good place to play,' Harrison continues. 'The audiences there are generally very nice, very polite, which would give us the opportunity to concentrate on the show without worrying about being slagged off by the audience.'

While the likelihood of Clapton & Co. being slagged off anywhere seems rather thin, Harrison admits to another reason for choosing Japan for his return to live performing. 'I have a lot of fans there,' he explains. 'They'd been asking me for twenty years to come and play and when I finally decided to go ahead, I felt like I really owed it to them.'

With the line-up and itinerary in place, the next step was repertoire. 'I put about thirty songs together on tape for the band,' Harrison continues. The selection criteria, he reveals, was simple. 'I picked the obvious hit records, like "Something", "My Sweet Lord", "Here Comes The Sun" and "Got My Mind Set On You". Then there were the ones with nostalgia appeal, like "Taxman", "I Want To Tell You", "Give Me Love" and "While My Guitar Gently Weeps", which, of course, had Eric on the original version. But I also threw in a few that I thought might be fun to perform live, like "Roll Over Beethoven" as well as some that had never been done in concert before, such as "Piggies" and "Cloud 9". During rehearsal we naturally pared the original thirty down to the ones that felt the best.'

It was an approach that yielded stunning results over a dozen concerts during a three-week period late last year. 'We really got down to the music,' Harrison asserts.

'We worked hard trying to do a better job each time out. The whole superstar aspect of performing has never really impressed me. The first four shows were enough for my ego. After that, it was just the fun of being back on stage and doing these songs again.'

It's a claim borne out in *Live In Japan*. The sheer pleasure of hearing the special selection of musical gems performed again by the man who made them great is matched, and exceeded, by the often electrifying interchange between this top-notch assemblage of talent. 'It's what playing live should be,' Harrison states simply.

With a superb concert document under his belt, Harrison is currently pondering his next project. 'It might be fun to tour with the Wilburys,' he allows, 'or go out again with this show and a new band. I did a benefit concert recently at the Royal Albert Hall and the reception was tremendous. Maybe it's time to do some playing in England and Europe ... maybe eventually even America.'

In the meantime, a deadpan Harrison concludes, he's grateful for the chance live performing has given him to quit smoking. To which might only be added ... whatever it takes, George.

Liverpool Institute High School For Boys

Reputedly Liverpool's premier grammar school, situated in Mount Street. George attended the school from September 1954, taking the No. 86 bus to school from Speke Boulevard, a journey that took an hour.

George didn't like his schooldays and was to say, 'That's when this darkness came in. Be here, stand there, shut up, sit down. You could punch people just to get it out of your system. It was the worse time of my life.'

He was to add, 'I used to do myself up in tight trousers, waistcoat and suede shoes, all very fashionable I reckoned, but the ones in charge had a different view of what should be worn.'

Another comment he made was, 'The worse thing was leaving junior school and going to the big grammar school ... that's when my frustrations began to start. The big school, Liverpool Institute, was a real pain in the neck. I knew then that the teachers were not the type of people to teach. The way they sent you out into the world was miserable.'

He was also to say that he hated being dictated to at the Innie. 'I was just trying to be myself. They were trying to turn everybody into rows of little toffees.'

George left the school with no formal qualifications. He didn't pass any of his O levels. He was to say, 'In the mocks I got two per cent, probably because I spelled my name right at the top.'

However, if he had not attended the 'Innie', George would never have become a Beatle, for the most important fact was that he met Paul McCartney, who was in a class a year ahead of him, at the school. Their friendship began when they got to know each other when they caught the same bus to school.

These days, the Institute has been transformed into a fame school, The Liverpool Institute of Performing Arts, which was launched by Paul.

Living In The Material World

Issued in Britain on Apple PAS 1006 on 21 June 1973, it was George's follow-up album to *All Things Must Pass* and reached No. 3 in the British charts. It was released in America on Apple SMAS 3410 on 30 May 1973 and topped the American charts, eventually selling three million copies worldwide.

George recorded most of the album between January and April 1973 at the Apple Studios in Savile Row. Musicians on the album, apart from George on guitar, included Ringo Starr and Jim Keltner on drums, Nicky Hopkins and Gary Wright on keyboards, Klaus Voormann on bass, Jim Horn on saxophone and flutes, John Barham on strings and Zakir Hussein on tabla. Drummer Jim Gordon appeared on the track 'Try Some, Buy Some'.

Tom Wilkes and Craig Braun designed the gatefold sleeve and there was a four-page insert of song lyrics. There were also two messages on the run-out groove area – HARE KRSNA and HARE RAMA.

The first single issued from the album was 'Give Me Love (Give Me Peace On Earth)', which topped the American singles chart at the same time that *Living In The Material World* was placed at No. 1 in the album chart, giving him his second double top in the US charts.

The tracks on the album were: Side One: 'Give Me Love (Give Me Peace On Earth)', 'Sue Me, Sue You Blues', 'The Light That Has

Lighted The World', 'Don't Let Me Wait Too Long', 'Who Can See It', 'Living In The Material World'. Side Two: 'The Lord Loves The One (That Loves The Lord)', 'Be Here Now', 'Try Some, Buy Some', 'The Day The World Gets 'Round', 'That Is All'.

London Standard Film Awards

Annual film awards sponsored by the *Evening Standard* newspaper. At the 1986 event, which took place at the Savoy Hotel, London, George and Denis O'Brien received an award on behalf of HandMade Films for their contribution to the British Film Industry.

George was dressed formally in a dinner jacket and bow tie. He received his honour from the Duchess of Kent and in good humour called her 'your Majesty'. She then gave him a kiss.

Lonely Man

A number composed by Mal Evans and Robert J. Purvis (of Splinter), which the duo Splinter performed in the nightclub sequence of the film *Little Malcolm And His Struggle Against The Eunuchs*. George co-produced it with Tom Scott and played guitar on the track using the name Hari Georgeson. Vocals were by Bill Elliott and Bob Purvis, Billy Preston was on organ, Jim Keltner on drums, Bill Dickinson on bass and John Taylor on Fender Rhodes.

The number was included on Splinter's debut album *Harder To Live*.

Long Long Long

A number composed by George, which was included on *The Beatles* double album. It lasts 3 minutes and 4 seconds and was recorded at Abbey Road Studios on 7 October 1968 with overdubbing on 8 and 9 October.

George observed that there was a bottle of wine on top of the Leslie speaker when they were recording. When Paul, who was playing Hammond organ, hit a particular note, it sent the Leslie vibrating and the bottle rattling – and this can be heard at the end of the recording. George also admitted that the chords came from Bob Dylan's 'Sad-Eyed Lady Of The Lowlands'.

Looking For My Life

A track from the *Brainwashed* album lasting 3 minutes and 49 seconds, with George on lead vocals, electric guitar, acoustic guitar and background vocals. Jeff Lynne was on acoustic guitar, 12-string guitar, piano, bass and background vocals with Dhani Harrison on electric guitar, acoustic guitar and background vocals and Jim Keltner on drums.

Love Comes To Everyone

A track from the 1979 album *George Harrison*, lasting 3 minutes and 31 seconds. It was issued in Britain on Dark Horse K17284 in May

1979 with 'Soft-Hearted Hana' on the flip. It didn't enter the British charts.

It was issued in America on Dark Horse DRC 8844 on 9 May 1979 with 'Soft Touch' on the flip. It also made no progress in the American charts.

Love You To

A number penned by George, which was included on the *Revolver* album, and recorded at Abbey Road Studios on 11 April 1966. George is double-tracked on lead vocal and sitar, and there is also another Indian instrument used, a tabla, played by Anil Bhagwat. The number is 2 minutes and 58 seconds in length.

In his book *I. Me. Mine.* George was to comment, '"Love You To" was one of the first tunes I wrote for sitar. "Norwegian Wood" was an accident as far as the sitar part was concerned, but this was the first song where I consciously tried to use the sitar and tabla on the basic track. I overdubbed the guitars and vocal later.'

Love's A State Of Mind

A single by Sylvia Griffin, released in Britain by Rocket Records on 27 May 1988. It included a slide guitar contribution from George that he'd recorded at his home studio FPSHOT, which producer Chris Thomas then overdubbed on the Griffin track.

LSD

Lysergic acid diethylamide, a hallucinogenic drug which acts directly on the brain, causing visions and heightened awareness of colours, sounds and textures, and altering people's perceptions.

George's first introduction to LSD was via a spiked drink. In January 1965 George and Patti and John and Cynthia were friends with their London dentist who lived in the Bayswater Road. One evening they were all invited to dinner at his house. After dinner, he had a neat line of sugar cubes that he dropped into their coffee. Patti didn't fancy drinking the coffee, but the dentist urged her to.

When they had settled into the drawing room he informed them that the sugar cubes had contained LSD and they were advised to sit back and experience it.

Both Patti and Cynthia were terrified and Patti whispered to George, 'Let's get the hell out of here.' They left, despite the dentist warning them that it would be dangerous to leave as they didn't know what would happen to them outside because they'd had no previous experience of the effects of LSD.

George told him they'd take their chances and they took a taxi to the Pickwick club where their friend Klaus Voormann was performing with his group Paddy, Klaus and Gibson. The dentist and his girlfriend followed them in another taxi.

At the Pickwick, the effects began to emerge and they began to experience distorting colours and pulsing sounds as weird sensations affected them. The dentist arrived and pleaded with them to come back to his place, but they thought he was the Devil and fled to the Ad Lib club.

John Lennon recalled the experience: 'I was insane going around London. We were cackling in the streets and Patti was shouting, "Let's break a window." It was insane. We were just out of our heads.

'When we finally got in the lift we all thought there was a fire, but it was just a little red light. We were all hot and hysterical, and when we arrived on the floor the lift stopped and the door opened, and we were all screaming.

'I had read somebody describing the effects of opium in the old days and I thought, "Fuck! It's happening." Then some singer came up to me and said, "Can I sit next to you?" And I said, "Only if you don't talk," because I just couldn't think.

'George somehow or other managed to drive us home in his Mini. We were going about ten miles an hour, but it seemed like a thousand, and Patti was saying, "Let's jump out and play football." It was just terrifying, but it was fantastic. I did some drawings at the time of four faces saying, "We all agree with you." I did a lot of drawing that night.'

George was fascinated by the experience and began to take LSD regularly, saying, 'It was like I had never tasted, smelled or heard anything before. For me it was like a flash. It just opened something inside of me, and I realised a lot of very heavy things. From that moment on, I wanted to have that depth and clarity of perception all the time.'

He said, 'LSD was just like lots of doors in my mind were flying open.'

Later he was to explain, 'It can help you get from A to B, but when you get to B, you see C. And you see that to get *really* high, you have to go it straight. So this was the disappointing thing about LSD.

'In the physical world we live in, there's always duality – good and bad, black and white, yes and no. There's always something equal and opposite to everything, and this is why you can't say LSD is good or it's bad, because it's both of them and it's neither of them altogether. People don't consider that. We've all got the same goal whether we realise it or not. We're all striving for something called God. Everyone is a potential Jesus Christ, really. We are all trying to get to where Christ got. And we're going to be in this world until we get there.

'The hippies are a good idea – love, flowers, and that is great – but when you see the other half of it, it's like anything. I love all these people, too, those who are honest and trying to find a bit of truth and to straighten out the untruths. I'm with them one hundred per cent, but when I see the bad side of it, I'm not so happy.'

Luera, Soledad

A female funeral director at the Hollywood Forever Cemetery. In December 2001 Luera was fired from her job after eight years, accused of putting a fake address on George's death certificate. She then threatened to sue Olivia Harrison, who had given her false information.

The place of death was listed as 1971 Coldwater Canyon, Beverly Hills, an address that doesn't exist. Olivia had given the address to Luera, whose job it was to fill out the official death report.

When she was fired, a colleague commented, 'Soledad is being made a scapegoat. She basically wrote down what Olivia told her was the address where George died.

'Soledad started talking to fellow employees and was fired for breach of confidentiality of the family's request and failure to notify the company of the incorrect address on the certificate. But she didn't know the address was wrong.'

Lumber, Jack

One of George's numerous pseudonyms. He used the name in the late 1970s when he and Olivia went on their holidays. He chose the name because *Monty Python*'s 'The Lumberjack Song' was a favourite of his.

Lumberjack Song, The

A *Monty Python's Flying Circus* number, which was re-recorded in a studio in 1975, produced by George 'Onothimagen' Harrison. It was included on *Monty Python Sings*, a compilation issued on 11 December 1989 by Virgin records, with release numbers: album MONT1, cassette MONTC1 and CD MONTCD1. When the *Monty Python* team were performing a three-week season at the City Center, New York, George dressed up in a Royal Canadian Mounted Police uniform and joined them on stage when they performed 'The Lumberjack Song'.

Lynne, Jeff

Jeff Lynne was born in Birmingham on 30 December 1947 and began his musical career in 1966 with Mike Sheridan and the Nightriders, who evolved into the Idle Race. For a short time he was with the Move. He next formed the Electric Light Orchestra and received great critical acclaim for his double album *Out Of The Blue* in 1978.

When George was considering a producer to work with it was Dave Edmunds who suggested Jeff Lynne to him. George asked Edmunds to contact Lynne and then invited him to dinner at Friar Park.

George recalled, 'We hung out a bit. The more we got to know each other, it just evolved into this thing. Jeff was the perfect choice. The great thing about Jeff was that he wanted to help me make my record.'

George was to add, 'Choosing Jeff to produce was part of a long process. I tried to think of someone who could complement my music without overpowering it, and also somebody I had respect for as a producer or songwriter. Then I thought, "Well, Jeff has a lot in common with me. I mean, a lot of his songs sound like the old pop songs or even like some old Beatle songs."

'I spent a year calling him and talking to him and hanging out with him. When it seemed like we were getting to be good buddies, I said, "Well, actually, I'm going to make an album." He said, "I'll help you a bit."'

He produced George's album *Cloud Nine* in 1987 and his friendship with George saw him become a member of the Traveling Wilburys.

One night, when they were having dinner, George asked him if he'd like to produce the next Beatles single – this was a new recording by George, Paul and Ringo using a demo tape by John Lennon, which Yoko Ono had given them to use for the recording. This was part of the *Anthology* project.

George said to Lynne, 'You fancy doing it, then? The Beatles one?' Lynne said, 'Yes, please.' Lynne jumped at the chance and was given 'Free As A Bird', which was just a piano demo at the time. After the single was released he was given two others to work on, 'Real Love' and 'Miss You'.

George said, 'Writing with Jeff Lynne is really the first time I've ever written with anyone. I wrote one time with Dylan back in '69. I wrote one with Eric Clapton. I've helped Ringo finish songs. But I'm not the type of songwriter that says, "Let's sit down and write." Every Beatles album that had a song of mine on it I wrote alone. John and Paul had been writing so much together. Once in a while I got a line from John when I was stuck. But at the same time I gave them lyrics. I helped out on "Eleanor Rigby". I wrote some of the lyrics to "Come Together".'

In an interview in January 2001, when talking about recording a new album to the German news agency DPA, George said that he wouldn't have Jeff producing it, commenting, 'I have stopped working with Jeff because I did not want him to make ELO albums out of my songs. On this album you can hear guitar, bass and drums, and no computers.'

In fact, Jeff began to work on what would be George's posthumous album *Brainwashed*. And in March 2002 he began to finish the songs George had left on demos, working with Dhani in Lynne's home studio for six months. *Brainwashed* was released in America on 19 November 2002 and reached No. 18 in the charts there.

George's comments from his January 2001 interview seem interesting when aligned with the comment Jeff made about *Brainwashed*: 'Sorry George, I made them a little bit posher than you may have wanted them.'

174 Macket's Lane

The house in Hunt's Cross, Liverpool 25 where the Harrison family moved when they left their Upton Road home in Speke. George's mother and father lived there until 1966 when he bought them a bungalow.

Madison Square Garden

The 20,000-seater in New York where George staged his Concert For Bangla Desh. The venue was also the site of George's end-of-tour concerts on Thursday 19 and Friday 20 December 1974.

On the first night Paul and Linda McCartney, Julian Lennon and Ringo Starr's manager Hilary Gerrard were in the audience.

Arrangements had originally been made for John Lennon to appear on stage with George, but this didn't happen due to the fact that John refused to sign agreement forms regarding the Beatles which had to be signed by midnight on the day of the first concert. George phoned May Pang, John's partner at the time, to complain, 'I started the tour without him and I'll finish it without him.'

However, John, together with May Pang, attended George's end-of-tour party at the Hippopotamus club in New York on Friday 20 December.

Commenting on the situation regarding his nonappearance and the fact that he wouldn't sign the agreement (he eventually signed it on Friday 27 December), John commented, 'George and I are still good pals and we always will be, but I was supposed to sign this thing on the day of his concert. He was pretty weird because he was in the middle of that tour and we hadn't communicated for a while because he doesn't live here. I've seen Paul a bit because he comes to New York a lot, and I'm always seeing Ringo in Los Angeles.

'Anyway, I was a bit nervous about going on stage, but I agreed to because it would have been mean of me not to go on with George after I'd gone on with Elton. I didn't sign the document on that day because my astrologer told me it wasn't the right day, tee hee!

'George was furious with me at the time because I hadn't signed it when I was supposed to, and somehow or other I was informed that I needn't bother to go to George's show. I was quite relieved in the end because there wasn't any time to rehearse and I didn't want it to be a case of just John jumping up and playing a few chords.

'I went to see him at Nassau and it was a good show. The band was great but Ravi wasn't there, so I didn't see the bit where the crowd is supposed to get restless. I just saw a good tight show. George's voice was shot but the atmosphere was good and the crowd was great.

'I saw George after the Garden show and we were friends again. But he was surrounded by the madhouse that's called "touring". I respect George but I think he made a mistake on the tour. Mistakes are easier to spot if you're not the person making them, so I don't want to come on like "I know better" 'cause I haven't done that . . . one of the basic mistakes seemed to be that the people wanted to hear old stuff. George wasn't prepared to do that, and I understand him. When I did that charity concert at Madison Square Garden, I was still riding high on *Imagine* so I was OK for material. But when I did 'Come Together' the house came down, which gave me an indication of what people wanted to hear.'

On the final night at Madison Square Garden, George slightly changed the words of 'Sue Me, Sue You Blues' to 'Bring your lawyer: Don't bring Klein.' Just before he performed 'This Is Life' he said, 'This is from everyone in the electric band and everyone in the Indian band. During the last fifty gigs, we had all the people who dug it, all the people who didn't dig it. All the ones who had too much ink in their pens. For everybody, this is it! God bless you all. It all comes out in the wash.'

George also appeared at the venue on Friday 16 October 1992 for a special thirtieth anniversary 'salute to Dylan' concert that was also aired on radio and screened on a pay-for-view cable channel. George was backed by an all-star band comprising Booker T, Steve Cropper and Jim Keltner under the direction of G.F. Smith.

George was wearing a purple sports coat and played an acoustic guitar when he performed 'If Not For You' and 'Absolutely Sweet Marie'. He then introduced Bob Dylan. He reappeared to join an all-star band that included Tom Petty and Dylan (members of the Traveling Wilburys) to perform 'My Back Pages' and sang lead on one of the verses. He shared the mic with Ron Wood and Johnny Cash on the number 'Knockin' On Heaven's Door'.

Maharishi Mahesh Yogi

Indian religion, philosophy, spirituality and music was to play a huge part in George's life through the men from the East who inspired him such as Ravi Shankar, Swami Prabhupada and the Maharishi Mahesh Yogi.

The Maharishi was born Mahesh Prasad Varma in India in 1918 and studied physics at the university of Allahabad. After graduating he spent the next thirteen years studying Sanskrit and the scriptures under Guru Dev.

Adopting the name Maharishi, which means 'great soul', he devised a way of making meditation more acceptable in the Western world via transcendental meditation.

Initially he arrived in London in 1959 and established the International Meditation Society, which later became known as the Spiritual Regeneration Movement.

It was Patti Harrison who originally became intrigued by the mysticism of India and meditation in particular. In February 1967 she attended a lecture on Spiritual Regeneration at Caxton Hall in London.

At the time Patti had time on her hands because, in addition to George being involved in Beatle matters, he had requested that she abandon her modelling career and even asked her to stop being involved in charity work.

The press nicknamed the Maharishi the 'giggling guru' due to his habit of giggling, and Patti talked George, John and Paul, with Cynthia and Jane Asher to attend a lecture on transcendental meditation he was giving on 24 August 1967 at the Hilton Hotel London (Ringo was in Queen Charlotte's Hospital with Maureen at the time). They paid their eight shillings at the door and listened to the lecture. When the Maharishi was made aware of his famous guests he granted them a private audience and then invited them to Bangor University College in North Wales at the weekend for a Bank Holiday course in transcendental meditation. John and George were very enthusiastic, although Paul wasn't and, when they told Ringo, he wasn't too keen, either, but agreed to go along. They all took a train from Euston station, although Cynthia Lennon broke down in tears when she missed the train.

George was to say, 'With meditation, you don't have to bother with all the trappings of traditional religion.' He also said, 'We've only just discovered what we can do as musicians, what thresholds we can cross. The future stretches out beyond our imagination.'

It was while they were at Bangor that they were told of the death of Brian Epstein. The Maharishi consoled them and George, now beginning to be influenced by his knowledge of Indian religions and spirituality, said, 'There is no such thing as death, only in the physical sense. He will return because he desired bliss so much.'

The Maharishi became the Beatles guru and he invited them to a lengthy course in meditation from February 1968 at his ashram in Rishikesh, India.

The Beatles' friend Alexis Mardas believed that the Maharishi was using them and intended to get them to sign part of their royalties over to him, so he began to seek out any scandal he could find. A nurse told him that the Maharishi had made advances to her, but George didn't believe him. However, when he told them that he'd approached some other women at the ashram and they'd confirmed it, George and John went to confront the Maharishi, being the only two Beatles left there as Ringo and Paul had abandoned the course and returned to London.

John Lennon was to say, 'There was this big hullabaloo about him trying to rape Mia Farrow or somebody and trying to get off with a few other women and things like that. We went to see him after we stayed up all night discussing "was it true or not true".

'When George started thinking it might be true there must be something in it.

'So we went to see the Maharishi, the whole gang of us, the next day, charged down to his hut, his bungalow, and as usual, when the dirty work came, I was the spokesman – whenever the dirty work came, I actually had to be leader – and I said, "We're leaving."

'"Why?" he asked, and all that shit and I said, "Well, if you're so cosmic, you'll know why."'

After Rishikesh George said, 'I'm not against spreading the word of meditation, but they started to go about it the wrong way, and made the whole thing seem a drag.'

In 1976 George was to say, 'I can see much clearer now what happened, and there was still just a lot of ignorance that went down. Maharishi was fantastic and I admire him – like Prabhupada – for being able, in spite of all the ridicule, to just keep on going.'

In April 1992 George appeared in concert at the Royal Albert Hall to raise funds for the Maharishi's Natural Law Party. He said, 'I still practice transcendental meditation and I think it's great. Maharishi only ever did good for us, and although I have not been with him physically, I never left him.'

Martin, George

The Beatles recording manager, born in London in 1926.

It's a matter of speculation, but was it a series of lucky incidents that led him to becoming known as 'the fifth Beatle'?

EMI had written to Brian Epstein rejecting the Beatles for their company. Their letter of rejection seemed final. The only A&R man with the company they hadn't approached about the Beatles was Martin, because his label Parlophone didn't really deal with pop records. The classically trained A&R man recorded jazz, classical and comedy records. The artists he recorded included Bernard Cribbins, the

Temperance Seven, Jimmy Shand, Sir Adrian Boult, Sir Malcolm Sargent and Cleo Laine.

Any pop records that did stray onto the label were few and far between and were always handed over to Ron Richards, Martin's assistant. At the time he recorded Shane Fenton (later to become Alvin Stardust) and Paul Gadd (later to become Gary Glitter), both of whom didn't actually achieve success until the 1970s 'Glam Rock' period. Martin didn't actually like pop music and had turned down Tommy Steele, who was then snapped up by Dick Rowe to become the biggest British rock'n'roll artist of the 1950s.

It was only by a coincidence when Brian Epstein went to the HMV shop to have acetates made that he was introduced to Syd Coleman, who phoned Martin's office to arrange an interview because he wanted the rights to some of the Beatles' songs. Even then things weren't straightforward and Epstein had to threaten EMI with a boycott of their records in all his stores before he was actually given a recording audition at Parlophone.

Even here, luck poked her head in. The Beatles were passed over to Ron Richards, the man who dealt with pop acts for the label – he is down on their original recording sheets as their A&R man. George Martin wasn't even present when the session began. During the session, engineer Norman Smith was interested to see they had original material such as 'Love Me Do' and sent tape operator Chris Neal down to the canteen to bring Martin up to the studio. Martin then took over. But for this incident, Richards may have remained their recording manager.

Although George Martin was an ideal recording manager for the Beatles, bringing his expertise to add to their talent, his main focus during the group's recording career was on material by John and Paul. He was never really interested in George's compositions and didn't spend the time and energy on them as he did on those by the two who he regarded as the Beatles' main stars. He was later to admit: 'I'm really sorry to say that I did not help George much with his songwriting. His early attempts did not show much promise. I tended to go with the blokes who were delivering the goods. I did look at his new material with a slightly jaundiced eye. When he would bring a new song along to me, I would say to myself, "I wonder if it's going to be any better than the last one?"'

When the *Sgt Pepper* album was being planned, Martin recalled, 'The first song George brought up for consideration was "Only A Northern Song". I had to tell George that as far as *Pepper* was concerned, I did not think his song would be good enough for what was shaping up as a really strong album. I suggested he come up with something a bit better. George was a bit bruised; it is never pleasant being rejected, even if you are friendly with the person who is doing the rejecting. When he came up with "Within You, Without You" it was a bit of a relief all around. I still didn't think it was a great song. The tune struck me as being a little bit of a dirge. But I found what George wanted to do with the song fascinating.'

Discussing George Martin on London Weekend Television's *The South Bank Show*, George said, 'I think we just grew through those years together, him as the straight man and us as the loonies; but he was always there for us to interpret our madness – we used to be slightly avant-garde on certain days of the week, and he would be there as the anchor person, to communicate that through the engineers on to the tape.'

Marwa Blues

A track from the *Brainwashed* album lasting 3 minutes and 41 seconds with George on slide guitar, keyboards and finger cymbals. Jeff Lynne was on acoustic guitar and keyboards, Ray Cooper on percussion, Dhani Harrison on acoustic guitar and Marc Mann was conductor and responsible for the string arrangement.

Mason, Dave

A former member of Traffic who first met the Beatles when he dropped in at the *Sgt Pepper* recording sessions.

He was one of the musicians invited to play acoustic guitar on the *All Things Must Pass* sessions. He also participated in some of the jam sessions during the recording, on numbers such as 'Plug Me In' and 'Thanks For The Pepperoni'.

Mason also appeared on some of the dates of the Delaney & Bonnie tour, when George played on it.

A few years later George recorded for Mason's *It's Like You Never Left* album. George was in Los Angeles where Mason was recording at the time and he just contacted George and asked him to come along and play on some of the tracks.

Musicians, and George in particular, often liked to drop in on sessions and play with fellow musicians. The only major problem in such circumstances is the 'men in suits' who point out that the artists are signed to different recording companies, or want to know what percentage the artist will get, while the artist himself just wants to return a favour or play for the fun of it. In these circumstances, George often used a pseudonym. On this occasion it was 'Son of Harry'.

Other artists on Mason's album included Stevie Wonder, Graham Nash and Jim Keltner.

Massott, Joe

A film producer who developed a friendship with George. One of his early works was a short film *Reflections Of Love – The Film Of Swinging London*, which he made in 1965. It starred Patti's sister Jenny Boyd.

George and John invited him to join them when they went to study Transcendental Meditation at the Maharishi Mahesh Yogi's ashram in Rishikesh. Joe also filmed them there and excerpts from his film were used in the Beatles *Anthology* TV series.

Joe was also responsible for George's first attempt at a movie soundtrack when he asked him to compose the film music for *Wonderwall*.

He was to comment, 'I had various choices. The Bee Gees were interested in doing something and came to Twickenham Studios to see me. It seemed the movie had created a vibe as Graham Nash also wanted to join in.

'George told me that he had been working on *Magical Mystery Tour* helping out, but that was Paul's project, that he would like to do something solo. So I told him he would have a free hand to do anything he liked musically. That was what interested him in particular.'

George was to recall, 'Joe Massott, the director, asked me would I do the music for his film and I said, "I don't know how to do music for films," and he said, "Anything you do I will have in the film," and those were the terms on which I agreed to do the work.

'I decided to do it as a mini-anthology of Indian music because I wanted to help turn the public on to Indian music.'

Although George had never written a soundtrack before, and because there were hundreds of cues, he was to say, 'I had a regular wind-up stopwatch and I watched the film to "spot-in" the music with the watch. I wrote the timings down in my book, then I'd go to Abbey Road, make up a piece, record it and when we'd synch it up at Twickenham it always worked, it was always right.'

Massott also approached George to compose music for the rock Western *Zachariah* in late 1969, but George declined.

Massott also directed the Led Zeppelin film *The Song Remains The Same*.

In 1998 Joe reissued *Wonderwall* on video, with a special book and also a 7″ single and CD with an additional number, 'In The First Place', which George had written for *Wonderwall* and recorded with the Remo Four in November 1967. When Joe was compiling material for his 'director's cut', George provided him with this number, which had originally been left off the original soundtrack.

The 'director's cut' video also included an unpublished John Lennon poem, spoken by actress Jane Birkin, which John had given to him when the two were both at the Maharishi Mahesh Yogi's ashram in India.

Material World Foundation

A charity that George set up in 1973 to support various agencies worldwide that aid poverty-stricken children.

Maya Love

The closing track on the first side of George's 1974 album *Dark Horse*.
It was also issued as the flipside of 'This Guitar (Can't Keep From
Crying)', an *Extra Texture (Read All About It)* track, in February 1976.

McCartney, Paul

James Paul McCartney was born at Walton Road Hospital, Liverpool
on 18 June 1942, the son of Mary and James McCartney. His brother
Michael was born eighteen months later.

Mary was a midwife and, as such, was able to obtain accommoda-
tion for the family at various addresses in Liverpool.

Paul passed his eleven-plus examinations and entered the grammar
school Liverpool Institute in 1957, where he was later to meet up with
George Harrison.

The relationship between George and Paul McCartney was initially
a good one. They originally travelled to Liverpool Institute together
when they both lived in Speke, prior to Paul and his family moving to
Forthlin Road.

Paul lived in Ardwick Road and George lived in Upton Green.
George recalled, 'It took from four o' clock to five to get home in the
evening to the outskirts of the Speke estate and it was on that bus
journey that I met Paul McCartney, because he, being at the same
school, had the same uniform and was going the same way as I was so
I started hanging out with him.'

At one time, when Paul was short of money, George's mum gave him
the bus fare. It was on the bus that George told Paul about his single
appearance with the Rebels, which impressed Paul.

George was a rebel at the Institute, a school he was never happy at.
Outward signs of his rebellion were obvious in the clothes he wore,
bright lime-green waistcoats to shock and a teddy-boy hairstyle.

Paul was a year ahead of George at the school, but their friendship
developed and they spent hours together discussing music and would
also practise together. George remembered, 'We used to play on our
own, not in any group, just listening to each other and pinching
anything from any other lad who could do better.'

At one time Paul introduced George to a friend of his. George immediately head-butted him and the boy fell to the ground. When Paul
asked him why he did it, George said that the boy wasn't worthy of
Paul's friendship.

When the Beatles began to achieve celebrity, one of George's
teachers, Arthur Evans, recalled, 'Harrison was the greatest surprise to
me of all during the Beatles' meteoric rise to fame. My memory of him
was of a very quiet, if not even introverted little boy who would sit in
the farthest corner and never say a word, or even look up.

'I'm not saying he was unintelligent, but you were always aware of
the presence of both Paul and [his brother] Michael in the classroom.

But Harrison hardly ever spoke. And I noticed that when they reached the pinnacle of their fame, he always stood about a foot behind the others. Which was in character with what appeared to be a rather retiring little boy. Obviously one doesn't know what friendships there were among schoolboys. But I was not aware that Paul and Harrison knew each other at all.'

One evening Paul cycled over to George's house in Speke to help in explaining the instructions in a guitar manual. Together they worked it out and they managed to play 'Don't You Rock Me Daddy-O'.

In the summer of 1957 Paul and George, accompanied by their guitars, went hitchhiking on the south coast. George recalled, 'When I was fourteen Paul and I went to Paignton in Devon on a hitchhiking holiday. It was a bit of a laugh too, because we ran out of money and had nowhere to sleep. So Paul suggested we sleep on the beach. Sand, however, is as hard as concrete when you lie on it all night.'

Paul took George to the Morgue, a skiffle club in Broadgreen, to meet members of his group the Quarry Men. Paul passed his guitar over to George, who picked his way through the introduction to 'Raunchy'. 'Can you play any more than that?' asked John Lennon, and George picked out another verse.

'Raunchy' by Bill Justis and his Orchestra was an instrumental hit in America in 1957, reaching No. 2 in the charts. Paul said of George, 'He would really play the guitar, particularly this piece called "Raunchy", which we all used to love. You see, if anyone could do something like that it was generally enough to get them in the group.' John was supposedly impressed by the guitar, but not by George. However, George was able to play 'Raunchy' again for John on a bus journey home following a gig at Wilson Hall, Garston on 6 February 1958 and soon began appearing with the Quarry Men when their regular guitarist Eric Griffiths didn't appear.

Paul allegedly plotted to get rid of Griffiths by arranging a rehearsal at Forthlin Road with himself, George, John and drummer Colin Hanton, but not inviting Griffiths. While they were rehearsing the phone rang. They suspected it was Eric, but the three guitarists made out that they were busy playing and made Hanton take the call and tell Griffiths that he had been replaced permanently.

Paul also recalled, 'I knew George long before John and any of the others. They were all from Woolton, the posh district, and we hailed from the Allerton set, which was more working class. George and I had got together to learn the guitar and we were chums, despite his tender years as it seemed to me then. In fact George was only nine months younger than I was but to me George was always my little mate.'

Paul often came round to George's house in Speke to rehearse with him. George recalled: 'Paul was very good with the harder chords, I must admit. After a time, though, we actually began playing real songs together, like 'Don't You Rock Me Daddy-O' and 'Besame Mucho'.

Paul knocked me out with his singing especially, although I remember him being a little embarrassed to really sing out, seeing we were stuck right in the middle of my parent's place with the whole family walking about. He said he felt funny singing about love and such around my dad. We must have both really been a sight. I bet the others were just about pissing themselves trying not to laugh.'

Paul said, 'He was a good mate and his mum let us use the place to rehearse. George was far ahead of us as a guitarist when we met, but that isn't saying very much because we were all raw beginners ourselves. George knows his own weaknesses as a musician. He cares, does what he can to improve all the time. He was always eager to learn.'

In the summer of 1958 George and Paul went hitchhiking again, this time to Wales. George commented, 'We ran out of cash again, and Paul had the idea that we could sleep at the police station in one of the cells. Unfortunately the police refused but did suggest we could kip in the grandstand of the local football club. With great difficulty we climbed the wall surrounding the football ground, and with even greater difficulty got to sleep on the concrete steps of the grandstand. Just as day was breaking, I woke to see the caretaker standing over us. "What are you doing in my grandstand?" he demanded. "S-sleeping," Paul croaked. "Well, you're not anymore!" We didn't need telling twice.'

That was the summer that they first recorded at Percy Philips' studio in Kensington recording Buddy Holly's 'That'll Be The Day' and a song that George and Paul wrote called 'In Spite Of All The Danger', the only example of the two of them as a writing team.

When the Quarry Men had re-formed for the Casbah residency, the relationship between Paul and George had shifted. Having spent so much time writing in collaboration with John, Paul was now closer to John and the earlier close friendship between George and Paul suffered. As Cynthia Lennon was to recall, 'George being much younger and not writing songs didn't have the same communication with them, but John and Paul couldn't stop playing together.'

The power behind the Beatles seemed to rest with Paul and John, with both George and the newcomer Ringo taking something of a back seat.

George eventually began writing again and his first song, 'Don't Bother Me', appeared in *A Hard Day's Night*, although he found it a battle to receive any serious attention for his songs – and he discovered that Paul was now even to challenge his expertise as a guitarist.

The tension between George and Paul was apparent during the recording of the *Rubber Soul* album, according to engineer Norman Smith who said, 'George was having to put up with an awful lot from Paul. We now had the luxury of four-track recording, so George would put his solo on afterwards. But as far as Paul was concerned, George could do no right – Paul was absolutely finicky.

'So what would happen was that on certain songs Paul himself played the solos. I would wonder what the hell was going on, because George would have done two or three takes, and to me they were really quite OK. But Paul would be saying, "No, no, no!" And he'd start quoting American records, telling him to play exactly as he'd heard on such-and-such a song. So we'd go back from the top and George would really get into it. Then would come Paul's comment, "OK, the first sixteen bars weren't bad. But that middle . . ." Then Paul would take over and do it himself – he always had a left-handed guitar with him.

'Subsequently, I discovered that George Harrison had been hating Paul's guts for this, but it didn't show itself. In fact, I take my hat off to George Harrison that he swallowed what he had to swallow in terms of criticism from Paul.'

On 10 January 1969, during the filming at Twickenham Studios of the movie that was to become *Let It Be*, George walked out on the Beatles. He had two main reasons: one because he felt that Paul was treating him as an inferior, the other following an argument with John in frustration at the omnipresent Yoko Ono being constantly in their face, making sure she was in every shot during the filming of 'Get Back'. Commenting on the episode with Paul, he said: 'Paul and I were trying to have an argument and the crew carried on filming and recording us. Anyway, after one of those first mornings, I couldn't stand it. I told Paul, "I'll play whatever you want me to play. Or I won't play at all. Whatever it is that'll please you. I'll do it." I decided this is it – it's not fun anymore; it's very unhappy being in this band; it's a load of crap. Thank you. I'm leaving.'

He was also to say, 'I just got fed up with the bad vibes and that arguments with Paul were being put on film. I didn't care if it was the Beatles, I was getting out. Getting home in that pissed-off mood I wrote the song 'Wah Wah', which was saying, "You've given me a bloody headache."'

The relationship continued to deteriorate after Paul took legal action to wind up the Beatles.

Despite that, George invited him to participate in the Concert For Bangla Desh. Paul said that he'd only agree to appear if the other three would drop their legal action against him which had been instigated because of his action to dissolve the Beatles partnership. This was unacceptable to George.

Some years later, both Paul and George made an appearance at the San Remo Festival in Italy. Although George had a strong relationship with Ringo, he still had reservations about his friendship with Paul, and because they didn't greet each other warmly at the San Remo Festival, George had to explain, 'We weren't avoiding each other. Neither of us knew each other was going to be there.' On arriving at Heathrow he told journalists that Paul was 'definitely a bit too moody for me'.

In the early 1980s, following some meetings to discuss business, George was able to say, 'Paul and I had not been friends for a number of years but lately we spent a lot of time really getting to know each other again.'

Later in the decade, George was to say, 'Paul has shown a superior attitude towards me, musically, for years. In normal circumstances, I had not let his attitudes bother me and, to get a peaceful life, I had always let him have his own way, even when this meant that songs, which I had composed, were not being recorded. When I had returned from the States, I was in a very happy frame of mind. But I quickly discovered that I was up against the same old Paul.'

In 1989 George was to say that he found Paul too moody for his liking, although he admitted, 'Our relationship is quite good, but there's no reunion of any Beatles.' He told the Associated Press: 'We have been having dinner together. We are friends now: it's the first time we have been this close for a long time. But it doesn't mean to say that we are going to make another group or anything. You know, I could go out and try to become a superstar, and I tell you, if I went to an agent and a manager and checked myself out and practised a bit, I could do it. But I don't really want to do that. That's being a kamikaze pop star, the tours and everything. I don't have to prove anything. I don't want to be in the business full time because I'm a gardener: I plant flowers and watch them grow.'

In 1993 the three surviving members of the Beatles met to plan their *Anthology* project, which was to occupy them for the next two years. Apart from a television series and a book, they agreed to record together again using some John Lennon demo tapes which Yoko Ono had given to them for the project.

In an interview with the British music magazine *Mojo*, published in June 1997, Paul discussed his relationship with George. He said, 'When we were working on "Free As A Bird" there were one or two little bits of tension, but it was actually cool for the record. For instance, I had a couple of ideas that he didn't like and he was right. I'm the first one to accept that, so that was OK. We did say then that we might work together in the future, but the truth is, after "Real Love", I think George has some business problems. It didn't do a lot for his moods over the last couple of years. He's been having a bit of a hard time, actually, he's not been that easy to get on with. I've rung him and maybe he hasn't rung back. No big deal. But when I ring Ringo, he rings back immediately, we're quite close that way. You know, I'll write George a letter and he might not reply to it. I don't think he means not to reply to it, but it makes me wonder whether he actually wants to do it or not. And if you're not sure, you back off a little. But I love him, he's a lovely guy.'

In November 2001, when George was at New York's Staten Island University Hospital, ill with cancer, Paul went to visit him. He talked with George for six hours, during which time Paul broke down and cried. They talked about all their years together, the ups and downs, and George was said to remain in good spirits because his beliefs had helped him to eliminate the fear of death.

McLaren F1
A car described as 'the finest driving machine yet built for the road'. George finally took delivery of his model in 1995, eighteen months after he'd originally ordered it. The supercar cost £540,000, had a top speed of 235mph and could go from 0–60mph in just 3.2 seconds.

Meditation
After George was introduced to meditation in the late 1960s due to meeting the Maharishi Mahesh Yogi, he practiced meditation for the rest of his life.

He was to say, 'Meditation is a natural process of tapping latent energy that's within us all. You can go on doing what you do normally but with a little bit of extra happiness, that's all. The idea is to transcend to a more subtle level of thought, to replace the things you think about as a rule with a special word or sound, which you keep repeating. The aim is to reach a level of pure consciousness. When your mind is a complete blank, it's beyond all previous experience!'

George considered it a good alternative to drugs. 'Certain drugs intensify the perception but that's all relatively superficial. Drugs don't get to the true you, the real self, in the way that meditation and yoga can.'

Mills, Hayley
A British actress, daughter of Sir John Mills, who found fame as the child star of a series of Disney films. When she was sixteen years old Hayley was considered for a part in *A Hard Day's Night*, providing some romantic interest for one of the Beatles. Then Walter Shenson decided against it. But George was later to escort her to a charity midnight premiere of *Charade* at the Regal, Henley-on-Thames.

Miss O'Dell
The flipside of 'Give Me Love (Give Me Peace On Earth)', which was issued in Britain on Apple R 5988 on 25 May 1973.

Lasting 2 minutes and 26 seconds, the number was inspired by Chris O'Dell, who worked for Apple Records. George penned the number while he was in Malibu, California in April 1971.

Monsters
A mail-order compilation double album issued in America on Warner Bros PRO A 796 in May 1979. It contained the number 'Not Guilty' from the *George Harrison* album.

Monument To British Rock, A

Volume One of an EMI compilation of rock classics by various artists. It was issued in Britain on Harvest EMTV 17 on 4 May 1979. 'My Sweet Lord' was included as the second track on Side One, the first time a number of George's had been included on a compilation album other than his own.

Morrison, Ruth

George's first girlfriend. They started going out together when George was fifteen.

During the summer of 1958 George was a member of a group called the Les Stewart Quartet. The Quarry Men hadn't played together for some months and had virtually disbanded, although John and Paul continued to meet and write songs together.

Ken Brown, a fellow member of the Les Stewart Quartet, remembered that George was head-over-heels for Ruth. The three of them were sitting together in Lowlands Club in Heyman's Green, where the group had a residency, and over coffee, Ruth suggested that Mrs Mona Best was opening a coffee bar called the Casbah, also in Heyman's Green, and that they should approach her as she was seeking a group to be resident at the club.

George and Ken Brown approached Mrs Best, who agreed to give them the residency, but when they approached Les Stewart he refused, complaining that Brown had spent too much time at the Casbah, helping them to prepare the club, and had neglected rehearsals with the group.

George and Brown then discussed what they should do, not wanting to let Mrs Best down. George recalled John and Paul and said he'd approach them. They agreed and, together with Ken Brown, the Quarry Men were re-formed and took up the residency.

Who knows, but for Ruth's suggestion, the Quarry Men might never have got together again and George might have remained with the Les Stewart Quartet.

Soon after, Ruth and her family moved down to Birmingham and she took up a career as a nurse.

Motor Racing

Throughout his life George had a passion for motor racing and became close friends with many major racing stars. His interest was aroused at the 1955 British Grand Prix at Aintree when he saw the Argentinian Fangio with his Mercedes team-mate Stirling Moss. He became a regular at Aintree.

George recalled the times in a 28 July 1979 interview with Chris Hockley of *Motor* magazine.

He said, 'I'm getting too well known at motor races now. It was my hobby, now it's getting like work again.' He was referring to the fact that now that fans knew he attended the races, autograph hunters always besieged him.

George explained, 'I can't remember why I started going to Aintree. I think I just saw a poster advertising a race. Anyway, I used to go there whether it was a big or small meeting, take my butties and sit on the Railway Straight embankment to watch the race. I went to a lot of bike meetings as well – I was a big fan of Geoff Duke. I had a box camera and went round taking pics of all the cars. If I could find an address I wrote away to the car factories and somewhere at home I've got pictures of all the old Vauxhalls, Connaughts and BRMs. All that stuff got lost when I went on the road with the Beatles, but I'm sure it's still in my Dad's attic.

'By the time I got any money at all I was seventeen or eighteen, getting a couple of quid a week from a few concerts in Liverpool. But I got so involved with rock'n'roll and the Beatles – we were on our way to making records and all that – that to tell you the truth I completely lost touch with motor racing apart from watching the odd bit on TV or reading magazines.'

In Monaco George met Jackie Stewart. He commented, 'Jackie did such a lot for the sport and was criticised for it. People moaned and groaned when he wore fireproof suits and talked about safety – things which are so obvious and practical now but at the time were being put down. Another thing was that he always projected the sport beyond just the racing enthusiasts, which I think is very important.'

George had a close relationship with numerous racing drivers. When Ayrton Senna, the Brazilian three-times Formula One world champion died, George said he was almost as shocked as when John Lennon died. He also sent a personal message to Senna's relatives.

George discussed his fascination with Formula One in an interview in *The Times* on 3 March 2001. He said, 'I used to go to watch motor-cycle racing at Aintree in Liverpool, and I saw a poster advertising sports-car racing. I used to go up to the Railway Straight at Aintree and my earliest memory of a car is a Jaguar XK120 racing a Mercedes-Benz 300SL.'

George mentioned that his favourite driver at the time was 'Juan Manuel Fangio in the 1950s. Another early memory was Fangio allowing Moss to pass him in the last fifty metres of the British Grand Prix at Aintree.' This occurred in 1955 when both drivers were driving Mercedes.

Discussing his favourite cars, George commented, 'I loved the Mercedes W196 from the 1950s, the Lotus 25 and Lotus 79, the Brabham BT52 and the Brabham BT46B and the McLaren MP4/4.'

Mentioning his own two cars, which were like racing models, he said, 'My McLaren F1 road car always gives me an awesome feeling when I am in it. Next favourite is my Rocket – for hooligans only! Bit of a contrast to my first cars, a Ford Anglia and Jaguar MkII.

Asked if he would have wanted to be a Formula One driver if he hadn't been involved in music, George replied, 'I don't think so. I have played guitar with Damon Hill and Jacques Villeneuve, drums with Eddie Jordan and taught Gerhard Berger the ukulele, but the Formula One supergroup I am really in is called FLB with Norbert Haug on accordion and lederhosen. I hear Max Mosley and Bernie Ecclestone are thinking of joining.'

From the 1970s onwards, George spent a great deal of time travelling the world attending the Formula One Grand Prix races at Silverstone, Melbourne, Long Beach and Brazil and it was an interest also shared by his wife Olivia.

Movie Life Of George, The

A Granada Television documentary with some performance sequences which had been filmed at Shepperton Film Studios on Sunday 1 October 1988, during the party to celebrate the tenth anniversary of HandMade Films. At the party George performed two Carl Perkins numbers, the first being 'Honey Don't'. Perkins had come all the way from America to join him and tell him that guitar playing was more important than movies, and the two of them played an acoustic version of 'That's Alright, Mama' with Joe Brown. A speech that George gave was included in the documentary, as was a clip from the HandMade film *Water* featuring George, Eric Clapton and Ringo Starr performing 'Freedom'. The sixty-minute documentary was broadcast on the ITV network on Sunday 8 January 1989.

Guests in the programme included Michael Palin, Eric Idle, John Cleese, Terry Gilliam, Bob Hoskins, Michael Caine, Robbie Coltrane and Billy Connolly.

Discussing why he didn't appear on screen any more, George commented, 'Some people are good at acting. I have enough trouble just trying to pretend to be me without trying to be somebody else.'

The Movie Life Of George was premiered in America on the Discovery Channel on 5 February 1990.

Mr Roadrunner

A programme directed by Geoff Wonfor, which was broadcast by Channel Four on Saturday 6 June 1992. It revolved around Jools Holland as he travels to Tennessee and Mississippi, pursued by the devil. He discovers George, holding a ukulele, who performs 'Between The Devil And The Deep Blue Sea', a number originally popularised by Cab Calloway. Apart from Holland on piano, the other musicians were Joe Brown on guitar, Gilson Lavis on stand-up bass, Herbie Flowers on tuba and Ray Cooper on drums.

MTV Videomusic Awards (1988)

An awards ceremony that took place at the Universal Amphitheatre, Los Angeles on Wednesday 7 September 1988. George had seven separate nominations. They were: Best Video Category, 'When We Was Fab'; Best Male Video, 'Got My Mind Set On You (chair version)'; Best Concept Video, 'When We Was Fab'; Best Special Effect, 'When We Was Fab' and 'Got My Mind Set On You (arcade version)'; Best Art Direction In A Video, 'Got My Mind Set On You (arcade version)'; Breakthrough Video, 'When We Was Fab'.

MuchMusic Live Interview

A television programme from the 24-hour MuchMusic television studio in Toronto, Canada.

George appeared on their *MuchMusic Live Interview* programme on Monday 28 March 1988 and was interviewed by Christopher Ward for 34 minutes, during which a number of subjects were covered including his first visit to America in 1963, his working relationship with Jeff Lynne and the use of Beatles numbers in commercials. He also mentioned that he'd bought a mono machine from EMI, used on the 'Paperback Writer' track, for £3.

In another brief exchange, Paul McCartney was discussed:

Ward: How did you feel when you heard the McCartney versions of the old songs in *Broad Street*?

George: I think they were OK. I didn't notice they were new versions. I only watched it once. I remember 'Ballroom Dancing', but I don't remember the old ones.

Ward: He said that he wanted to tackle some of the old ones, including, possibly, some of John Lennon's songs, like 'Beautiful Boy' and 'Imagine'. Does that surprise you that he would do that?

George: Paul?

Ward: Yes.

George: Maybe, because he ran out of good ones of his own!

Ward: Well, now we've got that on record.

George: Well, it's true.

My Sweet Lord

A track from the *All Things Must Pass* album, which was issued as a single in Britain on Apple R 5884 on 15 January 1971. George had originally announced that it would be released in November 1970, but changed his mind and the single was withdrawn because he didn't want it to conflict with sales of *All Things Must Pass*.

George wrote the number in December 1969 when he was touring with Delaney & Bonnie & Friends and it was recorded between May and August 1970 with Phil Spector co-producing.

The track is 4 minutes and 37 seconds in length. Peter Drake, who played steel guitar on the track, had been flown over from American at a cost of $10,000 to participate in the recording of the *All Things Must Pass* album. Apart from George and Drake, other musicians performing on the track were Klaus Voormann on bass guitar, Ringo Starr on drums, Gary Wright on piano and Badfinger on guitars.

Within two weeks it had sold 250,000 copies in Britain alone and topped the charts for six weeks, also becoming the first solo Beatles No. 1 hit. No promo had been prepared, so for the *Top Of The Pops* plug a clip of George singing it live from the *Concert For Bangla Desh* film was screened.

With 700,000 copies sold in Britain by February 1971, making it the top-selling single in Britain that year, it was also to be the third best-selling single by an ex-Beatle, after 'Mull Of Kintyre' by Paul McCartney and 'Imagine' by John Lennon.

The single also topped the charts in America, where it was released ahead of the *All Things Must Pass* album on Apple 2995 on 23 November 1970. It received a Gold Disc award on 14 December 1970 when it passed one million sales and it was No. 1 in the charts for four weeks.

The single was also a No. 1 hit in several other countries around the world, including Australia, Canada, Ireland and Holland.

The flipside of the British release was 'What Is Life' at 4 minutes and 20 seconds, while the flipside of the American single was 'Isn't It A Pity'.

When John Lennon heard the number he was quite impressed and commented, 'I'm starting to think there must be a God.'

George's achievement was marred in March 1971 when the music publishing company Bright Tunes Music Ltd, took legal action against George. They claimed that 'My Sweet Lord' plagiarised their Ronnie Mack number 'He's So Fine', which had been a hit for the Chiffons in 1963.

George's royalties were immediately frozen.

George denied the charge saying that his inspiration had been the Edwin Hawkins Singers' version of 'Oh Happy Day'.

At the time of the litigation, Allen Klein was managing George. In 1973, after he had ceased to represent George, Klein bought Bright Tunes Music Ltd after George had been found guilty of the infringement, but before damages had been determined. Klein had been expecting a large payout but received less than he had imagined because the court felt that Klein's act had been a breach of duty to his former client.

The case had continued for several years and a verdict was finally forthcoming in a New York court in November 1990. Judge Richard Owen said that Klein's company ABKCO would own the song for the world, except for the USA, UK and Canada, where George would own it. Harrison would pay Klein $270,020.

In his summing up, Owen had stated, 'Did Harrison deliberately use the music of "He's So Fine"? I do not believe he did so *deliberately*. Nevertheless, it is clear that "My Sweet Lord" is the very same song as

"He's So Fine" with different words, and Harrison had access to "He's So Fine". This is, under the law, infringement of copyright, and is no less so even though subconsciously accomplished.'

After the case, George wrote a song about the affair, 'This Song', which was included on his *Thirty Three & 1/3* album.

An account of the origin of George's number was included in the court proceedings, which were described by West Key Number System, an American company that published microfilm of legal cases:

'Harrison and his group, which include an American black gospel singer named Billy Preston, were in Copenhagen, Denmark on a singing engagement. There was a press conference involving the group going on backstage. Harrison slipped away from the press conference and went to a room upstairs and began "vamping" some guitar chords, fitting on the top chords he was playing the words "Hallelujah" and "Hare Krishna" in various ways.

'During the course of his vamping, he was alternating between what musicians call a Minor 11 chord and a Major V chord. At some point he went down to meet with others of the group, asking them to listen, which they did, and everyone began to join in, taking first "Hallelujah" and then "Hare Krishna" and putting them into four-part harmony.

'In any event, from this very free-flowing exchange of ideas, with Harrison playing his two chords and everyone singing "Hallelujah" and "Hare Krishna", there began to emerge the "My Sweet Lord" text idea, which Harrison sought to develop a little bit further during the following week as he was playing it on his guitar.

'Approximately one week later the entire group flew back to London because they had earlier booked time to go to a recording studio with Billy Preston to make an album. In the studio, Preston was the principal musician. Harrison did not play on the session. He had given Preston his basic motif with the idea that it be turned into a song, and went back and forth from the studio to the engineer's recording booth, supervising the recording "takes". Under circumstances that Harrison was utterly unable to recall, while everybody was working toward a finished song, in the recording studio, somehow or other the essential three notes of motif A reached polish form.'

Despite the fact that George said he was inspired by hearing 'Oh Happy Day' in June 1970 and the implication that Billy Preston had a large part to play, Delaney Bramlett has other things to say. The tour mentioned in the court report was not 'Harrison and his group', it was actually the Delaney & Bonnie & Friends tour', which George requested to be on.

Bramlett recalls that after one of the shows, 'George came over to me and said, "You write a lot of gospel songs. I'd like to know what inspires you to do that." And so I gave him my explanation. I told him, "I get things from the Bible, from what a preacher may say, or just the feelings I felt towards God." He said, "Well can you give me a for instance? How would you start?" So I grabbed my guitar and started playing the Chiffons' melody from "He's So Fine", and then sang the words, "My sweet Lord/ Oh my Lord/Oh my Lord/ I just wanna be with you . . ." George said OK, then I said, "Then you praise the Lord in your own way." Rita and Bonnie were there and so I told them when we got to this one part to sing "Hallelujah". They did. George said OK.'

When the single came out, Delaney said, 'I called up George and told him that I didn't mean for him to use the melody of "He's So Fine". He said, "Well, it's not exactly," and it really wasn't. He did put some curves in there but he did get sued.'

Bramlett had thought at the time that he'd been given a co-writing credit, but when he bought the record he discovered that this wasn't so. 'When I saw I wasn't credited, I called George and said, "George, I didn't see my name on the song." He promised me that it would be on the next printing of the record. I was never given credit on that song but he did admit that the song, to a large extent, was mine, and I never saw any money from it.'

He didn't pursue any legal action because he wanted to maintain his friendship with George, but was to say, 'We haven't spoken since all that came about. It makes me feel sad. There are no hard feelings from me. I believe, because we haven't spoken in years, that he felt worse about it than I did. I just think the whole thing was an oversight on his part. He just didn't follow through on it.'

Following George's death it was re-released in Britain by Parlophone on 14 January 2002 and in America by Capitol on 22 January 2002.

The re-release had a new cover featuring a photograph that George had taken himself of a water lily. There were also bonus tracks: an acoustic version of 'Let It Down' and 'My Sweet Lord 2000'.

It hit the top of the British charts on Sunday 20 January 2002, almost 31 years to the day when it first topped the singles chart. All proceeds from the new release went to the Material World Foundation, the charity George set up in 1973 to support agencies worldwide to aid poverty-stricken children.

It also made British chart history by topping the chart after the longest interval since its original release.

George discussed 'My Sweet Lord' with disc jockey Anne Nightingale in a lengthy interview prerecorded on Tuesday 1 February 1977.

He said, 'The first version of that was recorded with Billy Preston with the Edwin Hawkins Singers. That was good because the idea for the song came to me anyway based upon 'Oh Happy Day'. I was on the road with Delaney and Bonnie and Eric at the time in Sweden and I was just thinking of a way of how to combine "Hallelujah" and "Hare Krishna", which is just simplistically the West and the East. How to get everybody singing "Hallelujah, Hallelujah, Hallelujah" and then suddenly throw "Hare Krishna" in and catch them before they realised!

'That was really the idea, based upon "Oh Happy Day" by the Edwin Hawkins Singers. As it happened, they came to town and phoned up and said, "Do you want us to do any dates?" So we got them down to Olympic Studios. The original version of "My Sweet Lord" is with the Temptations, so we had their drummer, bass player and guitar, Billy on piano and organ and the Edwin Hawkins Singers. If you listen to that one, there is a point where I was trying to get the Edwin Hawkins Singers to sing "Hare Krishna". They are a funny group of people. They were saying, "What? What is this Hare Krishna?" Luckily, there was one young guy in there and he said, "You know, Hare Krishna. You have seen them out there, dancing in the street." And so, if you listen to that version, there is one place where they are going "Hallelujah, Hare Krishna". So I was happy. I got it in twice actually.

'It wasn't until my own version had been released and it was a hit, that trouble loomed large. The first thing I knew was when Klein said something. He said, "Somebody has made a recording." It was the company Bright Tunes; they had got this version recorded by Jodie Miller of "He's So Fine" which was really like, you know, putting the screws in. What they did was to change the chords of 'He's So Fine' and make them completely into the same chords as 'My Sweet Lord', because there is actually a slight difference, and then also put on top of it the slide guitar part. So it was really trying to rub it in, and I thought "God!" So then, all the people started hustling each other and the guy from Bright Tunes was demanding money and various things. I really didn't hear anything about it for years. The attorneys were supposedly settling the thing and in the end I said, "Look, it is just a lot of aggravation. Just give the guy some money." And so they were going to give him two hundred thousand dollars. I found out, last week, after it has been to court and has been a big scene, now the guy only gets fifty thousand! The judge made a slip after the court case. He just said to my attorney, "Actually, I like both the songs." My lawyer said to him, "What do you mean, both of the songs? You said, in your decision, that it's the same song." And he said, "Oooops! Sorry. What I mean is, I like the song with the two sets of lyrics."'

My Sweet Lord (2000)

A re-recording of George's famous hit, lasting 4 minutes and 58 seconds, which George included as a bonus on the *All Things Must Pass* reissue on double CD. Commenting on why he re-recorded it, he told Reuters, 'I just like the idea and the opportunity to freshen it up, because the point of "My Sweet Lord" is just to try and remind myself basically that there's more to life than the material world.'

George's son Dhani also plays acoustic guitar on the track.

Mysterioso, L'Angelo

The name George used when he played guitar on the track 'Never Tell Your Mother She's Out Of Tune' on the Jack Bruce album *Songs For A Tailor*. He had to use a pseudonym due to his contractual obligations with Apple Records that prevented him using his own name when playing with artists who weren't signed to the Beatles label.

Mystical One

The opening track of the second side of George's 1982 album *Gone Troppo*, lasting 3 minutes and 40 seconds. Joe Brown played mandolin on the track and also duets with George.

Natural Law Party, The

A political party launched by the Maharishi Mahesh Yogi to promote Transcendental Meditation, which entered the British General Election in 1992 under the slogan 'Election Is A National Celebration'. The Maharishi believed that a government that believed in Transcendental Meditation would help to solve problems of law and order and would also advise on a health prevention system using natural biological rhythms.

They were even allowed a General Election broadcast in which Yogic practitioners displayed 'yogic flying'.

George Harrison, who was still practising meditation, decided to help raise funds for the party by headlining a concert at the Royal Albert Hall on Monday 6 April 1992 entitled, 'The Natural Law Party Presents George Harrison And Friends – Inspiration To The Youth Of Great Britain – Election Is A Celebration.'

George had last appeared at the Albert Hall on 15 September 1963 with the Beatles in 'The Great Pop Prom'. This was his first full-length solo show in Britain.

He said, 'I am performing in this concert to support the Natural Law Party. I will vote for the Natural Law Party because I want a total change and not just a choice between left and right. The system we have now is obsolete and is not fulfilling the needs of the people. Times have changed and we need a new approach. I believe this party offers the only option to get out of our problems and create the beautiful nation we would all like to have. The general election should be a celebration of democracy and our right to vote. The Natural Law Party is turning this election into a wonderful national celebration and I am with them all the way.'

The party fielded 313 candidates in the election, which took place on Thursday 9 April 1992, although it lost its deposit in every seat.

At 7.30 p.m. Dr Jeffrey Clements came on stage to announce the Natural Law Party as 'a beautiful new sunshine for the nation'. He then introduced George, who wore a dark suit with a bright red shirt. He introduced pianist Joe Walsh who was joined by a band with Zak Starkey on a second drum kit. Their twenty-minute set ended with 'Rocky Mountain Way'. Gary Moore was introduced next, he'd played on the Traveling Wilburys' album and George had given him a number for his album *Still Got The Blues*. A brass section, vocalists, keyboardists, drummers and guitarists, now augmented the band.

Eric Clapton also performed with George at the concert and the 105-minute set mainly comprised the repertoire from their recent tour of Japan: 'I Want To Tell You', 'Old Brown Shoe', 'Taxman', 'Give Me Love (Give Me Peace On Earth)', 'Something', 'What Is Life', 'Piggies', 'Got My Mind Set On You', 'Cloud 9', 'Here Comes The Sun', 'My Sweet Lord', 'All Those Years Ago', 'Cheer Down', 'Isn't It A Pity' and 'Devil's Radio'. There was an encore with 'Roll Over Beethoven' and 'While My Guitar Gently Weeps', during which Ringo Starr arrived on stage to join them. After George left the stage, Ringo and the band jammed for five minutes and George reappeared with his son Dhani for another performance of 'Roll Over Beethoven', with most of the other musicians joining in, including Ringo Starr, Joe Walsh, Gary Moore, Zak Starkey, Tessa Niles, Greg Phillinganes, Mike Campbell, Katie Kissoon, Steve Ferrone, Andy Fairweather-Low, Ray Cooper, Will Lee and Chuck Leavell.

After the concert, George talked to a reporter from the *Liverpool Echo* and said, 'They were trying to get me on at the Liverpool Empire, but logistically it was proving difficult. Maybe I will come around and do a little tour sooner or later. I miss Liverpool in a nostalgic way and I actually drive through there occasionally. I have just been there a few months ago. I drive all the way around and just look at the places and say, "There's where I was born, there's where the Cavern got knocked down." What I miss about Liverpool is the people's humour. Everybody's a comedian and I like that. I am a comedian too.'

Never Get Over You

A track from the *Brainwashed* album lasting 3 minutes and 25 seconds, with George on lead vocals, electric guitar, acoustic guitar, mouseboy and background vocals. Jeff Lynne was on bass guitar, mouseboy tamer and piano and Jim Keltner on drums.

Never Without You

A tribute to George on Ringo's March, 2003 album *Ringo Rama*. It was co-written by Ringo, producer Mark Hudson and Gary Nicholson.

Ringo was to comment, 'It was my way, with the help of Gary and Mark, to say how much George meant to me and how much he will be remembered.'

The track also features Eric Clapton on guitar and Ringo said, 'I called Eric up and it was great to have him. Eric's on two tracks on the album, but I really wanted him on this song because George loved Eric and Eric loved George. I wanted Eric to come and play that solo because I only wanted people on the track who George knew and loved.'

New Morning

An album by Bob Dylan, produced by Bob Johnston. George had been invited by Dylan to attend his recording session for the album at Studio B in the Columbia Recording Studios in New York on Friday 1 May 1970. On arriving he took up the guitar and jammed on several numbers. Apart from Dylan and George, the other musicians were Charlie E. Daniels on bass, Russ Kunkel on drums and Bob Johnston on piano.

Newsnight

A BBC2 television programme. George prerecorded an interview for the show which was conducted by Robin Denselow at the HandMade Films office at 26 Cadogan Square, London. The show was transmitted on Friday 1 February 1985 and lasted for nineteen minutes, with George telling Denselow, 'I don't want to be a film star, I don't even want to be a pop star. I just want to live in peace.'

Nicky Horne's Music Scene

A brief music-news excerpt in the regional ITV television show *News At Six*.

On Monday 19 February 1979, Horne briefly interviewed George outside London Polytechnic and mainly quizzed him about his feelings towards the recently released feature film *Sgt Pepper's Lonely Hearts Club Band*. Horne asked George if he'd seen the movie.

'No, no. I'm not going to see it. Everybody tells me it's awful,' he replied.

Horne answered, 'Well, a lot of people have said it's awful. The thing is, how much control, if any, did you have over it?'

George said, 'We didn't have any control. I mean, there's been a lot of Beatles things, you know, like *John, Paul, Bert, Ringo, Ted* . . . and *Ringo* and *Sgt Pepper*, and all kinds of things like that, because the Fab Four were split and all over the world, then it was pretty easy to go and do things like that. But, I don't really think they're supposed to go and do things like that. All they needed was the songs, and ATV music owned most of the songs, so it was pretty easy to do that. But, I don't really think they're supposed to do that and, in fact, we've just got together a group of people to go and sue them all!'

The brief interview lasted three minutes and was screened that evening.

Nightingale, Anne
British disc jockey. Anne interviewed George at length at Broadcasting House, London on the morning of Tuesday 1 February 1977. The first part of the interview was broadcast on her show on Saturday 5 February and the second on Saturday 12 February 1977.

A number of topics were discussed including the controversy over 'My Sweet Lord', the Concert For Bangla Desh, George's solo recording, the Beatles break-up, the popularity of 'Something' and the romance between George's ex-wife Patti and Eric Clapton.

Surprisingly, George was quite forthright, explaining, 'Ever since 1963 I have not really had a private life. So one thing I found was that if you have got something to hide, you've got all these people buzzing round you, round your front door, all the time. Say, for example, if you split up with your wife and you're trying not to tell anybody, then there's people there who are trying to find something out. But if there's nothing to be known, then it is much easier in the long run. So consequently, since 1963/1964, the Beatles have been owned by the public, or Fleet Street, and we learned to live with that. I found that it was much easier just to tell people. What's the point in trying to hide something? It only means that they are going to be crawling around your garden, trying to get pictures of you and stuff. It's easier just to say, "Sure, I'm divorced," or whatever.'

Apart from the interview, musical interludes during the two shows included a version of 'Something' performed by the London Symphony Orchestra, 'Dispute And Violence' and 'Am I Missing You' by Ravi Shankar, Splinter's 'Costafine Town' and two versions of 'He's So Fine', one by the Chiffons, the other by Jodie Miller, the latter two numbers illustrating a point George was making in the interview about 'My Sweet Lord'.

Nobody's Child (single)
A Traveling Wilburys single. It was the first number recorded at their Friday 27 April 1990 recording session in Bel Air. Warner Bros issued it on the Wilbury records label in Britain on Monday 18 June 1990 in aid of the Romanian Angel Appeal. The flipside was 'Lumiere', a number by Dave Stewart. The 12″ and CD versions of the single also included a live version of Ringo Starr's 'With A Little Help From My Friends', which he performed at the Greek Theatre, Los Angeles on 4 September 1980.

Olivia had phoned George from Romania asking for his help and he immediately recorded this number with the Wilburys.

He said that he thought Bob Dylan's part in the song was: 'Just fantastic. It sounds so profound and meaningful. Bob had to leave after we'd done the basic track so the next day we put the vocal on. One go each. We just guessed which way would work best: Tom Petty started, I came in, Jeff Lynne did the choruses and Bob did the second half of the choruses on his own. Then we stuck on a little bit of keyboards and some bass, mixed it and it was completely finished in just two days after Olivia's call.'

The Beatles had originally recorded 'Nobody's Child' in Hamburg in 1962 when they backed Tony Sheridan at sessions recorded by Bert Kaempfert.

Nobody's Child: Romanian Angel Appeal

Olivia Harrison had formed a charity to aid orphan children in Romania. It was called the Romanian Angel Charity Appeal. A special charity album was issued in Britain on Warner Bros (vinyl: WX353; cassette WX 353c and CD 7599 26280-2) on 23 July 1990 and in America the following day.

While she was in Romania Olivia phoned George to ask if he could help in any way. The charity album was the result and George and the Traveling Wilburys had completed the track 'Nobody's Child' within two days of the phone call.

The album opened with the Traveling Wilburys' version of 'Nobody's Child'. Track five was the George Harrison/Paul Simon duet on 'Homeward Bound'. Track ten was the composition 'That Kind Of Woman' which Eric Clapton had recorded and track twelve was the Duane Eddy number 'The Trembler', recorded at George's Friar Park Studios, with George playing slide guitar.

George recalled that he asked Bruce Springsteen for a live track, but heard no more. He also tried to contact Michael Jackson, unsuccessfully. He recalled, 'I tried calling Michael Jackson because I got a message from his lawyer, who happened to be the same guy who did the Wilburys record deal. He said, "Michael Jackson wants to talk to you." He thought it was something to do with the fact that Paul and him are rowing about all the Beatles songs. Apparently, Michael wanted someone who used to be a Beatle to be his friend. Or something . . . but he never called me back.'

The album also included Eric Clapton's outtake of 'That Kind Of Woman' from his *Journeyman* album, a number on which George played. Ringo Starr and his All Starr Band contributed 'With A Little Help From My Friends'.

Stevie Winwood and Queen came up with tracks, but they were too late to be included on the album.

Not Guilty

A song penned by George in 1968 and recorded by the Beatles on 7 August 1968, but it was then left off *The Beatles* white album at the last minute.

There were more takes of this song than any other in the Beatles recording career – a total of 101.

Eric Clapton had also added a guitar track to it. George later re-recorded the number and it was included on the *George Harrison* album in 1979.

George was to comment, 'It was me getting pissed off with Lennon and McCartney for the grief I was catching during the making of this album. I said I wasn't guilty of getting in the way of their careers. I said I wasn't guilty of leading them astray in our all going to India to see the Maharishi. I was sticking up for myself and the song came off strong enough to be saved and utilised.'

O'Brien, Denis

A former accountant who once worked as a senior investment analyst with Rothschilds. Peter Sellers introduced him to George and they originally teamed up in 1973.

O'Brien then took over the management of George's financial affairs, looking after the royalties that came in for hits such as 'My Sweet Lord'. When George became involved in the film business when he sought to aid his friends at *Monty Python's Flying Circus* with *The Life Of Brian*, O'Brien helped George to set up his company HandMade Films.

In 1995 George took out a lawsuit against O'Brien because he believed that he had conned him out of £16 million, allegedly bringing him close to bankruptcy. He filed court papers in Los Angeles accusing O'Brien of:

- Setting up a tangled web of investments so complex that George was unable to keep track of his money.
- Allowing the value of those investments to nosedive through poor management and bad judgement.
- Secretly siphoning off millions of pounds to fund a jetset lifestyle that featured 'yachts and villas in various parts of the world'.
- Conning George into believing O'Brien shared liability for their company's bad debts when, in fact, George was on his own.

George commented to the press, 'I think the court papers tell the whole story – it's a long one and everything is contained in there.

'The action is proceeding and I'm letting my lawyers handle it. I'm not saying it's not been a strain, it's just something you cope with. I'll just get on with it. I'm really tired by the whole thing.'

The sixteen-page lawsuit was compiled by George's lawyer Bertram Fields, who claimed that O'Brien concealed from George the fact that HandMade Films had made massive losses.

The papers claimed: 'O'Brien encouraged and accepted Harrison's trust and confidence. Manipulating that unqualified trust, O'Brien urged Harrison to rely on him totally and to give him unchecked control of Harrison's affairs.

'Harrison did, in effect, place his entire financial life and wellbeing in O'Brien's hands.'

Commenting on HandMade Films, the papers pointed out, 'Through his improper and inept management he caused the organisation to lose huge sums of money.' They went on to say that O'Brien told George that in order to keep the film organisation as a going business it was necessary and advisable for Harrison personally to borrow massive amounts of money.

'Harrison did so, acting in reliance on O'Brien's advice, and thereby incurring personal liability in excess of $25 million.

'While acting as Harrison's manager and partner, O'Brien enriched himself and lived on a lavish scale at Harrison's expense, buying yachts and villas in various parts of the world.

'Harrison suffered enormous losses and liabilities as a result of O'Brien's improper and inept management and deceitful conduct.'

In January 1996 George won a partial victory when the Los Angeles Superior Court awarded him $11.6 million against O'Brien, almost half of the $25 million that George said was the extent of the debt caused by O'Brien for HandMade Films. Judge Kathryn Doi Todd pointed out that O'Brien was personally responsible for half of the debts and had also failed to sign documents relating to the various loans granted to the company.

In 2002, following George's death, a federal judge in St Louis decided that George should have been believed when he said he was too ill to appear at the bankruptcy court, when attempting to protect what he'd won in a Californian court case against O'Brien. His lawyers wanted George to give a deposition in St Louis but he refused to provide the court with a deposition of his condition, therefore the bankruptcy judge Barry Schermer rejected his claim. The new decision overturned the previous one and gave George's estate a potential $17 million victory.

Oasis

A popular British group of the 1990s, led by the brothers Noel and Liam Gallagher. They made no bones about their admiration of the Beatles and the Beatles obviously heavily influenced their music. Despite their position as champions of the Beatles music, they were quite upset by remarks that George made about the band.

Their major influence seemed to be John Lennon, although they didn't display any of his acerbic wit, despite a degree of tough, although rather inarticulate, talk.

Responding to George's criticism of Oasis during the *Chants Of India* interviews in Paris, in October 1997, during an MTV interview, Liam Gallagher turned on George, who had referred to him as 'the silly one'. Gallagher said, 'He doesn't know me, so what's he on about? It goes to show that after all that time in the Beatles and he's still stupid. How does he know I'm silly? I've got four GCSEs; I'm not silly. If that's his personal opinion, fair enough, you know what I mean? I still love the Beatles and I still love George Harrison as a songwriter, but as a person, he's a nipple. And if I ever meet him, I'll tell him. And if you're watching George – nipple!'

Then, on the Radio 1FM programme *Evening Session*, Liam continued the attack, threatening to physically assault George. He said, 'I'm gonna shoot me mouth off here – all these snakes coming out of the closets, all these old farts. I'll offer them out right here on radio. If they want to fight, be at Primrose Hill, Saturday morning, at twelve o'clock. I will beat the fuckin' living daylight shit out of them. That goes for George, Jagger, Richards and any other c*** that give me shit. If any of them old farts have got a problem with me then leave your Zimmer frames at home and I'll hold you up with a good right hook. They are jealous and senile and not getting enough fucking meat pies. If they want a fight, I'll beat them up.'

Old Brown Shoe

A number composed by George, which was the flipside of the Beatles single 'The Ballad Of John And Yoko'. It lasts 3 minutes and 17 seconds.

George had originally made a demo disco of the song on 25 February 1969 on which he played all the instruments himself. He then called in the Beatles for a session on 16 April.

On Cloud Nine

A sixty-minute Radio One special about George's album *Cloud Nine*, aired on Sunday 27 December 1987. George appeared on the programme for an interview and also played the unreleased recording 'Hottest Gang In Town', which had originally been planned for the *Shanghai Surprise* soundtrack.

One Meat Ball

A folk number by Josh White that George used to sing in his youth, along with other songs, now considered 'standards'. He commented, 'I would say that even the crap music that we hated – the late forties, early fifties American schmalz records like 'The Railroad Runs Through The Middle Of The House' or the British 'I'm A Blue Toothbrush, You're A Pink Toothbrush' – even that had some kind of influence on us.'

Only A Northern Song

A number composed by George, which was included on the *Yellow Submarine* album. It is 3 minutes and 20 seconds in length.

There is an apocryphal story that this number was the last song recorded for the film and the story goes that producer Al Brodax discovered that the film needed one more song. It was two o'clock in the morning and the London Symphony Orchestra were at Abbey Road Studios. George allegedly said he could write a song in an hour or so and returned later saying, 'Here Al. It's only a northern song.'

This is untrue. Not only were the London Symphony Orchestra not present at Abbey Road Studios that night, but recording on the number had originally begun when the Beatles made a first recording on Tuesday 14 February 1967, when the song had the working title of 'Not known'. Recording continued the following day and the title came about because fifty per cent of Northern Songs was owned by Dick James while John Lennon, Paul McCartney and NEMS Enterprises owned the rest. George was only a contracted songwriter to the company and wasn't happy with the arrangement.

It was initially recorded for the *Sgt Pepper* album, but was to end up on *Yellow Submarine*.

George was to say, '"Northern Song" was a joke relating to Liverpool, the Holy City in the North of England. In addition, the song was copyrighted Northern Songs Ltd, which I didn't own.'

Ono, Yoko

An avant-garde artist, born in Tokyo on 18 February 1933. She was fluent in English and when her family moved to America she was educated at the exclusive Sarah Lawrence School in Scarsdale.

She married Japanese pianist Toshi Ichiyanagi at the age of nineteen but she was reputedly regularly unfaithful and they were divorced in 1963. She married film producer Tony Cox and the couple had a daughter Kyoko.

They moved to London in 1966 and she began to make a reputation for various events called 'happenings', such as wrapping up one of the stone lions in Trafalgar Square, and making a film called *Bottoms*, which consisted entirely of close-ups of numerous bare bottoms of both sexes.

John Dunbar, a friend of John Lennon and partner in the Indica Gallery, invited John to an exhibition of Yoko's claiming that she performed a 'Bag Piece', in which she climbed into a bag with a friend and 'either fucked or didn't fuck'. This intrigued John and he went along to the exhibition.

People's versions of what happened that day varied. Yoko said she'd never heard of John or the Beatles, while others contend that she knew all about them and had set out to snare one of the Beatles herself. John's driver Les Anthony said that John didn't pay much attention to her at the exhibition and that when he left Yoko ran into the street after him.

Yoko began to pursue John with a vengeance and talked him into sponsoring her next exhibition 'The Half Wind Show' at the Lisson Gallery.

By the beginning of 1968 she had split from her husband and a few months later visited John at his Weybridge home when his wife Cynthia was on holiday in Greece. They went to bed together and made love. When Cynthia returned she realised that her marriage was over.

From that time onwards Yoko never left John's side and involved him in all her avant-garde pursuits. She was later to divorce her second husband and John became her No. 3.

George disliked Yoko Ono from the moment they met and he made his feelings plain. He was annoyed by her presence during *The Beatles* double album sessions and also when the group were at Twickenham Studios recording and filming the 'Get Back' project, which later became *Let It Be*. The omnipresent Ono began to irk him as she was always there, even accompanying John to the toilet in addition to getting the Beatles to back her on some wailing.

John was later to comment on George's dislike of Yoko saying, 'You sit through sixty sessions with the most big-headed, uptight people on earth and see what it's fucking like, and be insulted by these people just because you love someone. And George, shit, insulted her right to her face in the Apple office at the beginning. Just being "straightforward", you know – that game of "Well, I'm going to be upfront because this is what we've heard." And Dylan and a few people said she'd got a lousy name in New York, and you give off bad vibes.

'That's what George said to her and we both sat through it, and I didn't hit him, I don't know why, but I was always hoping that they would come around. I couldn't believe it, you know. And they all sat there with their wives, like a fucking jury. And judged us. Ringo was all right. So was Maureen, but the others really gave it to us.'

When John had settled in New York he commented on it again: 'I still can't believe the things George said to her. He told her that he'd heard from New York that she'd got a bad vibe. I should have smacked him in the mouth.'

When Paul filed his lawsuit for the dissolution of the Beatles, his statement read out in court said that one of the reasons George left the group was 'he could not get on with Yoko'.

John was invited to participate in the Concert For Bangla Desh and Allen Klein told him that he could use his own backing group. When it was mentioned that Yoko wanted to appear on stage with John, George wouldn't hear of it. He'd disliked her when he'd met her three years previously and hadn't changed his opinion. He abhorred her music and wouldn't agree to her performing. He told John, explaining to him that the concert was to raise money for charities and wasn't to be a showcase for Yoko's avant-garde singing.

Yoko was furious and in a struggle John's glasses were broken. He fled New York, taking the first flight to Europe, which landed him in Paris.

When John and Yoko moved to New York they made their headquarters at Allen Klein's offices at ABKCO. George turned up at the offices with a number of new songs he wanted to demonstrate to John. The two of them got guitars, went into an empty room and began to play and sing. American Apple executive Al Steckler recalled, 'Yoko barged in and saw what was going on and started doing her screeching. John said, "Get the fuck out of here!" He picked her up and took her, stumbling over a chair, and tossed her out of the door and slammed it. Then they went back to playing on their guitars.'

Yoko was in England in November 1983, primarily to discuss Apple business. She had a meeting with George, Paul and Ringo. An associate was to comment: 'The tension was still there. Yoko was not forgiven. Oh, Ringo was nice. He always was nice. And Paul was charming in the way that he could always be when he chose to. George still didn't care. He didn't like Yoko when John first met her and he didn't like her in London three years after John was dead. So nothing was accomplished at the meeting. What they had gotten together to talk about went right back on the shelf.'

Orbison, Roy

Singer born on 23 April 1936 in Vernon, Texas. He first came to prominence in Britain when his number 'Only The Lonely' topped the charts. The Beatles regarded Orbison as an influence, and when they made their first broadcast on radio on *Teenagers' Turn*, the number they opened with was Orbison's 'Dream Baby', sung by Paul.

He was booked to tour Britain from 18 May to 9 June 1963 on a bill with the Beatles. Originally he had his name topping the Beatles, even though they closed the show, which is the spot traditionally given to the bill-topper. After one week the billing was reversed.

When Roy toured with the Beatles in 1963, both he and George used to oversleep. He recalled, 'George and I missed the bus a lot. They left without us.'

They also chatted together about music and became good friends. However, they didn't meet up again until many years later.

He underwent heart surgery in 1979 and his career seemed on the wane. However, when Jeff Lynne began recording a Roy Orbison album *Mystery Girl* in 1988, George played guitar and sang backing vocals on the song 'I Won't Back Down'.

George met Lynne and Orbison over dinner and discussed a track he wanted to make. They ended up picking up Tom Petty and arriving at Bob Dylan's garage studios – and the Traveling Wilburys was born.

Roy became Lefty Wilbury and it was a terrific boost to his career. In the last interview before his death he was praising George for having persuaded him to join the Wilburys.

He died a sudden death from a massive heart attack in a Nashville hospital on 6 December 1988 at the age of 52.

George was to say, 'He was a sweet, sweet man. We loved Roy, and still do. He's out there, really, his spirit. You know life flows on within you and without you. He's around.'

His posthumous album *Mystery Girl* was issued in America on 1 February 1989 and in Britain on 30 January.

Ostin, Mo
Chairman of Warner Bros Records, who left the company in 1994 to become a consultant to Time-Warner. As a tribute the company issued a 6-CD promo-only sampler *Mo's Songs* (Warner Bros PRO-Mo-1994), issued on 20 December 1994. The song that opens the set was a number George wrote for him in March 1977, entitled 'Mo', in honour of Mo's fiftieth birthday. The number features acoustic and slide guitars, a full backing track and lyrics such as: 'They could've called him Clive or so. They didn't call him Joe – they called him Mo Mo Mo'. The number is 4 minutes and 54 seconds in length.

Other numbers on the set included 'All Those Years Ago' and the Traveling Wilburys' 'Handle With Care'.

2,200 copes were made and presented to Mo's friends and Warner Bros employees throughout America.

Out Of The Blue
The first and the longest of the 'Apple Jam' tracks on the *All Things Must Pass* triple album. Written by George, it is 11 minutes and 13 seconds in length.

Musicians on the track included George on guitar, Jim Gordon on drums, Carl Radle on bass, Bobby Whitlock on keyboards, Eric Clapton on guitar, Gary Wright on keyboards, Jim Price on trumpet and Bobby Keys on sax.

Palomino Club, The

A venue in North Hollywood, Los Angeles. Taj Mahal was performing at the club on Thursday 19 February 1987 when George, along with Bob Dylan, John Fogerty and Jesse Ed Davis joined Mahal on stage. The group then performed for two hours. George played 'Matchbox' with Taj Mahal, 'Blue Suede Shoes' with John Fogerty, 'Peggy Sue' with Bob Dylan and also 'Honey Don't', 'Watching The River Flow' and 'Dizzy Miss Lizzy'.

The entire performance was captured on the club's in-house video system.

Perkins, Carl

Carl Perkins was born in Ridgely, near Tiptonville, Tennessee on 9 April 1932.

He came to the attention of John, Paul and George via his 1955 number 'Blue Suede Shoes'. As a result, Perkins became one of the seminal influences on George's life, from the time George obtained Perkins' debut album *Dance Album Of Carl Perkins*.

Among the Perkins numbers in the group's stage repertoire were 'Blue Suede Shoes', 'Sure To Fall (In Love With You)', 'Your True Love' and 'Everybody's Trying To Be My Baby', with George taking the lead vocal on the latter two.

When the Silver Beetles went on their short tour of Scotland with Johnny Gentle in 1960, George adopted the alias Carl Harrison.

The Beatles recorded 'Matchbox' on 1 June 1964 and Perkins attended the session. Sadly, a jam session he joined in with the boys at the studio was not recorded. Later in the year they recorded two other Perkins numbers, 'Everybody's Trying To Be My Baby' and 'Honey

Don't'. Perkins was to say that the royalties from the Beatles' versions of his songs enabled him to buy a farm for his parents.

In 1985 he was invited to make a TV special in London and sent out a video invitation to George, Paul and Ringo to join him. Paul refused, George and Ringo accepted. The two then joined Perkins and other musicians, including Eric Clapton, Dave Edmunds and Roseanne Cash in *Carl Perkins & Friends: A Rockabilly Session*, recorded at Limehouse TV Studios, London on 21 October 1985. It was the first time that George and Ringo had performed together since the concert for Bangla Desh.

After the show, commenting on the first time he saw a photograph of the Beatles, he said, 'I thought they looked like girls, with that hair. But I liked their records right away. To me, there's always been something pure about four people on stage playing rock'n'roll.

'When I hear people like Eric Clapton and the Beatles say, "You're the reason I'm holding a guitar," it weakens my old knees. I don't hear myself in their playing. I do in some early Beatles songs, but they advanced it so much. That rockabilly sound wasn't as simple as I thought it was. If those guys were inspired by Carl Perkins, they took a simple note and stretched it from one end of the guitar to the other.'

George was to keep in touch with Perkins and the two of them also performed 'That's Alright Mama' in the documentary *The Movie Life Of George* and also played together at the Hard Rock Café in London in the early 1990s. In addition they worked on a song together.

Perkins' last album *Go Cat Go* was released by Dinosaur Records in 1996. This contained contributions from all four members of the Beatles. There was a live recording of John performing 'Blue Suede Shoes' at the Toronto Rock'n'Roll Revival Festival in 1969, Paul performing 'My Old Friend', recorded fifteen years earlier and previously unreleased, Ringo performing 'Matchbox' with his All Starr Band and George playing 'Distance Makes No Difference', a number he produced and played for Carl during some recording sessions at Friar Park.

Perkins had been fighting throat and tonsil cancer for some time at the time of his death at the age of 65 on 19 January 1998 in a Nashville hospital following a series of strokes.

George travelled to Jackson, Tennessee to attend the funeral, which was held at Lambeth University, Jackson on 23 January. Paul McCartney sent a video message, while at the end of the small tribute concert, George was invited onto the stage by Wynonna Judd and performed 'Your True Love', the Perkins number, on acoustic guitar, backed by Garth Brooks, Billy Ray Cyrus, Ricky Skaggs and three female backing singers.

Petty, Tom

Tom Petty was born in Gainesville, Florida on 20 October 1953. He formed his group the Heartbreakers in 1973. They toured with Bob Dylan in 1988 in Israel and Europe.

Petty became a member of the Traveling Wilburys when George arrived at his house to borrow a guitar. George had had dinner with Jeff Lynne and Roy Orbison, who Lynne was currently recording, and mentioned that he'd like Lynne to help him on a track for a B side for a *Cloud Nine* promotional single. George said they could rent a studio and write the song together, but Lynne suggested that they could record it at Bob Dylan's garage studio in Malibu. On the way they stopped at Tom Petty's house to borrow a guitar and he decided to join them and became a Wilbury. Charlie T. Wilbury to be precise!

George was later to play on Petty's album *Full Moon Fever*.

Petulengro, Eva

A noted British Romany clairvoyant who read George's hand in 1965. The results of her reading appeared in *Beatles Monthly* magazine. She was to say that George's lifelines showed that he would live to a ripe old age and fulfil much during this time, that he was fit and healthy and he would have no major health problems apart from the usual bouts of colds or flu. She said that the Line of the Sun predicted success in the arts and his travel lines suggested that he was going on many journeys in a few years time. She also stated that George would develop a different aspect of his career in the future, although it would not necessarily separate him from the other three Beatles.

Piggies

A track from *The Beatles* white album, 2 minutes and 3 seconds in length, which was recorded at Abbey Road on 19 September 1966 with overdubbing on 20 September and 10 October.

George had originally begun writing the number early in 1966, but had left it unfinished. He rediscovered the song at his parents' home and completed it. In his book *I. Me. Mine.* he explained, '"Piggies" is a social comment. I was stuck for one line in the middle until my mother came up with the lyric, "What they need is a damn good whacking!" which is a nice simple way of saying they need a good hiding. It needed to rhyme with "backing", "lacking" and had absolutely nothing to do with American policemen or California shagnastics.'

Commenting on the number, John Lennon said, 'I gave George a couple of lines about forks and knives and eating bacon.'

A concluding verse that George had written wasn't recorded.

This was one of the songs that Charles Manson took to be a secret message to him from the Beatles and he believed it warned of an imminent black revolution.

Pirate Song, The

A number co-written by Paul and Eric Idle and featured on Idle's comedy series *Rutland Weekend Television*, which was screened on BBC2 on Boxing Day, 1975. A clip of George's performance of the number was included in the BBC2 show *An Evening With Vic And Bob* on Monday 27 December 1993.

Pisces Fish

A track from the *Brainwashed* album lasting 4 minutes and 52 seconds, with George on lead vocals, electric guitar, acoustic guitar, bass guitar, ukulele and background vocals. Jeff Lynne was on electric guitar, keyboards and percussion while Dhani Harrison was on electric guitar and Jim Keltner on drums with Mike Moran and Marc Mann on additional keyboards.

George described it as a 'partially autobiographical rock hymn about learning to swim in the river and watch it flow'.

Pisshole Artists, The

A group who made an appearance in the English village of Pishill in December 1978. Their name was obviously a piss take on the name of the village. The group comprised George Harrison, Ian Paice, Jon Lord, Boz Burrell, Mick Ralphs and Simon Kirke.

PJ Vatican Blues (Last Saturday Night)

A track from the *Brainwashed* album lasting 2 minutes and 38 seconds with George on lead vocals, slide guitar, ukulele and background vocals. Jeff Lynne was on acoustic guitar, electric guitar, bass guitar, Wurlitzer and background vocals while Dhani Harrison was on acoustic guitar and background vocals and Jim Keltner on drums.

Plug Me In

A track from the *All Things Must Pass* triple album, penned by George at 3 minutes and 16 seconds in length. This is a jam session from the 'Apple Jam' part of the album and the musicians appearing on the track include Bobby Whitlock on keyboards, Carl Radle on bass, and George, Eric Clapton and Dave Mason on guitars.

Porky's Revenge 2

The third in the series of films about the conflict between a group of school kids and a local brothel-keeper.

George's involvement with the soundtrack of this movie came about through his friendship with Dave Edmunds. The two live close to each other and in 1984 Dave asked George if he could contribute to a soundtrack album he'd been asked to put together for 20th Century Fox. George suggested 'I Don't Want To Do It', a previously unreleased Bob Dylan number that George had recorded some time ago.

He worked on a re-recording with Edmunds and the song, which was 2 minutes and 51 second in length, was included on side one of the *Porky's Revenge* soundtrack album, issued in America by CBS on Columbia JS 39983 on Monday 14 March 1985 and in Britain on CBS

70265 on Friday 28 June 1985. A CD was issued in America on Mobile Fidelity MFCD-797 in November 1988.

A 7″ single, which was a different mix from the album, was issued on Columbia 38-04887 with Dave Edmunds' 'Queen Of The Hop' on the flip. There was also a 12″ promotional single issued to American radio stations.

Prabhupada, A.C. Bhaktivedanta Swami

It was in the late 1960s that George's devotion to Krishna became strong, and he was in awe of the founder of the International Society For Krishna Consciousness (ISKCON), His Divine Grace A.C. Bhaktivedanta Swami Prabhupada.

In 1922 the Swami, who had been born in Calcutta, began studying Bhakti Yoga and decided to devote the rest of his life to promoting the message of Krishna throughout the world by bringing the *magamantra* to the West. This became known as the 'Hare Krishna mantra', which is the repetition of Krishna's name, chanted as a form of meditation.

In September 1965, at the age of seventy, the Swami set off for America and in a few years had established over one hundred Krishna Consciousness centres in different parts of the world including the Radha Krishna Temple in London, which he founded in 1966.

While based in Manhattan's east side he attracted disciples with kirtanas. These were chanting sessions where visitors would chant, dance and clap at an ever increasing pace until the kirtana would eventually climax and come to a halt.

During his stay in America he made an album of the chanting of disciples, *Krishna Consciousness*. George obtained a copy and he said, 'It was like a door opened in my subconscious, maybe from a previous life.'

His followers visited the Apple HQ and met up with George, who arranged for them to meet up with the Beatles at Kinfauns. Over a vegetarian meal, during which they began chanting, George found that the movement in Britain did not have much money.

As a result he arranged for Apple to lease them a building in Bury Place, Holborn, London. Work on the building was suspended when neighbours complained about the noise of the renovation work and an independent inquiry took place.

On hearing from Syamasundar of George's generosity when he donated a further £2,000 for marble to the temple's altar, the Swami replied to him: 'It is understood from your letter that Mr George Harrison has a little sympathy for our movement, and if Krishna is actually satisfied on him surely he will be able to join us in pushing on the Sankirtan movement throughout the world. Somehow or other the Beatles have become the cynosure of the neighbouring European countries and America also. He is attracted to our philosophy and if Mr Harrison takes the leading part in organising a huge Sankirtan party consisting of the Beatles and our ISKCON boys, surely we shall change the face of the world so much politically harassed by the manoeuvres of the politicians.'

The Swami could see the potential benefits of George promoting the movement and wrote again to Syamasundar: 'I am so glad that George Harrison is composing songs like "Lord Whom We Have So Long Ignored". He is very thoughtful. When we actually meet I shall be able to compose very attractive songs for public reception. The public is in need of such songs, and if they are administered through nice agents like the Beatles, it will surely be a big success.'

It was George's suggestion that brought about the next step when he decided to record the devotional chant using members of the Radha Krishna Temple, telling them, 'I think it would be preferable if you guys got the money instead of us. It might actually be better if you made your own record for Apple. How about it?'

The initial session took place at George's bungalow, Kinfauns, with George participating on guitar and Billy Preston joining in on synthesizer.

Next a recording rehearsal took place at Trident Studios and the actual recording took place at Abbey Road Studios.

A disciple, Mukunda Das Goswami, was to recall, 'The first time we got together to record was at George's place on Claremont Drive in Esher. He had a very nice vegetarian meal provided and afterward we all chanted with him and Billy Preston.

'Bill was playing an early type of Moog synthesizer, George was playing his guitar and we were on drums and kartals. I remember us doing a bit of cooking together that night, and I think he may even have played us a Lenny Bruce record.'

Another disciple recalled the Abbey Road session: 'On the day of the recording about a dozen devotees, including some newly recruited Britishers, assembled at EMI recording studios on Abbey Road. When the first group of devotees arrived in George's white Mercedes, a crowd of teenagers began singing Hare Krishna to the tune popularised by the rock musical *Hair*.

'With Paul McCartney and his wife Linda operating the control console, the recording session began. Everyone worked quickly, making Side One of the 45-rpm record in about an hour.

'George played organ and Mukunda played *mridangam*. Yamuna sang the lead with Syamasundar backing her, with the other voices blending together in chorus.

'On the fourth take everything went smoothly, with Malati spontaneously hitting a brass gong at the end. Then they recorded the flipside of the record. Afterwards, George dubbed in the bass guitar and other voices. The devotees, engineers, everyone felt good about it. "This is going to be big," George promised.'

The single 'Hare Krishna Mantra' by the Radha Krishna Temple, was released in America on 22 August 1969 and in Britain on 29 August and reached No. 17 in the British charts. This was followed by 'Govinda', which was released in Britain on 6 March 1970 where it reached No. 23 and in America on 24 March. George also produced an album *The Radha Krsna Temple*, which was released in America on 21 May 1971 and in Britain on 28 May.

Due to the problems of the investigation over the Bury Street site, John Lennon suggested that they move into his mansion Tittenhurst Park until the matter was settled.

Prabhupada himself flew into London on 11 September 1969 and George was to travel to Heathrow to greet him. There was a short press conference at the airport and the Swami was then driven to Tittenhurst Park in John's white Rolls-Royce.

After lunch he invited George, John and Yoko Ono to join him. He indicated for Syamasundar to place a garland of carnations, which had been given to him at the airport, on George.

A lengthy conversation between them then took place, which was eventually to be published in book form.

Part of the conversation was as follows:

Prabhupada: You are anxious to bring about peace in the world. I've read some of your statements, and they show me that you're anxious to do something. Actually, every saintly person should try and bring peace, but we must know the process. What kind of philosophy are you following, may I ask?

Yoko: We don't follow anything. We are just living.

George: We've done meditation. Or I do my meditation – mantra meditation.

Prabhupada: Hare Krishna is also a mantra.

John: Ours is not a song, though. We heard it from Maharishi. A mantra each.

Prabhupada: His mantras are not public?

John: No. It's a secret.

Yoko: If Hare Krishna is such a strong, powerful mantra, is there any reason to chant anything else?

Prabhupada: There are other mantras, but Hare Krishna is especially recommended for this age.

John: If all mantras are just the name of God, then whether it's a secret mantra or an open mantra, it doesn't really make much difference, does it, which one you sing?

Prabhupada: It does make a difference. For instance, in a drug shop they sell many types of medicines for curing different diseases. But still you have to get a doctor's prescription in order to get a particular type of medicine. Otherwise the druggist won't supply you. You might go to the drug shop and say, 'I'm diseased. Please give me any medicine you have.' But the druggist will ask you, 'Where is your prescription?' Similarly, in this age, the Hare Krishna mantra is prescribed in the scriptures. And the great teacher Sri Chaitanya Mahaprabhu, whom we consider to be an incarnation of God, also prescribed it. Therefore, our principle is that everyone should follow the prescription of the great authorities.

Yoko: If the mantra itself has such power, does it matter where you receive it?

Prabhupada: Yes, it does matter. For instance, milk is nutritious. That's a fact everyone knows. But if milk is touched by the lips of a serpent, it is no longer nutritious. It becomes poisonous. If you don't receive the mantra through the proper channel, it may not really be spiritual.

John: But what if one of these masters who's not in the line says exactly the same thing as one who is? What if he says his mantra is coming from the Vedas and he seems to speak with as much authority as you?

Prabhupada: If the mantra is actually coming through a bona fide disciplic succession, then it will have the potency.

John: But the Hare Krishna mantra is the best one?

Prabhupada: Yes. We say that the Hare Krishna mantra is sufficient for one's perfection, for liberation.

George: Isn't it like flowers? Somebody may prefer roses, and somebody may like carnations better. Isn't it really a matter for the individual devotee to decide? One person may find that Hare Krishna is more beneficial to his spiritual progress, and yet another person may find that some other mantra may be more beneficial for him.

Prabhupada: But still there is a distinction. A fragrant rose is considered better than a flower without any scent. You may be attracted by one flower, and I may be attracted by another flower. But among the flowers a distinction can be made. There are many flowers that have no fragrance and many that do. Therefore, your attraction for a particular flower is not the solution to the question of which is actually better. In the same way, personal attraction is not the solution to choosing the best spiritual process. You've been speaking of the Maharishi. Hasn't he written some book on Bhagavad-Gita?

John: Yes, that's the one we've read.

Prabhupada: So, why is he using Krishna's book to put forward his own philosophy? Bhagavad-Gita is Krishna's book. Why is he taking Krishna's book?

John: Well, he didn't. He just translated it.

Prabhupada: Why? Because Krishna's book is very well respected.

John: I've also read part of another translation by Paramahansa Yogananda.

Prabhupada: Yes, all these men take advantage of Krishna's book to lend and air of authority to their own speculations. Vivekananda has done it, Sri Aurobindo has done it. Thousands of them have done it. But why do they use Bhagavad-Gita as the vehicle for their own ideas?

George: In the versions I've read, the authors all claim that theirs is the best. And sometimes I get something from one which I didn't get from another.

John: I found that the best thing for myself is to take a little bit from here and a little bit from there.

Yoko: I mean, we're not just saying that. We want to ask your advice. In other words, what is your answer to this question of authority?

Prabhupada: If we don't take the Gita from the authorised disciplic succession, it won't help us. In our introduction to Bhagavad-Gita we have carefully explained that aside from Krishna there is no authority, because Bhagavad-Gita was spoken by Krishna. Can you deny that?

John: What about Yogananda, Maharishi and all these other people who have translated the Gita? How are we to tell that their version isn't also Krishna's word?

Prabhupada: If you seriously want to understand this, you should study the original Sanskrit text.

John: Study Sanskrit? Oh, now you're talking.

George: But Vivekananda said that books, rituals, dogmas and temples are secondary details anyway. He said they're not the most important thing. You don't have to read the book in order to have the perception.

Prabhupada (laughing): Then why did Vivekananda write so many books?

The conversation continued for some time and was recorded and it was published by the Bhaktivedanta Book Trust in 1981 among the shoal of books published following John Lennon's murder, under the title *Lennon '69: Search For Liberation.*

George was to say of the Swami, 'He is my friend. He is my master who I have great respect for. It's like, if you want to learn how to ski, you go to somebody who'll teach you how to ski. I accept Prabhupada as qualified to teach people about Krishna.'

George even devoted a song to the Swami, 'The Lord Loves The One That Loves The Lord'.

George was very respectful of Indian spiritual leaders and before attending a meeting with the Swami in 1972 he removed his sock and said, 'I get so nervous when I am around his Divine grace – I just got my hair cut to see Prabhupada.'

Swami Prabhupada died on the evening of 17 November 1977 at the age of 81. Shortly before his death he took a gold ring from his finger, passed it on to a disciple and told him, 'Please give this to George Harrison. He was a good friend to us all. He loves Krishna sincerely and I love him. He was my archangel.'

George did, at one time, consider becoming a full-blooded Krishna devotee, shaving his head and adhering to the disciplines. However, Prabhupada had advocated training in self-purification, which meant that his followers did not eat meat, have illicit sex, gamble, or take intoxicants such as drugs, alcohol, coffee or cigarettes.

This would obviously have been too much for George, who had become involved in extramarital affairs, had sampled a variety of drugs, at one time became addicted to alcohol and was a heavy smoker.

However, his support and devotion to Prabhupada and Hare Krishna never wavered. With the problems caused by the building near the British Museum in Bury Street, in 1972 George bought Picket's Manor, an impressive building in seventeen acres of ground in Hertfordshire. He had it renovated as Bhaktivedanta Manor and donated it to the movement. Varshana Devi Dasi was to say, 'When George gave us the Manor, he gave us more than a few buildings. He provided a facility for many thousands of people to come for spiritual instruction and to worship God. Each year, over 15,000 British public-school students visit the Manor to learn about Vaishnava Hinduism.'

Preston, Billy

George first met Preston in Hamburg in 1962 when Preston was a member of Little Richard's band. The Gospel Rock keyboards player was born in Houston, Texas on 9 September 1946.

Preston was only fifteen when George befriended him in Hamburg and the two met again when Preston was in Britain touring with Ray Charles. He has also toured with Sam Cooke and was the regular keyboard player on the American rock show *Shindig*.

When there were some tensions between the members of the Beatles during the recording sessions on the 'Get Back' project, George thought of bringing Preston in to lessen the stressful atmosphere.

He received co-billing on the 'Get Back' single, which was the only time someone shared their name with the Beatles on a Beatles record. It led to some people referring to him as 'the fifth Beatle'.

Billy also performed on further Beatles tracks – 'Let It Be', 'I. Me. Mine.', 'I've Got A Feeling', 'Dig A Pony' and 'One After 909'.

Billy became one of the close friends of George's inner circle of musicians and he was to comment, 'George is wonderful. George is very spiritual. He's a very loving and humble person. He's a very good friend and he is like a brother to me.'

George also brought him into Apple records and did most of the co-producing on Preston's two albums for Apple, *That's The Way God Planned It* and *Encouraging Words*.

When he arrived for the first recording session, George said, 'I'm going to invite some of my friends over to play on the session.' His friends were Eric Clapton on guitar, Keith Richards on bass and Ginger Baker on drums. George produced Billy's single 'Everything's All Right' c/w 'I Want To Thank You'. He also recorded a Preston single of 'My Sweet Lord' c/w 'Long As I Got My Baby', with backing from the Edwin Hawkins Singers, six months before George released his own version.

When the hassles with Apple began following the presence of Allen Klein, Billy asked George to free him from his Apple contract. He'd been with Apple for three years.

Billy was one of the musicians on the Delaney And Bonnie And Friends Tour, which George joined in December 1969. He also appeared on *Concert For Bangla Desh* and on George's first American tour in 1974. Mentioning the tour, Preston said, 'He was definitely inspired after *Bangla Desh*. He wanted to do it again right away. But it took some time. He had to do a lot of thinking on this one because he had to get out there and be the one.'

George was later to invite him to play on his solo albums *All Things Must Pass*, *Thirty Three & 1/3* and others, in addition to hiring him as a musician on his Ravi Shankar Dark Horse record projects.

George also lent a hand on Preston's own albums by making guest appearances.

Prince's Trust Concerts 1987

Two benefit shows that took place at Wembley Arena, London on Friday 5 June and Saturday 6 June 1987, with Prince Charles and Princess Diana in attendance.

George and Ringo were surprise guests and appeared on both evenings, and on the first night they joined Ben E. King in a performance of 'Stand By Me'. On the second evening, supported by Eric Clapton, they performed 'While My Guitar Gently Weeps' and 'Here Comes The Sun' with Ringo then performing 'With A Little Help From My Friends'.

ITV screened edited highlights from the two shows on Saturday 20 June 1987, omitting George's performance of 'Here Comes The Sun'.

Radio One also broadcast a radio special on the concert on Friday 1 January 1988. A home video was also issued.

In America, the concerts were aired as a sixty-minute HBO special on Sunday 13 September 1987. HBO also broadcast further screenings on 16, 19, 21 and 25 September.

The HBO broadcast included backstage scenes omitted from the British TV airing and George is seen commenting: 'It's nerve-wracking. I haven't done a show in England since 1966 and the last time I did a concert tour was in 1974. So it makes you nervous when you don't perform all the time.'

Backstage, he is asked what he would play. He replied 'White Christmas' and 'I'm A Pink Toothbrush' and then turned to Ringo and said, 'What are you doing?' Ringo said, 'I'm collecting the money.'

Incidentally, in his first remark, George must have forgotten his British appearance with Delaney and Bonnie.

The home video of the concerts, featuring George and Ringo, were released on Tuesday 14 June 1988. This was an unusual release because it was issued by Kodak in a special three-pack offer which included a 74-minute Prince's Trust video and two blank three-hour tapes.

Promotional Records

In America major artists regularly record interviews that are pressed onto single or album discs or CDs and then distributed to radio stations throughout the country for disc jockeys to play.

During his career, George made two such records. The first was 'George Harrison Interview Record', which was issued in August 1974. This interview was conducted by Chuck Cassell and was mainly promoting Dark Horse Records and the initial releases on the label.

The second was 'A Personal Music Dialogue With George Harrison At Thirty Three & 1/3'. This also covered George's *Dark Horse* album, but included appropriate cues on the record for local disc jockeys to play tracks from the new album.

Pseudonyms

George's first use of a pseudonym took place in May 1960 when the Silver Beetles toured Scotland as a backing band to singer Johnny Gentle. George adopted the name Carl Harrison in tribute to Carl Perkins.

During his solo career George liked to make guest appearances on records by his friends but, due to contractual difficulties, in a number of cases he had to use pseudonyms. They included L'Angelo Mysterioso, George O'Hara, George Harrysong, Hari Georgeson, Jai Raj Harisein, and Spike and Nelson Wilbury.

He also used pseudonyms when travelling and booking into hotels.

Pure Smokey

A number inspired by Smokey Robinson and the Motown sound. The number, 3 minutes and 50 seconds in length, was included on the *Thirty Three & 1/3* album. George was to say, 'Just a while back I was thinking about personal records that I like to hear. And in the sixties we were really into Tamla Motown, just around the time it was first breaking. So I always liked Smokey Robinson and the Miracles in that period. And I found myself playing a lot of his records. And I dedicated a tune on the last album to Smokey, but I'd written this one at the same time as that song, which was "Ooh Baby". This song called "Pure Smokey" was really, that was the title of one of Smokey Robinson's albums. And it was really just like an idea that I had that sometimes when you like something and you never . . . if you never get to say to somebody that you appreciated it. And I thought I'd use this as a way of getting across a point of . . . I don't want to be late. I didn't want to die and realise I hadn't told my dad I like him or whatever. It's like that, and so I think I try and make a point of . . . if I really like something now I want to tell the person I like it rather than to find out that I should have done something and I never. And I just try and live like that now. So this song just says . . . in the past, like, I'd hesitate, I feel some joy, but before I show my thanks it became too late. And now all the way I want to find the time to stop to say, "Thank you Lord for giving us each new day." So it's really to say thanks for certain things. And so then it just goes into Smokey saying . . . because I got a lot of pleasure out of his records and so it's just a "thank you".'

Quarry Men, The

The skiffle group that developed into the Beatles. John Lennon originally formed it in March 1957 while he was still at Quarry Bank School in Liverpool. Although he was interested in rock'n'roll, he, like so many other British youngsters, thought that the instruments needed to play the music would be expensive. It was different with skiffle, which could almost be played with homemade instruments. John's guitar only cost his Aunt Mimi £17 and his mate Pete Shotton played a washboard. The duties on tea-chest bass were shared between some of John's other friends, initially Bill Smith, then alternating between Ivan Vaughan and Nigel Walley. There was Rod Davis on banjo, Eric Griffiths on guitar and Colin Hanton on drums.

On Saturday 22 June 1957, the Quarry Men were playing at the Woolton Village Fete when Paul McCartney entered their lives. He recalled, 'A mate of mine at school, Ivy Vaughan, had said, "Come along and see this group, they're great." We used to go to the fair together with these great jackets with flaps here, light blue with flecks in them.

'I went to see the group and loved it. It was a young group instead of dance music. John was obviously leading this thing – he had an acoustic guitar; brown wood with a hole, and a bit of a crew cut, with a little quiff. He didn't know the words for anything, he'd obviously only heard the records and not bought them, but I was pretty impressed.

'I met up with John backstage in this little church hall, and just picked up his guitar, which I had to play upside down, because I'm left-handed, and played "Twenty Flight Rock". They were all impressed because I knew all the words, then somebody played the piano, somebody sang "Long Tall Sally", and later they asked me to join.'

Nigel no longer played tea-chest bass as John asked him to become the group's manager. He had cards printed reading:

Country, Western, Rock'n'roll, Skiffle
   The Quarry Men
   Open for Engagements

In an effort to secure the group a booking at the popular jazz club the Cavern, which had opened that year, Nigel contacted the owner's father at the Lee Park Golf Club. He arranged for his son Alan Sytner to see the group and as a result they received a Cavern booking.

Paul was unable to join them on their first Cavern appearance on 7 August because he was away at scout camp with his brother Mike.

Paul's first appearance with them took place at the New Clubmoor Hall, a Conservative club, and Paul remembers, 'That night was a disaster because I got sticky fingers and blew the solo in "Guitar Boogie Shuffle", which is one of the easiest things in the world to play.'

Before the end of the year there had been other changes in personnel, with manager Nigel Walley leaving because of ill health and Rod Davis also quitting the group.

On Saturday 7 December 1957, George turned up to watch the group perform at Wilson Hall in Garston. He said, 'I'd been invited to see them play several times by Paul but for some reason never got round to it before.

'I remember being very impressed with John's big thick sideboards and trendy teddy-boy clothes. In a way, all that emotional rough stuff was simply a way for him to help separate the men from the boys, I think. I was never intimidated by him.

'Whenever he had a go at me I just gave him a little bit of his own right back.'

It was at their next gig at Wilson Hall on 6 February 1958 that George made enough of an impression to be asked to join the group. After the gig, George joined John and Paul on the bus for part of their way home. Paul said, 'George slipped quietly into one of the seats on this almost empty bus we were on, took out his guitar and went right into "Raunchy". Some days later I asked John, "Well, what do you think about George?" He gave it a second or two and then he replied, "Yeah, man, he'd be great." And that was that. George was in and we were on our way.'

The group now comprised John, Paul, George, Len Garry, Eric Griffiths and an occasional pianist John 'Duff' Lowe.

This was the outfit that made their first record at Percy Philips' studio at 53 Kensington, Liverpool on 12 July 1958. They recorded the Buddy Holly number 'That'll Be The Day' and an original number credited to Harrison/McCartney, 'In Spite Of All The Danger'.

The group could only afford one copy of the disc, which cost 17/6d. The copy was lent to each member of the group over a period of time and finally ended up in Lowe's hands when he left the group at the end of 1958.

The final gig of the year took place on 20 December when the Quarry Men played at the reception for the marriage of George's brother Harry to Irene McGann.

The first booking of the New Year also came via George's family. His father Harry, who was chairman of the Speke Bus Depot Social club, booked them to appear at the Club's New Year party on 1 January at Wilson Hall in Garston. Their only other booking took place on 24 January at Woolton Village Club.

The Quarry Men seemed to fade away, with no bookings and the members going their own way, with John and Paul spending their time writing together and George joining another band, The Les Stewart Quartet.

During the months between January and August, there had been no real contact between George and his fellow members of the Quarry Men. His new band comprised Les Stewart, Geoff Skinner, Ken Brown and himself, all on guitar and vocals. With some bands in those early days, a drummer wasn't included.

The group had a residency at Lowlands club in Hayman's Green in the West Derby area of Liverpool. At the time George was dating a girl called Ruth Morrison. Ruth informed George and Ken Brown that a new club was opening on the other side of Hayman's Green and were looking for a resident band. Brown went along to see the club owner, a woman called Mona Best, who agreed to them becoming the resident band and informed him that the club would be opening on Saturday 29 August 1959.

Brown went along to Stewart's house and sat in the lounge with Stewart and George and said that he'd managed to get them a residency at the new club. Stewart wasn't interested – he was angry at the fact that Brown had been missing rehearsals because he'd been helping out at the Casbah, to prepare them for the opening. He said that they wouldn't be playing at the new club.

George left Stewart's house with Brown and they discussed the situation. Brown suggested that they form another band and George said that he had two friends and could approach them and see if they were interested.

He then contacted John and Paul and they agreed, so a new band was formed with John, Paul, George and Ken Brown. They decided to utilise the former name of John's skiffle group, the Quarry Men. But for this incident, the Beatles would probably never have existed.

The group began their residency and, like the Les Stewart Quartet, didn't have the services of a drummer.

On their seventh appearance at the Casbah, on 10 October 1959,

another incident occurred which resulted in a group change. Ken
Brown was sacked.

He recalled, 'One night, just as we were due to start a Saturday
session, I felt a crippling pain in my leg. I could barely stand, but
insisted on doing something, so Mrs Best asked me to take the money
at the door and, for the first time, John, Paul and George played
without me.

'Just as everyone was going home I was in the club when Paul came
back down the steps. "Hey Ken, what's all this?" he said. "What?" I
asked him. "Mrs Best says she's paying you, even though you didn't
play with us tonight." "That's up to her," I replied, as Paul bounded
back up the stairs, still arguing with Mrs Best. They all came downstairs to me. "We think your fifteen bob should be divided between us,
as you didn't play tonight," said Paul. So of course I didn't agree. "All
right, that's it then!" shouted McCartney, and they stormed off down
the drive towards West Derby village, shouting that they would never
play the Casbah again.'

Well, at least John, Paul and George were together again and were to
remain that way. They didn't replace Brown, but were later to associate
themselves with the Casbah. (Think about it: name a club in Liverpool
with six letters, beginning with C, where the Beatles, under their original name of the Quarry Men, had a residency? Many people might
think – Cavern – but it was actually the Casbah.)

Following the incident at the club, the group decided to enter a
Carroll Levis 'TV Star Search' at the Empire Theatre, but dispensed
with the name the Quarry Men and called themselves Johnny And The
Moondogs.

Radha Krishna Temple

The Radha Krishna Temple in London was founded in July 1966 by His Divine Grace A.C. Bhaktivedanta Swami.

A member of Bhakti Yoga, he came to London to teach the meaning of love and trained devotees of the International Society For Krishna Consciousness in the process of self-purification. They follow four principles:

They must not eat meat, they must not have illicit sex, they must not gamble and they must not take any intoxicants, including drugs, coffee, tea or cigarettes.

Early sessions for the recording of the 'Hare Krishna Mantra' took place in 1969 at Kinfauns with George on guitar and Billy Preston on synthesizer. George then had the group attend a recording session at Trident Studios, which was mainly a rehearsal, and the final recording took place at Abbey Road Studios.

In addition to members of the London branch of the Temple, George played organ and Paul and Linda McCartney were operating the control console.

George described the record as a devotional chant. 'While the words don't alter, the tune that it is sung to doesn't matter. You could sing it to "Coming Round The Mountain" if you wanted to. All I've done on this is shorten it. The actual meaning of the words is not important, although there are various forms of addressing the spiritual Lord – God, if you like. They are more a sort of magical vibration to bring about a spiritual awareness.

'God has many names, I never know what to call him. This is just another way of finding spiritual communion.'

The single was released in Britain on Apple 25 on 6 March 1970 and in America on Apple 1821 on 24 March 1970. 'Prayer To The Spiritual Masters' was on the flip, another traditional manta, arranged, like the first, by Makunda Das Adhikary.

It reached No. 17 in Britain, was a chart-topper in Germany and Czechoslovakia and made the Top Ten in Japan, but had no impact in America.

George also produced an album *The Radha Krishna Temple*, which was issued in Britain on Apple SKAO 3376 on 21 May 1971 and in America on Apple SAPCOR 18 on 28 May 1971. The tracks were: Side One: 'Govinda', 'Sri Gurvastakam', 'Bhaja Bhakata/Arati', 'Hare Krishna Mantra'. Side Two: 'Sri Isopanisad', 'Bhaja Hunre Mana', 'Govinda Jaya Jaya'.

Raga (album)

The original soundtrack album to the film about Ravi Shankar. George produced it. The album was issued in America on Apple SWAO 3384 on 7 December 1971. The tracks were: Side One: 'Dawn To Dusk', Ravi Shankar; 'Vedic Hymns', Public Domain; 'Baba Teaching', Public Domain; 'Birth To Death', Ravi Shankar; 'Vinus House', Ravi Shankar; 'Gurur Bramha', Ravi Shankar; 'United Nations', Ravi Shankar and Yehudi Menuhin. Side Two: 'Medley'; 'Raga Parameshwari', Ravi Shankar; 'Rangeswhart', Ravi Shankar; 'Banaras Ghat', Ravi Shankar; 'Bombay School', Ravi Shankar; 'Kinnara School', Ravi Shankar'; 'Frenzy And Distortion', Ravi Shankar'; 'Raga Desh', Ravi Shankar.

Raga (film)

A film that was originally going to be called 'Messenger Out Of The East'. The film was released by Apple in 1971 and was a 96-minute documentary on Ravi Shankar.

George and Ravi held a press conference in Los Angeles to announce that the film would focus on Shankar's life and philosophy, taking in a general look at Indian religions and traditions. George made a brief appearance in the film taking a sitar lesson from Ravi. George also introduced Yehudi Menuhin, saying, 'Old friend Yehudi Menuhin, one of the great violinists, joins Shankar for an informal session while youthful George Harrison comes to the master to learn.'

The film was produced and directed by Howard Worth, with a screenplay by Nancy Becal. It was distributed by Apple Films and received its premiere at the Carnegie Hall cinema in New York on 23 November 1971.

Raga Mala: The Autobiography Of Ravi Shankar

Ravi Shankar took three years to write this 120,000-word book, heavily illustrated with over 200 photographs, which was published by Genesis Publications in the spring of 1998 in a limited edition of 2,000 copies.

Each copy was personally signed by Shankar and also contained two CDs with eighty minutes of exclusive material. He also recorded a half-hour piece 'Raga Tilak Kamond' specially for the book. The track 'I Am Missing You' includes both George and Ringo, there is 'Dakshini' an outtake from the *Chants Of India* sessions, which was produced by and features George. The other tracks were 'Charu Keshi' and 'Morning Love'.

George edited the book and wrote the introduction, mentioning Ravi's influence on his own spiritual development. He commented, 'By this time the Beatles had met so many people – prime ministers, celebrities, royalty – but I got to the point where I thought, "I'd like to meet somebody who could really impress me." And that was when I met Ravi. He was the first person who impressed me in a way that was beyond just being a famous celebrity. Ravi plugged me into the whole of reality. I mean, I met Elvis – Elvis impressed me when I was a kid, and impressed me when I met him because of the buzz of meeting Elvis – but you couldn't later go on round to him and say, "Elvis, what's happening in the universe."'

Rapido

A BBC2 television programme, presented by Antoine de Caunes. George pretaped an interview that was first screened on Wednesday 5 December 1990 and repeated on Monday 10 December 1990.

Here is an edited transcript:

George: Thank you, it's nice to be here with my Rap Rap Rap waistcoat.

Antoine: With his 1987 single 'When We was Fab', George Harrison momentarily reflected on his days with the Beatles, but he's quick to play down the legacy of the most famous band of all time.

George: We don't go around feeling like Supergroups or Superpeople – we're just people who happen to do this as a job and happen to have become well known for doing it. But apart from that, it's all in other people's heads ... all the mystic and the intrigue ... we're just like anybody else you know. It's no use talking to me, it's just like talking to you, it's the same, really.

Antoine: Paul McCartney recently attempted to diffuse the Beatles mystique by tackling it head on. His world tour and subsequent triple live album leaned heavily on old Beatles songs and George seems happy to leave him to it.

George: Yes. Well, his whole thing is doing a Beatles tour. Now he's decided to be the Beatles. I'm not interested. For me, it's the past and, you know, to be here now is my motto.

Antoine: It's ten years now since John Lennon's untimely death and the publicity surrounding what would have been John's

fiftieth birthday in October, with its accompanying publishing and
record spin-offs, leaves George uneasy, but he's resigned to the
inevitable.

George: It's a sad thing the way he died and, you know, it's OK,
really, for everybody loses people and I'd just like to say actually
it's only the physical thing which disappears. The soul keeps on
going and I sort of know that to be true – it's not something I've
made up to make myself feel good about it.

Antoine: Following a break from recording in the mid-eighties,
Harrison re-emerged in 1987 with the *Cloud Nine* album.
Although heavily involved with the Traveling Wilburys and more
recently the Romanian Angel Appeal, George has no definite plans
for another solo album.

George: The record deal I had, which I think was a five-record
deal, finished with *Cloud Nine* and it's sort of a nice feeling to
know that you're not obliged to do something – so that, therefore,
I can just do stuff I want, rather than because I've got a contractual obligation. So I've just been thinking – I don't have a record
deal at the moment.

Antoine: The Traveling Wilburys first came together on a one-
off project to record a B side for a George Harrison single, but
they enjoyed themselves so much they stuck around.

George: It was just a set of circumstances that got us all in the
same room together. We made one song and there was nothing
much we could do with that song on its own, so we decided we'd
do another nine songs on the basis that it only took us one day to
write one song. The time element with Bob being continually on
the road, we had about nine days with him and made the album.
So, anyway, it turned out very nice – turned out nice again – so we
thought we'd do another one. That's all, basically. Bob called and
said, 'When are we going to do a new one?' so we just set a date
when we all had time – which was April this year. We got together
and started from scratch this time and got in a room and just
wrote fifteen tunes, and just finished eleven.

Antoine: Contacted by George's wife, Olivia, on her return from
visiting the orphaned children in Romania, the Wilburys put their
unique blend of talents to work and recorded the single 'Nobody's
Child' within 24 hours.

George: Obviously, because it's me, Jeff Lynne, Tom Petty and
Bob Dylan, we do what we do, but when you mix it together, you
get us in a room – it's like it can happen with anybody if they can
basically get a unit together where they get off on each other's
company. You can hear the style of my guitar, you can hear my
voice the same as you can hear Dylan and all that. But the mix is
neither like anybody's solo record in particular.

Antoine: Despite their name, the Traveling Wilburys haven't

toured on the concert circuit, although George quite fancies the idea of the group playing live.

George: It would be good. I could imagine what it could be like on stage doing a show. It could be fun, there's no question about it. In fact, I don't know if we'd do it anyway. I'm a bit shy about touring, particularly because of the fact that it's such a big wind-up to do a tour. You can't just do a quick tour.

Rattled
A number from *The Traveling Wilburys Volume 1* on which Jeff Lynne takes the lead.

Rebels, The
A short-lived group formed by George in 1957. His mother Louise had originally given him £3 to buy a guitar off a boy from school, but this was upgraded when his mother saved up the housekeeping money and bought him a better instrument for £30.

George then formed a group which he called the Rebels, bringing in his brother Peter on guitar and vocals, their friend Arthur Kelly, also on guitar and vocals, and two other friends – one on mouth organ, the other on tea-chest bass.

George was to recall, 'I remember the Rebels had a tea chest with a lot of gnomes around it. One of my brothers had a five-shilling guitar, which had the back off. Apart from that it was all fine. Just my brother, some mates and me. I tried to lay down the law a bit, but they weren't having any of that.'

The group only ever experienced a single gig. This was to be an audition at the British Legion Club, Dam Wood Road, Speke, near to where George lived at the time.

Rehearsals had taken place at Arthur's house in Wavertree and in one of the bedrooms of George's house.

The boys were in for a shock when they arrived at the British Legion and discovered that the band who'd been booked officially to perform that evening hadn't turned up. The Rebels were asked to take their place and perform a lengthy set, which worried them, as they only knew two numbers. However, no one seemed to notice and the boys were pleased to receive a fee of ten shillings at the end of the evening.

George was able to tell his school friend Paul McCartney about the gig on the bus to school the next morning.

Recordings
George made an extensive amount of recordings during his long post-Beatles career. They included his canon of albums and singles, demo discs, unfinished songs, numbers he performed on television, radio shows, concerts and events (such as The Rock And Roll Hall Of Fame),

songs by other songwriters ranging from Bob Dylan and Carl Perkins
(the influence of both is apparent in this list) to Ravi Shankar and
Hoagy Carmichael, Traveling Wilburys numbers, sessions with other
artists such as Leon Russell and Gary Wright, outtakes, songs co-
penned with other artists, and numerous recordings that have never
made it onto official recordings but which have appeared over the years
on bootleg albums. If ever a 'George Harrison Anthology' were considered, there would be an incredible number of recordings to choose
from. Even a radio series similar to *The Lost Lennon Tapes* or Paul
McCartney's *Oobu Joobu* would not be difficult to assemble because of
the vast amount of material available.

Here is a basic list of most of the numbers that George recorded over
the years, many of which have not found their way onto the mainstream releases:

A.
'A Bit More Of You'; 'A Hard Rain's A-Gonna Fall'; 'Abandoned
Love'; 'Absolutely Sweet Marie'; 'All Along The Watchtower'; 'All I
Have To Do Is Dream'; 'All Things Must Pass'; 'All Those Years Ago';
'Amen'; 'Anourag'; 'The Answer's At The End'; 'Apple Jam'; 'Apple
Scruffs'; 'Art Of Dying'; 'Awaiting On You All'.

B.
'Baby Don't Run Away'; 'Backwards Tabla'; 'Backwards Tones';
'Bacon Fat'; 'Badge'; 'Ballad Of Sir Frankie Crisp'; 'Baltimore
Oriole'; 'Bangla Desh'; 'Bangla Dhun'; 'Barbara Ann'; 'Beautiful
Girl'; 'Behind That Locked Door'; 'The Bells Of Rhymney'; 'Between
The Devil And The Deep Blue Sea'; 'Beware Of Darkness'; 'Blood
From A Clone'; 'Blow Away'; 'Blowin' In The Wind'; 'Blue Moon Of
Kentucky'; 'Blue Suede Shoes'; 'Born On The Bayou'; 'Brainwashed';
'Breath Away From Heaven'; 'Bridge Over Troubled Water'; 'Bye Bye
Love'.

C.
'Can't Stop Thinking About You'; 'Checkin' Up On My Baby'; 'Cheer
Down'; 'Circles'; 'Cloud 9'; 'Cockamamie Business'; 'Congratulations';
'Cool Dry Place'; 'Corinna, Corinna'; 'Cosmic Empire'; 'Cowboy
Music'; 'Crackerbox Palace'; 'Crosscut Saw'; 'Crying'; 'Cupid'.

D.
'Da Doo Ron Ron'; 'Dark Horse'; 'Dark Sweet Lady'; 'The Day The
World Gets 'Round'; 'Dear One'; 'Deep Blue'; 'Dehra Dun'; 'The
Devil's Been Busy'; 'Devil's Radio'; 'Ding Dong'; 'Dirty World';
'Dispute And Violence'; 'Distance Makes No Difference With Love';
'Dizzy Miss Lizzy'; 'Don't Bother Me'; 'Don't Let Me Wait Too Long';
'Don't Think Twice, It's Alright'; 'Down To The River'; 'Dream Away';
'Dream Scene'; 'Drilling A Home'; 'Drive My Car'.

E.

'End Of The Line'; 'Every Grain Of Sand'; 'Everybody, Nobody'; 'Everybody's Trying To Be My Baby'; 'Extra Texture (Read All About It)'.

F.

'Fantasy Sequins'; 'Far East Man'; 'Farther On Down The Road'; 'Faster'; 'Fish On The Sand'; 'Fishing Blues'; 'Flying Hour'; 'Focus Of Attention'; 'For You Blue'; 'Freedom'.

G.

'Gat Kirwani'; 'Gates Of Eden'; 'Get Back'; 'Ghost Riders In The Sky'; 'Give Me Love (Give Me Peace On Earth)'; 'Glad All Over'; 'Glass Box'; 'Going Down To Golders Green'; 'Gone Troppo'; 'Gone, Gone, Gone'; 'Got My Mind Set On You'; 'Greasy Legs'; 'Greece'; 'Grey Cloudy Lies'; 'Group Lesson'; 'Guru Vandana'.

H.

'Handle With Care'; 'Hari's On Tour (Express)'; 'Heading For The Light'; 'Hear Me Lord'; 'Here Comes Emerson'; 'Here Comes The Moon'; 'Here Comes The Sun'; 'Hey Bo Diddley'; 'His Name Is Legs'; 'The Holdup'; 'Homeward Bound'; 'Honey Don't Honey Hush'; 'Honey, Just Allow Me One More Chance'; 'Hong Kong Blues'; 'Hottest Gong In Town'; 'Hound Dog'.

I.

'I Am Missing You'; '(I Can't Get No) Satisfaction'; 'I Dig Love'; 'I Don't Believe You (She Acts Like We Have Never Met)'; 'I Don't Care Any More'; 'I Don't Want To Do It'; 'I Live For You'; 'I Really Love You'; 'I Remember Jeep'; 'I Saw Her Standing There'; 'I Threw It All Away'; 'I Want To Tell You'; 'I'd Have You Anytime'; 'I'll Still Love You'; 'If I Needed Someone'; 'If Not For You'; 'If You Believe'; 'If You Belonged To Me'; 'In My Life'; 'In The First Place'; 'In The Midnight Hour'; 'In The Park'; 'India'; 'Indus'; 'Inside Out'; 'Isn't It A Pity'; 'It Don't Come Easy'; 'It Is He' (Jai Sri Krishna)'; 'It Takes A Lot To Laugh, It Takes A Train To Cry'; 'It's All Too Much'; 'It's Johnny's Birthday'; 'It's What You Value'.

J.

'Jai Sri Kalij'; 'Johnny B. Goode'; 'Jumping Jack Flash'; 'Just For Today'; 'Just Like A Woman'; 'Just Like Tom Thumb's Blues'.

K.

'Knock On Wood'; 'Knockin' On Heaven's Door'.

L.

'La Bamba'; 'Las Vegas Blues'; 'Last Night'; 'Lay His Head'; 'Learning How To Love You'; 'Let It Be Me'; 'Let It Down'; 'Let It Roll'; 'Life

Itself'; 'The Light That Has Lighted The World'; 'Like A Rolling
Stone'; 'Like A Ship'; 'Living In The Material World'; 'The Lord Loves
The One (That Loves The Lord)'; 'Love Comes To Everyone'; 'Love
Minus Zero/No Limit'; 'Love Scene'; 'Lucille'; 'The Lumberjack Song'.

M.
'Mama, You've Been On My Mind'; 'Margarita'; 'Matchbox';
'Maxine'; 'Maya Love'; 'Microbes'; 'Miss O'Dell'; 'Mo'; 'Mother
Divine'; 'Mr Tambourine Man'; 'My Back Pages'; 'My Sweet Lord';
'Mystical One'.

N.
'Naderdani'; 'New Blue Moon'; 'Night Train To Memphis'; 'No Time
Or Space'; 'Nobody Loves You (When You're Down And Out)';
'Nobody's Child'; 'No Alone Anymore'; 'Not Guilty'; 'Nothing From
Nothing'; 'Nowhere To Go'.

O.
'Old Brown Shoe'; 'Old Love'; 'Om Hare Om'; 'On The Bed'; 'One
Too Many Mornings'; 'Ooh Baby (You Know That I Love You)'; 'Out
Of The Blue'; 'Outa-Space'.

P.
'Party Seacombe'; 'Peggy Sue'; 'Pete Drake And His Amazing Talking
Guitar'; 'Piggies'; 'The Pirate Song'; 'Pisces Fish'; 'Plug Me In'; 'Poor
House'; 'Poor Little Girl'; 'Prabhujee'; 'Pretending'; 'Private
Instruction'; 'Proud Mary'; 'Pure Smokey'.

R.
'Rainy Day Women No. 12 & 35'; 'Rattled'; 'Red Lady Too'; 'Ride Of
The Valkyries'; 'Ride Rajbun'; 'Rock Island Line'; 'Rockin' Chair';
'Roll Over Beethoven'; 'Run Of The Mill'; 'Run So Far'; 'Runaway'.

S.
'Sat Singing'; 'Save The World'; 'See Yourself'; '7 Deadly Sins';
'Shanghai Surprise'; 'She Caught The Katy'; 'She's My Baby'; 'Shelter
In Your Love'; 'Sign On The Window'; 'Simply Shady'; 'Singing Om';
'Sitar Demonstration'; 'Ski-ing'; 'So Sad'; 'Soft Touch'; 'Soft-Hearted
Hana'; 'Someplace Else'; 'Something'; 'Song To Woody'; 'Soundstage
Of Mind'; 'Sour Milk Sea'; 'Stand By Me'; 'Stop In The Name Of
Love'; 'Sue Me, Sue You Blues'; 'Swordfencing'.

T.
'Tabla And Pakavaj'; 'Take Me As I Am'; 'Taxman'; 'Teardrops'; 'Tears
Of The World'; 'Tell Me What Has Happened To You'; 'Thanks For
The Pepperoni'; 'That Is All'; 'This Kind Of Woman'; 'That Which I

Have Lost'; 'That's All Right (Mama)'; 'That's The Way God Planned It'; 'That's The Way It Goes'; 'That's What It Takes'; 'Think For Yourself'; 'This Guitar (Can't Keep From Crying)'; 'This Is Love'; 'This Song'; 'Time Passes Slowly'; 'Tired Of Midnight Blue'; 'Tom Cat'; 'True Love'; 'Try Some, Buy Some'; 'Tweeter And The Monkey Man'; '12 Bar Bali'; 'Twist And Shout'; 'Two-Faced Man'.

U.
'Unconsciousness Rules'; 'Under The Boardwalk'; 'Under The Mersey Wall'; 'Unknown Delight'.

V.
'Vachaspati'; 'Valentine'.

W.
'Wah-Wah'; 'Wake Up My Love'; 'Watching The River Flow'; 'Went To See The Gypsy'; 'What Is Life'; 'When Every Song Is Sung'; 'When We Was Fab'; 'Whenever'; 'While My Guitar Gently Weeps'; 'Who Can See It'; 'Whole Lotta Shakin' Goin' On'; 'Wailbury Twist'; 'Will It Go Round In Circles'; 'Willie And The Hand Jive'; 'Window, Window'; 'Woman Don't You Cry For Me'; 'Wonderful Tonight'; 'Wonderwall To Be Here'; 'The World Is Waiting For the Sunrise'; 'World Of Stone'; 'Wreck Of The Hesperus'; 'Writing's On The Wall'.

Y.
'Yesterday'; 'You'; 'You Took My Breath Away'; 'You're Gonna Need Somebody On Your Bond'; 'Youngblood'; 'Your Love Is Forever'; 'Your True Love'.

Z.
'Zig Zag'; 'Zoom, Zoom, Zoom'.

Religion And Spirituality

As a child George was baptised a Roman Catholic, but he didn't follow the faith too closely. In fact, he seemed quite antagonistic towards it once he had become inspired by Eastern religions.

He was to say, 'After communion, I was supposed to have confirmation, but I thought, "I'm not going to bother with that, I'll just confirm it later myself. From then on, I avoided the church, but every Thursday a kid would come round to herald the arrival of the priest. They'd go round all the streets, knock on the door and shout, "The Priest's coming!" And we'd all go, "Oh shit!" and run like hell up the stairs and hide. My mother would have to open the door and he'd say, "Ah, hello Mrs Harrison, it's nice to see you again, so it is. Eh beJesus." She'd stuff two half-crowns in his sweaty little hand and off he'd go to build another church or pub.'

But most religions need contributions to build their places of worship and George gave more than two half-crowns to the Krishna movement.

Eastern spirituality was becoming fashionable in the West during the 1960s and while George found a calling in his love of Eastern religions, his attacks on the Catholic Church proved contradictory. Don't the chants in the Catholic Church find their equivalent in the chants to Krishna?

When he sings 'You don't need no rosary beads or them books to read' in the song 'Awaiting On You All' from the *All Things Must Pass* album, he is criticising the Catholic Church with its rosary beads and holy books. Yet George read books on Eastern religions such as the *Bhagavad Gita*, which consolidated his beliefs, and he even donated thousands of pounds towards the *Krishna Book*, an English translation by Sri Prabhupada – and there were even the equivalent of rosary beads. George said, 'Oh, yeah. I have my beads. I remember when I first got them, they were just big knobby globs of wood, but now I'm very glad to say that they're smooth from chanting a lot. I find it's very good to be touching them. It keeps another one of the senses fixed on God. Beads really help in that respect.'

The beads of Krishna devotees comprise 108 beads, each representing a Hare Krishna mantra, which is repeated 16 times a day, amounting to a total of 1,729 'Hare Krishnas'.

George even criticised the Catholic taking of the wafer and wine in Communion, yet he praised the similar *prasadam* of the Krishna devotees, saying, 'Well, we should try to see God in everything, so it helps so much having the food to taste. Let's face it, if God is in everything, why shouldn't you taste Him when you eat? I think that prasadam is a very important thing. Krishna is God, so He's absolute: His name, His form, prasadam, it's all Him. They say the way to a man's heart is through his stomach, so if you can get to a man's spirit soul by eating, and it works, why not do it?

'The idea is that prasadam is the sacrament the Christians talk about, only instead of just being a wafer, it's a whole feast, really, and the taste is so nice – it's out of this world.'

George was also critical of the church raising money and talked of the Pope owning 51% of General Motors, adding, 'The stock exchange is the only thing he's qualified to quote us.' Yet he didn't balk when the Maharishi was discussing the Beatles placing 10–15% of their yearly earnings in a Swiss bank in his name, and he quite generously left millions in his will to the Krishna movement. Without funds religions have a hard time to survive in this material world!

After meeting Ravi Shankar he became interested in Indian music, but following visits to India and the knowledge he gained from certain recommended books (*Autobiography Of A Yogi* by Paramahansa Yogananda and the *Bhagavad Gita* particularly influenced him), he became devoutly interested in Indian religions, including Hinduism. His interests also stretched from Krishna to transcendental meditation and his influences increased due to the 'men from the East' he admired and learned from, including Shankar, the Marahishi Mahesh Yogi and Prabhupada.

On the trip to India to learn guitar in 1966, he read a book by Swami Vivekananda called *Raja Yoga*. He said: 'As soon as I read that, I thought, "That's what I want to know!" They tried to bring me up as a Catholic, and for me it didn't deliver. But to read, "Each soul is divine. The goal is to manifest that divinity," was very important to me.'

His interest in Krishna philosophy grew and he also began searching for spiritual enlightenment. The American Krishna convert Syamasundar Das said, 'George was always the one who was really sincere about trying to know God. This wasn't just a casual sort of curious intellectual enquiry but rather a deep, deep longing for the truth.'

George said, 'Through Hinduism I feel a better person. I just get happier and happier. I now feel for a fact that I am unlimited and I am now more in control of my physical body.'

Discussing his experiences meditating at Rishikesh he described it as: 'A slowing down of the thought process followed by a blinding acceleration of consciousness.' Later, he added, 'It's something to do with feeling really tiny. But at the same time I also felt I was a whole thing as well. It was like being two completely different things at the same time. Soon this feeling would begin to vibrate right through me and started getting bigger and bigger and faster and faster. Before I knew what was happening it was going so far and so fast it was mind-boggling and I'd come out of it really scared. I used to get that experience a lot when we were recording *Abbey Road*. I'd go into this big empty studio, get into a soundbox and do my meditation. It was here I had a couple of indications that this was the same thing I went through as a kid.

'Ravi is probably the person who has influenced my life the most. Maybe he's not aware of it, but I really love Ravi and he's been like a father as well as a spiritual guide. I got involved with Hinduism because Ravi Shankar was a Hindu. And I came to understand what Christ really was through Hinduism. Down through the ages there has always been a spiritual path, it's been passed on and it always will be. It just so happens that India was the place where the seed was planted.'

George also tried to explain the truths he learned from Indian philosophies, saying, 'The Vedic system is all about enlightenment, basically, and music is one of the vehicles to gain enlightenment.'

In some ways, George proved to be more articulate in interviews than either John or Paul. His beliefs can be detected in some of the quotes he made.

George was to say, 'I believe in reincarnation. You keep coming back until you get it straight. The ultimate thing is to manifest divinity and become one with the Creator.'

This is basically similar to karma, in which the life you lead will determine how high you rise in your next life, the basis being that one should achieve a greater spirituality with each sojourn on the earth. George will probably have to serve a few more terms because in this life he succumbed to drugs, extramarital affairs and materialism.

George was also to comment sagely, 'Many people think that life is predestined. I think it is vaguely, but it's still up to you, which way your life is going to go. All I've ever done is to keep being me and it's all just worked out.'

He was even able to say, 'We were made John, Paul, George and Ringo, because of what we did last time; it was all here for us, on a plate. We're reaping what we sowed in our past life, whatever it was. That's really all there is to it, squire.'

George always believed in an afterlife, which is why he was able to achieve a degree of peace when he passed on. Commenting on the death of Brian Epstein, George said, 'There is no such thing as death, only in the physical sense. Life goes on. The important thing is that he is OK now.'

When he was attacked at his home in Friar Park in 1999, George began chanting the Hare Krishna mantra. This is because of the part in the Bhagavad-Gita which states: 'Whoever, at the end of his life, quits his body remembering me alone, at once attains my nature. Of this there is no doubt.'

George made a secret pilgrimage to Varanasi in India three months before he died during which he bathed in sacred water and prayed at the temple.

Among those present when he died were Syamasundar Das and Mukunda Goswami. They quietly chanted and sprinkled holy water from the Ganges on George's head, also placing a *Tulsi* leaf between his lips and a wreath of *Tulsi* leaves around his neck while they hummed verses from the Bhagavad-Gita.

The website for the *Brainwashed* album contains the words: 'There can be no question about the depth of Harrison's spiritual convictions, and *Brainwashed* makes that clear yet again. In his final years, Harrison confronted the imminence of his death, and that experience provides the foundation of this album, though not in a luridly explicit, confessional way. It's more like the events of his last years lent an inevitable gravity to issues Harrison had pondered for decades. When mortality stopped being a philosophical problem, but could be felt every moment in the beat of his pulse, these are the songs that George Harrison wrote.'

Rising Sun

A track from the *Brainwashed* album lasting 5 minutes and 27 seconds, with George on lead vocals, slide guitar, acoustic guitar and background vocals. Jeff Lynne is on bass guitar, electric guitar and piano with Dhani Harrison on Wurlitzer and Jim Keltner on drums.

Rock And Roll Hall Of Fame

The Beatles were inducted at the third annual Rock And Roll Hall of Fame event at the Waldorf Astoria Hotel in New York on 20 January 1988. George, Ringo, Yoko Ono, Julian and Sean were in attendance, although Paul declined the invitation. There were 700 guests at a cost of $1,000 per plate.

Mick Jagger inducted the Beatles, saying, 'We thought we were totally unique animals. Then we heard there was a group from Liverpool! They had long hair, scruffy clothes, but they had a record contract – I was almost sick!'

George was to make a short speech during which he said, 'I don't have much to say 'cause I'm the quiet Beatle. It's unfortunate Paul's not here 'cause he was the one with the speech in his pocket. We all know why John can't be here, I'm sure he would be. It's hard, really, to stand here supposedly representing the Beatles. But . . . it's all what's left, I'm afraid. But we all loved him so much, and we all love Paul very much.'

Numerous musicians, including George and Ringo, participated in a jam session with numbers such as 'Twist And Shout', 'All Along The Watchtower', 'Stop, In The Name of Love', 'Whole Lotta Shakin' Going' On', 'Down On Bayou', 'Like A Rolling Stone' and 'I Can't Get No Satisfaction'. George sang and played guitar. Among the many celebrities present, a number of them participating in the jam, were Bruce Springsteen, Billy Joel, Mick Jagger, Jeff Lynne, Neil Young, Jeff Beck, Bob Dylan, Steve van Zandt, John Fogerty, Dave Edmunds and Les Paul.

Rockabilly Session – Carl Perkins And Friends, A

When the 53-year-old Carl Perkins was offered the opportunity of his own television special to celebrate the thirtieth anniversary of his song 'Blue Suede Shoes', he sent out a video invitation to a number of musicians, including all three former Beatles.

On it, he said, 'Hello, I'm Carl Perkins. A lot older, a lot fatter than when you last saw me. I would certainly love to do a TV special one time in my life, something I have never done. I would certainly love to have you be a part of it. If you're interested, sign the endorsed card and I'll put it together.'

The hope of having all three ex-Beatles disappeared when Paul turned him down, but George and Ringo accepted, leading Carl to say, 'Two out of three ain't bad, though. It was exciting to get that close to it. It's never too late. I'll try again.'

Paul's excuse that he was working on a new album didn't really stand up, but Carl said, 'All three just will not publicly play. There is a blockage there. And there are some reasons I don't know and the world doesn't know.'

George's returned card had read, 'Carl Perkins has been my hero since I was a kid. How could I refuse him anything?'

The special was screened on Channel Four on New Year's Day 1986. It was premiered in America on the Cinemax channel on 5 January 1986 and included songs edited out of the Channel Four special. Other musicians who had responded to the invitation were Eric Clapton, Dave Edmunds, Rosanne Cash, Slim Jim Phantom, Lee Rocker, Earl Slick and Greg Perkins (Carl's son). In addition, there were the members of Edmunds' band: John David, Mickey Gee, David Charles and Geraint Watkins.

There was a three-hour rehearsal on 19 October and the programme was taped on 21 October at the Limehouse Television Studios in Canary Wharf, London.

Members of the 250-strong audience when the show was filmed included Olivia Harrison, Denis O'Brien, Barbara Bach, Jason and Lee Starkey, Patti Clapton and Ringo's manager Hilary Gerard.

Perkins was to say, 'George really got excited because he hadn't played in front of an audience for so long. Before he went on, he was real nervous, and I felt him freein' up right after he walked up there and I pitched him a guitar break that he wasn't expecting. I could tell by the grin on his face that his fears were leaving.'

After the show, Carl said that Olivia came to his dressing room to tell him that George was happy. 'Carl, I don't know what to say to you, because I saw my old George so happy tonight, I saw something there that I hadn't seen in a long time.'

Together with the other musicians they went to Friar Park for a party, helping themselves to the guitars on the walls to play together until the early hours of the morning. Perkins even recalled that George suggested that they tour together and that they should do an album together, along with Dave Edmunds.

Perkins was later to admit that prior to the show he hardly knew George and Ringo. 'I had only seen these two one time in my life, in 1964. A lot of people think that we were close because they recorded my songs, but we were not.'

The show opened with some backstage footage of George and Ringo embracing and Carl Perkins then performed 'Boppin' The Blues' and 'Cat Clothes', backed by Dave Edmunds and his band. He then turned to Edmunds to say they need a drummer. Edmunds said, 'Well, Ritchie's here,' and Ringo joined them and took the lead vocal on 'Honey Don't', commenting, 'It's been a long time,' when the number finished. Eric Clapton then joined Carl and Ringo on 'Matchbox'. Ringo left while Perkins and Clapton duetted on 'Mean Woman Blues', then Carl performed a solo with 'Turn Around'.

Perkins next introduced Rosanne Cash, daughter of Johnny Cash, saying, 'I rocked this girl when she was a baby and I'd like to rock *with* her right now,' and Rosanne played 'What Kinda Girl'.

George then appeared and performed 'Everybody's Trying To Be My Baby' and was joined by Edmunds to back Perkins on 'Your True Love', during which George sang some lead vocal and played a solo.

Then the musicians gathered to join Perkins in a medley of 'That's Alright Mama' and 'Blue Moon Of Kentucky'.

The group of musicians then played 'Glad All Over', 'Whole Lotta Shakin''' and 'Gone Gone Gone'. The final number was 'Blue Suede Shoes'.

One of the numbers left out of the transmission was George's rendition of 'Sure To Fall'.

Rocking Chair In Hawaii

A track from the *Brainwashed* album lasting 3 minutes and 7 seconds with George on lead vocals, dobro slide guitar, acoustic guitar, ukulele, keyboard and background vocals. Jeff Lynne played bass and Jim Keltner drums.

Rockline

A radio show from the Global Satellite Network, based in Los Angeles, which is syndicated to 200 radio stations throughout America from its KLOS-FM studio.

Together with Jeff Lynne, George appeared on the show on Wednesday 10 February 1988.

George hadn't intended to perform on the show but when he was asked, a member of the production team offered to lend him a Gretsch guitar and George agreed on condition that he could keep the guitar for his own collection.

He and Lynne then gave an acoustic performance and played 'Drive My Car', 'Here Comes The Sun', 'The Bells Of Rhymney', 'Mr Tambourine Man', 'Take Me As I Am', 'That's Alright (Mama)', 'Let It Be Me', 'Something' and 'Every Grain Of Sand'.

During another *Rockline* interview George discussed HandMade Films' plans, saying there would be no more low-budget films as in the past. 'I think that kind of market is largely gone, and if we want to stay in the film business, I think we have to kind of follow the Hollywood thing.'

Rockspeak

A British BBC Radio 1 programme, which featured an interview with George, conducted by disc jockey Alan Freeman, on Friday 6 December 1974. The thirty-minute interview had been recorded at Apple's James Street office and was broadcast at 10 p.m. The interview was re-edited, renamed *Rock Around The World* and syndicated to American radio stations in September 1975 to promote George's album *Extra Texture (Read All About It)*.

Romanian Angel Appeal, The

A charity launched by Olivia Harrison in April 1990 after she read reports about an AIDS epidemic among infants in Romania. She enlisted the help of the other Beatles wives, Barbara, Linda and Yoko, who immediately raised $100,000.

She mentioned her appeal to George when he was recording with the Traveling Wilburys in Los Angeles and they donated the track 'Nobody's Child' to the proposed charity album, as did Dave Stewart and Elton John. The Material World Charitable Foundation collected the money and during the first couple of weeks £25,000 was raised.

During the first week in April Olivia went to Romania for three days to see how she could benefit the orphans.

George told the *Daily Mail* newspaper that he had responded to the appeal the only way he could, by donating music, saying, 'If you are a plumber you can plumb a sink; if you are a musician, you can write a song; if you are a mother you can nurse a child. Everyone can help the children of Romania in their own way.'

'Nobody's Child' was recorded within 24 hours of Olivia telling George about the appeal. It was a country music song that had originally been popularised in Britain by Lonnie Donegan and recorded by the Beatles as a backing band to Tony Sheridan in Hamburg in 1962. It became the first single issued from the charity album and had been recorded by George, Bob Dylan, Jeff Lynne and Tom Petty.

It was Dylan who had suggested the tune and George obtained the lyrics of the first verse by phoning Joe Brown in London. They couldn't remember the second verse, so George improvised, making the lyrics more relevant to the situation in Romania, with words such as: 'In every town and village there are places just like this/With rows and rows of children, babies in their cribs/ They've long since stopped crying, as no one ever hears/ And no one's here to notice them or take away their fears.'

George said, 'There are so many things in the world that need doing and so many people who need help. But what can be more important than taking care of children.'

There was a 12″ single of the number with Dave Stewart's 'Lumiere' on the B side, a Ringo Starr live recording of 'With A Little Help From My Friends' and the George and Paul Simon duet of 'Homeward Bound' from the 1976 *Saturday Night Live* show.

Other artists contributing to the compilation album *Nobody's Child Romania Angel Appeal*, released by Warner Brothers, included Elton John, Eric Clapton, Edie Brickell, Guns N' Roses, Stevie Wonder, Van Morrison, Mike & The Mechanics, Donovan, Billy Idol, Duane Eddy and Rick Ocasek.

Olivia was to say, 'The money raised went on supplies, not administrative costs, and we paid these ourselves.' Ten trucks, together with 32 volunteers, left for Romania on 10 May with food, clothing and medical supplies.

Rubber Soul

George had two of his compositions featured on this album, 'Think For Yourself' and 'If I Needed Someone'.

There were tensions between George and Paul even at this stage of their recording career. Engineer Norman Smith related to journalist Chris Salewicz: 'With *Rubber Soul* the clash between John and Paul was becoming obvious. Also, George was having to put up with an awful lot from Paul. We now had the luxury of four-track recording, so George would put his solo on afterward. But as far as Paul was concerned, George could do no right – Paul was absolutely finicky.

'So what would happen was that on certain songs Paul himself played the solos. I would wonder what the hell was going on because George would have done two or three takes, and to me they were really quite OK. But Paul would be saying, "No, no, no!" And he'd start quoting American records, telling him to play exactly as he'd heard on such-and-such a song. So we'd go back from the top, and George would really get into it. Then would come Paul's comment, "OK, the first sixteen bars weren't bad, but that middle . . ." Then Paul would take over and do it himself – he always had a left-handed guitar with him.

'Subsequently, I discovered that George Harrison had been hating Paul's bloody guts for this, but it didn't show itself.'

Run Of The Mill

A track from the *All Things Must Pass* album lasting 2 minutes and 51 seconds.

When asked about the inspiration for the song on a web chat, George replied, 'There was an expression that came from Yorkshire where they made fabric. Run of the mill just means average. I was using that phrase more or less because the Beatles were just splitting up. I don't know if they had that expression in America.'

Run So Far

A track on the posthumous *Brainwashed* album, which was originally included on Eric Clapton's 1989 album *Journeyman*, with George featured on the track on guitar and vocals.

Rutland Weekend Television

On Saturday 13 December 1975, George recorded a Boxing Day edition of *Rutland Weekend Television* at the BBC Television Centre in Wood Green. The programme was 31 minutes in length and George appeared as a pirate called Bob. The programme also featured 'The Pirate Song', penned by George and Eric Idle.

San Remo Music Festival
A major annual Italian musical festival. George attended the festival on Friday 26 February 1988 where he was presented with an award for 'Video Of The Year' for 'When We Was Fab'. He appeared on stage for eleven minutes and while at the festival was to give some brief interviews to Italian television channels. In the evening he returned to Britain.

He was unaware that Paul McCartney was appearing at the festival the following day to perform with his new band. Neither did Paul know that George was appearing the day before him. Despite this, and the fact that they weren't present at San Remo at the same time, the *News Of The World* published a story claiming the two of them had a row at the festival.

Sat Singing
A number George wrote in 1979 and produced and recorded at Friar Park in March 1980, ostensibly for his *Somewhere In England* album. Originally it was set to be the opening track of side two, but a Warner Bros executive was unhappy with the finished master of *Somewhere In England* and ordered it to be reworked. George was furious, but wrote some further tracks while on holiday in Hawaii, replacing 'Sat Singing'.

The number was eventually issued on a four-track CD enclosed with the Genesis Publication *Songs By George Harrison* on 15 February 1988.

Saturday Night Live
An NBC television show. George recorded several songs for the show on Friday 19 November 1976 at Studio 8-H, 30 Rockefeller Plaza, New York.

On the eve of the show, during a press conference in the Dolly Madison Room of the Madison Hotel in Washington, George discussed his forthcoming appearance on *Saturday Night Live* and said he was aware of producer Lorne Michaels running joke of a $3,000 offer for the Beatles to appear.

He said, 'Part of it's on film, but I've got to sing some old tunes with Paul Simon. You know, I look forward to being on the show, except, unfortunately, I don't have time to rehearse anything. So God knows what we're going to do. Maybe Paul and I will do a tune on acoustics, because we can't rehearse with a band. I've got to do one of them tomorrow at lunchtime and then go straight down there and do it – I'm taping it tomorrow, 'cause I leave on the following day, Friday.'

He did acoustic performances of 'Here Comes The Sun' and 'Homeward Bound'. The promotional films for 'Crackerbox Palace' and 'This Song' were also shown. When George appeared with Paul Simon, the two recorded 'Bye Bye Love', 'Don't Let Me Wait Too Long', 'Yesterday', 'Bridge Over Troubled Water', 'Rock Island Line' and 'Flight Of The Valkyries'.

George was promoting his latest album *Thirty Three & 1/3* at the time and at the beginning of the show, which was broadcast the following day, he is seen asking produced Lorne Michaels if he could have the $3,000 which Michaels had promised for a Beatles reunion. Michaels told him, 'If it was up to me, you could have the money. But NBC wouldn't agree.'

Save The World

A number George wrote which was included on the *Somewhere In England* album, lasting 4 minutes and 54 seconds. George was to alter the number slightly four years later, adding some different lyrics to give Greenpeace a namecheck and remixing the track for the A&M compilation *Greenpeace*, released in June 1985.

Savoy Truffle

A number composed by George, which was included on *The Beatles* double album. It is 2 minutes and 52 seconds in length. Eric Clapton had inspired the number. George recalled, 'At the time he had a lot of cavities in his teeth and needed dental work. He always had toothache but he ate a lot of chocolates. He was over at my house and I had a box of 'Good News' chocolates on the table and wrote the song from the names on the lid.'

The number was recorded at Trident Studios on 3 October 1968 with overdubbing on 5, 11 and 14 October. In addition to the Beatles, there were some session musicians featured on the number playing two baritone and four tenor saxes.

Scott, Tom

A composer, arranger, producer, musician director and saxophonist who has been guest artist on over 500 recordings by major names, has composed the soundtrack music to films such as *Conquest Of The Planet Of The Apes* and *Stir Crazy* and TV shows such as *Starsky And Hutch*, *Cannon* and *Streets Of San Francisco* and has contributed to soundtracks of movies such as *Taxi Driver*, *Blade Runner* and *Toy Story 2*. He has been nominated for twelve Grammys and awarded two.

Scott had originally studied Indian music at high school under Harihar Rao, a former pupil of Ravi Shankar. Under his tutelage Scott spent a year studying Indian music.

When Ravi Shankar was commissioned to write the score for *Charlie*, a film with Cliff Robertson, he asked Harihar Rao if he could find him an orchestra of musicians who knew about Indian music – and one of those selected by Rao was Scott.

He was then asked to work on the album *Shankar, Family & Friends*, which George produced in 1974, and the same year was invited to take part in the *Dark Horse* tour.

He has also appeared on the albums *Extra Texture*, *Dark Horse*, *Thirty Three & 1/3* and *Somewhere In England* and was credited as assistant producer on the *George Harrison* album.

He was actually to take on the task of producer or co-producer on the *George Harrison* album, but soon after recordings began George contracted hepatitis and recordings were suspended for a while, so Scott returned to America and was therefore only credited as assistant producer.

Having made so many recordings at Friar Park, George then asked him to produce Splinter's second album *Harder To Live* for Dark Horse. George had originally produced one track, 'Lonely Man', and then asked Scott to complete the production of the album.

He has also appeared on albums by Ringo Starr and Paul McCartney, providing the sax solo on 'Listen To What The Man Said' on the *Venus And Mars* album.

George was also a guest on one of Scott's own albums, *New York Connection* in 1975. When Tom was recording the album in Los Angeles he heard that George was in town, phoned him and George agreed to play on the album, modestly telling Scott, 'You know, I'm not a real musician. I didn't really have any schooling or formal training.'

See Yourself

A number originally composed in 1967 in response to the media attacks on Paul McCartney's statements about LSD. George felt the media were hypocritical. At the time he didn't finish off the number but he eventually completed and recorded it in 1976 for his *Thirty Three &*

1/3 album. The number, which is the last track on side one, is 2 minutes and 47 seconds in length.

George was to say, 'Everybody who goes back and remembers that period will know that there was a big story in the press where somehow they'd found out – they'd heard that Paul had taken the *dreaded LSD*. And he said, "Well, look, whatever I say I'm going to tell the truth. And whatever I say I just want you to know that it's *you*, the media who are going to the people, who spread what I say."

'And they were saying, "Did you take it?" and he said, "Yes, I took it." And they put it all over the papers "Paul McCartney, etc." Then they all came after us all, saying "Have you had it? Have you had it?" And I said, "Sure, we had it years ago." But then there was an outcry saying, "You should have said you didn't take it." In effect they were saying, "You should have told a lie." They pushed the responsibility onto him for saying, "You're going to influence other people to take it." And he'd said out front that "it's going to be *your* responsibility, whatever I say."

'And so I just thought of that. "It's easier to tell a lie than it is to tell the truth." And off we go. "It's easier to criticise somebody else than to see yourself." Because people won't accept responsibility for themselves. And it's very often that we all, and I'm included, point our fingers at people and criticise or pass judgement on others, when first what we should do is try and see ourselves.'

Sgt Pepper's Lonely Hearts Club Band

Along with *Abbey Road*, an album that has one of the most identifiable cover images ever. George only had a single composition on the album, 'Within You, Without You'.

The galaxy of famous figures featured on that cover were not entirely the Beatles' own choices. Many of the characters selected by John and Paul weren't used, and a large number of the characters were chosen by Robert Fraser, an art gallery owner, and artist Peter Blake.

However, George's choices of four Indian yogis were included. Sri Yukteswar Giri was the author of 'The Holy Science', a treatise that dealt with the underlying unity of the Bible and the Hindu scriptures. He was also Sri Yogananda's guru. Sri ParamahansaYogananda was the person instrumental in introducing Indian thought and practice to America, being the first great Indian master to live in the West. He was also the author of *Autobiography Of A Yogi*, a book that so impressed George that he gave a copy to Henry Kissinger. George was to dedicate two songs on his *Thirty Three & 1/3* album to the Yogi – 'Dear One' and 'See Yourself'. The other yogis were Sri Lahiri Mahasaya and Sri Mahavatara Babaji.

John Lennon had chosen Mahatma Ghandi and a stand-up cut-out figure of him was already set up in the studio when EMI's Sir Joseph Lockwood arrived to see how the cover was progressing. He immediately banned the figure of Ghandi as he felt it might cause offence in India, one of EMI's major markets.

This seems a strange decision in the light of a group of George's Indian holy men appearing on the cover.

Shanghai Surprise (film)

A HandMade film that was the cause of a great deal of press coverage and controversy because it starred husband-and-wife team Madonna and Sean Penn. There were tales of disagreements on the set and George eventually had to set up and attend a press conference in an attempt to cool down the press speculation. Despite the ' major publicity, the film was a relative box-office flop.

It was premiered in New York on Tuesday 26 August 1986. George wrote some songs for the film and also composed the musical score with Michael Kamen, although he abandoned the idea of issuing a film soundtrack. However, five of his compositions were included in the soundtrack of the movie itself: 'Shanghai Surprise', 'Hottest Gong In Town', 'Someplace Else', 'Breath Away From Heaven' and 'Zig Zag'. 'Someplace Else' and 'Breath Away From Heaven' were later to surface on the *Cloud Nine* album.

In addition to the tracks he also co-wrote the film's incidental music with Michael Kamen.

He also made a cameo appearance in the movie and is glimpsed performing 'Hottest Gong In Town'.

The British premiere was on 17 October 1986.

There was also a 48-minute documentary on the making of the film called *Handmade In Hong Kong*, which included interviews with George and footage of him recording the movie soundtrack. Madonna and Sean Penn attempted to prevent its transmission on television. When they were unsuccessful they insisted on cuts being made, but George overruled them and it was screened in Britain on Channel 4 on Tuesday 7 October 1986 without any cuts.

Shanghai Surprise (press conference)

Here is a transcript of the press conference, which George and Madonna held in London on 6 March 1986.

George: Good afternoon. On behalf of us both and HandMade Films, welcome. I'd like to ask for maybe a bit of order. Whoever wants to ask a question, maybe you could say your name, what newspaper you're from, and also your intentions at the next general election.

Question: Madonna, what kind of boss is George Harrison and were you a Beatlemaniac?

Madonna: I wasn't a Beatlemaniac. I don't think I really appreciated their songs until I was much older. I was too young to really get caught up in the craze. But he's a great boss, very under-standing and sympathetic.

Question: What sort of advice has he given you?

Madonna: I think he's given me more advice on how to deal with the press than how to work in the movie.

Question: Is it fun working with your husband, Sean Penn?

Madonna: Of course it is. He's a pro. He's worked on several films and his experience has helped me.

Question: Has it caused any personal problems off set, do you argue at all?

George: Do you row with your wife?

Question: George, is it true you are playing a cameo role in the film?

George: Well, yes and no, really. There is one scene in a night-club with a band playing in the background, and because I'm writing the music to the film I decided it would be easier if I was the singer in the band.

Question: Mr Harrison, are you confident that this film is going to be as successful?

George: I think so, yeah.

Question: It seems as though it's a more ambitious film than *A Private Function*.

George: Well, it is certainly a larger budget film than *A Private Function*, but it's totally different to any of the previous films we've made. It's a sort of adventure film, slightly humorous. I think it's actually a very good-looking film. This will be the thing in the end because there has been so much written in the papers that has absolutely nothing to do with what the film is about, and these two people have spent the last couple of months working on this thing.

Question: George, when you hired Mr Penn, did you think that there would be ... let's face it, this film is surrounded by a lot of hype.

George: Well, you're the people who create the hype, let's not get that wrong.

Question: What I'm saying is, did you expect the sort of coverage you're getting?

George: I did expect a certain amount of commotion from the press, but I must admit I overestimated your intelligence.

Question: George, there's been a lot of reports that you've had to personally separate the warring factions on the set. Do you think this will affect the film adversely, and would you work with Sean Penn again?

George: Sure. I happen to like Sean very much because I don't see him like you. I see him as an actor who we hired and the role that he plays, and has played in the past – which is one of the reasons we chose him – is of a feisty young guy. That said, he's actually a human being who's very nice, and he's a talented actor. You just have to separate the two things, his job and his ability to do it and the sensationalism because he happened to marry Madonna.

Question: Why isn't Mr Penn here at this conference?

George: Because he's busy working.

Madonna: He's in more scenes than I am.

Question: Would some of the commotion have been cut down a bit if the original press conference hadn't been cancelled? Isn't this just one of the old Hollywood ways of getting publicity?

George: The press conference was postponed because after we returned from Hong Kong the schedule had to be reorganised and, let's face it, we're here to make a film, not to hold press conferences.

Question: One of the people from HandMade told me that the reason they cancelled it was that after the scene at the airport they didn't feel like giving the press an even break. Is that true?

George: Well, maybe that's true as well. I can't speak for whoever said that, you'll have to ask them. The purpose of this is to try and clarify some situation. I can see the attitude written all over your face. There's no actual point in you asking anything because you've already predetermined what it is you're going to say. I'd like to ask if there's anybody who is actually honest. That's what we want, a bit of honesty. Because if you want the truth, you'll get it. But I don't suppose that some people here are actually capable of recognising it when they see it.

Question: George, what do you think of the so-called British film revival? Did you see *Letter To Brezhnev* and do you have any plans to film in Liverpool?

George: Well, actually, *Letter To Brezhnev* resurrected my original belief in the character of the Liverpool people. It's a fantastic example of how someone with no money and no hope can actually get through that. I think it's fabulous. I've not spent a great deal of time in Liverpool over the years, but I'm happy to say that the film has revitalised my image of Liverpool people. I think the British Film Year was a good idea, just to try and stimulate more interest from the public. I think to a degree it helped a lot.

Question: Madonna, will you be singing on the soundtrack at all?

Madonna: I'm not really thinking about the musical aspects of the movie, I'm just trying to concentrate on the acting.

George: At this point I'm doing the music. If she wants to she's welcome, but she wasn't hired as a musician.

Question: Madonna, I wonder if either you or your husband would like to apologise for incidents which have involved bad behaviour on your behalf?

Madonna: I have nothing to apologise for.

George: I would add to that. Everything that's been written in the papers has been started by someone in the press, either the press photographer that sat on the hood of the car or the woman from the radio station who broke in and also the appalling behaviour of the journalist who actually stole photographs from the continuity woman. So there's nothing to apologise for. I think certain elements of the press should apologise and at the same time I hope that all of them who do have intelligence will recognise that they're not the ones who have made us angry.

Question: Do you think that situation has been antagonised by the enormous amount of security that's being used?

Madonna: We don't have an enormous amount of security.

Question: There is today.

George: Yes, today. If you'd been with us in the car trying to get in here, you'd realise it's like a bunch of animals. Absolute animals. Do you just want us to get torn apart and beaten up? Because that's really what those people are like.

Question: You must have realised what the British press are like. Do you regret shooting the last few weeks here rather than in the States?

George: It's a British film. You know, if you like we'll all go to Australia and make our movies there in the future. We'd like to make them in England. We'd like to be reasonable and we'd like you to be reasonable because it doesn't do anyone . . . I think in a way certain of the press have actually got in the way. You would have achieved more if you had a different attitude.

Question: But big stars come over here and make films perfectly well.

George: You know it's *you*, the press, who decide how big you want the stars to be. Let's face it, stars are actually people, human beings who have become famous for one thing or another and that is usually encouraged by the press to the point where the only thing left to do is to knock them. It's a historical fact and it's unfortunate that she happens to be going through that at this time.

Question: Surely it was worse in the sixties?

George: It was worse because it was a new experience to me. But now I don't give a damn what you say about me, because I know who I am and I know what I feel and I know you can't get me any more. The press can't get me. You can write your snide little things about me, but ultimately I'm all right. I know I'm all right. I don't care about those kind of snide remarks. I care about the truth.

Question: You depend on the media for publicity. Without the publicity no one would go to your films. So what are you standing there saying we're wrong to be here for?

George: I didn't say you were wrong to be here. I was just

making a point: he asked, 'Is it any different from the sixties?' and I said, 'Well, in the sixties it was a new experience for me, but now I've been through so much I've learned how to deal with it.' I didn't say anything about what you said.

Question: We have had loads of film stars over here, but have never had these sort of fights.

Madonna: When Robert De Niro comes to the airport, are there twenty photographers that sit on his limousine and don't allow him to leave the airport?

George: Those people, let's face it, are big stars but they're not news.

Question: But I've never seen scenes like this.

George: Yes, but it's been created by the press. All those photographers are out there to get as many pictures as they can because they sell them to everybody. They make money out of it and because she's hot they're trying to make as much money as they can.

Question: But that's why you hired her.

George: Yes, but we expected non-animals. You're all quite nice now, aren't you?

Question: Talking of animals, is it true that Sean Penn has been on the set giving orders . . .

George: What kind of introduction is that? That doesn't even deserve an answer.

Question: What about the incident at the airport?

George: That was the press jumping all over the car.

Question: It wasn't the press that were at fault, there were two other people who got involved who were plain-clothes detectives and they shouldn't have been involved.

George: But nevertheless he was trying to jump on the front of the car as it drove away. What do you expect? Whatever the facts, it is still something which doesn't really justify the amount of attention it's been given.

Question: How do the naked scenes fit into the film?

George: It's not that kind of movie.

Madonna: There are no naked women in the movie.

George: Lots of naked men, though!

Question: Madonna, do you care what's said about you in the press?

Madonna: I think what George meant was that he doesn't feel it any more when bad things are written about him.

George: I don't particularly want you to say more nasty things, but I've learned not to read them. It's just water off a duck's back. Otherwise we would all be ulcerated, wouldn't we? The sad thing is that people have got brains in their heads and maybe we should just try and use some of the other cells in our brains rather than the ones that are just to do with all this sensational stuff.

Question: What's your favourite scene in the movie?

George: I like it when she kills the monster from outer space!

Question: What state of production are the other current HandMade titles in?

George: We've got a number of films in the making, because we've been able to break even, or have been able to come up with the funding for certain films. Some of them are scripts that are being worked on. Others are in the casting stage. For instance, there's a film called *Travelling Man*, which has been in pre-production for a number of years.

Question: When did you first become aware of Madonna?

George: I don't know. A couple of years ago.

Madonna: When he wrote 'Lady Madonna'!

Question: Were you aware of her records?

George: Sure, I was aware of her with all the TV, videos and stuff. The first time I heard her was on the radio when I heard her singing something about 'living in the material world'.

Question: Madonna, I heard your management contract is up for sale. And George, would you like to buy it?

George: You're a little troublemaker, aren't you?

Question: Was this film written for Madonna and Sean Penn?

George: It wasn't. It was taken from a book called *Farraday's Flowers* and the producer wrote the screenplay. We talked about various possibilities for the casting and someone suggested Madonna. Apart from the fact that everyone knew she was a famous singer, if you saw *Desperately Seeking Susan* you know even Barry Norman agrees that there was some potential there. She got the screenplay, and Sean Penn, who had also worked with John Combs, the producer, on a couple of other films, read the screenplay and said that he would do it too. It was quite a coincidental thing. It wasn't any sort of huge plot to get these newly-wed people; I don't think they had even got married then. In a commercial sense, it was obviously good to have her in it because it's better than having someone nobody has ever heard of. But the rest of it was just luck. But I mean, lots of our films do have people no one's heard of. It's not any policy.

Question: How many actresses had you seen for the part?

George: I'm not too sure of that. I wasn't in the country at the time. There were obviously other considerations; I know there were for Sean's part. But there's no point in me giving you a list of people who I thought would play the part well.

Question: What are your responsibilities as executive producer?

George: Well, really, the part I've played in the past was to provide the film unit with the money, and apart from that, if there's any comment I would like to make on the screenplay or the casting. It varies from film to film. Some films I have very little to do with and others, like this one, I have a lot to do with. But there's no other way around it on this one because originally I was just going to do the music, but I got dragged in much more than I would normally. Usually I like a low-profile existence and it's been years since I got involved in the newspapers like this.

Question: George, are you happy with the progress of the film despite any difficulties you've had?

George: Whatever difficulties there have been are all behind us. I hope this press conference will help us to calm things down a little. I'm very pleased with what I'm seeing on the screen, which is the main thing. That's all I want, to get them to be able to complete shooting with the least problems.

Question: Is it true that there have been problems between director Jim Godard and Sean Penn?

Madonna: No, it's not true. ·

George: No more than in any other film, you know. Every film has discussions and debates as to how it should proceed.

Question: Do you tell the director to change camera angles?

Madonna: I don't tell anyone anything and neither does Sean.

George: I think most people look through the camera, because when you're on the other side it's handy to know what is actually in and out of the shot.

Question: Did you say it's been a great many years since you held a press conference?

George: Me, personally, yeah. I think 1974 was the last time I did anything like this. I just do gardening, you know. I like the nice quiet life.

Question: Despite it all, Madonna, are you happy?

Madonna: I am.

George: That's about it, thank you.

Madonna: We're not such a bad bunch of people are, we? Bye.

Shanghai Surprise (song)
A number penned by George as the theme song for the 1986 HandMade movie starring Madonna and Sean Penn. George recorded the number with Vicki Brown, the wife of musician Joe Brown. Vicki, the former Vicki Haseman, had been a member of the Vernons Girls and the Breakaways in the 1960s.

He'd planned issuing it as a single, but due to the bad performance of the film, the single was cancelled.

Shankar, Ravi
The most famous exponent of sitar playing in the West was born Ronindra Shankar in Varanasi (Benares), India on 7 April 1920. He was the youngest of five sons.

At the age of ten he moved to Paris with his brother Uday, who had a company of Hindu musicians and dancers there.

Ravi began his studies on the sitar at the age of eighteen in Maihar, India under the noted guru of Hindu classical music, Baba Allauddin Khan. Ravi married Baba's daughter Annapurna Devi in 1941.

Shankar was noted for his raga-based repertoire, appearing in concerts alongside musicians such as violinist Yehudi Menuhin, composer Philip Glass, flautist Jeanne-Pierre Rampal, jazz saxophonist Bud Shank and composers Zubin Mehta and Andre Previn.

George called him 'The Godfather of World Music', although that was also the title Tim White of *Billboard* magazine dubbed on George. In an interview in April 1972, Ravi commented, 'To me, he is like a son, like a younger brother, like a disciple all combined together. I have a very great love and affection for him.'

George said, 'After "Norwegian Wood" I met Ravi Shankar at a friend's house in London for dinner. He offered to give me instructions in the basics of the sitar, like how to sit, how to hold it, and the basic exercises. It was the first time I had ever really learned music with a bit of discipline. Then I started to listen to Indian music for the next two years, and hardly touched the guitar, except for recordings. Having all these material things, I wanted something more. And it happened that at just the time I wanted it, it came to me in the form of Ravi Shankar, Indian music and the whole Indian philosophy.'

They had met in 1965 at an Asian Music Circle dinner in London. Ravi was 45 years old at the time. He was then invited to the Harrison house in Claremont Drive, Esher to give him sitar lessons. Ravi brought along the noted tabla drummer Alla Rakah and George had invited John Lennon and Ringo Starr along. Ravi was pleased to perform for the small gathering of musicians and said, 'I felt very happy with my music and my little audience responded very warmly as we played.'

Ravi was invited to give George further lessons and he had had to explain to him, 'You must undergo many long years of study and practice of the basics before you play a single note properly.'

Ravi was surprised George had such a deep interest in music, philosophy and a spiritual quest and was pleased to discover that he loved Indian culture.

He said, 'The only solid lessons on sitar he had from me was in the summer and autumn of 1966, which he couldn't pursue as much as we both wanted. He was very talented and would have become a good sitar player if only he could have given some time.'

In 1995, Ravi was to say, 'When George came to me as a student in the 1960s, there was what I can only call an explosion in my life. My music became very popular and for many musicians I became a guru. Because of the drug scene it was a very difficult period. For me the sanctity of music is all – I have never needed drugs – and my energy went into telling young people that they didn't need them either. Rock stars came to me to learn, but George stood out from all of them.'

Discussing George in an interview with Don Heckman of the *LA Times* when promoting his *Chants Of India* CD, Shankar commented, 'In the beginning, when we met back in 1966, I found him very immature, naturally, because he was very young then. But still he had tremendous passion in wanting to know about India, Indian yogis, Indian music, Indian philosophy, Indian food and all that. And through the years, I thought, you know, this too shall pass. But I introduced him to this book *Autobiography Of A Yogi* by Paramahansa Yogananda, and that put him on a serious approach. Then he tried himself with Maharishi Mahesh Yogi and the Krishna people, but he always came back to me through music. In fact, it is mainly through music that I pushed him further and further, and today I find him to be so much into it, more than ever before – not in a superficial manner, but deeply into it. To me, George is, I don't know how to describe it, a son, a friend, someone very dear, and I love him very much. He has given me so much love and respect that my heart is full of it.'

Ravi, who has been given an honorary knighthood by Queen Elizabeth II, lives in Encinitas, California with his second wife Sukanya and their daughter Anoushka, who was born in London, who has become a famous musician in her own right.

From the time George first met Ravi, there have been many collaborations, including the film *Raga*, based on Ravi's first book *My Music, My Life*. George also produced the soundtrack to the film. George signed him to the Apple label where he co-produced his album *In Concert 1972*, and played on Ravi's album *Shankar, Family and Friends*. He also produced the 1975 album *Music Festival From India* and continued to be involved in various recordings such as *In Celebration* and *Chants Of India*. George also edited Ravi's Genesis book *Raga Mala*.

A major event that evolved from their friendship was the groundbreaking *Concert For Bangla Desh*. Ravi also appeared on George's 1974 North American tour.

Sheene, Barry

The legendary motorcycle racer, born in London in 1950.

George originally met him in 1977 at Long Beach, California. Sheene spotted George strolling around the garages and introduced himself. The two then began a long friendship that lasted until George's death.

George travelled to Thames Television Studios in Euston Road, London on Wednesday 25 January 1978 to appear as a surprise guest on *This Is Your Life*, this edition being a tribute to the racer. George declared his admiration for Sheene, and related how Barry had persuaded John Surtees to let him drive a circuit at Brands Hatch, but he also said, 'Before I met him, I thought Barry was a bit of a Midland Banker.' This is rhyming slang for 'wanker', but the show's host Eamonn Andrews misunderstood what George had said and asked his researchers why they hadn't told him that George had once been employed at the Midland Bank!

Regarding the incident at Brands Hatch, it was Sheene who took George along to try out John Surtees' supercharged TS19. At the time there was a need to wear fireproof clothing because of accidents that had occurred in Formula One racing.

George recalled, 'Barry persuaded John Surtees to let me have a go. But John said, "He's got no gear." So Barry rips off his fireproof vest and says to me, "Here you are, you can wear this." I just slipped on this sweaty old thing and borrowed John's crash helmet, got in the car and said, "I'm not going to go fast because I haven't even walked around Brands Hatch, let alone driven around!" So he said, "Oh, shit, you had better get in the road car."

'Well, we went bombing off round the track in his Mercedes and he was saying things like, "Keep it over to the left here; make sure the tail doesn't flick out too much here, fourth here," and so on. I was just hanging on for dear life. I got in the F1 car and thought, "Now, what did he say?" Then, while I was pulling away in the pit lane, trying not to stall it, I was thinking, "God, it's windy in the car." I hadn't even remembered to close my visor. It was like, wow, those wheels just dig in round the corners. I didn't go very fast. I just signed the chitty saying that if I killed myself, it wasn't John's fault.'

George was said to have once offered Sheene $280,000 *not* to take up Formula One racing, as he thought it too dangerous for him.

Sheene had his first drive in a Grand Prix car at Brands Hatch in August 1977 with George looking on. Once he did take up Grand Prix racing, George supported him and joined the Sheene camp at the French Grand Prix.

He actually wrote a song about Sheene, although he never recorded it. He did include a dedication to Barry on his 1979 album *George Harrison*.

Following the attack on George by Michael Abram with Olivia coming to the rescue, Sheene commented, 'Olivia is a martial arts expert and a real brave lady.' When George died he wrote in his regular *Bike* magazine column: 'If anybody could make a laugh of it, it's George, so I'm sure he's having fun wherever he is.'

Sheene himself died of cancer on 10 March 2003.

Shelter In Your Love

An unreleased song, one of several that George and Alvin Lee co-wrote in December 1985. George made a studio demo of the number which has since appeared on a number of bootleg albums.

Simmonds, Kathy

British model and actress who appeared in the movie *The Touchables* as one of a quartet of girls who kidnap a pop idol and imprison him in a plastic, see-through dome. Robert Freeman, the photographer whose photographs were to appear on Beatles albums, directed the film.

Kathy had had an affair with Rod Stewart and next had an affair with Harry Nilsson. A photo of her appears on the gatefold sleeve of Nilsson's album, *A Little Touch Of Nilsson In The Night*.

During 1974, when George and Patti's marriage was in difficulty, with Patti having an affair with Eric Clapton, George began an affair with Kathy.

The two of them spent several weeks together in a villa at St George's Bay in Grenada. Kathy believed that the romance was serious. Then George suddenly left her, flying to Los Angeles to discuss his forthcoming American tour.

Rather than the beginning of a long-term relationship, it had turned out to be a short-term affair.

Simon, Paul

A major American singer-songwriter, who was originally part of the duo Simon & Garfunkel, before turning solo.

On 19 November 1976 George and Paul recorded two numbers together for the NBC programme *Saturday Night Live*. They sat on stools, side by side, and performed 'Homeward Bound' and 'Here Comes The Sun'.

In 1990, when Olivia became involved in the plight of the Romanian orphans, she phoned George to ask for his help. He immediately began planning a charity album, which was released as *Nobody's Child* and began phoning his friends for their participation.

He recalled, 'I rang Paul Simon who was right in the middle of an album which he's been working on for so long but he said, "I don't really have the time." So I said, "If you can't do it, I understand, but remember we did that *Saturday Night Live*. When we played together? Do you have any objections to me using the version we did of 'Homeward Bound' on that?"

'We'd done "Here Comes The Sun" as well but I was fairly conscious of not making it my album.'

Simon visited George at Friar Park in October 2000. George took him round the estate showing him his gardens and in the evening, after dinner, George performed a miniconcert for him playing Hawaiian music on several ukuleles.

Simply Shady

A track on the 1974 *Dark Horse* album lasting 4 minutes and 35 seconds. George penned the number in India and was inspired by his split with Patti.

Simpsons, The

George provided the voice-over for his own appearance in the highly successful cartoon series *The Simpsons*. His brief appearance took place in episode 9F21, which was premiered in America on the Fox TV network on Thursday 30 September 1993.

The episode was entitled 'Homer's Barbershop Quartet'.

It was scripted by Jeff Martin who said, 'It was an easy episode to write. We essentially presented a compressed history of the Beatles.'

The Simpsons are at a 'swap meet' and among the items on Marge's booth is her painting of Ringo (from the episode where Ringo had a cameo). Bart and Lisa rummage through a batch of old records and come across *Meet The Be-Sharps*, which has a picture of their dad on the cover.

Homer recalls his youthful days in the Be-Sharps, a barbershop vocal group with himself, Principal Skinner, Apu and Chief Wiggum.

The quartet are discovered by a British agent, Nigel, who takes them over and decides Chief Wiggum can't really sing too well and replaces him with Barney, Homer's drinking buddy. He also decides that Apu's last Indian name Nahasapemapetalon is too long.

When the group are trying to find a name for themselves, Principal Skinner says, 'We've got to have something that's funny at first, but less funny each time you hear it.'

They record 'Baby On Board' and Nigel enters the studio saying, 'Gentlemen, you've just made your first number one.' He also suggests to Homer that he keeps his marriage to Marge a secret.

Arriving at Kennedy Airport they are besieged by fans. One reporter asks, 'Principal Skinner, you've been referred to as the funny one. Is that true?' 'Yes. Yes it is,' says Skinner – and everyone breaks out in hysterics.

The group win a Grammy award for their *Meet The Be-Sharps* album, presented to them by David Crosby.

In the after-the-ceremony party, Homer briefly meets George.

George: Hello, Homer, I'm George Harrison.
Homer: Oh my God. Oh my God! Where did you get that brownie?
George: Over there. There's a big pile of them.
Homer (who downs the whole bunch): Oh, ma-an.
George: Well, what a nice fellow.

In it, there are many parallels to the Beatles' career. Moe's Tavern had previously been called Moe's Cavern, Barney replaced Wiggum, just as Ringo replaced Pete Best, their *Meet The Be-Sharps* album cover mirrors the *Meet The Beatles* cover, and so on.

At home Homer shows Bart and Lisa his collection of Be-Sharps memorabilia, including a Be-Sharps lunch box.

'I can't believe you're still not popular.' says Lisa.

'What'd you do, screw up like the Beatles and say you were bigger than Jesus?' asks Bart.

'All the time,' says Homer. 'It was the title of our second album.'

He holds up a copy of *Bigger Than Jesus*, which pictures the four walking across the Abbey Road zebra crossing, with Barney in his bare feet.

The group has problems – a shabby-looking Be-Sharps, without Barney, are seen singing a jingle.

'And where's Barney?' asks an angry Homer.

'Oh, he's with his new girlfriend, the Japanese conceptual artist,' says Skinner.

Barney arrives, dressed in black and wearing granny glasses, accompanied by a Yoko look-alike.

'Barbershop is in danger of growing stale. I'm taking it to straaange new places,' he says.

The group decide to quit and Barney returns to Moe's bar with his girlfriend. He orders a beer, and she says, 'I'd like a single plum floating in perfume, served in a man's cap.'

After relating his story, Homer decides to arrange a reunion of the Be-Sharps and they reunite for a concert on the roof of Moe's place. As they perform, George pulls up in his limousine, rolls down the window, looks at them and says, 'It's been done.'

As the credits roll, Homer says, 'I'd like to thank you on behalf of the group, and I hope we passed the audition.'

The episode was directed by Mark Kirklandt.

In another episode of *The Simpsons*, Apu pulls out a record *The Concert Against Bangla Desh*. It is almost an exact copy of the design of the original album with the exception that a mushroom cloud has replaced the image of the little boy.

Sitar

George was to play this Indian stringed instrument on the Beatles tracks 'Norwegian Wood' and 'Within You Without You'.

When George first met Ravi Shankar in 1966 at an Asian Music Circle dinner party in London, he asked if Ravi could teach him how to play the sitar. The following week Shankar arrived at George's house in Esher and, George was to recall, 'He showed me the basics. How to hold the sitar, how to sit in the correct position, how to wear the pick on your finger and how to begin playing.'

He also commented, 'There are so many exercises just for the way you hit the string and others for bending the notes. You must practise scales by pulling the strings until the pitch is perfect. It's murder on your fingers.'

For that first meeting George had invited John and Ringo along to watch and Ravi had also brought a famous tabla player, Alla Rakah.

Following the second lesson, Ravi suggested that he should go to

India for further tuition. He was to say, 'From the moment we met, George was asking questions and I felt he was genuinely interested in Indian music and religion. Then George expressed a desire to learn the sitar from me. I asked him if he could give time and total energy to work harder on it. He said he would do his best.'

Ravi was also to add, 'George is still just a beginner, but he is an enthusiastic and ambitious student, because he realises that the sitar itself is an evolvement from Indian culture.

'It might take a lifetime of learning before he is a great master of the instrument, but if he progresses in the same way that he has been doing, his understanding will lead him to a medium of greatness on the sitar. But it takes a lifetime to learn. I have been studying since I was a very little boy in India and I am still learning.'

A great deal of discipline is needed to play the instrument and lessons include yoga exercises due to the fact that the player is required to sit for long periods. He also has to hold what is a cumbersome instrument and have the base seated securely in the base of his foot. This is initially very painful until the musician learns to play properly.

George was instructed to sit cross-legged on the floor and had to support the vertical instrument with his hands at different heights along its neck. He was also instructed to close his eyes to enable him to learn the layout of the instrument.

John Lennon was to comment, 'I wouldn't have George's patience, I'd get angry and kick the thing.'

On their return from Manila in the Philippines, the Beatles stopped off in New Delhi, India for three days where George bought himself a new sitar.

Following the Beatles' North American tour, George took Patti to India where they booked into the Taj Mahal Hotel in Bombay as Mr & Mrs Sam Wells. From the middle of September until the third week of October, George was practising the sitar for seven hours every day at Ravi Shankar's class. George was to say, 'I did a lot of sitaring in a nice peaceful way and it was good.'

Ravi said, 'George is a wonderful student and it will not be long before he masters the sitar.'

At a press conference during the trip, George was to comment, 'The urge to be something more than a mere Beatle provoked me to come to India. By learning to play the sitar, I can give Beatle fans a little more.' He also said, 'I find the philosophy and culture of the East natural and real, unlike Western philosophy which at a central stage reached a dead end. I think the Westerners who say the East is a mystery are a narrow-minded lot, not ready to accept its greatness.'

George spent endless hours between 1965 and 1968 practising on sitar under Ravi's supervision, but was neglecting his ability as a guitarist. His friend Eric Clapton noticed this and gave George a Les Paul guitar, hoping it would spark his interest again.

Ravi also noticed it and pointed it out to George, who realised that he would never be a great sitar player, but needed to improve as a guitarist, leading to George abandoning the sitar and returning to playing guitar.

Skiffle: The Definitive Inside Story
A book by Chas McDevitt, published in 1997. George penned a fore-word in which he wrote, 'I have a lot to thank skiffle for. Without it being so simple, I may not have put in so much time with the guitar, enabling me to learn more of the instrument as I progressed, and without a guitar I would not have had a career.'

Smith, Gary
A diet guru George attended in the 1990s. He also advised the racing driver Emerson Fittipaldi. Smith was founder of the Aspen Wellness Group. His low-fat, complex-carbohydrate diet emphasises whole grains, whole-wheat pastas, fruit and vegetables with beans.

Smith, 'Legs' Larry
The former drummer with the Bonzo Dog Doo-Dah Band, born in Oxford on 18 January 1940.

He was part of the 'Henley Pack', the group of musicians in the area who became part of George's circle of close friends. Not only was he a regular guest at Friar Park, but was also invited as a house guest at George's home in Maui, Hawaii.

'Legs' was a somewhat eccentric character, who amused George greatly. He even immortalised him in the song 'His Name Is Legs (Ladies and Gentlemen)' on the *Extra Texture* album. George also commissioned him to illustrate his *Gone Troppo* album.

In 1983, Legs was to recall, 'I go through periods of being absolutely drunk and periods of great sobriety, and this, happily is my sober period coming up. I always do things in tens, so I spent ten years drinking, and now I'm on my second year of being sober. I'm beginning to work a bit more these days, and last year I was offered the chance to design an album cover for George. In fact, design the entire campaign, which included a lot of things: the songbook, two posters and basically overseeing the whole *Gone Troppo* campaign. Actually I should say it in an Australian accent because "Gone troppo" literally means "Gone a bit loony".

'It was a wonderful thing to do, it was a great few months working on it. I kept whizzing over to George's every couple of weeks. As the album tracks were forming, so were the designs and stuff in my head. George took a real interest in the process. Of course, he already knew a lot about the process of making album covers, obviously, because he's done so many, but he was very involved in this one.'

In 1983 George also involved Legs in the HandMade film *Bullshot* and had him singing the theme song.

So Sad (No Love Of His Own)
A number that George first began writing in New York in 1972. He gave it to guitarist Alvin Lee and Mylon Lefevere, a gospel-rocker from Georgia, in 1973 for their November album *The Road To Freedom*. George included it on his *Dark Horse* album the following year, under the shorter title 'So Sad'.

Soft-Hearted Hana
A track from the 1979 *George Harrison* album lasting 3 minutes and 59 seconds. George began writing the number in Los Angeles and completed the lyrics in February 1978. The number was partly recorded in a pub in Henley.

It also featured as the flipside of the single 'Love Comes To Everyone'.

Soft Touch
A song George wrote about his son Dhani while he was in the Virgin Islands. It was included on the 1979 *George Harrison* album and is 3 minutes and 57 seconds in length.

Some Come Running
A 1990 album by Jim Capaldi. George was a guest on the track 'Oh Lord, Why Lord' and also appeared in the promotional video.

Something
This was the only song by George to be issued as the A side of a Beatles single.

The number was recorded during *The Beatles* double album sessions in 1968. George had taped a demo on 25 February 1969 and the Beatles then recorded it on 16 April. It was recorded again on 2 May with overdubbing on 5 May 5, 11 and 16 July and 15 August. The song is 2 minutes and 58 seconds in length.

It wasn't used on *The Beatles* double album but was included on the *Abbey Road* album and also released as a single in Britain on 31 October 1969. It was the first British single to be taken from an album that had already been released, although it only reached No. 18 in the British charts.

It was released as a single in America on 6 October 1969 and reached No. 3 in the charts.

Both John Lennon and Paul McCartney considered it the best track on the *Abbey Road* album.

Ungenerously, John was to comment in his Playboy interview: '"Something" was the first time he ever got an A side, because Paul and I always wrote both sides anyway. Not because we were keeping him out, because, simply, his material wasn't up to scratch.' That might have been John's point of view, but the Lennon and McCartney juggling to get their own songs onto the singles and albums did close George out, whatever the quality of his material, as proved by their lack of interest in his classic 'While My Guitar Gently Weeps'.

It was Allen Klein who insisted on 'Something' being issued as a single. But for his intervention, George may never have had the A side of a Beatles single.

The first line was inspired by a track on James Taylor's first Apple album *Something In The Way She Moves*. For a time, as a joke, George had opened with the lines, 'Something in the way she moves/attracts me like a pomegranate.'

George said it was 'probably the nicest melody line I've ever written'.

In his *I. Me. Mine.* book, George was to recall, '"Something" was written on the piano while we were making the White album. I had a break while Paul was doing some overdubbing so I went into an empty studio and began to write. That's really all there is to it, except the middle took some time to sort out. It didn't go on the White album because we'd already finished all the tracks. I gave it to Joe Cocker a year before I did it.'

There were over 150 versions of the number recorded within the first decade following its release, making it second only to 'Yesterday'. Frank Sinatra was to say that 'Something' was 'the greatest love song of the past fifty years'. Sinatra included it in his repertoire, although in a number of performances he inaccurately credited it to Lennon and McCartney.

Shirley Bassey recorded it in 1976 and her version reached No. 4 in the British charts.

George was to say, 'It's probably got a range of five notes which fits most singers needs best. This, I suppose, is my most successful song with over 150 cover versions. My favourite version is the one by James Brown – that was excellent. When I wrote it, in my mind I heard Ray Charles singing it, and he did do it some years later. I like Smokey Robinson's version too.'

'Something' also received an Ivor Novello Award as 'Best Song musically and lyrically'.

In 1997, George discussed the inclusion of 'Something' on the Beatles *Anthology*.

'That was a song I wrote back during the White album. There was a moment that I wasn't doing anything while we were making the white album and I wrote it on the piano in Studio One in Abbey Road and it sounded like it was so obvious to me from a piano point of view, the notes, the way they followed on, that I couldn't believe that nobody had ever written that before. You know, as with any song that's really popular, there's a lot of cover versions of it, and I've never counted them up, but there was many versions of that, like Smokey Robinson and the Miracles and James Brown and not many people know about the James Brown version, but it was a hell of a record. It was really good.

'Then it became pretty tricky to do the bridge and make it all work and musically for it all to get back out of the bridge. The arrangement took me quite a while to get it finished.'

Somewhere In England

The third Dark Horse album to be released by Warner Brothers, but not without major problems.

Originally, a release date of 29 October 1980 had been set, which, incidentally, coincided with the release of John Lennon's *Double Fantasy*.

However, when Derek Taylor presented the finished album to Warner's they said that it was 'lifeless' and sent it back demanding 'improvements'. George was furious, but decided to comply and returned to the studio and recorded a further four songs.

During this time John Lennon was murdered, which led to George altering the record further from the original line-up of numbers.

He was able to voice his opinion of the record industry 'men in suits' who had called the album 'lifeless' on the opening track, 'Blood From A Clone'.

Warner's also vetoed the original cover design, which had a satellite photograph of England merging with a profile of George's face. Caroline Irwin took the new cover of George sitting in front of 'Holland Park Avenue Study' and there is a dedication to John Lennon on the inner sleeve.

The original album had George as the sole producer, but the revised album co-credited George with Ray Cooper, who was also percussionist.

Other musicians featured included Ringo Starr, Jim Keltner and Dave Mattacks on drums; Willie Weeks and Herbie Flowers on bass; Neil Larson, Gary Brooker, Al Kooper, Mike Moran and Ray Cooper on keyboards and synthesizers; Tom Scott on lyricon and horns; Herbie Flowers on tuba and Alla Rakah on tabla.

The album was issued in Britain on Dark Horse K 56870 on Friday 5 June 1981. It had already been issued in America on Monday 1 June 1981. It was to reach No. 11 in the American charts and No. 13 in the British charts.

The track 'All Those Years Ago' had been rewritten due to John's death and also included contributions from Paul McCartney and Ringo Starr. George penned all the numbers with the exception of 'Hong Kong Blues' and 'Baltimore Oriole'. Hoagy Carmichael wrote those two numbers.

The four tracks removed from the original were released on the CDs that came with George's two Genesis book projects. They were 'Flying Hour', 'Lay His Head', 'Sat Singing' and 'Tears Of The World'.

The tracks finally included on the album were: Side One: 'Blood From A Clone', 'Unconsciousness Rules', 'Life Itself', 'All Those Years Ago', 'Baltimore Oriole'. Side Two: 'Teardrops', 'That Which I Have Lost', 'Writing's On The Wall', 'Hong Kong Blues', 'Save The World'.

Songs From The Material World

A tribute album issued by Kotch Records on 25 February 2002. Artists featured performing numbers by George include Roger McGuinn, Dave Davies, Peter Green, Bonnie Bramlett, Julian Lennon, Todd Rundgren, Leslie West, Donovan, Al Kooper, They Might Be Giants, Wayne Kramer, Midge Ure, Masters of Reality, Simon Townshend, Jay Bennett, Marc Ford, and the Smithereens.

Songs Of George Harrison, The

The first of two books published by Genesis in 1987 and 1992 respectively. *The Songs Of George Harrison* was issued in a limited edition priced at £235, with each copy personally signed by George and containing the four numbers that were omitted from his *Somewhere In England* album, 'Flying Hour', 'Lay His Head', 'Sat Singing' and 'Tears Of The World', and a demo of 'Life Itself', which was available on either a 7" vinyl EP or 5" CD.

Songs Of George Harrison 2

Published by Genesis in 1992, it contained lyrics to 59 numbers, illustrated and hand-lettered by Keith West. There was a foreword by Ringo Starr and a 'middleword' by Harry Nilsson. Also enclosed was a 5" CD or 7" vinyl record featuring four numbers, including a demo version of 'Life Itself', a memorable number from the *Somewhere In England* album. The other numbers were 'Hottest Gang In Town' (a leftover from the *Shanghai Surprise* project), 'Tears Of The World' (one of the four tracks Warner Bros Records rejected for the *Somewhere In England* album) and 'Hari's On Tour (Express) (a live recording of the opening track from the *Dark Horse* album).

It was issued in a limited edition of 2,500 copies, all individually signed by George and Keith West.

Songwriting

It is interesting to note that George was really the first member of the Beatles to have input in early recordings. The very first record that the group made, while they were still known as the Quarry Men, was recorded at Percy Philips' studio in Kensington, Liverpool in 1958. One side comprised Buddy Holly's 'That'll Be The Day'; the other was an original composition, 'In Spite Of All The Danger', which was credited as a Harrison/McCartney composition. It's a pity we don't have further information about this number, although in recent years Paul now claims that it was mostly his work. If John and Paul were writing together, why wasn't it a Lennon/McCartney number that they recorded on their first session? How did the number come about? Did George and Paul initially begin writing together? Did they make it up on the spot? Who thought of the title? Only Paul now could provide such information, although at times Paul tends to be a revisionist and he and George disagree about their own perspective on events in the early career of the Beatles, as can be seen in their *Anthology* television series.

Nevertheless, the Harrison/McCartney team came before the Lennon and McCartney one.

Then, when the group made their first professional recordings in Hamburg with Bert Kaempfert, backing Tony Sheridan, they requested that they record some of their own numbers. The only one they recorded was 'Cry For A Shadow', a Harrison/Lennon composition. We know that it was an instrumental that George wrote in the Shadows style after a challenge from Rory Storm, but what was John's input? John was mainly the wordsmith, George the guitarist. Whatever the contribution of either, the second original Beatles composition to be recorded was a George Harrison and John Lennon one. At the time Kaempfert, the recording manager, felt that George's instrumental composition was better than the numbers by Lennon and McCartney that were played to him.

The cover story of the 20 July 1961 issue of *Mersey Beat* announced news of their Hamburg recordings and the first time mention in print of an original Beatles song being recorded was one by George.

This is what led Bill Harry to begin to pester George about his songwriting in 1963. By that time the Beatles music was centred around Lennon and McCartney numbers. Harry pointed out that George was the first Beatle to be credited in print as a songwriter, so why wasn't he writing songs? Eventually, at the Beatles appearance at the ABC, Blackpool, George told Harry that his pestering had resulted in him writing 'Don't Bother Me', the number that reintroduced him as a Beatles songwriter. In his *I. Me. Mine.* he mentions writing the number in a hotel room in Bournemouth while ill, although this doesn't contradict the original inspiration for the song, as he began writing it one time when intending to go to a Liverpool club and realising he'd be badgered about his songwriting again. He could have then finished it at a later time, which he did with a number of his songs.

Once he gained his confidence in writing again, he had great difficulty in getting his material recorded by the Beatles due to the lobbying by John and Paul to have their numbers recorded. George was to say, 'The usual thing was that we'd do fourteen of their tunes, and then they'd condescend to listen to one of mine.'

George told *Rolling Stone* about the problems he had getting his songs on Beatles albums, saying, 'It was like having diarrhoea and not being allowed to go to the toilet.'

In an interview with the *Sunday Mirror* he said that John and Paul were egomaniacs who stifled his talent. He claimed that many of the songs he wrote after the group had disbanded were better than their greatest hits. He said, 'Paul and John were obviously talented and they were a great duo, but they also had massive egos which left little room for others. I felt ignored and undervalued for years. Not all the songs released back then were good, far from it. Since the split I have written songs which are just as good, if not better than the best of the Beatles. The difference is that the Beatles songs would go to the top of the chart in a matter of days.'

On another occasion he recalled, 'I used to have a hang-up about telling John, Paul and Ringo I had a song for the albums, because I felt mentally, at that time, as if I was trying to compete. And in a way, the standard of the songs had to be good, because theirs were very good. I don't want the Beatles to be recording rubbish for my sake, just because I wrote it. On the other hand, *I* don't want to record rubbish, just because *they* wrote it. The group comes first. It took time for me to get more confidence as a songwriter, and now I don't care if they don't like it. I can shrug it off. Sometimes it's a matter of whoever pushes hardest gets the most tunes on the album, then it's down to personalities. And more often, I just leave it until somebody would like to do one of my tunes.'

While in Toronto, Canada on Monday 28 March 1988, George held a press conference and was asked to comment on a remark by Paul McCartney that he'd like to write some songs with him. George replied, 'Yes, Paul has suggested that maybe he and me should write something again. I mean it's pretty funny really. I mean, I've only been there about thirty years in Paul's life and now he wants to write with me. But maybe it would be quite interesting to do that. There's a thing with Paul, one minute he says one thing and he's really charming and the next minute, he's all uptight. We all go through that, good and bad stuff. But, by now, we've got to find the centre.'

In 1965, discussing his songwriting activities with the *New Musical Express*, he said, 'I'm getting tape recorders – like Johnny and Paul have – fixed up into a sort of home studio. They can overdub vocal and instrumental tracks so that when they get an idea for a song they can make a demo record for themselves. I want to do the same.'

In 1966 *Beatles Monthly* asked him if he was becoming more confident as a songwriter. He told them, 'Naturally. You get more confident as you progress. In the old days I used to say to myself, "I'm sure I can write," but it was difficult because of John and Paul. Their standard of writing has bettered over the years, so it was very hard for me to come straight to the top – on par with them, instead of building up like they did.' He also commented, 'I've thrown away about thirty songs, they may have been all right if I'd worked on them, but I didn't think they were strong enough.

'My main trouble is the lyrics. I can't seem to write down what I want to say – it doesn't come over literally, so I compromise, usually far too much I suppose. I find that everything makes a song, not just the melody as so many people seem to think, but the words, the technique – the lot.'

Following his first Beatles song, 'Don't Bother Me', George next had the numbers 'I Need You' and 'You Like Me Too Much' on the *Help!* Album. *Rubber Soul* saw him with two more album tracks, 'Think For Yourself' and 'If I Needed Someone', the latter also becoming part of the Beatles stage act. The number also provided a Top 20 hit for the Hollies, although George was to criticise their version.

Revolver featured his track 'Love You To', in which George is the only Beatle who participates, engaging Indian session musicians to back him. His inspirations in both music and lyrics was now strongly influenced by the East and this was to increase as his relationships with Ravi Shankar and the Maharishi Mahesh Yogi developed. Another composition by George on the album is 'Taxman', which described his feelings about governments literally engaging in 'legal theft', something which irked him his entire life. His third track on the album was 'I Want To Tell You'.

The *Sgt Pepper* album saw him with only one track, 'Within You Without You', another Eastern-influenced number in which he was once again backed by Indian musicians.

His contribution to the *Magical Mystery Tour* EP was 'Blue Jay Way', inspired by Derek Taylor.

March 1968 saw George's first ever composition to be featured on a single when 'The Inner Light' became the flipside of 'Lady Madonna'.

During their sojourn in Rishikesh, it wasn't only John and Paul who were prolific in their songwriting. George also wrote a considerable number of songs during the stay at the Maharishi Mahesh Yogi's ashram. *The Beatles* white album contained many of the numbers written there, although they were mainly by John and Paul. However, George did manage to get four of his numbers on to the double album. They were the classic 'While My Guitar Gently Weeps', 'Piggies', 'Savoy Truffle' and 'Long Long Long'.

While with the Beatles he was also to involve himself in two solo projects, the film soundtrack *Wonderwall* and the experimental album *Electronic Sound*.

Two of George's tracks are to be found on the *Yellow Submarine* album, 'Only A Northern Song' and 'It's All Too Much'.

George's composition 'Old Brown Shoe' then found itself on the flipside of 'The Ballad Of John And Yoko'. In 1969 the *Abbey Road* album included two of George's songs, 'Something' and 'Here Comes The Sun', proving once and for all how he had matured as a songwriter in his own right. They were arguably two of the best songs on the entire album. 'Something' became the third most covered Beatles singles after

'Yesterday' and 'Imagine'. Allen Klein decided to provide George with his only A side of a Beatles single when he chose 'Something' as their new release.

The Beatles final album *Let It Be* also saw the inclusion of two of George's songs, 'I. Me. Mine.' and 'For You Blue'.

Out of around two hundred Beatles compositions that the group recorded, George's contributions amounted to barely twenty. He had so many numbers written which he couldn't get onto the Beatles albums that he was able to issue a triple album *All Things Must Pass* and become the first ex-Beatle to top the charts with both an album and a single.

Following the court case revolving around 'My Sweet Lord'/'He's So Fine', George began to be increasingly worried in case he subconsciously wrote anything that seemed similar to an existing song. Influences of other songs *have* been detected in many songwriters' works, which is not surprising and not exactly plagiarism. It has been claimed, for instance, that the Jam copied the opening riff from George's 'Taxman' for their 'Start' single, and no one could deny that the melody of John Lennon's 'Happy Xmas (War Is Over)' is almost identical to the traditional tune 'Stewball'. Whether it really was Delaney Bramlett who virtually composed 'My Sweet Lord' as he says, is open to speculation as George is no longer around to deny it. Another obvious influence in one of George's compositions has to be the Apple artist James Taylor, who recorded a song for Apple Records called 'Something In The Way She Moves', which became the first line of George's classic hit 'Something'.

There were lengthy periods during George's life when he didn't write any songs at all. During interviews to promote the Beatles *Anthology 2* he revealed that the business problems he'd had with his former manager Denis O'Brien had kept him from songwriting. He said, 'Those years from the end of 1991 have been like hell, so it's just recently that I've written some new tunes, and I'm trying to find the time to not have to deal with all these accountants and lawyers.'

Discussing his songs, George said, 'Of my songs, "Here Comes The Sun" and "Something" are probably the biggest. Frank Sinatra, who sings it with his "Stick around, Jack", says "Something" is the greatest love song of all time. At last count, which was years ago, there were 140 covers of "Something". Sinatra, Smokey Robinson, Ray Charles. My personal favourite is the version by James Brown. It was one of his B sides. I have it on my jukebox at home. It's absolutely brilliant. "Taxman" was done not too long ago by Berry Gordy's son, so I've done all right.'

It was George who had facsimiles of the songs he wrote, together with his personal comments on their origins, presented in the book *I. Me. Mine*. He was also to continue to present facsimiles and stories of his songwriting in two further Genesis books *The Songs Of George Harrison* and *The Songs Of George Harrison 2*.

Sooty goes To Hawaii

A song George wrote in February 1978 during his nine-week holiday in Hawaii.

Soundstage Of Mind

A composition that George wrote in October 1974 during the rehearsals for his first American tour on the soundstage at A&M Studios. He was to play the number intermittently during the tour. When he appeared in Fort Worth, Texas, on 22 November, George announced the number on stage, saying it was 'just a boogie-woogie tune for you, which we haven't written the words to yet and it's one we made up on the soundstage rehearsal.'

Sour Milk Sea

A number that George composed during meditation sessions at Rishikesh.

He considered it 'too spiritual' for the Beatles to record, but produced a recording of the number with Jackie Lomax in 1968.

It featured an incredible line-up, with George on rhythm, Paul McCartney on bass, Ringo Starr on drums, Eric Clapton on lead guitar and Nicky Hopkins on piano.

It was Jackie's first Apple single and one of the first four Apple releases. The single was issued in America on Apple 1802 on 26 August 1968 and in Britain on 6 September 1968 on Apple 3. The number is 3 minutes and 51 seconds in length and 'The Eagle Laughs At You', penned by Lomax, was on the flip.

South Bank Show, The

The London Weekend television arts programme featured Ravi Shankar on 12 August 2001. George was also featured, as was a clip from the film *Raga* and the recording of *Chants Of India* at Friar Park Studios in 1997.

Spector, Phil

A legendary record producer, born Harvey Philip Spector in the Bronx, New York on 26 December 1940. He was inspired to enter the record business after hearing British skiffle king Lonnie Donegan's 'Rock Island Line'.

He had numerous hits and his records impressed the Beatles. When he visited Britain in 1964 with the Ronettes they were invited to a party at Decca publicity man Tony Hall's flat. Spector began discussing his records with the Beatles, telling them about the sessions and who was on them, and a good atmosphere developed between them. George and Estelle Bennett slipped away together to an upstairs room.

A week after the party the Beatles were due to fly to America to appear on the *Ed Sullivan Show*. Not knowing what to expect in New York, they called Phil and asked him how they should handle things. Then they asked him if he'd fly to New York with them.

Spector was always terrified of flying, but he was to recall at a later date that the flight was a lot of fun. He said, 'It was probably the only time I flew that I wasn't afraid, because I knew that they weren't going to get killed in a plane.

'That plane was really an awful trip. I mean there were 28 or 30 minutes where the plane dropped thousands of feet over the ocean. It scared the shit out of me, but there were 140 people on board who were all press and Beatles right-hand men and left-hand men, and we just sat together and talked about the Apollo and all that jive. Lennon was with his first wife, and he was very quiet. Paul asked a lot of questions. George was wonderful. It was a nice trip.'

When they arrived at JFK airport they asked Phil a favour. He recalled, 'It's really funny but they were terribly frightened to get off the plane. They were really frightened of America. They said, "You go first." Because the whole thing about Kennedy scared them very, very much. They really thought it would be possible for somebody to be there and want to kill them.'

The Beatles stayed in touch with Spector over the years – unaware that he'd always held the hope of being able to produce a Beatles album. When he released the single 'River Deep, Mountain High' George wrote a cover blurb for it: '"River Deep, Mountain High" is a perfect record from start to finish. You couldn't improve on it.'

Phil also hoped to revive his wife Ronnie's career and George co-produced 'Try Some, Buy Some' with her. George had penned the number and he co-wrote the flipside 'Tandoori Chicken' with Spector, but the record was unsuccessful. However Apple were to release *Phil Spector's Christmas Album* in December 1972.

In January 1969 the Beatles began working on a project they called 'Get Back', which was to be a documentary film and a soundtrack album. They despaired of it and left the tapes on a shelf at Apple, with George Martin refusing to begin mixing the tapes. John Lennon said, 'Nobody would look at it.'

Spector was invited to London to see if he could sort out the mess of the 'Get Back' tapes, a seemingly thankless task of over thirty hours of unmixed recording tape. He arrived in London in January 1970 and booked into the Inn On The Park hotel with the Beatles' American plugger Pete Bennett and Spector's bodyguard George Brand. Initially, to see if he was up to the job, John had asked him to produce a Plastic Ono Band single 'Instant Karma'. John was pleased with Spector's production, but Spector wasn't happy with it and said he wanted to work on it further. John refused and issued the single in Britain. When it was issued in America it was a much smoother production – Phil had remixed it again without John knowing.

As a result of the success of 'Instant Karma' in America, Allen Klein booked Spector to go ahead on the 'Get Back' tapes, with no restrictions. During February and March he worked tirelessly in the Apple Studio basement, adding strings and choirs to the various tracks.

George was soon to begin work on his solo album and asked Spector to produce it.

When Paul heard what had been done to his track 'The Long And Winding Road', which he'd intended to be a very simple production, he was furious and demanded that Spector's changes be junked. Klein ignored him and released the Spector-produced 'The Long And Winding Road' as the first single from the project, now renamed *Let It Be*. Paul never forgave Spector for what he'd done and in the court papers requesting the winding up of the Beatles partnership, he cited that what had been done to that track was evidence of a conspiracy to 'ruin my career artistically'.

When the album was released, it was critically mauled in some quarters and George Martin had some stinging comments to make, causing Spector to say, 'It was no favour to me to give me George Martin's job because I don't consider him in my league. He's an arranger, that's all. As far as *Let It Be*, he left it in a deplorable condition, and it was not satisfactory to any of them, they did not want it out as it was. So John said, "Let Phil do it," and I said, "Fine." Then I said, "Would anybody like to get involved in it, work with me?" "No." They didn't care. But they did have the right to say, "We don't want it out," and they didn't say that.'

Due to the criticism he received, Spector commented, 'Everybody was saying, "Oh Beatles, don't break up, give us something to remember you by," and you give it to them and then the critics just knock the shit out of it. "It's awful, it's this, it's that." But it's your Beatles, your great Beatles! Forget my name, if my name hadn't been on the album there wouldn't have been all that. George told me that, John, everyone. That's the dues you have to pay. It was nothing to me. I had my reputation before the Beatles were around. They knew that and I knew that. I knew who I was and what I was before I met the Beatles.'

In May, Spector went into the studio with George and during the next six months they worked on the triple album *All Things Must Pass* with an array of fine musicians including Eric Clapton, Billy Preston, Ringo Starr, Dave Mason and Bobby Keys. Preston recalled, 'He was unique the way he worked. He would use a lot of keyboards playing the same chord to make it big and strong. We would do it several times in different octaves and it was monotonous as hell. But he was making it the Phil Spector sound. Myself, I was never really a fan of his sound. I thought it worked on the Ronettes stuff, it worked on certain things but not on others. But with George's stuff it was perfect.'

Of the session, Preston said, 'It was a lot of laughs. Phil didn't seek to overtake George or anything. He would hold court and all you could do was laugh because he had the floor and Phil looked like a cartoon to me, a funny little guy with a funny little voice, loony but a lot of fun. And he was brilliant. I still don't know how he got the echo like he did; he'd record with an echo in the room and that was the only time I ever saw that, man. He had every machine going at once and he knew what every one was doing in relation to the others. It was a circus and he was the ringleader.'

All Things Must Pass was released in November 1970 and topped the charts on both sides of the Atlantic.

George next commissioned him to record the Concert For Bangla Desh. At Madison Square Garden that night Spector got into an argument with the security police backstage and they began to hit him with their clubs. 'I'm Phil Spector. Don't you know who I am!' he was screaming at them. George heard and called Pete Bennett, 'They're beating up Phil' and they rushed forward into the guards and dragged Phil away.

Bennett recalled, 'I got in there and I grabbed him and put his head under my arm so they couldn't beat on his head. I said, "What are you doing? He's our producer!" and one of the guys says, "I don't care who he is, he's a nasty son of a bitch."'

Spector next produced John's *Imagine* album.

George engaged him to work on his *Living In The Material World* album, but the experience was a tense one. George told Timothy White: 'Phil worked on the second solo album. By that I mean he was around. Again, he kept falling over and breaking his ankles, wrists. The guy who was his helper was having heart attacks. Phil was never there. I literally used to have to go and break into the hotel to get him. I'd go along the roof at the Inn On The Park in London and climb in his window yelling, "Come on! We're supposed to be making a record!" He'd say, "Oh, OK." And then he used to have eighteen cherry brandies before he could get himself down to the studio. I got so tired of that because I needed somebody to help. I was ending up with more work than if I'd just been doing it on my own.'

Spector, Ronnie

The former Veronica Burnett, who was a member of the Ronettes, the hit recording group with Phil Spector's Philles label. Ronnie became Spector's wife in 1968.

In her autobiography *Be My Baby*, Ronnie recalled that she first met the Beatles in 1964 at a London party and, together with her sister Estelle, went on a few dates with George and John Lennon, although at one time their mother came along on the date.

When the Ronettes were booked to appear on the Beatles 1966 tour of the USA, Phil wouldn't let her appear and had her replaced by her cousin Elaine. It was said to be because he was jealous that she would form a relationship with John Lennon.

When Spector began recording at Apple he decided to take the opportunity of relaunching his wife via the Beatles Company and had her fly over to London in 1971 and sign with Apple. He wanted her to record for Apple under the name Veronica, but George and John insisted she use the name she was better known by – Ronnie.

The initial idea was for her to record an album and the sessions began at Abbey Road Studios in February 1971, co-produced by George and Phil Spector, with George using a number of the musicians he'd engaged to record with him for the *All Things Must Pass* album.

George wrote two numbers especially for Ronnie; one was 'You', the other was 'Try Some, Buy Some'. He also co-wrote another number for her with Spector, 'Tandoori Chicken'.

A single, 'Try Some Buy Some' c/w 'Tandoori Chicken', was released in Britain on Apple 33 on 16 April 1971 and in America on Apple 1832 on 19 April 1971. This was co-produced by George, who played guitar on both tracks.

Ronnie didn't like the song and complained about it and the record wasn't a success. On 'Tandoori Chicken', in addition to Paul playing guitar, John Lennon provided backing vocals.

Her career with Apple Records was brief, no album was completed and only the one single was released.

Speed On

A number on Nicky Hopkins' album *Tin Man Was A Dreamer*, on which George provided a guitar solo.

Splinter

A duo from South Shields, comprising Bill Elliott and Bob Purvis, who were discovered by Mal Evans.

He was looking for a group to play in the nightclub scene of the film *Little Malcolm And His Struggle Against The Eunuchs*. In their scene they performed the film's theme song 'Lonely Man', produced by George. Bill Elliott sang on John Lennon's Elastic Oz Band's 'God Save Us'.

George signed them to his Dark Horse Records label next and had them record an album at FPSHOT, co-produced by him and Tom Scott, called *Harder To Live* from which the single 'Costafine Town' was issued. It reached No. 17 in the British charts.

Springsteen, Bruce

When George was compiling the charity album *Nobody's Child* to raise funds to aid Romanian orphans, he contacted Springsteen to see if he would contribute a live track. George said it was 'because he's got millions of unused live tracks. But he never came through with it. I'd heard a rumour that I'd approached him to join the Wilburys, but that isn't true.'

Star Club Tapes

At the New Year's Eve festivities at the Star Club at the close of 1962, during the Beatles last appearance at the Hamburg venue, Adrian Barber, at the request of Kingsize Taylor, recorded the Beatles' performances on tape.

During the 1970s Kingsize Taylor, still in possession of the tapes, teamed up with Alan Williams and the tapes were acquired by Paul Murphy of Lingasong music, who released the tapes in album form. Apple went to court to oppose the release, but lost the case.

In 1998, due to changes in the copyright law, Apple once again sought to prevent their release when Lingasong Music announced the imminent release of the tapes in the CD format.

The case opened at the High Court in London on Tuesday 5 May 1998 with Mr Justice Neuberger presiding.

The following day George appeared in court to represent the Beatles' side of the case, saying, 'I drew the short straw and was the one who had to go to court for Apple.' George was referring to the fact that Ringo was abroad at the time and had submitted his evidence in writing while Paul was excused attendance due to Linda's recent death.

Lingasong had claimed that John Lennon was the leader of the group and had given his permission for the Beatles to be recorded. George denied this saying, 'We had a democratic thing going between us. Everyone had to agree with everything that was done, whether it was a concert in Liverpool or to go to Hamburg.'

George pointed out that when he first joined the Beatles, John had turned to him for musical advice. 'I taught John the guitar. He had a little guitar with three strings tuned like a banjo. I had to show him all the chords. When I first met him I was very young, but so was he. He was seventeen and I was maybe fourteen or fifteen. But by the time we were in Hamburg, I'd grown up a lot, and I could certainly hold my own against him.'

George also pointed out, 'He was the loudest, the noisiest and the oldest. He could be wrong about something but try and win the argument just by being loud.'

Regarding the claim that Taylor had permission to record the Beatles, George said, 'To my mind, there was never any recording equipment there at all. Maybe he had it in a cupboard. Whatever he says, we didn't see it. We didn't ask him to do it, we never heard them, we never had anything to do with them – and that's the story.'

Discussing the Star Club itself, George recalled, 'It was a really rough place, and the waiters used to let off tear gas to get rid of the sailors if a fight started. I kept well out of it. But there were also some quite nice people who went to the club. They weren't all gangsters and transvestites – there were teenagers and art students. But by 2 a.m. on Saturday, it was hell.'

Mentioning Kingsize Taylor, George said, 'He was a leader of another group. In those days, everyone was friendly, but we only saw one another if they happened to play the same club at the same time. If we weren't, we didn't see him from one month to the next. He wasn't a friend we hung around with.'

George also pointed out that, even if John had given Taylor his permission, it wasn't legal for the tape to be turned into an album. 'One drunken person recording another bunch of drunks does not constitute a business deal. It just didn't happen. It certainly didn't take place in my company or my lifetime. Neither Paul or Ringo heard it, either. The only person who allegedly heard anything about it is the one who is dead, who can't actually come here and say it's a load of rubbish.

'If we had been sitting around the table and Ted Taylor was saying, "Hey lads, I am going to record you and I'll make this live record that will come back to haunt you for the rest of your lives," and John was saying, "Great, you can do it," then I would have said, "You are not recording me." We had a record contract and we were on a roll. The last thing we needed was one little bedroom recording to come out.'

Describing the tapes as 'the crummiest recording ever made in our name', he added, 'There was no organised recording. It was a wild affair. We were just a whole bunch of drunken musicians grabbing guitars. And if Teddy Taylor just happened to have a tape recorder and decided to plug it in and tape us, that still doesn't constitute the right to put out a record. It's not whether he bought a pint of beer for John, it's whether people are allowed to make a recording without permission. I could go out tonight and tape Mick Jagger – but that doesn't mean I could go out and sell it. The bottom line is that John didn't give permission, and even if he had, he couldn't have given it for all of us. We were a democratic band.'

George mentioned their early days in Liverpool saying it was 'a lot of teenagers getting drunk and playing rock'n'roll. That's how it was. It was just a wild thing.'

He mentioned the advice from people that they shouldn't drink and smoke on stage and present themselves like Cliff Richard and the Shadows – this was actually the advice of Brian Epstein. 'We had black leather. We were a bit more funky than Cliff and the Shadows. But there was always this thing about the Rolling Stones being more funky than the Beatles.'

Discussing the sacking of Pete Best, he said that the drummer was a loner who didn't fit in with the other Beatles and when Ringo Starr replaced him that was 'the last piece in the jigsaw puzzle'. This didn't give any further enlightenment on the mystery of the sacking. It's possible that George was the chief instigator, as he was a good friend of Ringo and didn't get on well with Best.

He admitted not remembering much from the early days of their career, saying, 'Unlike the experts who wallow in Beatles trivia, I spend a lot of time getting the junk out of my mind through meditation, so I don't know or remember – I don't *want* to know or remember – every last detail, because it was trivial pursuit.'

Mr Justice Neuberger was particularly impressed by George's testimony and praised his convincing evidence when he ruled that the Lingasong CD of the Hamburg tapes should not be released, that the recording should be given to the Beatles' solicitors, and that all of the Beatles' costs should be paid by Lingasong Music Ltd.

Starkey, Maureen

Formerly Ringo Starr's wife, Maureen was born Maureen Cox in Liverpool on 4 August 1946. She became an assistant hairdresser at the Ashley du Pre salon when she was fifteen and the following year met Ringo Starr. The two began 'going steady', but when Ringo moved to London he began dating model Vicki Hodge. When he had a tonsillectomy at University College Hospital Maureen travelled to London, visited him in hospital and spent Christmas with him. She became pregnant and the two were married on 11 February 1965.

In 1983, in his book *The Love You Make*, former Apple executive Peter Grant made certain claims about an affair between George and Maureen.

When John and Yoko left for America, Ringo bought Tittenhurst Park. They invited George and Patti to join them for a meal one night. According to Brown, when the meal was finished, George blurted out that he was in love with Maureen. Maureen became terribly embarrassed, Ringo stormed off and Patti burst into tears and locked herself in the bathroom. After a while, George and Patti left.

That part of the story seems to be true, as even Maureen recalled that she started clearing the dining table after the meal and George approached Ringo and said, 'I have to talk to you. I'm deeply in love with Maureen and I have been for three years.'

There is no confirmation of what Brown alleges happened next. He wrote that a few weeks after the abortive dinner incident, Patti returned home from a shopping spree in London and found George in the bedroom with Maureen.

Maureen and Patti were to neither confirm nor deny the incident, but when George was asked why he'd slept with his friend's wife, he shrugged his shoulders and said, 'Incest.'

Both marriages were to break down. Maureen and Ringo began to live virtually separate lives until their divorce in 1975 and Patti was to desert George for his best friend Eric Clapton.

It says much for the friendships of all concerned that Ringo and George, and George and Eric continued their relationships despite the infidelities.

Ringo was to marry actress Barbara Bach, Eric to marry Patti, but later divorce her, George married Olivia Arias and Maureen married Isaac Tigrett of the Hard Rock Café chain. She died at the age of 47 on

30 December 1995 at the Fred Hutchinson Cancer Research Center in Seattle.

Starr, Ringo

Ringo Starr was born Richard Starkey at his parents' home in Madryn Street, Dingle, Liverpool. Throughout his early years he suffered a number of illnesses and operations and spent a great deal of his time in hospitals, with the result that his education suffered. When he returned to his school to obtain a certificate to confirm that he'd left, he said, 'They didn't even remember I'd been there.'

In 1957 he formed the Eddie Clayton Skiffle Group with some friends and then joined the Darktown Skiffle Group. In March 1959 he became drummer with Al Caldwell's Texans, who were to become one of Liverpool's leading groups, Rory Storm and the Hurricanes.

When the Beatles went on their first trip to Germany in 1960, they moved from the Indra club to the Kaiserkeller club and the Hurricanes arrived from Liverpool to top the bill over them. At the time, George described Ringo as 'the nasty one with his little grey streak of hair'.

It was while they were in Germany that they made a recording at the Akustic Studio on which John, George, Paul and Ringo played together for the first time.

When *Mersey Beat* held it's first annual poll to determine the leading groups in Liverpool, Rory Storm and the Hurricanes had the most votes, but forty of them were disqualified and the Beatles were declared the winners.

In 1962 the Beatles decided to get rid of Pete Best, their drummer of two years. By this time George, in particular, had developed a strong friendship with Ringo and he was asked to join the group. At the time he had just received an offer to join Kingsize Taylor and the Dominoes at £20 a week. The Beatles offered him £25 and he decided to go where the money was! People in Liverpool began calling him 'The Luckiest Man In The World'.

When Ringo made his debut with the Beatles at the Cavern, George received a black eye. This was possibly because *Mersey Beat* had reported that George had visited Ringo's house – and people assumed that he was the one who had lobbied to have Ringo to replace Best.

Ringo was instructed to rid himself of the grey streak and have his hair styled into the moptop. When he first arrived at Abbey Road Studios to record, Paul McCartney, George Martin and Ron Richards weren't happy with his playing and a session drummer, Andy White, was booked for the next recording session. However, Ringo was to prove a remarkable drummer.

When the Beatles were about to embark on their world tour and Ringo had to be hospitalised with tonsillitis, George said, 'I was dead set against carrying on without Ringo. Imagine, the Beatles without Ringo Starr! Anyway, I bowed to the pressure and off we went, but I was none too pleased, even though Jimmy (Nicol, Ringo's temporary replacement) was actually quite a nice guy.'

Although George was to become associated with the film industry later in his career, it was through HandMade Films and his position as executive producer. On the other hand, Ringo also had initial success on film and appeared in more movies than any of the other Beatles.

Apart from the Beatles movies they included *Candy*, *The Magic Christian*, *Blindman*, *200 Motels*, *Born To Boogie*, *Son Of Dracula*, *That'll Be The Day*, *Harry And Ringo's Night Out*, *Lisztomania*, *Sextette*, *The Last Waltz*, *The Kids Are Alright*, *Caveman* and *Give My Regards To Broad Street*.

In his private life he married his Liverpool girlfriend Maureen Cox. The marriage became troubled when Ringo and Maureen joined George and Patti for dinner one night at Friar Park. George suddenly disclosed that he was in love with Maureen. Ringo fled the mansion with his wife. A couple of weeks later Patti arrived home from a shopping trip to find Maureen in bed with George.

Ringo and Maureen were divorced in July 1975 and Ringo was to marry actress Barbara Bach.

He was out of the limelight for a few years due to problems with alcohol, and had to attend a drying-out clinic with his wife.

Ringo then found a very lucrative outlet providing the voice-overs for the children's television series *Thomas The Tank Engine*, which reputedly earned him millions.

He launched his first All-Starr Band in 1989 and has continued to appear with various line-ups of the band ever since.

Stuck Inside A Cloud

A track from the *Brainwashed* album lasting 4 minutes and 4 seconds with George on lead vocals, slide guitar, acoustic guitar and background vocals. Jeff Lynne was on bass guitar, electric guitar and piano, Dhani Harrison on Wurlitzer and Jim Keltner on drums.

Sue You Sue Me Blues

A number George wrote when Paul McCartney was suing his fellow Beatles. He included it on the *Living In The Material World* album. It is 4 minutes and 38 seconds in length.

He also gave the number to Jesse Ed Davis who issued it as a single in January 1972.

Sunshine Life For Me (Sail Away Raymond)

A country style number composed by George when he was visiting Donovan in Ireland. He gave the song to Ringo for his *Ringo* album.

Tana Mana

A 'new age' CD from the Ravi Shankar Project that was released in America in June 1987 and issued in Britain by Ariola/BMG on 9 February 1990. George made guest appearances on the CD, which was recorded at George's FPSHOT Studios. The fifth track is called 'Friar Park' and George plays autoharp and synthesizer on it.

Taxman

A number penned by George, which was included on the *Revolver* album. It is 2 minutes and 35 seconds in length and was recorded in a day. The song was George's way of complaining that 95% of his income was taken by the Inland Revenue. He said, 'Are we to be punished like this for working hard?'

George didn't believe people should be taxed and in some instances he regarded it as little more than legal theft.

In the song he mentions British prime ministers Harold Wilson and Edward Heath.

John Lennon was to comment, 'I remember the day he called to ask me to help on "Taxman", one of his bigger songs. I threw in a few one-liners to help the song along because that's what he asked for. He came to me because he couldn't go to Paul McCartney because Paul wouldn't have helped him at that period. I didn't really want to help him. I thought, "Oh no, don't tell me I have to work on George's stuff." But because I loved him and didn't want to hurt him, when he called, I just sort of held my tongue and said, "OK".'

In 1984 Rockwell recorded a version of 'Taxman'. Rockwell is the pseudonym of Berry Gordy's son, Kennedy Gordy. The single was issued on Motown on 7″ (TMG 1345) and 12″ (TMGT 1345).

Taylor, Derek

Derek was a member of the Beatles close inner circle. He first met them in Manchester on 30 May 1963 when he was a reporter for the northern edition of the *Daily Express* newspaper and reviewed their concert at the Odeon, Manchester. He began to write about the Beatles regularly for the newspaper and became known as their 'Beatles man'.

Together with John Buchanan, the Manchester editor of the paper, he visited Brian Epstein to suggest that they ghost a column by a member of the Beatles. It was Derek who suggested that George should be the one as he seemed nice and was pleasant to talk to. Epstein said, 'How interesting. A rather nice idea. It would be good for George, it would give him an interest, an extra interest. John and Paul have their songwriting and Ringo is rather new.' It was agreed that Derek should ghost the column for George and he flew to Paris on 14 January 1964 to begin writing the column.

Brian Epstein next engaged him to ghostwrite his book *A Cellarful Of Noise* and he became Brian's personal assistant. A dispute with Epstein brought about his resignation and for a time he moved to America, where he became press agent for various bands, including the Byrds and the Beach Boys, in addition to helping organise the Monterey Pop Festival.

When the Beatles launched Apple, they appealed to Derek to join them and he became Apple's press officer. At one time he and George decided to collaborate on writing a Broadway musical based on the Apple press office, but they later abandoned the idea because Derek felt he couldn't write the script.

Derek was generally closer to George and he assisted George with his book *I. Me. Mine.* while George reciprocated to promote Derek's autobiography, *Fifty Years Adrift* and travelled to Australia and New Zealand in November 1985 to promote Derek's book with him. Derek also became George's press aide.

An example of their closeness is revealed by the fact that on 15 September 1978 George bought Brundon Hill, a house one mile from the market town of Sudbury, for Derek Taylor and his family. It cost £67,000.

At one time, Derek and his wife Joan were to join George in Los Angeles, but they got lost in the fog, an incident that proved the inspiration for George's 'Blue Jay Way'.

Derek died at his Suffolk home on Sunday 7 September 1997, after battling for some time with cancer. He was 65 years old. George was the only member of the Beatles who attended his funeral.

Taylor, James

An American singer/songwriter, signed to the Apple label by Peter Asher. His first Apple album contained his self-penned number 'Something In The Way She Moves', which is likely to have inspired

George because he used the phrase as the first line of his song 'Something'.

Teardrops
The second single to be issued from the *Somewhere In England* album, released in Britain on Dark Horse K 17837 on 31 July 1981 with 'Save The World' on the flip. It is 4 minutes and 1 second in length. Although it was issued in a picture sleeve, it failed to register in the British charts. It also failed to enter the American charts following its release there on Dark Horse DRC 79825 on 24 July 1981.

Thanks For The Pepperoni
A track from the *All Things Must Pass* triple album, penned by George. It's the last track of the 'Apple Jam' section and features the basic Derek & The Dominoes line-up – Jim Gordon, Carl Radle, Bobby Whitlock and Eric Clapton backing George.

That Kind Of Woman
A number penned by George, which Eric Clapton recorded for his *Journeyman* album. The number wasn't used then, but Clapton's version was released the following year in the Romanian Angel Appeal album, *Nobody's Child*. Gary Moore, another of George's friends, also recorded it and issued it as a single and included it on his 1990 album *Still Got The Blues*.

That's The Way It Goes
A number that appeared on the May 1982 album *Gone Troppo* in Britain. George, Ray Cooper and Phil McDonald produced the 3-minute 32-second track. It was remixed by George and Jeff Lynne and included as a bonus track on the CD and the 12″ version of 'When We Was Fab', which was released in Britain in January 1988.

Think For Yourself
A number composed by George and recorded by the Beatles at Abbey Road on 8 November 1965. It was included on the *Rubber Soul* album and is 2 minutes and 14 seconds in length. Commenting on the song in his book *I. Me. Mine.* George said, '"Think For Yourself" must be about "somebody" from the sound of it – but all this time later I don't quite recall who inspired that tune. Probably the government.'

There was a fuzz effect on the track that Paul McCartney achieved by playing his Rickenbacker bass through a distortion box.

Thirty Three & 1/3
George's first album on his own Dark Horse label, issued in Britain on Dark Horse K 56319 on 19 November 1976 where it reached No. 25 in the charts. It was issued in America on Dark Horse DH 3005 on 24 November 1976 and reached No. 11 in the charts.

This was the album that was the cause of the split with distributors A&M Records. The contract had stated that the album should be ready for release on 15 June 1976 (George's 33 & 1/3 birthday). However, George had hepatitis and was too ill to complete the album on schedule. As a result, A&M records sued him for $10 million for failing to deliver. It was suspected that A&M were using this as an opportunity to drop Dark Horse as they considered it to be uncommercial. A settlement was finally agreed and George then did a deal with Warner Brothers.

George was able to complete the album at his FPSHOT studios during the summer of 1976 and Warner Brothers released it on 19 November 1976.

With the exception of the Cole Porter song 'True Love', George penned all the numbers. He also co-produced the album with Tom Scott.

Musicians on the album included Tom Scott on saxophones, flute and lyricon, Willie Weeks on bass, Alvin Taylor on drums, Gary Wright on keyboards, Richard Tee on piano, organ and Fender Rhodes, Billy Preston on piano, organ and synthesizer, David Foster on Fender Rhodes and clavinet, Emil Richards on marimba and George on guitar, synthesizers and percussion.

Bob Cato designed the gatefold sleeve.

The tracks were: Side One: 'Woman Don't You Cry For Me', 'Dear One', 'Beautiful Girl', 'This Song', 'See Yourself'. Side Two: 'It's What You Value', 'True Love', 'Pure Smokey', 'Crackerbox Palace', 'Learning How To Love You'.

This Guitar (Can't Keep From Crying)

A song that George wrote during a holiday in Hawaii, and basically a continuation of 'While My Guitar Gently Weeps'. It lasts for 4 minutes and 4 seconds and was included on the 1974 *Extra Texture (Read All About It)* album. It was also released as a single in Britain on Apple R 6012 on 6 February 1976 at 3 minutes and 45 seconds. 'Maya Love', a track from the *Dark Horse* album, was on the flip.

It didn't reach the British charts.

It was issued in America on Apple 1885 on 8 December 1975. It became the first single by George not to enter the American charts. It was also the last single by George to appear on the Apple label.

This Is Love

The third single to be released from the *Cloud Nine* album. It was issued in Britain on 13 June 1988 in three different formats: the 7″ single on Dark Horse W 7913 with 'Breath Away From Heaven', the 12″ single on W 79131 with 'This Is Love', 'Breath Away From Heaven' and 'All Those Years Ago', and the 3″ CD-single on W 7913 CD with 'This Is Love', 'Breath Away From Heaven', 'All Those Years Ago' and 'Hong Kong Blues'.

The promo for the single was filmed at George's home in Maui, Hawaii at a picnic for friends and family held in George's backyard. The promo made its debut on MTV on 16 May 1988.

This Morning

A CBS television show. George and Ravi Shankar were in America promoting the *Chants Of India* album and were interviewed for the programme on Thursday 12 June 1997.

Here is a transcript:

Q: You said as a Beatle you had met captains of industry, politicians and royalty, yet no one impressed you until you met Ravi.

George: That's true, yes.

Q: Why?

George: During that time, you know, we met just about everybody and I just thought, well, I'm looking for something really beyond just the ordinary, the mundane, and that's where I wanted somebody to impress me and, you know, I didn't expect it to be this little Indian man but, you know, good things come in small packages.

Q: Now it's your turn Ravi. You've called him many things. Three words that stand out: friend, disciple, son.

Ravi: At present, chum, because he makes me laugh more than anyone else.

Q: What is it like having him in the studio with you?

Ravi: This was a great experience. He helped me so much in real producing. It's being there in the recording booth from the very beginning – balancing to editing, mixing and everything.

Q: Ravi, in this country when we hear chants, we tend to think of Gregorian chants. We think of religious chants. This album is not like that. This is more mainstream.

Ravi: I chose the chants which are not so much into religion. No matter who listens to it feels that special spiritual feeling.

George: Something like this is totally new. It's like 'and now for something completely different' and, you know, I think it's worthy. It's something that I believe in and I think it's a benefit if people during the day, you know, everybody gets stressed out and this music is particularly inclined to calm you down. It's an antidote to stress.

Q: You brought your mates Paul and John to India in the sixties to hear his music and to taste the culture. They left, you stayed. I'm speaking more, your soul stayed, as it were. Why do you think that is?

George: Well, from my point of view, it's the only place to be really. For every human is a quest to find the answer to: why are we here? Who am I? Where did I come from? Where am I going?

That to me became the most important thing in my life. Everything else is secondary. So for me there is no alternative.

This Song

A single lasting 3 minutes and 50 seconds that was issued in Britain on Dark Horse K 16856 on 19 November 1976 with 'Learning How To Love You' on the flip. It was released at the same time as George's *Thirty Three & 1/3* album.

It was also George's first American Dark Horse single when it was issued on Dark Horse DRC 8294 on 15 November 1976. It reached No. 25 in the American charts.

The number was to air George's frustration about the 'My Sweet Lord'/ 'He's So Fine' copyright case and has a short spoken piece by Eric Idle in the middle.

George was to say, 'Look, I'd be willing every time I write a song if somebody will have a computer and I can just go up to the thing and sing my new song into it and the computer will say, "Sorry" or "Yes OK". I'm willing to do that, because the last thing I want to do is keep spending the rest of my life in court or being faced with that problem.

'Once you get people thinking "Oh, well, they beat Harrison on 'My Sweet Lord', let's sue," they can sue the world! It made me so paranoid about writing. And I thought, "God, I don't even want to touch the guitar or piano in case it's touching somebody's note. Somebody might own that note, so you'd better watch out."'

Time Bandits

HandMade Films' next venture following *The Life Of Brian* was to finance the 1981 release *Time Bandits*, which had been co-scripted by Michael Palin and Terry Gilliam.

It concerns a group of dwarfs who have stolen a map of the Universe, and it relates how they set out through gaps in the structure of time in search of treasure, accompanied by Kevin, a twentieth-century schoolboy. During their adventures they encounter King Agamemnon (Sean Connery) battling the Minotaur, Napoleon (Ian Holm) sacking Italy and Robin Hood (John Cleese) in Sherwood Forest. There is a climactic battle between Good and Evil, enacted by Sir Ralph Richardson and David Warner.

George composed the tune 'Only A Dream Away' for the film, of which he was executive producer. The number was later included as a track on his *Gone Troppo* album.

Titelman, Russ

An American record producer. When George approached Warner Bros in Burbank regarding his projected *George Harrison* album, he asked three of the staff producers, Titelman, Ted Templeman and Lenny Waronker to comment on his demos. George felt he received such encouragement from Titelman that he asked him to co-produce the album with him.

Tours

Unlike Paul – or even Ringo – George did not embark on many tours during his solo career.

On Wednesday 23 October 1974 he held a press conference at the Beverly Wilshire Hotel in Los Angeles to discuss his first American solo tour, saying, 'I tried to squeeze in some concerts before Christmas, although all the places were booked out. Really, the feeling in the band was that we should do a gig in London.'

It appeared that the press were rather more interested in discussing the Beatles than the tour and George was asked what his relationship with John and Paul was like. 'It's very good,' he said. 'I haven't seen John since he's been in the States. I spoke to him a lot on the telephone. He's in great shape. I met Paul recently, and everything is very friendly. It doesn't mean everybody is going to form a band.' He was asked if he was amazed at how much the Beatles still meant to people and replied, 'Not really. I mean, it's nice. I realise that the Beatles did fill a space in the sixties. All the people that the Beatles meant something to have grown up. It's like anything you've grown up with, you get attached to things. I understand the Beatles, in many ways, did nice things and it's appreciated that the people still like them. They want to hold on to something. People are afraid of change. You can't live in the past.'

When he was asked if he was involved in negotiations to get the Beatles back together again he said, 'It's all a fantasy, putting the Beatles back together again. If we ever do that, it's because everyone is broke. I'd rather have Willie Weeks on bass than Paul McCartney. With all respect to Paul, since the Beatles I've been in a box, taking me years to be able to play with other musicians. Paul is a fine bass player, but he's a bit overpowering at times. I'd join a band with John Lennon any day, but I couldn't join a band with Paul McCartney. That's not personal, but from a musical point of view.'

At another press conference to discuss the tour, he answered various questions from reporters:

Q: Why did you decide to return to America?

George: I've been back here many times. This is the first time I've been back to work, though. It's also the first time I've had an H-I visa since '71.

Q: What was the reason for your not having the H-1?

George: I had the same problem as John Lennon. I was busted for marijuana way back in '67.

Q: Would you ever consider touring Mexico?

George: I wouldn't mind. I mean, I would go anywhere. This is really a test. I either finish this tour ecstatically happy and want to go on tour everywhere, or I'll end up just going back to my cave again for another five years.

Q: Could you tell us your feelings and expectations for the upcoming tour?

George: I think if I had more time I'd be panic-stricken, but I don't really have the time to get worried about it.

Q: Are you getting divorced from Patti?

George: No. I mean, that's as silly as marriage.

Q: Can you foresee a time when you'll give up your musical objectives?

George: I can see a time when I'd give up this sort of madness, but music – I mean, *everything* is based upon music. I'll never stop my music.

Q: What direction is your music going in now?

George: Haven't got a clue. I mean, it's getting a bit funkier, especially with Willy Weeks and all them.

Q: What's your attitude about drugs now?

George: Drugs? What drugs? Aspirins or what are you talking about? I mean, I think it's awful when it ruins people. What do you define as a drug? Like whisky? I don't want to advocate anything because it's so difficult to get into America these days.

At the beginning of his 1974 North American tour George was still suffering from laryngitis. Reviewers, critical of his failing voice, dubbed it the 'Dark Hoarse' tour and many said that, because he'd been suffering from throat problems prior to the tour, he should have postponed it until his voice was better. Critics also bemoaned the fact that George was reluctant to play Beatles songs, only doing a couple at the urging of Ravi Shankar. They also seemed unhappy at the amount of Indian music in the repertoire.

His accompanying musicians were Ravi Shankar, Billy Preston, Tom Scott, Jim Horn, Chuck Findley, Robben Ford, Andy Newmark, Emil Richards and Willie Weeks.

The repertoire for this tour comprised: 'Hari's On Tour (Express)', 'The Lord Loves The One (That Loves The Lord)', 'For You Blue', 'Something', 'While My Guitar Gently Weeps', 'Will It Go Round In Circles?', 'Sue Me, Sue You Blues', 'Who Can See It?', 'Zoom, Zoom, Zoom', 'Jai Sri Kalij', 'Naderdani', 'Vachaspati', 'Anourag', 'Dispute And Violence', 'I Am Missing You', 'Give Me Love (Give Me Peace On Earth)', 'Soundstage Of Mind', 'In My Life', 'Tom Cat', 'Maya Love', 'Outa Space', 'Dark Horse', 'What Is Life?', 'My Sweet Lord'.

At the start of each concert, George played *Monty Python's* 'The Lumberjack Song' over the PA system. He also rewrote some of the lyrics to the Lennon and McCartney number 'In My Life'.

George's rapport with the audience was often not very good. At the show in Los Angeles on 11 November he said to the audience, 'I don't know how it feels down there, but from up here, you seem pretty dead.' When someone placed flowers on the stage, he kicked them off. When a policeman was involved in a tussle with a woman in the audience at the Providence show, George shouted, 'Hey, man, hey you! Leave her alone for Christ's sake. We're trying to do a bloody show. We didn't come here for a fight.'

750,000 people saw the tour, which brought in around $4 million. Although the tour was taped every night and filming also took place, the proposed double album and film of the tour was scrapped.

The dates were:

Saturday 2 November. Pacific Coliseum, Vancouver, British Columbia, Canada.

Monday 4 November. Seattle Center Coliseum, Seattle, Washington.

Wednesday 6 November. Cow Palace, San Francisco, California.

Thursday 7 November. Cow Palace, San Francisco, California.

Friday 8 November. The Oakland/Alameda County Coliseum Arena, Oakland, California.

Sunday 10 November. Long Beach Arena, Long Beach, California.

Monday 11 November. The Forum, Los Angeles, California.

Tuesday 12 November. The Forum, Los Angeles, California.

Thursday 14 November. Tucson Community Center, Tucson, Arizona.

Saturday 16 November. Salt Palace, Salt Lake City, Utah.

Monday 18 November. Denver Coliseum, Denver, Colorado.

Wednesday 20 November. The Arena, St Louis, Missouri.

Thursday 21 November. Assembly Center, Tulsa, Oklahoma.

Friday 22 November. Tarrant County Convention Center, Fort Worth, Texas.

Sunday 24 November. Hofheinz Pavilion, Houston, Texas.

Tuesday 26 November. LSU Assembly Center, Baton Rouge, Louisiana.

Wednesday 27 November. Mid-South Coliseum, Memphis, Tennessee.

Thursday 28 November. The Omni Coliseum, Atlanta, Georgia.

Saturday 30 November. Chicago Stadium, Chicago, Illinois.

Wednesday 4 December. Olympia Stadium, Detroit, Michigan.

Friday 6 December. Maple Leaf Gardens, Toronto, Ontario, Canada.

Sunday 8 December. The Forum, Montreal, Quebec, Canada.

Tuesday 10 December. Boston Garden, Boston, Massachusetts.

Wednesday 11 December. Providence Civic Center, Providence, Rhode Island.

Friday 13 December. Capitol Center, Largo, Maryland.

Sunday 15 December. Nassau Coliseum, Uniondale, Long Island.

Monday 16 December. The Spectrum, Philadelphia.

Tuesday 17 December. The Spectrum, Philadelphia.

Thursday 19 December. Madison Square Garden, New York City, New York.

Friday 20 December. Madison Square Garden, New York City, New York.

George never really liked touring, and there was then a very long gap of seventeen years between his first American tour and his tour of Japan, called 'Rock Legends: George Harrison And Eric Clapton And His Band'.

This was George's first concert tour since his 1974 Dark Horse Tour, and it was George's first visit to Japan since he appeared there with the Beatles in 1966. The tour took place from Sunday 1 December to Tuesday 17 December 1991 and comprised just twelve concerts at six venues. It was also Eric's first live appearance since his four-year-old son died from an accidental fall from a Manhattan hotel earlier that year on 20 March.

George was backed by Eric's backing band who were: Nathan East on bass guitar, Steve Ferrone on drums, Chuck Leavell on keyboards, Greg Phillinganes on keyboards, Ray Cooper on percussion, Andy Fairweather-Low on guitar and Katie Kissoon and Tessa Niles on backing vocals.

Discussing how the tour came about in the 17 October 1991 edition of *Rolling Stone* magazine, Eric commented, 'George and I have been friends for a long time and we've always seemed to be around when one of us needed the other. And when I was on tour last year, especially in the Third World and South America and places like that, people kept asking me about George, about how he was and what he was doing. And when I got back to England, I reported all this to George, and he started talking, on a very light-hearted level, about going on the road. And then, when I looked at my schedule for this year, I saw that I was deliberately not planning to work very much, but I had all this stuff standing by, like lights and sound, and the best band in the world. And I thought, "Well, why not?" And I put it to George that he goes out with us. All he's got to do essentially is walk out on the stage and strum an electric guitar, and we'll do everything else. Nothing for him to worry about, and I put it to him, and he was delighted and scared at the same time – really scared to death. Because it's been a long time. I mean, fifteen years or so, since his last American tour.'

In an interview with the British Q magazine, Eric said, 'I don't think he's ever had the experience of playing for an audience with a great band. The Beatles played to ten-year-old kids who screamed their heads off. He's stopped smoking, he's got himself into fighting-fit shape, he's got my lighting, my sound, my band. It's a crack team. We're going to Japan where the world spotlight won't be on him and he probably won't get a bad review. It's a great opportunity. If he doesn't do it now he probably never will.'

Interesting comments from Clapton, considering the years the Beatles paid their dues, endless hours in Hamburg (those tough audiences certainly weren't ten-year-olds), the numerous hours playing in venues throughout Liverpool (those audiences didn't comprise ten-year-olds either), prompting John Lennon to say that their best years as a performing group were in Hamburg and Liverpool – he would be surprised at the dismissive remarks from Clapton about those formative years as a live band!

George, together with Eric Clapton, held a press conference at the Capitol Tokyo Hilton at 1 p.m. on Friday 29 November 1991 prior to their Japanese tour. The conference was held in the hotel's Red Pearl room and there were 500 reporters in attendance. Immediately prior to the conference the two posed for photographers in the White Pearl room.

George: Short message, hello. Very nice to be here after such a long time.

Eric: Yes, it's nice to be back in Japan, this time with a friend. I love to come to this country. I come as often as I can and will continue to do so. I hope this will be a success and hope you will enjoy it.

Q: What attracts you to each other?

George: Well, it's very difficult; it's simple, but difficult, because something mutual that you like ... you can say it's the way he bends the strings or the way he says 'Hello'. It's difficult to say. It's just an attraction we have, an attraction in our lives and it's also the way he bends the notes. Was that good enough?

Eric: Well, George is senior to me by, what, I don't know, a year?

George: I'm about thirty. How old are you?

Eric: Seventy-nine. But I've always thought that he's a great songwriter, a great musician, a very unique man; and he gave up smoking, I have to respect him for that. I think he's very brave to come here because he hasn't worked on the stage for a long time and it can be a very frightening experience, but I think it will be rewarding. But I always thought of George as being a little like the elder brother I never had, so I respect his judgement and his values and I think he's a wonderful man. I like the way he bends the strings, too. He's a great slide player, most of all he's a fantastic slide player.

Q: What do you think about Prime Minister Major?

Eric: Very anonymous. He seems to be OK, but he just seems to be rather bland.

George: I've not met him. I've only seen him a couple of times on TV, because I gave up watching television as well as smoking and I also gave up reading newspapers. So I don't really know much about him, but I still think he's better than Mrs Thatcher.

Q: How did the idea of a tour come about and why did you come to Japan?

George: Well, the reason that I came to Japan was because Eric suggested to me that this time of year would be good if I wanted to do a concert tour. He was not working and his band was available to become my band. That was one reason why I thought about working, because Eric asked me. And the reason we came to Japan was, he likes Japan and he suggested that we come here. That was the first question. To convey to the fans, really, just whatever the meaning of the songs are, if they have some meaning for the fans of Japan. I've had a lot of mail over twenty-five years from Japan. Very nice letters from the Japanese people and they seem to like – or the ones who write, anyway – seem to like my records. So I just hope they like the live music as much as they like the records.

Q: How were the songs chosen?

George: They were chosen by either the fact that they were hit singles or that it had a feeling for me that it would be good to put on – like the song, 'Taxman' – it's a song that goes regardless of if it's the sixties, seventies, eighties, nineties. There's always a taxman, so if the song seems to fit ... Just what I felt would be reminiscent, like, 'If I Needed Someone' I sang at the Budokan twenty-six years ago, maybe, so might as well sing it at the Dome twenty-six years later. The rest were mainly singles or a selection from different albums going right from 1965 until last year.

Q: Will you play 'Roll Over Beethoven'?

George: Yes. It's very popular in Japan.

Q: What would you like to do in Japan?

George: Well, I'd like to see all the bits I didn't see last time. That's maybe from the hotel to the Tokyo Dome and back. I'd like to go to Kyoto and see some temples and some gardens although it's not the best time of the year to see the gardens. But still, I may not come back for another twenty-six years so I'd better go now. And maybe go to the electric shop and buy an electric toothbrush or something.

Q: Why is your song 'Tears Of The World' not included in your book *Songs by George Harrison*?

George: It fell out on the way to Japan. I don't know, really. You should write to the publisher and ask him. Or, you'll have to buy volume two. The publisher of the book is coming to the Tokyo Dome, so I'll tell him.

Q: Will the Beatles reunite?

George: No. It can't be possible because the Beatles don't exist especially now that John Lennon is not alive. It just happens, every time Paul needs some publicity he announces to the press we're getting back together again. I wouldn't pay much attention to that.

Q: Eric, what are your plans?

Eric: When this is finished, I go back for Christmas and then I'll start a world tour next year. I don't know what George will do. Maybe he will start a world tour on his own, I don't know.

George: Who knows, we'll have to wait and see.

Q: December ninth, the anniversary of John's death, takes place during your tour. Do you plan to do anything special on that day?

George: I'll have to look at the itinerary. We'd have to be doing a concert or if not we'll be travelling to a concert. But we won't be doing anything other than singing songs. We won't be doing anything special. No, the day doesn't have any special meaning to me.

Eric: I think the fact that George will be playing is tribute enough.

George: It's not that I don't respect that day John Lennon got killed or anything, I'm just not into days. I don't remember my own birthday, I don't remember anniversaries or anything. I'm just not into remembering days.

Q: What changes have you experienced since you were last in Japan?

George: Everything has changed over twenty-five years. First of all, I'm much younger now than I used to be. I think I can sing better, I can play better and I can be a happier person. Everything's changed.

Q: Are you planning to play 'Layla'?

Eric: I don't think so, unless there's some kind of riot or public outcry and we have to play it. I've played it at nearly every show for the past twenty so it doesn't bother me not to play it now and then. George has only given me a very limited space, so I'm going to try and do a couple of new songs. But, it's all negotiable, don't worry.

George: I don't mind if he does it.

Eric: We'll see, we'll see.

George: Thank you all very much, it's nice to be here.

Following the conference the PA system played 'Got My Mind Set On You'.

George's repertoire for the tour was: 'I Want To Tell You', 'Old Brown Shoe', 'Taxman', 'Give Me Love (Give Me Peace On Earth)', 'If I Needed Someone', 'Fish On The Sand', 'Love Comes To Everyone', 'What Is Life', 'Dark Horse', 'Piggies', 'Pretending', 'Old Love', 'Badger', 'Wonderful Tonight', 'Got My Mind Set On You', 'Cloud 9', 'Here Comes The Sun', 'My Sweet Lord', 'All Those Years Ago', 'Cheer Down', 'Devil's Radio', 'Isn't It A Pity', 'While My Guitar Gently Weeps', 'Roll Over Beethoven'.

During the tour the guitars he used were a Roy Buchanan Bluesmaster electric guitar No. 6; a Gibson J-200 custom acoustic guitar; a gold Fender 12-string electric guitar; a red Fender Stratocaster Eric Clapton model and a Gibson Les Paul Standard '60.

The itinerary was:

Sunday 1 December 1991. Yokohama, Japan.
Monday 2 December 1991. Osaka, Japan.
Tuesday 3 December 1991. Osaka, Japan.
Thursday 5 December 1991. Nagoya, Japan.
Friday 6 December 1991. Hiroshima, Japan.
Monday 9 December 1991. Fukuoka, Japan.
Tuesday 10 December 1991. Osaka, Japan.
Wednesday 11 December 1991. Osaka, Japan.
Thursday 12 December 1991. Osaka, Japan.
Saturday 14 December 1991. Tokyo, Japan.
Sunday 15 December 1991. Tokyo, Japan.
Tuesday 17 December 1991. Tokyo, Japan.

The tour was to gross £9.7 million.

Traveling Wilburys, The

When George was in Los Angeles in the spring of 1988 putting together tracks for a single to be released from the *Cloud Nine* album, he felt that he needed a new song to include as a bonus track on the 12″ single due for European release.

He contacted Jeff Lynne, who was co-producing with him, to participate in a song writing session. He also phoned Bob Dylan, who lived nearby, to ask if they could record the number at Dylan's recording studio, which was in his garage. George had left his guitar at Tom Petty's house a few nights earlier, so he invited Petty along. When Lynne arrived Roy Orbison accompanied him – Jeff had been working on Roy's album *Mystery Girl* at the time.

While George and Jeff worked on the song, Dylan prepared a barbecue.

George recalled, 'I looked behind the garage door and there was a cardboard box with "Handle With Care" on it.'

Then, all five musicians began to pitch in with suggestions for the number. George was to recall, 'I thought of the first line, then everyone was writing words with Dylan saying some hysterical things. Then we thought, "If Roy Orbison's coming along, we might as well have a lovely bit for him." So we wrote that, then just sang it. The next day we added electric guitar and bass, and mixed it. It was instant.'

The number was called 'Handle With Care'. When WEA Records heard the completed track they considered it to be too good to throw away as a B side, so George put it aside. He then thought it would be a good idea if they turned the collaboration into a full-scale album project.

For the next ten days the five musicians began writing together in

Dylan's garden and recording in his garage. What developed was the album *The Traveling Wilburys Volume 1*.

George and Jeff returned to England, where they added the final overdubs, and the album was issued in October 1988, soon after the release of the single 'Handle With Care'.

Michael Palin wrote the sleeve notes for the album. The tracks are: Side One: 'Handle With Care', 'Dirty World', 'Rattled', 'Last Night', 'Not Alone Anymore'. Side Two: 'Congratulations', 'Heading For The Light', 'Margarita', 'Tweeter And The Monkey Man', 'End Of The Line'.

It was issued in America on 25 October 1988 with the catalogue numbers: album Wilbury 4 25796, cassette Wilbury 1 25796 and CD Wilbury 2 25796. It was issued in Britain on the same date on Wilbury WX224.

The name Wilbury had been a suggestion from George and Jeff. While they had been recording *Cloud Nine*, when there were any technical problems with their equipment they said that gremlins were at work and they called them 'Wilburys' – it was an in-joke. George suggested they call themselves the Trembling Wilburys, but Dylan preferred the Traveling Wilburys.

They then decided to create a little history. They would masquerade as half-brothers, all sons of Charles Truscott Wilbury Senior. Bob Dylan was Lucky Wilbury or Boo Wilbury. Jeff Lynne was Otis Wilbury or Clayton Wilbury. Tom Petty was Charlie T. Jr or Muddy Wilbury. Roy Orbison was Lefty Wilbury and George was Nelson Wilbury or Spike Wilbury.

The other musicians who participated were referred to as 'the Sideburys'. They comprised Jim Keltner on drums, Jim Horn on sax and Ray Cooper on percussion. Ian Wallace played tom-toms on the 'Handle With Care' track.

After the death of Orbison it was rumoured that Del Shannon might replace him in the group. When told about the rumours, Shannon said, 'At the moment it's not likely to happen until the band gets back together from doing their own individual stuff. If they decide on a second album, I'd be interested.'

The Wilburys did go ahead and make a second album, but only as a quartet as they felt that Roy Orbison couldn't be replaced.

George said, 'You can't really replace somebody like Roy. As far as another member goes, I don't think it's that important. If some magic little thing happens, maybe there will be somebody. You could really have any number of Wilburys. The basic idea is attitude. For now, it's just us four.'

George joined Bob Dylan, Jeff Lynne and Tom Petty in Bel Air to record the album from Friday 27 April until Tuesday 15 May 1990. George only submitted one of his numbers, 'Maxine', but this was rejected and he had none of his own compositions on the album.

The first number recorded was 'Nobody's Child', a number that the Beatles had originally backed Tony Sheridan on in Hamburg in 1962. This was at the suggestion of Bob Dylan when George mentioned Olivia's Romanian Angel Appeal and the idea that they should donate a track.

There was no *Traveling Wilburys Volume 2* – their second and final album was called *Traveling Wilburys Volume 3*, due to the fact that a bootleg album called *Traveling Wilburys Volume 2* had already been released.

It was released on 29 October 1990 in both Britain and America. The UK release was on Wilbury WX384 and the American on Wilbury 9 26324-2. It comprised the tracks: 'She's My Baby', 'Inside Out', 'If You Belonged To Me', 'The Devil's Been Busy', '7 Deadly Sins', 'Poor House', 'Where Were You Last Night?', 'You Took My Breath Away' and 'Wilbury Twist'.

There were a number of singles released. 'Handle With Care' c/w 'Margarita' was the first (and, in the British release, a bonus track on an extended 'Handle With Care' issued in October 1988). 'End Of The Line' was released in February 1989 with an extended mix of 'End Of The Line', plus 'Congratulations'. 'Nobody's Child' was released in aid of the Romanian Orphans appeal in June 1990. 'She's My Baby' c/w the instrumental 'New Blue Moon' and 'Runaway' followed the same year and the final single was issued in March 1991 with 'Wilbury Twist' c/w 'New Blue Moon (Instrumental)' and 'Cool Dry Place'.

It was recorded at Wilbury Mountain Studio, Bel Air, California between March and May 1990 and at FPSHOT in July 1990.

It featured Tom Petty as Muddy Wilbury on acoustic and lead and backing vocals; Bob Dylan as Boo Wilbury on acoustic guitar, harmonica and lead and backing vocals; Jeff Lynne on acoustic guitar, bass, keyboards and lead and backing vocals; and George Harrison as Spike Wilbury on acoustic and electric guitars, mandolin, sitar and lead and backing vocals.

Other musicians included Jim Keltner on drums and percussion, Ray Cooper on percussion and Jim Horn on saxophones.

Gary Moore, under the name Ken Wilbury, played lead guitar on the opening track, 'She's My Baby'. The other tracks were: 'Inside Out', 'If You Belonged To Me', 'The Devil's Been Busy', '7 Deadly Sins', 'Poor House', 'Where Were You Last Night?', 'Cool Dry Place', 'New Blue Moon', 'You Took My Breath Away', 'Wilbury Twist', 'Runaway', 'Maxine', 'Like A Ship' and 'Nobody's Child'.

Following his tour of Japan, his first in seventeen years, George began to talk of a Traveling Wilburys tour, but it never happened.

He commented, 'That would be something I'd like to experience. I've always played around in my own mind what a Wilburys tour could be. Would each person do a solo set and then do Wilburys at the end, or would we all go right on from beginning to end and make everything

Wilburys? It's an intriguing thought. We could have a great band up there and the four of us could play acoustic if we wanted to. We could all sing 'Blowin' In The Wind', and Bob could sing 'Something'. Or we could just sing our individual songs and make them Wilbury tunes, as if we'd recorded them that way. Whatever it was, we could do it.'

Tom Petty also commented on the lack of a tour, since people said they were the *Traveling* Wilburys: 'I think it would work, if we wanted to do it. I don't think we ever considered it, really. There were a lot of nights when the conversation would roll around to that. But I don't think anybody ever took it seriously. I think it would ruin it in a way. Then you're obligated to be responsible, and it's not in the character of that group. It would make it very formal, and that would be the wrong spirit.'

A third album also wasn't to be, even though George said, 'There is definitely going to be another Wilbury album – volume 5. Each one of us enjoyed it so much.'

Sadly, it wasn't to be. Following the death of Roy Orbison, there were rumours of Del Shannon replacing him, of using unreleased tapes from Carl Perkins, but another album never materialised.

Neither did a Wilburys film. George was to say, 'We were trying to make a Wilbury film. We were going to film all the songs, it was all read – we had the studios booked, we had director David Leland, and every song filmed in a different location. Unfortunately Roy died, but I'd still like to do it sometime.'

Tribute To George Harrison

A sixty-minute video tribute by the Hare Krishna movement in the Bhaktivedanta Video Library series from Illumination television, issued in 2002, mainly concerning George's devotion to Hare Krishna and his association with Bhaktivedanta Manor, which he bought for the movement. It contained reminiscences by Krishna devotees and friends of George, including Syamasundar Dasa and Garudas Dasa.

George is shown visiting the manor in 1993, playing harmonium and leading devotees into the Hare Krishna Mantra, then he begins to perform it himself. He is seen praying at the temple and as he is leaving a devotee says, 'You changed our lives.'

George turns to him and says, 'You changed mine also!'

There are various other memories and tributes and the video claims that the number 'Something' was written about George's meeting with Prabhupada, but he then changed the lyric from 'he' to 'she'.

Troy, Doris

An American singer, whose major hit was 'Just One Look' in 1963. She visited Britain in 1969 and acted as a backing vocalist on a number of records for artists such as Tom Jones and Engelbert Humperdinck.

It was Madeleine Bell who arranged for her to be a backup singer on

Billy Preston's 'That's The Way God Planned It', which George produced. George asked her if she was signed to any record label and when she admitted she wasn't he offered her an Apple Records contract. Within a few days she had signed three Apple contracts – one as an artist, one as a producer and a third as a writer. George then produced 'Ain't That Cute' as her Apple debut single in February 1970 and he and Billy Preston played on the flipside, 'Vaya Con Dios'.

Her second single was 'Jacob's Ladder', a traditional number that was arranged by George, and he and Preston once again played on the flipside of the record, the Lennon and McCartney number 'Get Back'.

Her eponymous Apple album was self-produced, although it included the number 'Ain't That Cute', which George and Doris had co-written and George had produced. The track 'Give Me Back My Dynamite' was also co-written by George and Doris and the tracks 'Gonna Get My Baby Back' and 'You Give Me Joy Joy' were written by George, Doris, Ringo Starr and Stephen Stills.

The records weren't successful and Doris returned to the States in 1974.

True Love

A number penned by Cole Porter and originally featured in the 1956 film *High Society*. It was the only song not written by George to be included on the 1976 album *Thirty Three & 1/3* and is 2 minutes and 43 seconds in length.

It was also issued as a single in Britain on Dark Horse K 16896 on 18 February 1977 with 'Pure Smokey' on the flip. It failed to make any impact on the charts and wasn't issued as a single in America.

George reworked the number and was actually to comment at the time, 'Oh, you know, Cole Porter got the chords wrong! No, he wrote some very very fine songs and I think we used to sing that tune in the past when we used to play in Hamburg in Germany. We had to play like eight hours a night, so we used to play every song we'd ever imagined. This is going back a bit, like 1959 it was, I think. And we used to do whatever we heard and whatever we could come up with in order to try not to repeat too many. Of course we had our favourites, which we'd play a couple of times in the night, but save for the main sets which were when most of the crowd were there. But I think somewhere down the line we might even have done that song. But I don't know. Just this summer I was sitting around with the guitar and that song came into my mind and I just started playing it. And I thought then that it's so off-the-wall really and it's such a nice song. It's a very simple melody and very simple words, only about four words in it! And yet it's a nice song, it's a love song, it's an 'up' song and I just like the tune. And I just thought I'd fiddle it about a bit, with the chords . . . and then I just heard that arrangement, that it could be done just like that. That song could be done any way really, it's very adaptable. I mean, Bing's version sounds like he needs speeding up a bit or winding up! I don't know, it sounds a bit dreary. And I think this way, it's got a bit more life in it.'

Note: The Beatles weren't in Hamburg in 1959, of course. They went over the following year.

Try Some, Buy Some

One of two songs George wrote specially for Ronnie Spector when she was signed to Apple. He also co-produced the number with Phil Spector and played guitar on it.

The single was released in Britain on Apple 33 on 16 April 1971 and in America on Apple 1832 on 19 April 1971, but failed to make an impact, only reaching No. 77 in the American charts and receiving no chart placing in Britain.

Ronnie didn't like the song and said that she didn't understand a word of it. The flipside was 'Tandoori Chicken', co-written by George and Phil Spector, which Ronnie said was 'even weirder' than the A side.

Later, George decided to take away Ronnie's vocal from the recording and, using the original backing track, recorded the number himself and included it on his 1973 album *Living In The Material World*.

Unconsciousness Rules

A number composed by George that he included on his 1981 album *Somewhere In England*. It is 3 minutes and 3 seconds in length.

Under The Red Sky

A Bob Dylan album released by CBS in the UK on 17 September 1996 on CBS 467188-1 in vinyl, CBS 467188-4 on cassette and CBS 467188-2 on CD. It was issued in the US on 11 September. George appears on the title track playing slide guitar.

UNICEF Award

George was the recipient of the UNICEF Award on Tuesday 9 February 1982. He was presented with the award in Los Angeles by Hugh Downes, chairman of the US committee for UNICEF. The award was for his 1971 concert for Bangla Desh. At the same time George received a citation for 'Outstanding Contribution To The World's Children'.

George commented, 'It's nice to know you can achieve these sort of things. Even though the concert was over ten years ago and the public has probably forgotten about the problems of Bangladesh, the children still probably need help and the money will have significant impact.'

Unknown Delight

A track, penned by George, on his 1982 album *Gone Troppo*. It lasts for 4 minutes and 15 seconds and features vocal backing from Willie Greene, Bobby King and Pico Payne. Gary Brooker also plays synthesizer.

Van Eaton, Lon And Derrek

The brothers were former members of an American band called Jacob's Creek, which disbanded in March 1971. The two began writing and recording their own material and their manager Robin Garb sent the tapes to several recording companies, including Apple. Apple A&R man Tony King brought the tapes to the attention of George, who liked the material. John Lennon and Ringo Starr agreed and the duo was signed to Apple and flew to London to record their first album.

George produced their first number, 'Sweet Music', which became their first American single, issued on Apple 1845 on 6 March 1972. Klaus Voormann produced the flipside, 'Song Of Songs'.

Apple also released their album *Brother*, which contained the track 'Sweet Music', but they were present at a stage when Apple was crumbling and its main focus was on releases by the Beatles, so they moved to A&M Records.

A&M Records at the time was distributing George's new label 'Dark Horse' and the brothers were asked to back George on his *Dark Horse* album. Derrek recalled, 'That was around the time when Dark Horse was at A&M and George said come along and sing. I mean, to help us out, you know.'

Derrek also said, 'I remember once I was in George's sports car in Los Angeles and Dark Horse was at A&M, you know, that old Charlie Chaplin lot. We were speeding along and we pull up and he's got his whole offices and everything in there and the guard says, "Well, I'm not letting you in without a pass."'

Wah-Wah

A track from the *All Things Must Pass* triple album. It was penned by George and is 5 minutes and 34 seconds in length.

George originally wrote the song after he walked out on the Beatles on 10 January 1969, primarily following arguments with Paul.

He said, 'I just got fed up with the bad vibes and that arguments with Paul were being put on film. I didn't care if it was the Beatles, I was getting out. Getting home in that pissed-off mood, I wrote that song. "Wah-Wah" was saying, "You've given me a bloody headache!"'

Wake Up My Love

A single issued in Britain on Dark Horse 929864-7 on Monday 8 November 1982. It was the opening track from George's *Gone Troppo* album, and his only single release during the year. George refused to promote the single and it didn't chart in Britain. 'Greece' was on the flip. It was released in America on Dark Horse 7-29864 on the same day as the album, Wednesday 27 October 1982, also with 'Greece' on the flip. It reached its highest position, No. 53, on 4 December. It was produced by George, Ray Cooper and Phil McDonald and is 3 minutes and 33 seconds in length. A 12″ promotional single version was also released in America on Dark Horse PRO A-1075.

Water

A HandMade comedy which starred Michael Caine, Billy Connolly and Leonard Rossiter. Shortly before the film went into production, a major part of the funding was withdrawn and George had to dig deep in his pockets.

George was the executive producer and appeared in a cameo with

Ringo Starr and Eric Clapton in a charity concert sequence for the United Nations in the Singing Rebels Band during a performance of 'Freedom'. The sequence was filmed at Shepperton Studios, London.

Two other songs in the film, sung by Jimmy Helms, were co-written by George, who plays guitar on the soundtrack.

The first, 'Celebration', was written in collaboration with Mike Moran, while the second, 'Focus Of Attention', was penned by George, Moran and Dick Clement.

The film was premiered at the Odeon, Leicester Square on Friday 18 January 1985.

WDHA-FM

An American radio station, also known as 'The Rock of New Jersey', which presented a regular Beatles show hosted by Ken Michaels. On 21 February 1993 they presented a poll of their listeners' all-time favourite George Harrison songs. They were: (1) 'Something', (2) 'While My Guitar Gently Weeps', (3) 'Here Comes The Sun', (4) 'What Is Life?', (5) 'My Sweet Lord', (6) 'Give Me Love', (7) 'If I Needed Someone', (8) 'Blow Away', (9) 'Your Love Is Forever', (10) 'When We Was Fab', (11) 'Don't Let Me Wait Too Long', (12) 'Love Comes To Everyone', (13) 'I Need You', (14) 'All Things Must Pass', (15) 'All Those Years Ago', (16) 'Isn't It A Pity?', (17) 'Taxman', (18) 'Awaiting On You All', (19) 'Crackerbox Palace', (20) 'This Is Love'.

Weeks, Willie

An American country music bass player and session musician, who had appeared on albums by a host of artists including the Rolling Stones, Stevie Wonder, Rod Stewart and David Bowie.

George hired him to play on four of his albums: *Living In The Material World*, *Dark Horse*, *George Harrison* and *Somewhere In England*.

West 57th Street

An American television programme. On Saturday 12 December 1987 it featured an interview with George to promote his *Cloud Nine* album.

The interview, conducted by British journalist Selina Scott, lasted for fourteen minutes and included shots of George with Bob Hoskins during the editing of the film *Mona Lisa*. Philip Norman, author of *Shout!* was also on hand to add some comments.

Selina asked George about comments John Lennon made in his September 1980 interview with *Playboy* magazine:

Selina: In an interview before his death, John said he was really hurt by you, that you never mentioned in your autobiography any of the influence that he had on you.

George: He was annoyed 'cause I didn't say that he'd written one line of this song 'Taxman'. But I also didn't say how I wrote two lines of

'Come Together' or three lines of 'Eleanor Rigby', you know. I wasn't
getting into any of that. I think, in the balance, I would have had more
things to be niggled with him about than he would have had with me.

Selina: He said that you idolised him as a young boy.

George: That's what he thought. I liked him very much. He was a
groove. He was a good lad. But, at the same time, he misread me. He
didn't realise who I was, and this was one of the main faults of John
and Paul. They were so busy being John and Paul, they failed to realise
who else was around at the time.

Philip Norman: The Beatles is not a normal story! It's a supernatural
story. The pressure was supernatural – and George has recovered from
it. He's the one that we're going to have to ask about the Beatles.
There's no one else left to ask now, because McCartney won't tell you,
Ringo can't tell you, and John isn't here.

Selina: When you say Paul won't tell you, what do you mean?

Philip: He rewrites history all the time.

Selina: And Ringo can't tell you?

Philip: He doesn't know. He drank the drinks, he smoked the joints,
he had the girls and he drummed the drums. That was Ringo.

What Is Life?

A track from George's solo debut album *All Things Must Pass*, which
was 4 minutes and 20 seconds in length.

Another version of the recording was included as a bonus track on
the two-CD re-release of *All Things Must Pass* in 1991.

George was to comment, 'When we were going through all the tapes,
I just found this version that was like a rough mix on which I tried
having this piccolo trumpet player like the guy who played on "Penny
Lane". It wasn't actually the same bloke but I wanted that sound. So I
had an oboe and a piccolo trumpet and I had this part for them all
written out but they couldn't play it the same; they couldn't do this
kind of "hush" phrase, and they played it very staccato like a classical
player. So I must have just recorded them on it, then rough-mixed it,
and then ditched that.'

When Every Song Is Sung

A song penned by George, which was originally called 'Whenever' and
intended for Shirley Bassey. Ronnie Spector and Leon Russell also
attempted it.

'When Every Song Is Sung' was written and produced by George in
1972. In August of that year he recorded it at Friar Park with Cilla
Black, backed by Ringo on drums and Eric Clapton on guitar, along
with another song called 'You've Gotta Stay With Me'. Cilla had taken
a day off from Blackpool summer season on a Sunday, had an appointment with a dentist earlier that day and she wasn't in the mood to
record. She tried it again in 1974 with another producer. When she met

George in a vegetarian restaurant in London, they discussed recording it again. It had been retitled 'I'll Still Love You' and was re-recorded by Ringo for his *Rotogravure* album in 1976.

When We Was Fab

The second single to be released from the *Cloud Nine* album. The number 'Zig Zag' was on the flipside. It was issued in Britain on 25 January 1988 in 7″ and 12″ formats. The 7″ was on Dark Horse W8131 with just the two tracks. The 12″, on Dark Horse W8131T, had an extended version of 'When We Was Fab', 'Zig Zag', 'That's The Way It Goes (Remix)' and 'When We Was Fab (Reverse End)'.

The CD and 12″ with bonus tracks were issued only in Britain.

The promo was shot in Britain in December 1987 and Ringo and Elton John appeared alongside George. Paul McCartney refused to be in the video.

While My Guitar Gently Weeps

A number composed by George, which was included on *The Beatles* double album. It is 4 minutes and 41 seconds in length.

He recalled, 'I decided to write a song based on the first thing I saw upon opening any book. I picked up a book at random, opened it, saw "gently weeps", then laid the book down again and started the song.'

George felt that John and Paul turned a deaf ear to 'While My Guitar Gently Weeps', one of 23 songs taped during demo sessions at George's house. Recording began on 25 July 1968. 'I worked on that song with John, Paul and Ringo one day and they were not interested in it at all. And I knew inside of me that it was a nice song.'

During July 25 he taped a solo version.

Because of the apathy he'd received, George invited Eric Clapton to participate in the recording. The two were driving into London from Surrey on 6 September when George suggested it. Clapton said, 'I can't do that. Nobody ever plays on Beatles records.'

George insisted and took him into Abbey Road where Eric played the guitar solo on his Les Paul.

EMI's Brian Gibson was to comment, 'Eric behaved like any session musician, very quiet, just got on and played. That was it. There were no theatrics involved. I remember Eric telling George that Cream's approach to the recording would be to rehearse, rehearse, rehearse, spending very little time in the studio itself, whereas the Beatles approach seemed to be to record, record, record, and then eventually get the right one. The sessions were their rehearsals.'

Later, George was to say, 'It made them all try a bit harder; they were all on their best behaviour.'

White, Timothy

The editor-in-chief of *Billboard* magazine, who interviewed George on several occasions. George said that White was his favourite journalist.

He did an in-depth interview with George for the Saturday 5 December 1992 issue of *Billboard*, which sported George on the cover. This was to tie in with the fact that George had been awarded the first *Billboard* 'Century Award'.

White discussed George's spiritual life at length and a number of previously unpublished facts were to emerge. George told White, 'You may want to give a bit of warning to the Beatles fanatics about these details – since they're different from what's been published up until now – or you might never hear the end of it.' One of these facts was that George said his birthday was actually 24 February 1943 and not 25 February – which he had been celebrating as his birthday for nearly fifty years. He was born at 11.42 p.m.

In another interview published in *Billboard* on Saturday 9 March 1996, George told White: 'After all these years of lawyers that I got sucked into after having to handle my own business and find out what happened to it after Denis O'Brien abandoned ship, I've hardly ever picked up the guitar, other than doing the recent Beatles stuff and all the Beatles editing.

'It's a help (winning the lawsuit), but I didn't actually get any money. We've got to follow him to the ends of the earth, getting the case registered in every different area where he could have any assets. It's one thing winning, but actually getting the money is another thing.

'Those years from the end of 1991 have been like hell, so it's just recently that I've written some new tunes, and I'm trying to find the time not to deal with all these accountants and lawyers. O'Brien did put me unnecessarily through a real ugly scene. If I could have had a record recorded during the year, that would be quite nice, and I've got a few tunes that are decent.'

Wilkes, Tom

An album-cover artist who designed the covers of George's first four solo albums.

Wilkes has designed sleeves for artists ranging from the Rolling Stones to the Mamas and the Papas and also designed the poster for the Monterey Pop Festival in 1967. Until 1970 he worked in the creative department of A&M Records.

He received a letter from George and Phil Spector asking him to design the package for *All Things Must Pass*. Then George asked him to become involved in the *Bangla Desh* project, which he just worked on for expenses with his associates in Camouflage Productions. George flew them into New York and they did all the photography and put the whole package together.

For the *All Things Must Pass* package, George flew Wilkes and his photographer partner Barry Feinstein to England and they arrived at Friar Park, where they explored the ground, looking for ideas. They found various gnomes lying around and when George came along in his Wellingtons, they began taking the photographs. Pictures from the session were also used on the picture sleeves for 'What Is Life?' and 'My Sweet Lord'.

For the *Concert For Bangla Desh* sleeve Wilkes selected a press agency photo of a starving child and did extensive airbrushing prior to completing the design. Together with his partner Barry and Alan Pariser, the man who organised the Monterey Pop Festival, they prepared the entire package, together with a booklet, free of charge.

Wilkes also designed the cover of *Living In The Material World*, which used a Kirlian photograph of the aura of George's hand on the cover. Thelma Moss of the Parapsychological Department at UCLA took this. When the photograph was taken, George was holding a Hindi medal in his hand.

For the *Dark Horse* album, George gave Wilkes one of his school photographs and asked him to put it on the cover, but to make it look East Indian, so Wilkes painted a watercolour, which produced the Indian effect.

Wilkes, together with Craig Braun, was also commissioned to design the *Red* and *Blue* Beatle anthologies.

Will

There have been different reports regarding George's will and the money he left. One report stated that in his will George left £99,226,700, which was reduced to £98,916,400 after expenses had been deducted. The money was to be divided between Olivia and family members. However, 40% was said to have gone to the Inland Revenue in death duties.

Other reports alleged that he left £200m, the majority of which was left to his wife Olivia and son Dhani. It was claimed that the will also said that up to 10% of George's wealth was to be distributed to the International Society for Krishna Consciousness. George had supported this organisation both spiritually and financially for thirty years. The organisation was also to benefit from earnings from George's future royalties. A major donation was also left to Bhaktivedanta Manor, which George had bought for the Krishna movement in Britain. It was also said that £5 million was to be distributed to charities in aid of children in poor African countries.

Within You, Without You

A number penned by George, which was included on the *Sgt Pepper's Lonely Hearts Club Band* album. It is 5 minutes in length.

George wrote the song one evening after having dinner at Klaus Voormann's house. He was to recall, 'Klaus Voormann had a harmonium in his house, which I hadn't played before. I was doodling on it, playing to amuse myself, when "Within You, Without You" started to come. The tune came initially, and then I got the first line. It came out of what we'd been discussing that evening.'

The number was recorded at Abbey Road Studios on 15 March 1967, with overdubbing taking place on 22 March and 3 April.

Apart from singing lead vocal, George played a tamboura, as did Neil Aspinall.

George had also invited a number of Indian musicians to the session and their instruments were: a dilruba (a bowed instrument), tamboura, tabla and swordmandel (a zither-like instrument). There were also eight violinists and three cellists.

George Martin, who produced and arranged the session, commented, 'I worked very closely on the scoring of it, using a string orchestra, and he brought in some friends from the Indian Music Association to play special instruments. I was introduced to the dilruba, an Indian violin, in playing which a lot of sliding techniques are used. This meant that in scoring for that track I had to make the string players play very much like Indian musicians, bending the notes, and with slurs between one note and the next.'

John Lennon was to say that 'Within You, Without You' was 'one of George's best songs. One of my favourites of his, too. He's clear on that song. His mind and his music are clear. There is his innate talent; he brought that sound together.'

Woman Don't You Cry For Me

George penned this number while he was touring with Delaney And Bonnie in December 1969. It is the opening track on the *Thirty Three & 1/3* album and is 3 minutes and 15 seconds in length.

Discussing the inspiration for the song, George said, 'Eric Clapton really was a big influence to help me get back into the guitar because I went through a period when I just played sitar for years and I never played any guitar. I just forgot about it. And Eric ... I was friendly with Eric and he gave me this great guitar and I really got back involved. And I started to try and play slide, slide guitar. I always wanted to sort of be able to catch up a bit on my guitar playing, because by that time, with not playing it for so long – and we'd given up playing live dates – I was very rusty and all kinds of players, little kids coming up, eight years old, playing the best licks you've ever heard. So I felt a bit sort of behind and I got back involved with the guitar due to Eric. And I always admired him as a guitar player and as a friend. And that song really just is a couple of chords, but played more in the country rock sort of thing with slide guitar for me old pal Clapper.'

Wonderwall (album)

A movie soundtrack album by George, making him the first member of the Beatles to compose a complete soundtrack for a film. Although the soundtrack was issued under George's name, he only composed and produced and didn't play on any of the tracks.

He was initially asked to become involved in composing the soundtrack by director Joe Massott in 1967, although Massott had originally approached the Bee Gees, who declined the project. George began work on it after the *Magical Mystery Tour* in late 1967, deciding on an instrumental soundtrack, and produced a series of home demos after viewing an unfinished version of the film.

He then gathered a number of musicians using Abbey Road and the De Lane Lea Recording Studio in Kingsway. He produced two numbers in Abbey Road's Studio 2 on Wednesday 22 November 1967 under the working titles 'India' and 'Swordfencing', utilising the talents of two flautists, Richard Adeney and Jack Ellory, together with a tabla player. The following day he was recording in Studio 3 and the musicians used included two oboists, one trumpeter and two flautists.

The complete personnel of musicians at the various London sessions were: John Barham, piano, flugelhorn; Tommy Reilly, harmonica; Colin Manley, guitar, steel guitar; Tony Ashton, jangle piano, organ; Phil Rogers, bass; Roy Dyke, drums.

He recorded another session at Abbey Road's Studio 2 on 5 January. On 7 January 1968, George flew to India and spent five days at the EMI Studios in Bombay. Musicians at the Bombay sessions included: Ashish Khan, sarod; Mahapurush Mistra, tabla, pakavaj; Sharod and Hanuman Jadev, shanghais; Sambu-Das, Indril Bhattacharya, Shankar Ghosh, sitars; Chandra Shakher, surbahar; Shiv Kumar Shermar, santoor; S.R. Kenkare, flute; Vanaik Vora, thar-shanhai, Rij Ram Desad, harmonium, tablatarang.

The album became the first LP released on the Apple label on Friday 1 November 1968 on Apple SAPCOR 1 and in America on 2 December 1968 on Apple ST 3350, where it reached No. 49 in the charts.

The tracks were: Side One: 'Microbes', 'Red Lady Too', 'Tabla and Pakavaj', 'In The Park', 'Drilling A Home', 'Guru Vandana', 'Greasy Legs', 'Ski-ing', 'Gat Kirwani', 'Dream Scene'. Side Two: 'Party Secombe', 'Love Scene', 'Crying', 'Cowboy Music', 'Fantasy Sequins', 'On The Bed', 'Glass Box', 'Wonderwall To Be Here', 'Singing Om'.

Bob Gill, John Kelly and Alan Aldridge designed the album sleeve, with a front-cover illustration by Bob Gill.

Wonderwall (film)

George provided the soundtrack of this film, directed by Joe Massott and starring Jane Birkin, Jack MacGowran and Iain Quarrier. The story revolves around Oscar, a scientist who works for the water board, who accidentally creates a hole in his wall and watches a young model and her photographer boyfriend, who live next door, a plot not unlike the Henry Barbousse novel *L'Enfer*. The Fool also provided designs.

Wonderwall was premiered at the Cannes Film Festival on 17 May 1968 with George and Patti and Ringo and Maureen in attendance. The British release was on 12 January 1969.

Rhino Home Video in America released the film in DVD format in 1996. Apart from the feature film, the limited edition box set contained a 120-page book, a 7" vinyl single ('In The First Place' by the Remo Four), plus a CD single of the same number, a *Wonderwall* poster, a 66-page screenplay and colour stickers.

Wood, Ronnie

A former member of the Faces, who is now a member of the Rolling Stones. When he was still with the Faces, he and his wife Chrissie were invited as George's guests at Friar Park mansion for a month in October 1973. During the month, Wood reportedly had a liaison with George's wife Patti and on Monday 26 November 1973 he issued a statement: 'My romance with Patti Boyd is definitely on. Things will be sorted out in a few days. Until then, I naturally can't say very much. We're going to talk it out between us and hope to get a happy arrangement. Meanwhile, Patti has gone back to her home and will be talking to George about it. I won't be seeing her today.'

When George read the statement, he said, 'Whatever Ronnie Wood has got to say about anything, certainly about us, it has nothing to do with Patti or me. Got that? It has nothing to do with us – her or me!'

This caused the press to speculate that George and Patti's marriage was near breaking point.

Some years later, on Sunday 22 January 1984, Chrissie exposed the relationship in a *News Of the World* interview in which she said it had been a matter of wife swapping, with her and George going on holiday together to Portugal and Switzerland and Ronnie and Patti holidaying in the Bahamas together.

Work It Out

A 1990 album by brass musician Jim Horn, who had played on a number of George's albums. George, Jeff Lynne and Tom Petty all featured on the recording.

World Of Stone

The flipside of 'You', which was included on the 1976 album *Extra Texture*, but had been written a few years previously. George recorded the basic track on 2 May 1975 with Jesse Ed Davis, Jim Keltner and David Foster. The overdubbing took place on 2 June with Paul Stallworth, Davis and Foster.

Wrack My Brain

A number composed by George that he gave to Ringo for his *Stop And Smell The Roses* album. George also produced the song and played both lead and acoustic guitars. Ringo played drums, of course, and the other musicians were Herbie Flowers on bass and tuba, Al Cooper on piano and electric guitar and Ray Cooper on piano, percussion, synthesizer and lead guitar. George and Cooper supplied the backing vocals.

The number was also issued as a single in Britain on RCA 166 on 13 November 1981 with 'Drumming Is My Madness' on the flip, although it didn't chart. It was issued in America on Boardwalk NB7-11-30 on 27 October 1981 where it reached No. 38 in the charts.

Wright, Gary
A former member of Spooky Tooth, who became a close friend and associate of George's and appeared on a number of his albums, beginning with *All Things Must Pass*. He had met George previously, but it was through Klaus Voormann that he attended the sessions and began to participate.

When Gary recorded an album with his group Wonderwheel at Apple Studios in 1972, George played on the track 'Goodbye Goodbye Sunday'.

Their friendship developed and Gary visited India with George, during which he met his guru, Paramahansa Yogananda. Gary told journalist Rick Glover, 'And from that meeting, eventually everything I do, the way I think, the way I feel has never been the same. So I am eternally grateful for the events that led me to that meeting.'

Wright has played on virtually all of George's albums from *All Things Must Pass* to *Cloud Nine*. They co-wrote the songs 'If You Believe' and 'That's What It Takes', and also appeared together on *The Dick Cavett Show* in America on 23 November 1971 when George played slide guitar with Wonderwheel on 'Two-Faced Man'. George had also been a guest on three of Gary's albums, *Footprint*, *Who Am I?* and *First Signs Of Life*.

In late August 1972 George, sans Patti, spent a week's holiday with Gary and his wife Christina at a villa they'd rented in Portugal. Gary commented, 'George is just driving around Portugal and the south of France, staying with friends and at hotels. He seems to be enjoying himself. He's writing lots of new things and he seems to be having a good time.'

Commenting on the fact that Patti wasn't with George because she was at Friar Park overseeing renovation work, he said, 'Sometimes, George goes off on his own. Sometimes he takes Patti with him but I think he just felt like a holiday and wanted to get away.'

Writing's On The Wall
The flipside of 'All Those Years Ago'. It is 3 minutes and 55 seconds in length.

You

'You' was one of two numbers specially written by George for Ronnie Spector after she'd signed to Apple Records. The track was co-produced by George and Phil Spector.

A projected album of the material by Ronnie Spector was never completed, so George recorded 'You' as a single, issued in 1975, and also used it as the opening track on his *Extra Texture* album.

It was also issued as a single in Britain on Apple R 6007 on 12 September 1975 in a full colour picture sleeve. 'World Of Stone' was on the flip. It reached No. 38 in the British charts. It was issued in America on Apple 1884 on 15 September 1975 and reached No. 20 in the charts.

You Know What To Do (aka You'll Know What To Do)

A group number found in the Abbey Road vaults which was included on Disc Two of *Anthology One* in 1995. It had been George's second number following 'Don't Bother Me'. Paul commented, 'I do believe there will be a bunch of people interested in hearing the George Harrison song from thirty years ago that no one to this day has heard – it's not the greatest thing George ever wrote, but it's an undiscovered nugget. If you find a little Egyptian pot, it doesn't have to be the greatest Egyptian pot. The fact that it is Egyptian is enough.'

You Like Me Too Much

A number penned by George, which the Beatles recorded for the *Help!* album on Wednesday 17 February 1965. It was 2 minutes and 25 seconds in length. George Martin played a Steinway grand piano on the track.

It was included on the American album *Beatles VI*, released on 14 June 1965 and it next appeared on the *Help!* album on 6 August 1965. The following March it was included on the 'Yesterday' EP.

Your Love Is Forever
A track on the 1979 *George Harrison* album lasting 3 minutes and 43 seconds. It was also featured as the flipside of the single 'Faster'.

Yu, Dr Zion
An acupuncturist, based in California. When George's health began to suffer in 1976, he put his faith in uttering chants. His health continued to deteriorate and Olivia insisted that he see a doctor. He was then diagnosed as having serum hepatitis and had also suffered some liver damage. Vitamins were prescribed, but George didn't respond.

Olivia then contacted Dr Yu, having a recommendation from her younger brother Peter, who had been treated by him following a motorcycle accident.

The treatment worked. After several visits, George's health began to improve, and within a few months he was completely cured.

Zig Zag

A number written and produced by George with Jeff Lynne. It appeared on the soundtrack of the *Shanghai Surprise* film. The number was later used as the flipside of 'When We Was Fab' in January 1988.